Saddam Hussein's Ba'th Party
Inside an Authoritarian Regime

The Ba'th Party came to power in 1968 and remained for thirty-five years until the 2003 U.S.-led invasion. Under the leadership of Saddam Hussein, who became president of Iraq in 1979, a powerful authoritarian regime was created based on a system of violence and an extraordinary surveillance network, as well as rewards and incentives for supporters of the regime. The true horrors of this regime have been exposed for the first time through a massive archive of government documents captured by the United States after the fall of Saddam Hussein. It is these documents that form the basis of this extraordinarily revealing book and that have been translated and analyzed by Joseph Sassoon, an Iraqi-born scholar and seasoned commentator on the Middle East. What they uncover are the secrets of the innermost workings of Saddam Hussein's Revolutionary Command Council, how the party was structured, how it operated via its network of informers, and how the system of rewards functioned. Saddam Hussein's authority was dominant. His decision was final, whether arbitrating the promotion of a junior official or the death of a rival or a member of his family. As this gripping portrayal of Saddam Hussein's Iraq demonstrates, the regime was every bit as authoritarian and brutal as Stalin's Soviet Union, Mao's China, and Qadhafi's Libya.

Joseph Sassoon is Adjunct Professor at the Center for Contemporary Arabic Studies at Georgetown University and Senior Associate Member at St Antony's College, Oxford. He is the author of several books, including *Economic Policy in Iraq, 1932–1950* (1987) and *The Iraqi Refugees: The New Crisis in the Middle East* (2009).

D1521226

Saddam Hussein's Ba'th Party

Inside an Authoritarian Regime

JOSEPH SASSOON

CAMBRIDGE UNIVERSITY PRESS
Cambridge, New York, Melbourne, Madrid, Cape Town,
Singapore, São Paulo, Delhi, Tokyo, Mexico City

Cambridge University Press
32 Avenue of the Americas, New York, NY 10013-2473, USA

www.cambridge.org
Information on this title: www.cambridge.org/9780521149150

First published 2012

Printed in the United States of America

A catalog record for this publication is available from the British Library.

Library of Congress Cataloging in Publication data
Sassoon, Joseph.
Saddam Hussein's Ba'th Party : inside an authoritarian regime / Joseph Sassoon.
p. cm.
Includes bibliographical references and index.
ISBN 978-0-521-19301-6 (hardback) – ISBN 978-0-521-14915-0 (paperback)
1. Hizb al-Ba'th al-'Arabi al-Ishtiraki (Iraq)   2. Iraq – Politics and
government – 1979–1991.   3. Iraq – Politics and government – 1921–2003.
4. Hussein, Saddam, 1937–2006.   I. Title
JQ1849.A98B378   2011
324.2567'083–dc23   2011025076

ISBN 978-0-521-19301-6 Hardback
ISBN 978-0-521-14915-0 Paperback

To Helen

Contents

List of Figures and Tables

Figures

Tables

Acknowledgments

The idea for this book germinated from a discussion with Dina Khoury. Once I began the mammoth task of working on the documents, we had countless conversations about deciphering their intricacies and placing them in context for the period under study. For this and her wonderful friendship, I owe a debt of gratitude. I also wish to thank profusely Hassan Mneimneh, a director of the Iraq Memory Foundation, who probably knows more than any other person about those documents and was extremely helpful.

Many people gave me valuable advice and read and commented on some of the chapters, especially Roger Owen, Eugene Rogan, and Peter Sluglett. I am truly grateful to all of them for helping me despite their busy schedules. Timothy Garton Ash guided me through the maze of literature on the Soviet Union and communist Europe. Kevin Woods read one chapter and assisted me in navigating my way through the National Defense University (NDU) records. David Palkki and Joseph Simons at NDU are a dream team for any researcher, and I thank all these people.

I would also like to acknowledge the staff at the Hoover Institute who worked hard to make the archives accessible to researchers, despite all the difficulties. I am grateful to Richard Sousa, director of the library and archives; Haidar Hadi; and Ahmad Dhia' for their help, and I appreciate the encouragement of Kanan Makiya, founder of the Iraq Memory Foundation.

At Georgetown University many of my colleagues at the Center for Contemporary Arab Studies (CCAS) provided advice and support and patiently put up with my stream of stories about the regime and Saddam Hussein. In particular, I would like to thank Rochelle Davis for her advice and friendship. Samer Shehata from CCAS, Bruce Hoffman from the Center of Peace and Security Studies, and Elliott Colla from the department of Arabic and Islamic Studies were all sources of encouragement.

In the last six months of writing this book, during the 2010–11 academic year, I was fortunate enough to be at the Woodrow Wilson International Center for Scholars in Washington, DC, a true haven for researchers. I would like to express my gratitude to the Center for giving me this wonderful opportunity, and special thanks are due to Robert Litwak and Haleh Esfendiari. The exemplary service at the Center's library under Janet Spikes was an invaluable resource, and many of the Center's scholars, with their different specialties, stimulated my thinking by an exchange of ideas, for which I am grateful. I benefited greatly from Martin Dimitrov's friendship and intellect, which led to a new project on comparisons between the Ba'th regime and Bulgaria under communism.

I owe a special debt to the many Iraqis whom I interviewed. They were generous with their time, patient in explaining the inner workings of the system, and willing to share their personal stories, and I owe them a special debt of gratitude. In particular, I thank Lieutenant General Ra'ad al-Hamdani and his family for their hospitality; they became friends in the course of writing this book.

Others helped me in different ways, and I would like to acknowledge Dina Hussein and Anne-Laure Malauzat for their help in the research for secondary material. Virginia Myers deserves special thanks for her skills in editing the manuscript. My editor at Cambridge University Press, Marigold Acland, accompanied this project from its nascence and offered valuable advice, and I am grateful to Joy Mizan, senior editorial assistant, for her attentive and caring service. Laura Wilmot did an excellent job copyediting the manuscript despite a tight schedule.

Friends and family were a constant source of encouragement and support. My lifelong friend Terry Somekh was always ready to discuss the project. My mother continues to be inspirational with her love and care. Living in Washington, DC, added the extra bonus of being near my daughter Rachel, who witnessed this project from the start and whose encouragement means a lot to me.

Last but not least, I would like to thank Helen Jackson for her love, patience, and willingness to devote an endless number of hours to helping me, especially with the tables, footnotes, and bibliography, when this manuscript was in its final stages. There are truly no words to express my gratitude, and this book is dedicated to her.

Note on Transliteration

Transliteration has been kept as simple and as consistent as possible. I have used a modified system of transliteration according to the *International Journal of Middle East* but have eliminated diacritical and long vowel markers with the exception of the ʿain (ʿ) and the hamza (ʾ). For that reason the three Arab letters of *dhal*, *dhad*, and *dhaʾ* are written as *dh* for simplicity. Arabic names and geographical names that have entered into English were kept as such to make it easier for the general reader.

List of Abbreviations

BRCC	*Ba'th Regional Command Collection*
CRRC	*Conflict Records Research Center*
GDP	gross domestic product
GFIW	General Federation of Iraqi Women
GNP	gross national product
HRW	Human Rights Watch
ID	Iraqi dinar
IIS	Iraqi Intelligence Service
IPC	Iraq Petroleum Company
KDP	Kurdish Democratic Party
NIDS	*North Iraq Dataset*
OPEC	Organization of the Petroleum Exporting Countries
PUK	Patriotic Union of Kurdistan
RCC	Revolutionary Command Council
SRG	Special Republican Guard
SSO	Special Security Organization
UN	United Nations

Glossary

amin sir	secretary general
al-amn al-'am	General Security
al-amn al-'askari	Military Security
ashbal Saddam	Saddam's Cubs
asir murtadd	turncoat prisoner
asir mutamayyiz	distinguished prisoner of war
asir samid	steadfast/loyal prisoner
baba Saddam	Daddy Saddam
bay'a	pledge of allegiance
diwan	presidential offices
fida'iyyu Saddam	fedayeen Saddam (those who are willing to sacrifice themselves for Saddam)
al-fi'at al-'umriyya	the age structure
fir', firu'	branch/branches
firqa, firaq	division/divisions
futuwwa	Youth Organization
al-hamla al-'imaniyya	the faith campaign
al-haras al-jamhuri al-khass	Special Republican Guard (SRG)
al-haras al-qawmi	National Guard
al-himaya	special presidential protection unit
hizb al-Ba'th al-'Arabi al-ishtiraki	Arab Ba'th Socialist Party
hizb al-Da'wa	Da'wa Party

ikramiyya	bonus
imtiyazat	privileges
intifada	uprising
intima'	membership
intisab	affiliation
al-istikhbarat al-'askariyya al-'amma	General Military Intelligence
ittihad al-Saddamiyyin	Union of Saddamists
jaysh al-quds	the Jerusalem/Quds Army
al-jaysh al-sha'bi	the Popular Army
jidariyyat	murals
jihaz al-amn al-khass	Special Security Organization (SSO)
jihaz al-mukhabarat al-'Iraqiyya	Iraqi Intelligence Service (IIS)
jihaz hunain	former intelligence and security arm of the Ba'th Party
jil Saddam	Saddam's generation
al-kasb al-hizbi	party recruitment
madrasat al-i'dad al-hizbi	Party Preparatory School
al-mafariz al-khassa	special squads
majlis al-amn al-qawmi	National Security Council
al-makatib al-'askariyya	military bureaus
makatib istishariyya	consultancy bureaus
maktab amanat sir al-qutr	Party Secretariat
al-milad al-maymun	the Auspicious Birthday
mu'ayyid	sympathizer
mudiriyat al-harakat al-'askariyya	Directorate of Military Logistics
mujahidin	strugglers
mukarram	venerated
mukhtars	mayors
munadhammat al-munadhilin	Organization for Party Veterans
munadhammat al-sabirin	Organization for Party Pensioners
murafiq	adjutant or aide-de-camp
murashih	candidate
muta'awan	collaborator
al-mu'tamin	the trusted one (a term used for informers)
al-nashat al-watani	the national activity

nasir	supporter
nasir mutaqaddim	advanced supporter
nawt al-istihqaq al-ʿali	Badge of High Esteem
nawt al-shajaʿa	Badge of Bravery
qadisiyyat Saddam	euphemism for the Iran–Iraq War of 1980–1988
al-qaʾid	the leader
qanun al-tahajjum	Law of Assault
al-qiyada al-qawmiyya	National Command
al-qiyada al-qutriyya	Regional Command
raqaba shaʿbiyya	popular surveillance
riddat tishrin	the apostasy of November 1963
al-saff al-watani	national alignment
safhat al-ghadr wa al-khiyana	the page of betrayal and treachery (euphemism for the 1991 intifada)
shahadat al-jinsiyya	certificate of nationality
sharat al-hizb	Party Insignia
sharat umm al-maʿarik	Mother of All Battles Insignia
shuʿba, shuʿab	section, sections
shuʿbat al-istikhbarat al-ʿaskariyya	Section of Military Intelligence
tabaʿiyya Iraniyya	Iranian nationality or origin
al-takafful al-hizbi	party responsibility
al-taliʿa	the Vanguards
tandhim, tandhimat	structure, structures
tardid al-qasm	oath reiteration
tawjih fikri	intellectual guidance
al-thaqafa al-ʿamma	general culture
al-thaqafa al-hizbiyya	political education
ʿudhu ʿamil	active member
ʿudhu firʿ	branch member
ʿudhu firqa	division member
ʿudhu mutadarrib	apprenticed member
ʿudhu shuʿba	section member
umm al-maʿarik	Mother of All Battles (term for the First Gulf War)
waqf, awqaf	religious endowment, usually of land
wasaya al-raʾis	commands of the president

wisam al-rafidain	Medal of the Land of the Two Rivers
yawm al-nakhwa	Day of Military Training
yawm al-raya	Day of the Banner
yawm al-shahid	Day of the Martyr
yawm al-zahf al-kabir	Day of the Big March
al-za'im al-awhad	the sole leader

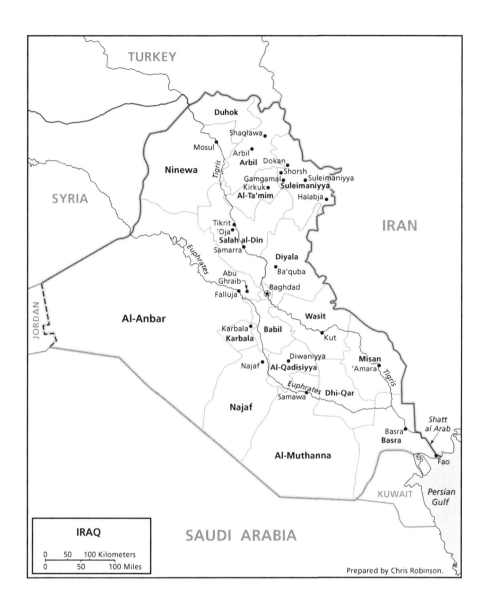

TURKEY

SYRIA

JORDAN

Duhok

Shaqlawa

Mosul

Arbil
Arbil
Dokan
Shorsh
Suleimaniyya
Gamgamal
Suleimaniyya
Kirkuk
Al-Ta'mim
Halabja

Ninewa

Tikrit
'Oja
Salah al-Din
Samarra

Diyala
Ba'quba

Abu
Ghraib
Baghdad
Falluja

Al-Anbar

Wasit

Karbala
Babil
Kut
Karbala

Diwaniyya
Misan
Najaf
Al-Qadisiyya
'Amara

Euphrates
Dhi-Qar
Samawa

Najaf

Al-Muthanna

IRAN

Basra
Basra

*Shatt
al Arab*

Fao

KUWAIT

*Persian
Gulf*

SAUDI ARABIA

IRAQ

0   50   100 Kilometers
0   50   100 Miles

Prepared by Chris Robinson.

Introduction

This book is an attempt to understand the inner workings of a modern Arab state from its own meticulous records rather than journalistic or secondary sources. For the first time, we are able to delve into the functioning of a one-party Arab state in the grip of a powerful authoritarian ideology. This is neither a history of the Ba'th Party nor of Iraq, but a study of the party's activities and modus operandi when it ruled the country between 1968 and 2003.

The research relies primarily on the massive archive of government documents captured by the United States after the fall of Saddam Hussein in April 2003. The records of the Ba'th Party, the intelligence services – mainly the Special Security Organization (SSO) – the presidential *diwan* (offices), and the Ministry of Information, as well as the audiotapes of meetings of the Revolutionary Command Council (RCC) and the leadership, found in the Conflict Records Research Center (CRRC), provide unparalleled insights into the ideology and structure of Saddam Hussein's regime. Whereas the documents reveal the decisions made, the tapes capture the spontaneity of private discussions among the country's leaders.

Most of these documents have come to light for the first time.[1] Some relate to the 2.4 million pages of the *North Iraq Dataset* (*NIDS*), which has already been partly published. The pages were sent to the United

---

[1] The Iraq Memory Foundation, *Prospectus 2008* (Washington, DC: 2008). There has been much controversy about the ownership of those documents. It is my understanding that they are currently in the custody of the Hoover Institute, but it has been agreed that the legal owner is the government of Iraq. The originals (which I have never seen, as all researchers have access only to digitized copies) will be returned to Baghdad when an agreement has been reached on timing.

States in May 1992 and August 1993, in two shipments of eighteen tons of official Iraqi state documents that had been captured by Kurdish groups during their March 1991 uprising.

The new material sourced for this book consists of about 6 million pages of documents of the *Ba'th Regional Command Collection* (*BRCC*), taken to Washington, DC, by the Iraq Memory Foundation under the direction of expatriate Iraqi scholar Kanan Makiya. About a third of both sets of documents were handwritten; typewriters were either not widely available or considered a "dangerous weapon" if they fell into enemy hands. All the documents have been digitized and are currently housed at the Hoover Institute, at Stanford University, or, in the case of many of the digitized *NIDS* files relating to the Iraqi Secret Police, at the University of Colorado at Boulder. The audiotapes are stored at the National Defense University in Washington, DC, and are indeed a treasure trove, conveying an intimate sense of how Saddam Hussein and the RCC conducted the business of the country.

Since Hanna Batatu published his magisterial work about Iraq,[2] most of our knowledge of Iraq has been based on secondary sources. Many books have dealt with different aspects of Iraq's history, and some excellent books such as those by Charles Tripp, Phoebe Marr, and Peter Sluglett have given us an extensive overview of Iraq's history.[3] Among the important works of significance to this study is the landmark work by Kanan Makiya, *Republic of Fear*, which exposed the repression of the Ba'th regime.[4] The book, however, focused mainly on fear and violence and almost ignored the incredibly extensive system of rewards that allowed Saddam Hussein's Ba'th Party to stay in power for such a long time. Similarly, important aspects, such as the resistance to the regime, were not emphasized. Other works added to our knowledge of certain essential elements in the history of the period such as tribalism and the political discourse under the Ba'th. Many of those works overstated the Sunni–Shi'i

---

[2] Hanna Batatu, *The Old Social Classes and the Revolutionary Movements of Iraq: A Study of Iraq's Old Landed and Commercial Classes and of Its Communists, Ba'thists, and Free Officers* (Princeton, NJ: Princeton University Press, 1978).

[3] Charles Tripp, *A History of Iraq*, paperback edn. (Cambridge University Press, 2000); Phebe Marr, *The Modern History of Iraq*, 2nd edn. (Boulder, CO: Westview Press, 2004); Peter Sluglett, *Britain in Iraq: Contriving King and Country 1914–1932*, paperback edn. (New York: Columbia University Press, 2007); Marion Farouk-Sluglett and Peter Sluglett, *Iraq Since 1958: From Revolution to Dictatorship* (London: KPI, 1987).

[4] Kanan Makiya, *Republic of Fear: The Politics of Modern Iraq*, paperback edn. (Berkeley: University of California Press, 1998). Originally the book was published under the pseudonym Samir al-Khalil.

chasm, although the documents clearly indicate that Saddam Hussein was almost "egalitarian" in his treatment of anyone considered or suspected of disloyalty, and that many Shiʿis were part of the system to the end.[5] While newspapers, the speeches of Saddam Hussein, and the Baʿth literature are critical to our comprehension of the period, the documents, in numerous instances, clearly indicate that the declared policies and speeches had other dimensions of which we were unaware. One example is the treatment of religiosity in the 1990s: the regime publicly launched a faith campaign but simultaneously, behind the scenes, continued to be anti-religious and to repress any sign of real religiosity. The documents allow us a more nuanced understanding of this period and of how the party played a fundamental role in every aspect of life in Iraq.

These fascinating records illustrate in minute detail how the different arms of the state functioned, and how the intelligence services gathered information, recruited informers, and carried out their surveillance of society. Reports were filed by all levels of the party hierarchy and were meticulously cross-referenced. From these records and countless memos we can build a unique picture of Saddam Hussein and his regime. Human Rights Watch (HRW) published a selection of the reports on its website and graphically described the "bureaucracy of repression" portrayed in these documents. The description is applicable to the majority of the documents:

> The language is numbingly dry, the format highly formalistic.... Written thus, the documents bespeak the daily tedium of career civil servants hewing closely to established bureaucratic procedure. The all-pervasive Iraqi bureaucracy manifests itself in another fashion: through the simple mechanism of referencing, the documents are linked to one another in a vast and complex administrative web. Official decrees are issued from high and passed down the ranks.... In a fashion, the meticulous cross-referencing that is characteristic of the Iraqi documents simply reflects the complexity of daily life in a sophisticated modern state.[6]

Although the regime laid strong emphasis on filing, we do not have much information about the filing system they used. We do know that filing continued uninterrupted during the First Gulf War and even for a couple

---

[5] See, for example, Amatzia Baram, *Culture, History and Ideology in the Formation of Baʿthist Iraq, 1968–89* (New York: St. Martin's Press, 1991), p. 15. Baram discussed "the near-disappearance of the Shiʿi element from the first rank of its leadership, and apparently from the lower echelons as well" by the late 1980s.

[6] Human Rights Watch, *Bureaucracy of Repression: The Iraqi Government in Its Own Words*, February 1, 1994, http://www.hrw.org/en/reports/1994/02/01/bureaucracy-repression (accessed November 10, 2010).

of weeks after the invasion of 2003 began.[7] The regime created its own terminology and expanded it over time. For example, *mu'tamin* (the trusted one) became the term for an informer; *ʿarus al-thawrat* (the bride of all revolutions) was the coup d'état of February 8, 1963, which catapulted the Baʿth into power for the first time; and numerous metaphors referred to special days of celebration and to organizations, such as *munadhammat al-munadhilin* (the Organization for Party Veterans), which was an organization for retired senior Baʿthists.

During the Baʿth's thirty-five-year rule, the party underwent many changes in response to the turbulent events that the country faced. In the 1970s, a time of relative economic prosperity, the party expanded its base dramatically and concentrated on recruiting new members from all sectors of the population. In northern Iraq, its operations against the Kurdish insurgency were closely coordinated with the security organizations, and the party's myriad branches were active in the Arabization of the region and in recruiting informers.

The 1980s were dominated by the Iran–Iraq War, and the party's political machine focused on attracting young people into the armed forces and popular militias. Deserters and prisoners of war were dealt with harshly, particularly from the mid-1980s onward, and the regime remained heavily engaged militarily in Kurdistan. In the 1990s, the devastating results of the First Gulf War were followed by uprisings in the Kurdish north and the Shiʿi south. Neither the party nor the security organizations were prepared for these and their ramifications. Despite this intelligence failure to anticipate the reaction of the civilian population in those two regions, the documents do not indicate a fundamental change in the party's role or that it was weakened, as some have argued. The active participation of a Party Secretariat member in every committee continued until the 2003 invasion, and the correspondence of the presidential *diwan*, the SSO, and the Baʿth Regional Command offers ample evidence that the party continued to be involved in implementing every decision. Furthermore, party recruitment, although flagging in certain areas, continued to increase. In fact, the number of those affiliated with the party grew substantially between 1991 and 2003.

Decision making in the 1980s and 1990s became centralized in the presidential *diwan*, but in both decades the party was deeply involved in micromanaging the country. During the 1990s the party also had

---

[7] For an interesting discussion of the systems of filing and their importance, see Ilana Feldman, *Governing Gaza: Bureaucracy, Authority, and the Work of Rule, 1917–1967* (Durham, NC: Duke University Press, 2008), pp. 31–61.

to contend with the repercussions of the severe international sanctions imposed on Iraq, and it was preoccupied with defensive preparations for the 2003 invasion. Moreover, the documents clearly illustrate the Ba'th Party's vital role in intelligence gathering. After the 1991 uprising the regime understood that it must extend its control of both the civilian and military populations to anticipate such events and, more importantly, to crush any nascent opposition. Therefore, during the regime's final decade, the security services were expanded, especially the SSO and the party's apparatus that monitored security. Last but not least, the party's considerable political and media resources were the driving force behind Saddam Hussein's personality cult.

In describing the activities of the Ba'th regime, this book draws many comparisons with the one-party regimes that ruled Eastern Europe and the Soviet Union, and between Saddam Hussein and leaders like Stalin. However, the differences also need to be highlighted. First of all, although terms such as *authoritarian*, *tyrannical*, and *dictatorship* are applicable to Iraq, *totalitarian* is not. Iraq differed from totalitarian regimes in a number of respects, the most important being the absence of any policy to transform the country and its economy into a centrally managed society – a command economy; furthermore, no attempts were made to emulate Stalin's draconian measures to industrialize the Soviet Union.[8]

Second, Iraq was unique because of its history. The country was involved in two major wars: the eight-year conflict with Iran from 1980 to 1988 and the First Gulf War in 1991, the latter precipitated by Iraq's invasion of Kuwait. Iraq was then subjected to almost thirteen years of sanctions, and until 1991 its army was engaged in recurrent military confrontations with the Kurds and then a major civilian uprising at the end of the 1991 War. Another fundamental difference was that, unlike East Germany or Hungary, the regime did not enjoy the protection of a patron superpower that could intervene to crush opposition.[9] Thus, it had to be

---

[8] For discussion of this topic, see definitions of *authoritarian* and *totalitarian* in Patrick O'Neil, *Essentials of Comparative Politics* (New York: W. W. Norton, 2004), pp. 12–13; for specific discussions on Iraq, see Achim Rohde, *State–Society Relations in Ba'thist Iraq: Facing Dictatorship* (London: Routledge, 2010), pp. 14–16; Hazem Saghieh, "Saddam Hussein, quel totalitarisme?" [Saddam Hussein: What Totalitarianism?] in Chris Kutschera (ed.), *Le Livre Noir de Saddam Hussein* [The Black Book of Saddam Hussein] (Paris: Oh! Editions, 2005), pp. 119–38. See also the section of Chapter 8 on the economy.

[9] For an interesting comparison with the Soviet Union's involvement in setting up the Stasi and dealing with the 1953 uprising in East Germany, see Gary Bruce, "The Prelude to Nationwide Surveillance in East Germany: Stasi Operations and Threat Perceptions, 1945-1953," *Journal of Cold War Studies*, vol. 5, no. 2 (Spring 2003), pp. 3-31.

self-reliant in ensuring "coup-proofing" and needed to co-opt large segments of the population to strengthen its power base. Indeed, in contrast to communist regimes, repression and violence did not decrease with the regime's longevity.

Finally, a comparison of Saddam Hussein's personality cult with, for example, Stalin's is complicated by the latter's successful record as a war leader. Stalin managed to orchestrate victory for his country in the Second World War in spite of massive loss of life and was seen as a heroic figure by his people. Saddam Hussein, on the other hand, took Iraq into a long and bloody war against Iran without achieving tangible results. He then invaded Kuwait, which led to the devastation of his country and to the imposition of severe sanctions that lasted until the final day of the Ba'th regime. Notwithstanding these differences, the international comparisons put into context many of the policies discussed in this book and are a reminder that Saddam Hussein and the Ba'th leadership copied or adapted many tactics from similar regimes in the Middle East and beyond.

The uniqueness of the Ba'th regime, however, is that in spite of the turbulent path it followed for thirty-five years it managed to survive against all odds. This book reveals how the Ba'th Party systematically penetrated every stratum of society and built an impressive political machine more powerful than any other group in Iraq, which drew large numbers of people into its sphere of influence. While using extreme violence and terror against its citizens, the regime created a notable parallel system of rewards for its supporters and succeeded in underscoring the necessity and importance of universal support. Another distinctive characteristic was flexibility; Saddam Hussein did not hesitate to change a policy even if it meant a complete reversal of his declared beliefs and actions. He did so in regard to tribalism, religion, and the status of women, and this trait was both his strength and his weakness.

Nevertheless, Saddam Hussein was consistent in his belief in coercive power, and his "repeated and extended episodes of war-making" had "pervasive effects on the dynamics of Iraqi politics, the organization of state and economy, and on state–society relations."[10] His own failure as a youth to be accepted into a military college may have made him determined to prove that he was a great military strategist, even at an immense cost in Iraqi lives. He had an instinctive empathy with the

---

[10] Isam al-Khafaji, "War as a Vehicle for the Rise and Demise of a State-Controlled Society: The Case of Ba'thist Iraq," in Steven Heydemann (ed.), *War, Institutions, and Social Change in the Middle East* (Berkeley: University of California Press, 2000), p. 259.

worldview expressed by Georges Clemenceau: "Ma politique étrangère et ma politique intérieure, c'est tout un. Politique intérieure, je fais la guerre; politique étrangère, je fais la guerre. Je fais toujours la guerre."[11]

In Iraq, the party was one of three pillars of government, together with the military and the bureaucracy, but it was the most important. This differed from the contemporaneous Ba'th regime in Syria, where the army was far more central because of the military background of the party's leaders. In Iraq, Saddam Hussein deliberately weakened the military as part of his coup-proofing, and the party became the essential core of the political system's command and control. The ideological domination of the armed forces began immediately after the party seized power on July 30, 1968, and the party machinery soon operated in all military ranks.[12] Historically, Iraq had developed a competent civil service that managed day-to-day administration, although the party slowly but surely crept into this bureaucracy and succeeded in bending it to serve its own political ends. Remarkably, the state bureaucracy continued to function during the decades of instability, even though the senior management of every ministry fell into the hands of Ba'thists. By the early 1980s, bolstered by his personality cult, Saddam Hussein had become the final decision maker on almost every important issue. Although the presidential *diwan* became a center for processing data before decisions were made, the party stayed involved at all levels and orchestrated the execution of major decisions made by Saddam Hussein and the RCC.

Yet the centralization of power and Saddam Hussein's dominating personality cannot on their own explain the regime's durability. Its underlying strength was derived from the remarkable symbiosis that developed between the leader and the party, which kept the regime functioning in spite of its several disastrous decisions. Saddam Hussein was very shrewd at manipulating the rivalries between different blocs of the Ba'th while concentrating state power in his own hands. But he saw the need for a central narrative that could unify as well as control the population, and for an apparatus to create a personality cult that would elevate him to untouchable status. Thus, failures were always blamed on others, never

---

[11] Clemenceau was prime minister of France before and during World War I. This excerpt is from a speech he gave in the French Chamber of Deputies on March 8, 1918. "My foreign policy and internal policy, it is all one. Internal policy, I make war; external policy, I make war. I always make war." http://www.assemblee-nationale.fr/histoire/Clemenceau1918.asp.

[12] For an interesting perspective on the infiltration of the army, see Taha Yasin's autobiography, which is part of his party file in *BRCC*, 002-3-7 (277–280).

on the president, and even by 2003 there were no signs of a fundamental change in the regime's potency or influence.

Although Saddam Hussein was astute in dealing with internal affairs, he was less successful at understanding foreign powers. His inability to grasp the implications of invading Kuwait and his belief that the United States and coalition forces would not invade Iraq are two blatant examples of his misjudgment. In a pattern familiar to other dictators, the presentations of intelligence information and ideas by members of the inner circle became colored by the leader's own view, by the presenters' anticipation of what he really wanted to hear, or by fear of offending him.

The apparatus of repression that developed in Iraq under the Ba'th regime and that facilitated its durability affected the country deeply. Yet it would be wrong to assume that compliance was based primarily on fear and the threat of violence. For repression to be effective, "a substantial section of society must identify with or even approve its activities."[13] Indeed, informers were not always hired under duress; they were attracted by the rewards and opportunities offered. Young men competed eagerly for coveted jobs in the intelligence services that brought them power and benefits, and many men and women from across the socioeconomic spectrum became part of the Ba'thist system for this reason. Others sincerely believed that the Ba'th ideology could solve the country's many problems. In the multidimensional relationship between the leadership and the Iraqi people, repression and rewards were used in tandem to entrench the regime in power, and they cast a long shadow across Iraqi society.

The regime's success lay also in its ability to attract large numbers of supporters and make them feel vested in the system. In its recruitment policy, which was a major element of Ba'thification, the party sought to achieve a good percentage of women members and, more importantly, to overcome the aging of its cadre by attracting the younger generation. A great deal of pressure to join the party was brought to bear on citizens, and some became members under duress, but many joined voluntarily, through conviction or from a desire to benefit from being a Ba'thist. The documents abound with evidence of citizens applying to join or rejoin the party. The vast majority of party affiliates, however, played little active role, because of the party's rigid hierarchy: only the upper echelons of membership were effectively involved in executing policies. Even so, a complex web of checks and counterchecks ensured that the privileged

---

[13] Richard Overy, *The Dictators: Hitler's Germany and Stalin's Russia*, paperback edn. (London: Penguin, 2005), p. 208.

few could not become too powerful. Above them, the Party Secretariat monitored every far-flung branch, which in turn controlled every aspect of civil and military life in the country.

A high priority of the Ba'th Party and its branches was the political indoctrination of members. Ba'thification of the masses was no less important, with special attention paid to the youth. By the 1990s, however, the Ba'th Party ideology and its emphasis on political and cultural education became centered on Saddam Hussein's personality cult. *Jil Saddam* – Saddam's generation – was imbued with Ba'th philosophy in every direct and indirect way. As time went on, the lines between cultural education and political education became blurred, causing severe damage to the quality of education and literature in Iraq.

From cradle to grave, it is hard to find any aspect of state or society in which the party did not wield some influence. Economically, it was in charge of allocating resources and granting contracts, a role that increased after sanctions were imposed, because the party had to police the rationing system. It used these powers to manage all imports and exports and to cement its economic control and political penetration of society. Apart from some short-lived attempts at socialism, the private sector functioned and even prospered at times. But, as part of Ba'thification, all professional and trade unions were subordinated to the party, and their real role was to be the eyes and ears of the regime in the different professions and to report any politically hostile activity.

In setting the background for the period under study, one has to look at Ba'th ideology and its role in creating an authoritarian regime. The word order of the party's motto – unity, freedom, and socialism – was significant. The party's emphasis on unity was central to its founding fathers, Michel 'Aflaq and Salah al-Din al-Bitar. Its main slogan, "One Arab nation with an eternal mission," was inscribed on all major party documents. However, the ill-prepared unification between Syria and Egypt in 1958, followed by its swift collapse in 1961, led many Ba'thists in Syria, particularly army officers, to resent the idea of unity, given the way they were treated by the dominant Egyptians. The Iraqi Ba'th Party realized early on that Arab unity could not be achieved in the way that the party had imagined in the early 1960s. Hence, no effort was made to pursue it, and unity became a mere slogan.[14]

[14] See an interview of Saddam Hussein with *al-Tadhamun*, London, February 6, 1988, translated in Foreign Broadcast Information Service (FBIS-NES-88-029). The interview with one of his biographers, the journalist Fuad Matar, is dated January 30, 1988.

Furthermore, the rift with Syria was definitely an impetus to deem-
phasize the party's zeal for pan-Arabism in favor of Iraqi patriotism.[15]
Freedom, the second word of the motto, is essential from the perspective of this book in understanding authoritarianism in Iraq. Freedom, in
the Ba'th jargon, meant people's democracy rather than a parliamentary
democracy. The issue of freedom was rarely discussed in the party's corri-
dors, and Saddam Hussein argued that Ba'th Party branch members were
free to choose their delegates, and that this in itself represented democracy and freedom. Indeed, both the Syrian and Iraqi Ba'th parties focused
far more on staying in power than allowing a free society. The failure
of the Ba'th in Iraq in 1963 to hold on to power further underlined the
practicality of governance that in turn rendered the ideology of freedom
hollow. The two Ba'th parties paid attention to their own region only
and created "authoritarian centralized governments, which rested heavily on military power."[16] Essentially, the party's ideology was at odds
with Western democracy because of its belief that democracy became "a
mere façade to conceal the tyranny, falsification and exploitation [by] the
reactionary classes."[17]

As for socialism, the party "believed in socialism as a means for the
total and radical liberation of the Arab individual."[18] In reality, however, apart from some nationalization of industries by both regimes in
Syria and Iraq, and distribution of land seized from large landowners,
there was cohabitation with the private sector, and the ideology's flexibility allowed the private sector in Iraq to grow for most of the period
under study. The party's ideology was malleable in other areas as well. In
the 1970s, Saddam Hussein called for wide-ranging reforms that would
enable women to study and become economically active. However, by
the mid-1980s these opportunities were curtailed as a consequence of the
war against Iran and Saddam Hussein's obsessive fear of Khomeinism. He
also reversed his policy on religion. Once the nationwide faith campaign
had been launched to promote religiosity, women were encouraged to
stay at home and produce children, in part to reduce Iran's demographic
superiority and to make up for the huge loss of life in the Iran–Iraq War.
Saddam Hussein's view of religion was complex, but not ambiguous.

---

[15] Baram, *Culture, History and Ideology*, pp. 14–16.
[16] John F. Devlin, *The Ba'th Party: A History from Its Origins to 1966* (Stanford, CA:
    Hoover Institution, 1976), p. 227.
[17] Arab Ba'th Socialist Party, *Some Theoretical Principles: Approved by the Six National
    Congress October 1963* (Beirut: Dar al-Tali'a, 1974), p. 48.
[18] *Ibid*.

He grew up in a secular environment, led a party with a secular socialist ideology, and was always suspicious of religious men. The facade of a faith campaign did not stop the continual repression of religious groups, be they Wahhabists or Shi'is.

Ironically, Saddam Hussein and the United States were natural allies in that they shared the same enemies: religious fanaticism and Iran. The Iraq Survey Group noted that "Saddam did not consider the United States a natural adversary, as he did Iran and Israel."[19] Documents predating the 9/11 attack clearly indicate the regime's concerns about Islamic fundamentalism and its potential impact on Iraqi youth. Wahhabism was banned from the early 1990s, and the death penalty imposed on its followers.[20] However, the Ba'th regime defined Iraqis not by their religion but by their support and loyalty to the party – unlike the situation after 2003. Kurds, Shi'is, and Christians were all part of the system and were involved in its operations and intelligence services. Yet religious activities of any kind were considered dangerous, and all mosques were kept under surveillance.

The centrality of loyalty for Saddam Hussein and the Ba'th Party led inevitably to a significant reliance on tribal, family, and kin associations. The intelligence services, for instance, recruited relatively large numbers from clans that owed total loyalty to Saddam Hussein. This was a fundamental difference from any communist system, as neither Stalin nor Mao placed many family members in senior roles in the party, the army, or the intelligence services. Many believe that Saddam Hussein was grooming his younger son, Qusay, as his successor, given that he had already appointed him head of the senior intelligence service (SSO) and of the Republican Guard.

In its structure the Ba'th Party was similar in many ways to the Soviet Communist Party. With its expansion in size and governing responsibilities, centralization of power and bureaucratization of the party mechanism became essential for its effectiveness. Every major party decision was channeled through *maktab amanat sir al-qutr* (the Party Secretariat), which was in essence the party's board of directors and whose functions and hierarchy were drawn up in a clear and detailed way. The Secretariat oversaw the running of every party branch, which in turn controlled

---

[19] Iraq Survey Group, *Regime Strategic Intent*, vol. I, Comprehensive Report of the Special Advisor to the Director of Central Intelligence, September 30, 2004, p. 31.

[20] Wahhabism is a Muslim sect founded in Arabia in the eighteenth century and revived by ibn-Saud in the twentieth century.

and collected information about every aspect of civil and military life throughout the country. Gathering information was a formidable task. The transmission of information to the leadership was often imperfect, because of sheer volume, but it was also sometimes deliberately inaccurate or embellished to hide inefficiencies or overstated promises made by the local leadership. For Iraqis, negotiating the bureaucracy's hierarchical structure was a long and arduous experience. Decision making was cumbersome and inefficient, but at the same time it allowed Saddam Hussein to govern without fear of powerful rivals emerging. He was also a manipulator par excellence of his aides and associates.

In many ways the party's structure was similar to that of a large corporation in how it recruited new members, created new branches, amalgamated branches to increase efficiency, and encouraged competition among branches and members. This echoed an observation made fifty years ago that the rank-and-file members of the Soviet Communist Party were almost as powerless within the total structure as the possessor of a single share in a publicly traded company in the West.[21] Not unlike a successful large corporation, everyone from the top to the bottom of the hierarchy was under constant pressure to perform and to make sure that his or her contribution was noticed by superiors. The clear hierarchies made it easier to categorize individuals and to allocate the corresponding rewards to members who were efficient and loyal. In the atmosphere of sanctions and economic deterioration in the 1990s this became even more important. Another key ingredient of the party's durability was its strong internal discipline and its iron grip on members. The party wanted to know everything possible about each affiliate; party members, as well as army officers, had to receive approval prior to marriage from the Party's Secretariat.

My study of authoritarianism in Iraq is divided into eight chapters. Chapter 1 is historical, based on secondary material that puts the rise of the Ba'th Party in context. Chapter 2 details the party structure and hierarchical organization and discusses the party's wide range of functions and its finances. The myriad rules and regulations, consistent with its disciplinary style, ranged from the sublime to the ridiculous but helped to undergird the party's control. By using an actual file, I re-create the life of a typical loyal member who joined at a young age. The chapter also examines recruitment and the Ba'th's ideologically driven political and cultural education policies.

[21] Alfred G. Meyer, "USSR, Incorporated," *Slavic Review*, vol. 20, no. 3 (October 1961), pp. 369–76.

Chapter 3 deals with the Ba'th branches, which were scattered strategically across the country. Until now, the paucity of original documents has led to a tendency to focus on the Party Secretariat or its leadership. In reality, the branches played an essential role in maintaining the party's control and vigilance in every corner of Iraq. They were deeply engaged in security, cultural, and recruitment activities; in relations with the public; and in financial matters, and they competed fiercely with one another to attract the attention of senior officials in Baghdad. Some fascinating handwritten minutes from a cell in a northern town allow a reconstruction of how one small Ba'th Party group dealt with its problems when the country was embroiled in a war with Iran and in conflict with local Kurds.

Chapter 4 discusses the security organizations. The Ba'th was closely connected to the intelligence machinery, and most documents were copied to the Party Secretariat. For the first time, an account is presented of the SSO – the main intelligence agency from the early 1990s, headed by Saddam Hussein's son Qusay – based on its own documents. Reading these documents is like entering an Orwellian world in which everyone intently watched everyone else. The chapter also discusses information gathering and the role of informers, many of whom were volunteers – either for rewards or, in the case of a few, for malicious personal reasons. Unlike for Eastern Europe or the Soviet Union, very little work has been done on informers in authoritarian regimes in the Middle East, who are usually perceived as acting under coercion.

In order to curb the historical influence of the armed forces, the party created military bureaus, and the relationship between the party and the army is discussed in Chapter 5. As in the Soviet Union, party commissars were stationed in every army unit to keep an eye on soldiers and officers and were involved in all military decisions despite their limited knowledge. Ba'thification of the army was also imposed by controlling the entrance procedures to military institutions. Several popular armies were created to bolster the country's defenses and to reduce reliance on the traditional army. The chapter also covers the issues of deserters and prisoners of war, and the elaborate honoring of martyrs.

It is impossible to explain this period without understanding Saddam Hussein's personality, his decision making, his character, his modus operandi, and above all his personality cult, which is the subject of Chapter 6. In the last twenty years of the regime, Iraq became synonymous with Saddam Hussein, who was elevated to a feared and venerated leader through the party's sophisticated bureaucracy.

Chapter 7 explores control and resistance and the parallel systems of punishments and rewards. There is no doubt that fear and violence played a critical role in sustaining the regime, but I conclude that without the comprehensive system of rewards, it would not have lasted so long. At the same time, given its known brutality, the number of those willing to resist the regime at great cost to themselves and their families is remarkable, and is a fruitful field for further research.

Chapter 8 examines the Ba'th Party's bureaucratic machine and decision-making process and portrays civilian life under the Ba'th: how the regime managed the economy, the unions, its policies on women and religion, and its intensive political education of children, youth, and students.

Although the Ba'th regime, with its bloody memories, has passed into history, it is incumbent on all researchers to protect the identity of many people still alive and living in Iraq. The policy in this book has been strict: no names of any individuals are mentioned unless they are well known in the public sphere, such as senior officials and Saddam Hussein's immediate family.

It should be emphasized, however, that the documents do not give a complete picture. First of all, in the looting of government offices after the invasion, many documents were stolen, as Rory Stewart, the governor of Misan province in 2004, recorded:

> Those who had stolen the intelligence files read them and noted the addresses and sold the contents door to door. Documents started at a few dollars a sheet. You could collect the manila files like stamps and see who had reported on you at school and at work, or which neighbour's [*sic*] report had led them to take your father away, and where he had been held and for how long, and what he had said in that time, on the official record, and what was the grounds for trial, and who sentenced him, and who carried it out, and where he was buried. And if a family wouldn't pay you enough for revealing the contents, another family would pay you for the opposite.[22]

Second, many orders were given orally by Saddam Hussein and lack any documentation. For that reason I listened to hundreds of hours of the audiotapes to get a fuller understanding of the system, and I interviewed a number of Iraqi generals and senior Ba'th members who were willing to share information and answer my many questions. Some of those

---

[22] Rory Stewart, *Occupational Hazards: My Time Governing in Iraq* (London: Picador, 2006), p. 233.

interviewees had no qualms about their names being published. Third, I did not have access to the archives of other important departments, such as the Ministries of Defense, Foreign Affairs, and Interior, or the local police. Fourth, it is almost impossible to chart the historical development of every topic, because the archives were not arranged chronologically, and many gaps exist. Finally, many areas were not covered in this study, and it is hoped that other scholars will continue exploring the multitude of subjects in the documents and will expand our understanding of Iraq's recent history.

I

The Rise of the Baʿth Party

On July 17, 1968, *hizb al-Baʿth al-ʿArabi al-ishtiraki* (the Arab Baʿth Socialist Party) launched a successful coup d'état and began its thirty-five-year domination of Iraq. The ascent of the Baʿth Party, five years after its first brief interlude in power, was the result of a combination of historical, economic, and social factors that had led to instability and repeated power vacuums in the decades leading up to July 1968.

Modern Iraq was created from the amalgamation of the three provinces of Baghdad, Basra, and Mosul, which constituted Mesopotamia and had been part of the Ottoman Empire for more than four centuries. When the First World War broke out, the British felt the need to protect their burgeoning oil and political interests in the region and launched a military campaign in Iraq. By 1918 they had come to control the three provinces but soon found out that ruling the country proved significantly more difficult than occupying it. Iraq became a British mandate from 1920 until independence was granted in 1932, and King Faisal was installed as its first monarch in 1921.[1]

Iraqi nationalists initially rose up against foreign control in summer 1920, sparked by the announcement of the mandate a couple of months earlier. This revolt was a turning point in the history of Iraqi nationalism, but it did not alter the nature of the occupation. The British continued to shape Iraqi institutions and tribal hierarchies throughout the 1920s and 1930s. However, although the mandate created the modern state of Iraq, it failed to establish nationhood among the three provinces that had been

---

[1] Many books cover the modern history of Iraq. The account here is partly based on Marr, *The Modern History of Iraq*; Tripp, *A History of Iraq*; and Sluglett, *Britain in Iraq*.

cobbled together, and successive Iraqi governments faced considerable challenges in dealing with the rich diversity of ethnic and religious groups, regional affiliations, and languages within their borders.

During the 1920s, governments changed frequently, and political parties functioned on the basis of alliances between different individuals and groups attempting to further their interests. "The ideological and moral bankruptcy of the political system was glaringly evident, particularly to those who were excluded from full participation in it."[2] Indeed, the mandate – perhaps understandably given the country's internal fractures and the overarching British interests – made "the state the principal arena for the multiple struggles that would constitute a distinctively Iraqi politics."[3] The implications were that those who controlled the state commanded its resources and allocated privileges to their supporters. The mandate continued officially until 1932, when the Kingdom of Iraq was granted independence under King Faisal I.[4]

The interwar period was characterized by the rise of pan-Arabism, an ideology influenced by the educationalist Sati' al-Husri, whose advocacy of Arab nationalism influenced an entire generation through his position as the director general of education.[5] Al-Husri emphasized the Arabic language, Arab nationalism, and Arabic history, negating a sense of national Iraqi identity and generally excluding non-Arab (and, to some extent, non-Sunni) Iraqis from his plans to educate the younger generation.[6] This period was fraught with communal tensions, tribal rebellions, and the increasing intrusion of the army into politics. When the Assyrian minority in northern Iraq demanded more autonomy, this was seen as a challenge to Iraq's national unity, and the army under Bakr Sidqi, the general in

---

[2] Peter Sluglett, "Le parti Baas: panarabisme, national-socialisme et dictature," in Kutschera (ed.), *Le Livre Noir*, p. 82.

[3] Tripp, *A History of Iraq*, p. 75.

[4] Iraq was admitted to the League of Nations in October 1932. Most members of the Permanent Mandates Commission, which oversaw the administration of the mandated territories, were not convinced that Iraq was ready to be "released from the Mandate." For the negotiations leading to Iraq's admission to the League of Nations, see Susan Pedersen, "Getting Out of Iraq – in 1932: The League of Nations and the Road to Normative Statehood," *American Historical Review*, vol. 115, no. 4 (October 2010), pp. 975–1000.

[5] For more details about al-Husri's education policy and his influence, see Orit Bashkin, *The Other Iraq: Pluralism and Culture in Hashemite Iraq* (Stanford, CA: Stanford University Press, 2009), pp. 231–33, 249–54.

[6] For a review of this period, see Peter Wien, *Iraqi Arab Nationalism: Authoritarian, Totalitarian, and Pro-Fascist Inclinations, 1932–1941* (London and New York: Routledge, 2006).

charge of the Mosul area, massacred hundreds of Assyrians in August
1933. Having gained prominence, Sidqi launched Iraq's first coup d'état
in October 1936, thus signaling the active entry of the military into politics
and creating a precedent for the use of violence to settle political disputes.[7]

The next historical milestone that influenced Saddam Hussein and
Ba'th ideology was the coup d'état of April 1941. Bakr Sidqi was assassinated in 1937, ten months after his successful coup, and the country
entered a period of instability. Another coup took place in 1938, installing
Nuri al-Sa'id as prime minister. The 1941 coup, unlike previous ones, was
targeted against the monarchy itself, rather than just replacing a prime
minister. The regent, 'Abd al-Ilah, appointed because King Faisal II was
still a minor, was deposed, and Rashid 'Ali al-Kaylani formed a cabinet
with the support of four colonels, known as the "Golden Square." Britain,
in the midst of the Second World War, asked permission for its troops to
cross through Iraq, in accordance with the Anglo–Iraqi Treaty of 1930,
which was designed to protect its interests in the region. Under pressure
from the colonels, Rashid 'Ali denied the British request, thus reneging on
the treaty. Hostilities between the two nations broke out, and there was
a brief period of fighting – known as the Anglo–Iraqi War – which lasted
for thirty days. Iraqi forces succumbed to British military pressure, especially from the Royal Air Force. A power vacuum existed for a couple of
days between the collapse of the government and the reestablishment of
British control over the country, which continued directly and indirectly
until 1958.

One consequence of this vacuum was two days of carnage against the
Jewish community of Baghdad, regarded as pro-British, which lasted until
order was reestablished. After the war, the four colonels were tried and
hanged, thus becoming martyrs in the eyes of many Iraqi nationalists.[8]
Saddam Hussein recounted in his books that when he was a young boy
his uncle told him numerous stories about the courage and patriotism of
those colonels, and that he looked up to them as role models.

The 1948 war in Palestine, between the newly independent Israeli state
and surrounding Arab countries, had a profound impact on Iraq and the

---

[7] Although the coup was named after Bakr Sidqi, the mastermind behind it was Hikmat
Suleiman, a politician with high ambitions. For more details, see Marr, *The Modern
History of Iraq*, pp. 44–47; Tripp, *A History of Iraq*, pp. 84–94.

[8] For extensive details about the coup and its implications, see Tripp, *A History of Iraq*,
pp. 99–107; Reeva S. Simon, *Iraq Between the Two World Wars: The Creation and
Implementation of a Nationalist Ideology* (New York: Columbia University Press, 1986),
pp. 145–65.

Arab world. Pan-Arab policy was strengthened and pro-British policies discredited, with calls for independence from British influence increasing by the day. The Iraqi Jewish community, which numbered more than 150,000 and played an important role in the country's commercial and cultural life, dwindled to about 30,000, leaving a void in the business world that was filled mostly by Shi'i merchants.

In the 1950s, the dramatic increase in oil revenues stimulated economic development, which enabled the government to embark on large construction projects. On numerous occasions, demands to improve labor conditions turned into violent demonstrations. Many of the strikes were planned by the Communist Party, which was the most organized political entity outside the government and enjoyed a loyal following. In 1952, the overthrow of the monarchy in Egypt galvanized Iraqi officers into contemplating an overthrow of their own monarchy. While Iraq was making progress in terms of social welfare, frustrations surrounding its foreign policy were increasing. These reached a breaking point during the Suez War of 1956, when Egypt was attacked by Britain, France, and Israel. Iraqis felt that their country could no longer stay on the side of the British, and young officers were encouraged to instigate the revolution that led to the declaration of Iraq as a republic on July 14, 1958.

During this period the Ba'th Party emerged in Iraq. Established in Syria in 1943 by a small circle of young intellectuals and led by Michel 'Aflaq, a Christian, and Salah al-Din al-Bitar, a Sunni Muslim, the Ba'th, which means resurrection or revival, saw itself as an Arab rather than a Syrian party. 'Aflaq told the historian Hanna Batatu that everyone "sensed that there was a vacuum, that the old leadership had gone bankrupt...that a new movement had to be set on foot."[9] The events in Palestine in 1948 increased the new party's appeal, and its leaders saw the gaps between governments and their peoples in the Arab world as an opportunity to expand their political base. Its popularity benefited from the fact that the Iraqi Communist Party was tainted by the Soviet Union's decision to recognize Israel. Ba'th ideology reached Iraq in the late 1940s and found receptive ears among university students. Fu'ad al-Rikabi became the leader of the Iraqi party in 1951, and young members were gradually recruited, including Saddam Hussein in 1956. The party regarded itself as "the vanguard and leader of the 'Arab Revolution.'"[10] Even by 1955,

[9] Batatu, *The Old Social Classes*, p. 726.
[10] Amatzia Baram, "Qawmiyya and Wataniyya in Ba'thi Iraq: The Search for a New Balance," *Middle Eastern Studies*, vol. 19, no. 2 (April 1983), p. 188.

however, its members numbered only about 300, and its influence among army officers was limited.

Following in the footsteps of the Egyptian Free Officers, Iraq's Free Officers launched the July 1958 revolution that toppled the monarchy, created the Iraqi republic, and inaugurated a new era in Iraq's history of coups d'état and instability. The swift success of the coup was due more to feelings of resentment and the desire for change on the part of large segments of the population rather than to devotion to a consistent ideology or a coherent group of activists.[11] The violent end of the royal family and of Prime Minister Nuri al-Sa'id instituted the use of public violence to resolve political disputes. Indeed, the public trials of senior officials of the monarchy that were broadcast on television were yet another pointer to the future; the proceedings of many of these trials became a farce, interrupted by people waving ropes and calling for the hanging of certain ministers and officers.[12] Under the circumstances, it is surprising that only a handful of those arrested were actually executed.

The two leaders of the 1958 revolution among the Free Officers were Brigadier 'Abd al-Karim Qasim and Colonel 'Abd al-Salam 'Arif. A rift soon developed between them, and their struggle for power became "a clash of personality and ideals."[13] Qasim emerged as the leader after skillfully maneuvering between nationalists and communists and not allowing either side to become too powerful. 'Arif, who supported a union with Egypt, was arrested and sentenced to death,[14] and for a while the communists seemed to be gaining power. The 1958 revolution allowed them to come into the open for the first time and to play a part in running the country.

In March 1959 the underlying tensions erupted in the Mosul Revolt, led by a pro-unionist army officer, and the turmoil symbolized the complexity of the various conflicts that permeated Iraqi politics and society. Supported by Egypt, which by then was openly hostile to Qasim's regime, the revolt was poorly planned and easily crushed by Iraqi troops loyal to Qasim. Its aftermath, however, left a deep scar on Iraq's history; Kurds attacked Turkomans who supported the revolt, and communists

---

[11] Batatu, *The Old Social Classes*, pp. 805–06.

[12] See Tripp, *A History of Iraq*, p. 168, for more details on the People's Court; see also Farouk-Sluglett and Sluglett, *Iraq Since 1958*, pp. 63–64.

[13] Farouk-Sluglett and Sluglett, *Iraq Since 1958*, p. 50. 'Arif was much more committed to Arab unity, whereas Qasim – supported by the communists – rejected the idea of immediate unity.

[14] The sentence was not ratified by Qasim, and Colonel 'Arif stayed in jail until 1961.

massacred nationalists. Looting in Mosul and summary executions reflected the deep fissures between Kurds and Arabs, peasants and land-lords, communists and nationalists.[15]

Qasim began to view the communists as a threat to his regime and gradually curtailed their power, but they were left with little alternative except to support him to the end, because they saw him as their best option. Over the years, the Communist Party played an important role in Iraq's political history, even though it was almost perpetually in oppo-sition. It attracted many followers during the 1940s, 1950s, and early 1960s, including members of religious minorities and a large number of intellectuals. This caused concern not only for the monarchy but also for the West, as it paralleled the intensification of the Cold War during the 1950s.[16] But, by late 1959, the influence of the communists in Iraq had peaked.

The same year, 1959, witnessed an attempt to assassinate Qasim. On October 7, a group of young Ba'thists, including Saddam Hussein, attempted to shoot Qasim as his car drove along its daily route along the famous Rashid Street. Although Qasim was injured, he recovered quickly, and many of the plotters, including Saddam Hussein, fled the country. Others were arrested, and their trial brought the Ba'th Party to public attention for the first time. After initially fleeing to Syria, Saddam Hus-sein moved to Cairo, using his time there to further his education while staying in close touch with other Iraqi exiles in Egypt. The unsuccess-ful attempt to assassinate Qasim later became mythologized in Saddam Hussein's personality cult, glorifying him and his associates (see Chapter 6). Another intriguing aspect of the affair was that Saddam Hussein was bewildered by Qasim's choice of the same route every day with only min-imum protection – usually a driver and one or two bodyguards.[17] This practice was of course reversed when the Ba'th came to power in 1968; Saddam Hussein was determined that no one would be able to break through the security barriers with which he surrounded himself.

Once Qasim had gained the upper hand against 'Arif, he became known in the media as the "sole leader," and although a personality cult

---

[15] For extensive coverage of the events, see Batatu, *The Old Social Classes*, pp. 866–89; Farouk-Sluglett and Sluglett, *Iraq Since 1958*, pp. 66–70.

[16] For an extensive history of the Communist Party, see Tareq Y. Ismael, *The Rise and Fall of the Communist Party of Iraq* (Cambridge University Press, 2008).

[17] Saddam Hussein, *Rijal wa madina* [Men and a City], *riwaya li-katibiha* [a Novel by Its Author] (Baghdad: Ministry of Culture, n.d.), p. 231–32. Interestingly Saddam Hussein believed that this was due to Qasim's megalomania.

did not develop to the same extent around him as did for Saddam Hussein, the fact remained that the Iraqi people became accustomed to having the same leader for four years and to realizing that authority began and ended with him. Qasim's approach of playing different political groups against one another, including some that supported him, alienated many of his natural allies, the Kurds in particular. His war against the Kurds, with whom he had initially attempted to be reconciled, was the first of many campaigns conducted by successive Iraqi governments until 1991, in attempts to crush the guerillas ensconced in the northern mountains, who enjoyed the support of the local population.

Yet Qasim – in stark contrast to Saddam Hussein – forgave many of those who plotted against him, commuted many death sentences issued by the People's Court, and pardoned 'Arif, who would later become president. As the Slugletts put it: "Qasim's failings, serious as they were, can scarcely be discussed in the same terms as the venality, savagery and wanton brutality characteristic of many of the regimes which followed his own."[18] Although the record of Qasim's regime was mixed, there is little doubt that much-needed social reform was launched and that his regime helped to make society somewhat more egalitarian, after decades of monarchical rule during which large landlords not only controlled agricultural land but had inordinate influence over the country's politics. In fact, it could be argued that the 1950s were characterized by the growing gap on the one hand between the monarchy and its supporters and on the other hand between the many political, economic, and social groups in the urban centers of the country. More than any of the rulers before or after him, Qasim was sensitive to the diversity of Iraq and the need to create some cohesion among the different groups.

The 1958 revolution had a long-lasting impact on Iraqi society; the social hierarchy was modified and a new middle class emerged. Between 1958 and 1963, Iraq moved away from the concept of Arab unity and established friendly relations with the Soviet bloc, unlike its previous orientation in the British and American orbit. But the greatest failure of that period was that no politically representative institutions or appropriate processes to govern Iraq were created, and the rule of law was damaged by the show trials. Qasim's inability to delegate authority to any other institution or executive organ set the stage for a powerful, politically skillful group to seize the opportunity and define the management of the

[18] Farouk-Sluglett and Sluglett, *Iraq Since 1958*, p. 83.

country. As Tripp succinctly said, Qasim "ruled as an autocrat and died as one, helping thus to reproduce the exclusive structures of Iraqi politics and their authoritarian impulse."[19]

The military became an active player in politics, intervening time and again, generating more instability, and backing successive authoritarian regimes.[20] Indeed, all regimes from 1958 onward had to focus their attention on coup-proofing, but only Saddam Hussein truly mastered that art, having carefully observed the turbulent events in his country between 1958 and 1968. To secure the loyalty of the military, all regimes after 1958 appeased the officer corps and granted it more privileges. It was therefore "not surprising that the youth who had no chance of pursuing a career in such prestigious fields as medicine or engineering would look to the officer corps."[21]

The year 1963, described by Batatu as "the bitterest of years,"[22] witnessed violence, assassinations, coups d'état, and changes of regime and exposed the elements of instability in Iraq at their most raw. Airplanes and tanks were used in the heart of Baghdad by the Ba'thists and their allies, forcing Qasim to surrender at his headquarters in the Ministry of Defense on February 9, 1963, almost a day after the revolt against him began. Qasim and a few close aides were given a summary trial, and all were executed shortly afterward by firing squad. Overnight, the "sole leader" of the country became "the enemy of the people," and his body and those of his associates were shown repeatedly on Iraqi television to prove to their supporters that Qasim's regime had come to an end. In the ensuing violence, Batatu estimated that about 5,000 communists were killed in the two days from February 8 to 10 as part of the relentless hunt by *al-haras al-qawmi* (the National Guard), a militia created by the Ba'th Party.[23] The new regime that came to power drew its support from

---

[19] Tripp, *A History of Iraq*, p. 170.
[20] Marr, *The Modern History of Iraq*, p. 112.
[21] Al-Khafaji, "War as a Vehicle," p. 265.
[22] Batatu, *The Old Social Classes*, pp. 974–94. Batatu was referring in particular to the tragic days of February 8–10, which witnessed violent collisions between different Iraqi groups.
[23] *Ibid.* See also Ismael, *The Rise and Fall*, pp. 106–09. Many writers discussed the CIA connection to the coup and the lists of communists it gave to the Ba'th leadership. Aburish blamed "Western connivance against Iraq" for the continuing inability to establish a stable government in the country. See Saïd K. Aburish, *Saddam Hussein: The Politics of Revenge* (New York: Bloomsbury, 2000), p. 58. See also the Conclusion, which discusses the United States and Saddam Hussein.

"a small but determined group of plotters able to draw on wider elements of disaffection in the military."[24]

The Ba'th's first nine months in office, between February 8 and November 18, 1963, are important for understanding the party's structure and the system it developed when it returned to power in 1968. The experience gained in 1963 was a significant turning point in the history of the Ba'th; it was the first real test of applying the party's ideology to the country's economic, social, and political problems. In 1963, the party realized that it was the highest constitutional authority, but that it did not have the necessary support networks in place.[25] Hence, after 1968, the Ba'th made strenuous efforts to create solid local support, and under Saddam Hussein's leadership it built powerful security organizations that could crush any resistance in its infancy. In 1963, the number of Ba'th Party members was estimated to be a mere 3,000, but after 1968 its leadership put in place a number of efficient systems to penetrate society and to expand the party's power base.[26]

The party also devoted considerable energy to analyzing the lessons of its first experience in power and concentrated on reversing its failures both ideologically and practically.[27] The party saw that its militia, the National Guard, had not enhanced its reputation; on the contrary, it left a damaging impression on the population. Thus, in 1968, the party refrained from setting up a militia until it had established itself and could organize a popular army fully under party control and discipline.

Saddam Hussein learned three bitter lessons from 1963 that he was determined not to repeat: to avoid ideological splits within the party and any competition for leadership; to weaken the military to prevent coups d'état; and finally, to control the levers of power, such as the security organizations, as this was critical to retaining political control.[28] Nevertheless, there were similarities between the first and second periods of Ba'th rule. In both of them, the party used ruthless methods to rid itself of its enemies. Although socialism was part and parcel of Ba'th ideology,

[24] Marr, *The Modern History of Iraq*, p. 113.
[25] Hani al-Fukayki, *Awkar al-hazima: Tajribati fi hizb al-Ba'th al-'Iraqi* [The Dens of Defeat: My Experience in the Iraqi Ba'th Party] (London: Riyadh al-Rayyis, 1993), p. 310.
[26] Aburish, *Saddam Hussein*, p. 60.
[27] See, for example, Hizb al-Ba'th al-'Arabi al-Ishtiraki, *Lamahat min nidhal al-Ba'th 1947–1977* [Glimpses from the Ba'th's Struggle, 1947–1977], 4th edn. (Baghdad: Ministry of Information and Culture, 1986), pp. 87–111.
[28] Marr, *The Modern History of Iraq*, pp. 119–23.

it was not enforced in either period, and military conflicts with the Kurds characterized both eras.

During the initial period after the party took over in 1963, there was a sense of anarchy throughout the country. Five years later, in 1968, the leadership was resolved not to tolerate such a chaotic atmosphere. However, in 1963 the party had no experience in governing the country, and its leadership was far from united on the course it should follow in almost every important respect, with the exception of rooting out communists. One ex-Ba'thist describes vividly in his memoirs the fissiparousness of the party leadership and the running tension between older military officers and young party militants. Friction between the two political factions of the party, the so-called rightists and leftists, was mostly concentrated around the issues of unity with Egypt and the nature of social and economic reforms, but to a large extent it turned into a clash of personalities and hunger for power.[29] As one of the Ba'th leaders at the time later told Phebe Marr: "We were not prepared for power. We had spent all of our time underground, preparing for conspiracy."[30] Another member emphasized that the secrecy under which the party operated "caused the rise of personal rivalries and tendencies and the abandonment of the principle of collective leadership."[31] The eighth regional congress summed up the lessons of that period:

> The leadership of the 1963 revolution [i.e., the leadership of the party at that time] failed to practice its role as a leadership of a revolutionary party. The party machine was left without precise and comprehensive central guidance. The party consequently was unable to act as a vanguard revolutionary institution leading the revolution as it should, regardless of the prevailing circumstances and the risks. It lost the initiative, and thus regression became simple and possible.[32]

Having learned from the lessons of the 1963 debacle, a well-oiled machine was constructed with a centralized hierarchy providing detailed guidance on every aspect of life in the country, as described in the next chapter.

---

[29] Al-Fukayki, *Awkar al-hazima*, pp. 273–75, 307–15.

[30] Marr, *The Modern History of Iraq*, p. 121. Marr quotes Talib Shabib, who was considered a moderate amid the two competing camps in the party.

[31] Kamel S. Abu Jaber, *The Arab Ba'th Socialist Party: History, Ideology and Organization* (Syracuse, NY: Syracuse University Press, 1966), p. 84.

[32] Arab Ba'th Socialist Party, *Revolutionary Iraq 1968–1973: The Political Report Adopted by the Eighth Regional Congress of the Arab Ba'th Socialist Party–Iraq* (Baghdad: The Party, 1974), p. 60.

Another outcome of the 1963 period was the increasing deterioration of relations between the Iraqi and Syrian Ba'th Parties. This was partly the result of the continual meddling of the movement's cofounder, Michel 'Aflaq, in the politics of both countries, but it mostly resulted from "the desire of the Syrian rulers to monopolize Ba'thi legitimacy" and prevent their supporters from shifting alliance to the Iraqi wing.[33]

'Abd al-Salam 'Arif, who had been pardoned by Qasim, became president after the February 1963 coup; even though he was not a Ba'thist, he manipulated the Ba'th Party into giving him the presidency. In November that year he engineered another coup to oust the Ba'th Party from power, and a new page in Iraq's history began, with the reign of the 'Arif brothers ('Abd al-Salam, 1963 to 1966; 'Abd al-Rahman, 1966 to July 1968). As Batatu explains, the "coalition of military Ba'thists, 'Arefites, and Nasserites was a coalition of competing groups, and therefore inherently unstable," and the Ba'thists lost in this contest.[34]

'Arif not only forced the party out of power by exploiting its lack of popularity – a consequence of the excesses committed by the party's militia – but also deprived it of its three official slogans. In a speech on February 13, 1967, 'Arif declared, "Freedom, Socialism, and Unity are the monopoly of no one. They represent the goals of sincere national and nationalist forces."[35] 'Arif managed to consolidate his power shortly after November 1963, and personalities like Ahmad Hasan al-Bakr were pushed aside while Ba'th rightists or members who had been on the sidelines were co-opted into the new regime. This is important because, as discussed later, the party and its security organizations paid much attention to the behavior of members after November 1963, and application forms for party membership inquired about the whereabouts and activities of each applicant at that time.

Creating the Republican Guard as a praetorian militia within the army presaged the centralization of systems of power and personal loyalty that was ruthlessly perfected under Saddam Hussein. Whereas 'Arif relied on army officers whom he could trust, Saddam Hussein replaced them with his civilian comrades from the party, to whom he granted military titles. Most members of the new regime were admirers of President Nasser

---

33 Eberhard Kienle, *Ba'th v Ba'th: The Conflict between Syria and Iraq 1968–1989* (London: I. B. Tauris, 1991), p. 170.

34 Batatu, *The Old Social Classes*, p. 1030.

35 S. L. Egerton, British Embassy, Baghdad, to D. Montgomery, Eastern Department, Foreign Affairs, February 14, 1967, FO EQ1/6, 1016/2/67. Accessed via Cengage Learning EMEA, Middle East Online Series 2: Iraq 1914–1974.

of Egypt, or else Arab nationalists, but 'Arif's policy combined strong pan-Arab nationalism with a social conservatism derived from his devout Muslim faith. He was antagonistic toward the Kurds and the Shi'is. In 1963, for instance, he repeatedly ordered the military to crush the Kurdish independence movement, and in leadership meetings he described the Shi'is with the derogatory term *shu'ubiyyun* and opposed Qasim's policy of opening the regime's doors to all Iraqis irrespective of ethnicity and religion.[36]

On the economic front, measures were adopted by the government, headed by Tahir Yahya, to pave the way for union with Egypt. Banks, insurance companies, and large corporations were nationalized, although middle-sized companies were left in private hands.[37] These surprising moves were not met with enthusiasm by the business community, nor did they resolve any of Iraq's economic problems, which resembled those of many developing countries attempting to navigate between import-substitution manufacturing on the one hand and the needs of the agricultural sector on the other.

The continuing clash between Iraq's Nasserites and the more moderate nationalists continued. Meanwhile, by 1965 Egypt and Iraq were becoming less enthusiastic about a union, as both countries realized the pragmatic obstacles involved. The Nasserites lost their influence when a coup by the Nasserite prime minister was foiled by supporters of 'Arif.[38] In spite of the proposed union, bilateral relations with Egypt were as turbulent as other aspects of Iraq's history; only a year earlier, a Ba'th plot was discovered in the armed forces, and Egypt sent troops as a sign of its support of 'Arif's regime.[39]

Because of the political maneuvers against him, 'Arif felt the need to expand his support base. Although he was not as authoritarian as Qasim, 'Arif's policy of co-opting other groups apart from the armed

[36] Al-Fukayki, *Awkar al-hazima*, p. 273. *Shu'ubiyya* dates back to the Abbasid period and seems to have denoted a non-Arab (*'ajami*) tribal connection. See Ofra Bengio, *Saddam's Word: Political Discourse in Iraq* (Oxford University Press, 1998), p. 103.

[37] For a detailed survey of the period of the 'Arif brothers, see Michael Eppel, *Iraq from Monarchy to Tyranny: From the Hashemites to the Rise of Saddam* (Gainesville, FL: University of Florida, 2004), pp. 219–40. Both Marr and Eppel argue that the brain behind those economic measures was Khayr al-Din al-Hasib, governor of the Central Bank of Iraq, who was impressed by the Egyptian model.

[38] Farouk-Sluglett and Sluglett, *Iraq Since 1958*, pp. 96–97.

[39] For an extensive review of the union attempts between Iraq and Egypt and Iraq's relations with Syria and Egypt, see Malik Mufti, *Sovereign Creations: Pan-Arabism and Political Order in Syria and Iraq* (Ithaca, NY: Cornell University Press, 1996).

forces resonated well with Saddam Hussein after 1968. Tribal sheikhs were "incorporated into a web of patron-client relations, eased by the revenues available to the central government through the export of oil."[40] By sponsoring tribalism and by recruiting many of his supporters and members of the Republican Guard from his own tribe, al-Jumaila, 'Arif set an example for Saddam Hussein to follow several years later.

Feeling secure in his position, he appointed a civilian prime minister, for the first time since the 1958 revolution. 'Abd al-Rahman al-Bazzaz, an Arab nationalist and a former dean of the faculty of law at the University of Baghdad, formed a government with more civilians than military men. He stressed the rule of law, initiated economic and foreign policy measures that began to change Iraq's image abroad, and created optimism within the country. Economically, al-Bazzaz shifted from the nationalization measures of previous governments and launched plans to support the private sector. Unfortunately for Iraqis, civilian rule did not last long. In April 1966, 'Abd al-Salam 'Arif was killed in a helicopter crash caused by a sandstorm and was replaced by his brother, 'Abd al-Rahman 'Arif, who was chief of staff at the time.

The government was engaged in yet another war against the Kurds, and al-Bazzaz, who was reappointed prime minister by the new president, was determined to find a solution. However, neither his decision to accede to the Kurds' demands nor his liberalization policies endeared him to the military or to the Nasserites. The day after the publication of the agreement with the Kurds, an attempted coup took place. The Nasserites who had organized it were defeated, but not before they managed to bomb the presidential palace after gaining control of some air force bases.[41] Thus, the short period of reform and civilian rule came to an end. Al-Bazzaz was replaced by prime ministers who were all military men, proving once again their indispensability. Unlike his brother, the newly installed 'Arif was not capable of consolidating the patronage system that had been established, and rivalries began to surface among the different factions in the country in a struggle for power. Amid this volatile political climate, the military defeat of Arab armies by Israel in the June 1967 War sent shudders through Iraq, as well as other Arab countries. Although Iraq was not a key state in this war and suffered few losses, the consequences of the defeat were enormous and led to a weakening of the legitimacy of military regimes as the most effective form of Arab government.

[40] Tripp, *A History of Iraq*, p. 181.
[41] Eppel, *Iraq from Monarchy to Tyranny*, pp. 225–30.

Economically, while "socialism" was an integral part of the policies of both 'Arif brothers, few socialist measures were implemented apart from the 1964 nationalization measures. In fact, there was constant confusion in the business community about the tenets of national policy, and substantial assets were smuggled abroad.[42] With each change of government came a new direction in economic planning, and this was exacerbated when the fall of Qasim prevented any of these plans from coming to full fruition.[43] Nevertheless, according to the Slugletts, although not much was achieved to reform the structure of the economy, the private sector managed to survive the instability of the 1960s and even expanded its activities.[44]

At the same time, significant progress was achieved in the oil industry. Iraq asserted its influence versus the Iraq Petroleum Company (IPC), which was a consortium of foreign oil companies, and granted the right to drill oil in territories not covered by the IPC to the Iraqi National Oil Company. The first step in controlling Iraq's oil resources began during Qasim's era, when the government expropriated most of the IPC's concessions. Creating Iraq's own oil company was a second step, and the process culminated in the nationalization of the IPC in 1972–73 under Saddam Hussein's tutelage. The broader industrialization of the country, however, moved ahead only slowly: the average growth for industrial production for the years 1962–69 was a modest 5.2 percent, compared to about 11 percent for 1953–58.[45] Overall, the economy stagnated, and the country's reliance on oil revenues continued, with oil accounting for more than 90 percent of exports. At the end of the 1960s, the economic situation was aptly summed up by Alnasrawi:

> The political instability and the frequent occurrence of coups d'etat [*sic*] since 1958 have inflicted heavy human, political, social, and economic damages on a country striving for progress. This instability delayed the implementation of agrarian reform, discouraged industrial and agricultural development efforts, increased the economy's dependence on the oil sector . . . and finally led to virtual economic stagnation.[46]

---

[42] Farouk-Sluglett and Sluglett, *Iraq Since 1958*, p. 220. See also pp. 219–27 for an overview of the economy and society under the 'Arif brothers.

[43] Hossein Askari and John Thomas Cummings, *Middle East Economies in the 1970s: A Comparative Approach* (New York: Praeger, 1976), pp. 435–37.

[44] Farouk-Sluglett and Sluglett, *Iraq Since 1958*, p. 220.

[45] Joseph Sassoon, "Industrialization in Iraq 1958–1968," *Ha-Mizrah he-Hadash*, vol. 30, (1981), p. 46.

[46] Abbas Alnasrawi, *Financing Economic Development in Iraq: The Role of Oil in a Middle Eastern Economy* (New York: Praeger, 1967), p. 160.

After losing power in November 1963 the Ba'th Party was in crisis. Its leaders were split among themselves, each side blaming the other for the failures of this first term in office. 'Aflaq intervened, and a new national leadership was created, with Ahmad Hasan al-Bakr and Saddam Hussein in the Regional Command, the party's top decision-making body. This was a major accomplishment for the young Saddam Hussein, who was not very well known and still in his twenties. From the beginning he wanted to extend his control of the party, and he took advantage of his appointment as the head of its intelligence and security arm, known as *jihaz hunain*. In September 1964, when the Ba'th's attempted coup against 'Arif failed, Saddam Hussein was among many leaders who were imprisoned. He was incarcerated for about two years until he managed to escape, although it seems that conditions were not as harsh as those that awaited his enemies years later. He was able to see his family and his six-month-old son, 'Uday, and he sent messages to al-Bakr concealed in the baby's clothing.[47]

'Arif was either too forgiving or felt sufficiently secure in his position to seek retribution; hence a dual policy developed whereby some Ba'th members were persecuted while others were allowed to carry on relatively unhindered. 'Abd al-Rahman 'Arif, aware of his own political weakness, met regularly with al-Bakr and tried to enlist the Ba'th as part of a national coalition. No serious efforts were made to capture Saddam Hussein after his escape, and by the end of 1966, at the age of twenty-nine, he became deputy secretary general of the party.

The rift between the Ba'th parties in Syria and Iraq widened. In February 1966, a military coup by the party's left wing in Syria forced 'Aflaq and the Syrian leadership to seek refuge in Iraq. From that point on, despite short periods of rapprochement, the chasm between the so-called left wing in Syria and the right wing supported by al-Bakr and Saddam Hussein was never bridged. The Iraqi Ba'th, realizing the diminishing appeal both of Nasserism and of pan-Arabism – particularly after June 1967 – took a critical stand against Nasser and his policies in the Arab world, thus gaining popularity among the nationalists in Iraq. Indeed, the weakness of Arabism in Iraq compared with Syria was one of the distinguishing features of the two ideologies.[48] Regional competition continued, with Saddam Hussein determined never to allow the Syrian branch to become

[47] Fuad Matar, *Saddam Hussein: The Man, the Cause, and the Future* (London: Third World Centre, 1981), p. 46.
[48] Sluglett, "Le parti Baas," p. 96.

the Ba'th headquarters in the Arab world.[49] 'Aflaq remained in Iraq until his death and was treated with utmost respect by Saddam Hussein as the founding father of the party. Antagonism between the two countries continued to deepen to the extent that Ba'thist Syria joined the coalition to liberate Kuwait from Iraq's occupation in 1991.[50]

The Iraqi Ba'th consolidated its organization, taking advantage of the political uncertainty and the crisis in political confidence that shook Iraq at the end of 1967; the public disappointment with the 'Arif brothers, particularly after the 1967 War, which undermined their legitimacy; the diminishing attractiveness of pan-Arabism; the weakening of the communists that had begun in 1963; and finally the growing interest in Ba'th ideology, which lacked detailed specifics but could appeal to large sectors of the population. Describing the period prior to the July 1968 coup, the political report of the eighth regional congress stated that "the past phase has been like a difficult birth, full of experiences, problems, success, failure, progress and retreat."[51] In reality, the Ba'th policy between November 1963 and July 1968 focused on how to seize power, rather than on constructing political programs to attract new members.[52] The party's new leadership distanced itself from those who were identified with the February–November 1963 period, such as 'Ali Salih al-Sa'di, and managed to strengthen its support within the military and civil structures, the latter orchestrated by Saddam Hussein.

The infighting within the 'Arif regime persisted, while a standstill in the war against the Kurds created further frustration among the officer corps. The Ba'thists were in touch with many senior officers, leading to an arrangement with Colonel 'Abd al-Razzaq al-Nayif, director of military intelligence, and Colonel 'Abd al-Rahman al-Da'ud, commander of the Republican Guard, whereby the two sides would withdraw their support from 'Arif. On July 17, 1968, 'Arif was forced to resign but was allowed to go into exile because he did not present any real threat to the party. Years later Saddam Hussein would recount the peaceful transition of

---

[49] For more details on the ideological rift between the two countries, see Kienle, *Ba'th v Ba'th*.

[50] For discussion of the rift between the two parties, see John F. Devlin, "The Baath Party: Rise and Metamorphosis," *American Historical Review*, vol. 96, no. 5 (December 1991), pp. 1396–1407.

[51] The Arab Ba'th Socialist Party, *Revolutionary Iraq*, p. 54.

[52] Marion Farouk-Sluglett and Peter Sluglett, "From Gang to Elite: The Iraqi Ba'th Party's Consolidation of Power 1968–1975," *Peuples Mediterranéens*, no. 40 (July–September 1987), p. 90.

power and express his pride that not a single drop of blood was shed. A seven-man revolutionary council was set up, consisting only of military personnel, and the Ba'th Party, conscious of its mistakes and rivalries in 1963, moved quickly to consolidate its support among the military. Thirteen days after this first peaceful coup, the two colonels and another independent (Sa'dun Ghaidan) were exiled or appointed as ambassadors, and the Ba'th takeover was complete.[53]

The Ba'th Party cleverly exploited the numerous vacuums of power in the country and the Iraqi people's desire for a strong and stable state that would launch their country into modernity and develop its potential. As the Slugletts wrote of the pre-1968 period: "All hope of the establishment of any form of democratic political life based on representative institutions had been crushed, and a system had emerged that had no other source of legitimacy except that conferred by military force and the possession of a monopoly of the means of coercion."[54] The lack of stability in the turbulent years between 1958 and 1968 brought another element to the fore: political violence. Using force became an accepted way of solving political disagreements, even among members of the same party or faction. Both Qasim, to some extent, and the first 'Arif, to a far greater extent, did not hesitate to send their enemies, sometimes even people who had been their close colleagues, to the gallows.[55] Although Saddam Hussein and the Ba'th Party were to take political violence and brutality to a new level after 1968, the basis for this was laid after the revolution of July 1958 and in particular after 1963. Hani al-Fukayki, a member of the Ba'th Regional Command and the party's political bureau in the 1960s, was more honest that many when discussing this period:

> I used to frequently visit the centers of interrogation and the prison in *qasr al-nihaya* [the palace of the end].... Although I did not personally participate in the torture of any of the suspects or accused, I do not remember condemning or denouncing torture, as I believed, like other revolutionaries of that era, that protecting the revolution and the party was above all other considerations and that humiliating and annihilating the enemy were core aspects of the revolutionary path.[56]

---

[53] For more extensive details of the events of July 17 and July 30, see Farouk-Sluglett and Sluglett, *Iraq Since 1958*, pp. 108–16; Tripp. *A History of Iraq*, pp. 185–92.

[54] Farouk-Sluglett and Sluglett, *Iraq Since 1958*, p. 93.

[55] In July 1963, 'Arif argued strongly for the execution of 450 officers who were accused of being Qasimites or communists during Qasim's era. See al-Fukayki, *Awkar al-hazima*, pp. 278–80.

[56] Al-Fukayki, *Awkar al-hazima*, p. 276.

This brief overview has shown that Iraq's troubled history in the twentieth century was marked by recurrent power vacuums among different interest groups. Their rivalries hindered the country's development, in particular the exploitation of its natural resources and considerable human resources and talents. Indeed, much of the affliction that dominated the period 1968–2003 originated in the 1960s: 'Arif's emphasis on tribalism, on building client groups, and on managing the state's resources to allow those in power to cater to the needs of their patronage networks and his setting up of large security organizations to coerce opponents. As we will see in the following chapters, the Ba'th leadership perfected all these aspects to its advantage and reigned for three and a half decades. The party, and in particular Saddam Hussein, understood the nation's yearning for stability and prosperity and exploited it to create an authoritarian regime and a personality cult on the basis of seemingly persuasive promises of a brighter future.

2

Party Structure and Organization

The development of the Ba'th Party's apparatus during its thirty-five-year rule enabled it to survive intraparty struggles, two devastating wars, a period of severe sanctions, and major battles against the Kurds and the Shi'is during the intifada of 1991. As the long arm of Saddam Hussein, the party became an impressive and formidable organization that played a central role in sustaining the power of the regime. In its structure, membership, and recruitment, and in its political education campaign, the Ba'th Party was characteristic of ruling parties in other tyrannical regimes.

The Party Structure

The Ba'th Party played a crucial role in decision making in Iraq, and in many ways its structure was similar to that of the Communist Party in the Soviet Union. Both societies could be termed mono-organizational, because all activities were run by hierarchies of appointed officials under a single command.[1] As the Ba'th Party expanded in size and governing responsibilities, bureaucratization became critical for its success. Ba'th documents clearly show that there was an elaborate division of labor and, like the Soviet system, goals and decisions were formulated at the apex of the pyramid, so that "organizational success depends on each participant precisely performing his tasks as prescribed, without his needing

[1] T. H. Rigby, "Stalinism and the Mono-Organizational Society," in Robert C. Tucker (ed.), *Stalinism: Essays in Historical Interpretation* (New Brunswick, NJ: Transaction, 1999), pp. 53–76.

to understand the system as a whole or even support its goals."[2] This was important, given that Iraq officially became a Ba'thist country after the party came to power in 1968:

> We have to emphasize that this society is led by a party, and that party is the Arab Ba'th Socialist Party... which leads [the people] in its values, its organizations, and also leads it in its ideas and its policies.... Thus it is necessary that the party's values and ideologies are at the forefront of these activities, and throughout the country's decision-making apparatus.[3]

In order to ensure that the party permeated and controlled every facet of life in Iraq, its members occupied most of the important positions in the country. In 1974, the political report of the eighth regional congress of the party declared that it had succeeded "in consolidating its leadership ... to an extent that makes it capable of safeguarding the regime and apply its programmes." However, the report admitted that "the phase was not free of many errors and negative aspects." Among these errors were "steps by the party in placing party members in sensitive government posts [that] were necessary but produced some negative results."[4]

Centralization of power was a key element of Ba'th strategy. The eighth congress report announced that the second most important task facing the revolution, after liquidating foreign intelligence networks and agents, was "to build a strong and central national authority."[5] Hence, every major decision in the ruling party was centralized through *maktab amanat sir al-qutr* (the Party Secretariat), in essence the party's board of directors. In a memo distributed by the RCC to all ministries, it decreed that all "correspondence between state ministries and party organizations are to be sent through the Party Secretariat."[6]

The functions and specialization of the Party Secretariat were drawn up in a clear and meticulous way. The Secretariat hierarchy was formulated according to a directive distributed by the office of the president, and the functions of each department and section were clearly defined.[7]

---

[2] *Ibid.*, p. 54.
[3] Saddam Hussein, *al-Thawra wa al-tarbiya al-wataniyya* [The Revolution and the National Education] (Baghdad: al-Maktaba al-Wataniyya, 1977), pp. 12–13.
[4] The Arab Ba'th Socialist Party, *Revolutionary Iraq*, pp. 66–67.
[5] *Ibid.*, pp. 74–77.
[6] RCC to All Ministries, "Circulation," January 16, 1978, *NIDS*, PUK 034, Box 0191 (100067).
[7] Ruling 10R Issued by Saddam Hussein to All Concerned, December 26, 2001, *BRCC*, 010-2-1 (007–034).

The Secretariat encompassed every branch within the party, which in turn controlled every aspect of civil and military life in the country (see Appendix I). The complexity of the hierarchical structure that needed to be negotiated to reach any small ruling that affected the party, or Iraqi citizens, showed the depth of bureaucratization. Needless to say, decision making was cumbersome and inefficient, but at the same time it gave Saddam Hussein the ability to govern without having to fear that too much power would fall into the hands of rivals.

The Department for Organizational and Political Affairs was probably the most important within the organization, as it prepared the material for discussions based on the orders of the party's secretary general (Saddam Hussein) and then proceeded to carry out those orders. In addition, it was responsible for following up on political matters with all branches of the party. One of its subsections, the private information section, had the job of collating information on any candidate applying for a significant position within the party or the government apparatus.[8] Some departments dealt with admission to military colleges, higher education institutions, and the Saddam Institute for the Study of the Qur'an, which was used to influence religious life in the country.[9] The control of admissions to these institutions was paramount for the party to establish and expand its authority at all levels of society and to prevent other parties from increasing their influence with students or military cadets.

Organizationally, *al-qiyada al-qutriyya* (the Regional Command) was the highest authority of the party in Iraq after its split from the Syrian Ba'th Party in 1966. Originally, *al-qiyada al-qawmiyya* (the National Command) was the executive body in charge of the different regional commands in the Arab world, and although it continued to function, its powers became increasingly symbolic.[10] Membership in *al-qiyada al-qutriyya* ranged from nineteen to twenty-one members.[11] In early 2001,

---

[8] *Ibid.*

[9] See Appendix I. For the role of the institute, see Chapter 8, the section on religion.

[10] The National Command was composed of ten members in 2001: Saddam Hussein and three members of the Quartet, in addition to six representatives of other Arab Ba'th parties from Jordan, Yemen, Lebanon, Sudan, Tunisia, and Syria. *Conflict Records Research Center (CRRC)*, SH-BATH-D-000-144.

[11] In May 2001, the number of members was nineteen. For the full list, see David Baran, *Vivre la tyrannie et lui survivre: L'Irak en transition* [Life and Survival under Tyranny: Iraq in Transition] (Paris: Mille et une nuits, 2004), p. 151. The only woman member was Huda Salih Mahdi 'Ammash. In 1977, the Regional Command was increased to twenty-one members. See Farouk-Sluglett and Sluglett, *Iraq Since 1958*, p. 208.

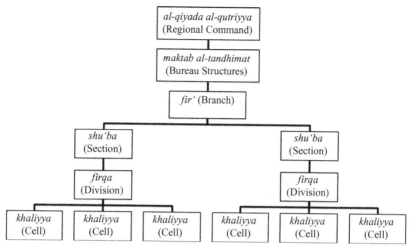

FIGURE 1. Structure of the Command of the Iraqi Baʿth Party. *Source:* Helms, *Iraq*, p. 84; Matar, *Saddam Hussein*, pp. 203–04.

its six most important members were Saddam Hussein, the Quartet (comprising ʿIzzat al-Duri, Taha Yasin Ramadan, Tariq ʿAziz, and ʿAli Hasan al-Majid), and Qusay Saddam Hussein. As Figure 1 shows, under the Regional Command were *maktab al-tandhimat* ("bureau structures," shortened to *tandhim*, or "structures," in the party jargon) whereby all party activities in one large geographic area were gathered under a single roof.[12] With the expansion of the party, the number of these structures grew; for instance, until 1989, there were six *tandhimat*: five that covered geographic areas (Baghdad, the center, the north, al-Furat, and the south) and one for the military bureaus. By 2002, there were seventeen *tandhimat*, which were subdivided into *firuʿ* (branches), which acted as the next layer in the hierarchy and supervised the activities of the sections, divisions, and cells. There were frequent spin-offs and amalgamations of these branches and sections during the party's thirty-five-year rule, and by late 2002, sixty-nine branches were reporting on their own activities and those of their subdivisions (see Appendix II).[13]

The number of sections and divisions varied from one province to another, and as membership increased, new sections and divisions were

---

[12] Christine Moss Helms, *Iraq: Eastern Flank of the Arab World* (Washington, DC: Brookings Institution, 1984), pp. 83–86; Matar, *Saddam Hussein*, pp. 203–04.

[13] Some of the party's studies relied on information from only a limited number of branches. For example, one study discussed activities of only twenty branches. See Bureau of Information and Studies to Party Secretariat, January 14, 2002, *BRCC*, 010-2-5 (006).

created. For example, in Misan province, there were 5 *shu'ab* (sections) in 1989, but by 2002 the number had risen to 20; these sections in turn had 93 *firaq* (divisions).[14] According to data from September 2002 (Appendix II), there were 4,468 party offices (branches, sections, and divisions) throughout the country, in addition to more than 32,000 cells.

Expansion occupied the minds of the party leaders: should they split sections and divisions that were getting too large or open new ones in order to boost recruitment and increase the party's membership base?[15] This was also an important issue for party personnel, as the leadership encouraged competition among different elements of the organization, and subdividing part of a section would mean, by definition, weakening it compared to other sections and thus reducing the power of those running it. As Appendix II indicates, excluding the military bureaus, the two *tandhimat* of Baghdad contained the largest number of sections, totaling 114 (57 sections each), whereas in the provinces, Salah al-Din had the highest number, with 57 sections, compared to Karbala, which had only 17 sections.

The Party's Functions

In order to consolidate its control over Iraqi society, the Ba'th Party reached into every aspect of life. Internally, party secretaries had an obligation to encourage the development and strengthen the devotion of members. They were responsible for party education, conducting elections, planning and coordinating meetings and conferences, implementing all party and leadership decrees, enforcing discipline, and making sure that the party played a significant role in every military unit.

Nationally, the party's most critical function was to be the eyes and ears of the regime in every corner of the country. With the passage of time, the party's influence over the security forces, the army, government bureaucracy (economy, education, health, etc.), and labor and professional unions, as well as over the creation of the cult personality of Saddam Hussein, was overwhelming. From the 1990s, the party became involved in food distribution, in pursuing and apprehending deserters,

---

[14] *BRCC*, July 31, 1989, 021-1-4 (135–136); Party Secretariat to Ministry of Awqaf, "Holy Books," October 5, 2002, *BRCC*, 011-1-4 (26). The party was distributing the Qur'an to all its affiliates as part of the faith campaign.

[15] See, for example, a summary of the meeting of Saddam Hussein with the Party Secretariat of al-Karkh branch in Baghdad in *al-Qadisiyya* newspaper, June 10, 2002.

and, finally, in the preparations to resist the American-led invasion of 2003.

Like any large corporation, every section and division had to file an annual report presenting its achievements in the format prescribed by the Party Secretariat. Each section had to put together statistics on current membership, recruitment of new members, conferences and meetings arranged with other sections, future prospects, cultural activities and forums, and popular events such as celebrations or special occasions dictated by the leadership. In addition, the sections carried out security activities, which included training members and capturing the regime's enemies.[16]

In regard to security matters, the branches and sections enjoyed considerable power; they took over many traditional police functions, mainly outside Baghdad, and were legally authorized to incarcerate suspects using extrajudicial procedures. Among its major functions, the party was responsible for collecting information about its opponents both inside and outside Iraq. Activities in northern Iraq illustrate how the Ba'th structure worked. The party cadre was in charge of arresting agents of the Kurdish Democratic Party (KDP), tracking the activities of its members outside Iraq, reporting on the different tribes in the area and ensuring their loyalty, recruiting informers, and encouraging the local population to provide information about the regime's enemies. Party members were also active in remote areas of Kurdistan, in supplying food or helping with literacy campaigns, in an attempt to reduce the influence of the KDP and its agents.[17]

The Arabization of northern Iraq was another important objective for Ba'th officials. This was done, first, by relocating Ba'th members to the north. In one example, based on a document dating back to 1983, 231 party personnel from across all ranks and 350 teachers were resettled in different parts of Kurdistan to increase the party's influence.[18] The second feature of Arabization was preventing those who left Kurdistan

---

[16] Party Secretariat of al-Karkh Branch to All Sections, "Forms," June 11, 2001, *BRCC*, 003-2-5 (285–296).

[17] Mandali Intelligence to Intelligence Headquarters, "Quarterly Report on Terrorists' Activities, July–September 1981," September 10, 1981, *NIDS*, KDP 033, Box 2344 (090000–090025). See also Head of Committee for Combating Enemy Activities, Arbil Province to Party Secretariat in the North, December 3, 1988, *NIDS*, PUK 008, Box 32; Secretary of Sanjar Division to Party Secretariat in the North, December 25, 1987, *NIDS*, PUK 040, Box 242.

[18] Party Secretariat to RCC, "Transfers," August 25, 1983, *BRCC*, 165-5-5 (385–390).

from returning to their homes unless they were loyal to the regime or became active members of the party. The party developed a system to check the origin of every citizen who wanted to relocate to the north, to ensure that they were not Kurdish or Persian, belonged to the right tribe, and had clean records.[19]

When an American-led invasion was looming toward the end of 2002, the party galvanized itself into preparation for the war. Intelligence reports were regularly supplied about the meetings of Kurdish activists outside Iraq working for either the Barazani or the Talabani groups.[20] Movements of individuals belonging to the Kurdish parties, who, according to those reports, were being trained by American officers, were monitored carefully.[21] Similarly, news of the arrival in the north of 500 people carrying Iraqi passports who belonged to *hizb al-da'wa* (Da'wa Party) and were allegedly sponsored by American intelligence agencies was dispatched by local activists to party headquarters.[22]

The party, through its military and armament department (see Appendix I), was also in charge of coordinating the distribution of arms to the party faithful, training as many people as possible to fight the invading armies, encouraging young men to join *fida'iyyu Saddam* (fedayeen Saddam, or "those who are willing to sacrifice themselves for Saddam"), and preparing and storing food and oil supplies for emergency use. The party also played a critical role in pursuing and arresting deserters, using its wide network of informers throughout the country (see Chapter 4). In the 1990s, when Saddam Hussein diverged from his original anti-tribal ideology and adopted a more pro-tribal policy,[23] the party became

---

[19] Party Secretariat to the Ministry of Interior, December 8, 1980, *BRCC*, 017-1-5 (115; 368; 398; 470–471).

[20] Mas'ud al-Barazani and Jalal al-Talabani led the two main Kurdish parties, the Kurdish Democratic Party (KDP) and the Patriotic Union of Kurdistan (PUK), respectively. For more information, see Gareth R. V. Stansfield, "The Kurdish Dilemma: The Golden Era Threatened," in Toby Dodge and Steven Simon (eds.), *Iraq at the Crossroads: State and Society in the Shadow of Regime Change*, Adelphi Papers 354 (Oxford University Press, 2003), pp. 131–48.

[21] Ninewa Party Secretariat to Party Secretariat, June 20, 2002, *BRCC*, 006-4-1 (231–233).

[22] *Ibid.*, May 7, 2002, *BRCC*, 006-4-1 (236).

[23] Amatzia Baram, "Neo-Tribalism in Iraq: Saddam Hussein's Tribal Policies 1991–96," *International Journal of Middle East Studies*, vol. 29, no. 1 (February 1997), pp. 1–31. Saddam Hussein, after the Ba'th came to power in 1968, rejected tribalism and saw it as a remnant of colonialism, but in the late 1980s he altered that view drastically and endorsed tribalism.

involved in solving issues arising with various tribes and accommodating their demands.[24]

Like any successful concern, the Ba'th Party needed to ensure that it was run on a financially sound basis, and it paid a lot of attention to its finances. Apart from the generous allocation by the RCC, the party collected fees and contributions from its members. Fees were commensurate with rank: in 1998, for example, a supporter would pay only 25 Iraqi dinar (ID) (about $0.03), whereas a branch member had to pay ID3,000 (roughly $3).[25] Fees were an important element in the party's balance sheet, and this was reflected in copious correspondence from the senior leadership urging branch secretaries to make sure fees were collected on time, while simultaneously encouraging members to make additional contributions. Much emphasis was placed on the financial condition of members, and there was an insistence that all information about personal finances should be accurate. The party also required that any change in a comrade's financial status had to be reported immediately.[26] The concern was that any deterioration in members' financial situation could lead to their becoming vulnerable and a possible security risk.

Saddam Hussein understood well the importance of finances in the successful running of the party. According to Jawad Hashim, who was minister of planning and an economic advisor to the RCC, Saddam Hussein decided to retain in Ba'th coffers the 5 percent of Iraq's oil revenues owned previously by the Gulbenkian Foundation, which had been nationalized in 1973. In a meeting attended by Hashim, the minister of finance, and the governor of the Central Bank, Saddam Hussein said,

> The Ba'th Party came to Iraq to govern for 300 years, and in order to continue in that role, and in case it would be removed in a military coup d'état, it has to have serious financial resources outside Iraq.... We do not want to repeat the mistakes of 1963 when our regime fell and we faced serious financial difficulties.... Thus, I am asking you men of finance and economy to figure out how to earmark the share of the nationalized Gulbenkian for the party.[27]

[24] Party Secretariat to Secretaries of Branches, "Decision," October 26, 1993, *BRCC*, 033-1-6 (279).

[25] Party Secretariat to Headquarters of All Branches, June 3, 1998, *BRCC*, 003-4-4 (322–323).

[26] Party Secretariat to All Branches, "Financial Situation," September 7, 1989, *BRCC*, 003-3-7 (006).

[27] Jawad Hashim, *Mudhakkarat wazir 'Iraqi ma'a al-Bakr wa Saddam: Dhikrayat fi al-siyasa al-'Iraqiyya 1967–2000* [Memoirs of an Iraqi Minister with al-Bakr and Saddam: Reflections on Iraqi Politics, 1967–2000] (Beirut: al-Saqi, 2003), pp. 148–49.

By Hashim's estimates, the revenues accumulated outside Iraq in the party's secret accounts could have reached about $10 billion by 1989, without including annual returns from its investments.[28]

The party was also involved in activities outside Iraq, either as an intelligence-gathering machine (see Chapter 4) or to help build and organize Baʿth branches in Arab countries. Saddam Hussein was of the opinion that Iraqi members should help Baʿth organizations in neighboring countries but that it would be preferable to have local leaders once they gained the right "qualifications and characteristics." He felt that a Baʿthist's duty was to abide by his or her duties: "Suppose we have 100 Baʿthists, they could be of use to our party branches here in Iraq or even abroad. Assign them, let them go, let them get transferred, let them get arrested, that is a Baʿthist duty. He should not neglect his duties."[29]

Party Discipline

The Baʿth Party in Iraq, like the Soviet Communists or the ruling party in any authoritarian regime, had to instill discipline in order to carry out the will of its leaders. "Party members are expected to inspire others by their exemplary behavior, sense of discipline, political consciousness, and willingness to sacrifice themselves in the interests of the Party and state."[30]

Saddam Hussein was a great believer in discipline, and in the novels he wrote (always published anonymously as "A Novel by Its Author," although their real authorship was understood by all people in Iraq), he reiterated his belief that lack of organization and poor preparation are behind every failure.[31] His predilection for party discipline is highlighted in many documents; he believed that discipline should take precedence over everything else for military cadets and for young party members.[32]

---

[28] *Ibid.*, p. 149.

[29] Audiotape of a discussion of RCC and senior party leadership, 1992 (no specific date), *CRRC*, SH-SHTP-A-000-830.

[30] Merle Fainsod, *How Russia Is Ruled*, revised edn. (Cambridge, MA: Harvard University Press, 1963), p. 493.

[31] Saddam Hussein, *Rijal wa madina*, pp. 252–53.

[32] See, for example, a report prepared following Saddam Hussein's orders to investigate the reasons for the lack of training of students in military camps and the high number of absentees. The report highlighted the lack of discipline and underlined the leader's teachings on this issue. Presidential *diwan* to Party Secretariat, "Decision of a Committee," September 22, 1986, *BRCC*, 003-2-7 (112–120).

Consistent with its disciplinary style, the party issued a myriad of rules and regulations ranging from the sublime to the ridiculous. Stiff measures were taken against corruption and abuses of power by senior members. In one case, a senior member obtained a license for a friend to open a bar (and was paid for that service): he was disciplined and demoted.[33] In another case, a branch member who produced exaggerated written reports was demoted due to his lack of credibility.[34] Sometimes punishments were for abuses of power by party members against members of security services.[35] Senior members were scorned if they used their party vehicles for private trips.[36] Party members were expected to arrive at their jobs punctually and to stay until the end of working hours. Lists were collected of those arriving late or leaving before the end of their shift; a note was made in their files, and in many cases either they were reprimanded immediately or the issue came up in their annual reviews.[37] It is important to note that although corruption was rampant and the Ba'th committed many abuses of power, its members, both junior and senior, never knew whether they would be punished for their actions. This lack of certainty acted as a restrictive control and was efficient as prescriptive control.

Control over the lives of members took other forms: they had to receive approval from the Party Secretariat before marriage, as did army officers; each member had to complete a form with information about his or her prospective spouse and the spouse's family, even if the spouse was also a party member. In an internal document on checking marriage approval forms, party branches were ordered "to check thoroughly the Arabic origin of not only the prospective wife but also her family, and no approval should be given to members who plan to marry [someone] from a non-Arab origin."[38] Once the war with Iran erupted, the party

---

[33] Presidential Advisor for Party Affairs to Party Secretariat, "Investigation," March 23, 1989, *BRCC*, 021-1-2 (181).

[34] Party Secretariat to Presidential *diwan*, "Behavior of a Member," December 13, 1994, *BRCC*, 119-4-8 (152).

[35] Military Intelligence Services to Party Secretariat, "Attack," June 24, 1996, *BRCC*, 021-1-2 (80).

[36] Al-Karkh Branch, Baghdad to All, "Vehicle Usage," October 20, 2001, *BRCC*, 004-1-3 (124).

[37] Party Secretariat to All Branches, "Late Employees," January 16, 1993, *BRCC*, 004-5-4; Al-Karkh Branch to Musa Section, "Absence of a Member from His Shift," August 19, 2001, *BRCC*, 003-2-5 (25).

[38] Party Secretariat to All Secretaries of Branches, November 14, 1983, *BRCC*, 003-3-5 (11); see also *NIDS*, PUK 038, Box 147 (900027).

had to confront the issue of affiliates who were of *taba'iyya Iraniyya* (Iranian nationality). One memo from the Party Secretariat, addressed directly to Saddam Hussein, informed him that "the party suffers from the existence of members who are not originally Arabs as this might constitute a danger to the party in the future." The memo recommended that no member of Iranian origin should be given "the honor of membership." Saddam Hussein wrote in the margins: "1) [I] Agree with the opinion of the Party Secretariat; 2) To be discussed in the Command meeting."[39] Many of those on whom the party refused to bestow membership were loyal Ba'thists. One man joined the party in 1958 and was arrested after the collapse of the first Ba'th regime in November 1963. Although five members wrote recommendations about him, he was refused membership due to his Iranian origins. Another had joined the party in 1965 and in spite of the fact that he was arrested in 1963 due to his pro-Ba'th activities, his full membership had been turned down frequently for the same reason.[40] In none of those documents was the word *Shi'i* mentioned, and the writers simply refer to it using the term *taba'iyya Iraniyya*. By 1987, toward the end of the war with Iran, based on direct orders from Saddam Hussein, the party began checking the nationality of anyone applying to join the party to determine if they were definitely Iraqi in origin.[41] In one documented case, the father of the applicant was found to have immigrated to Iraq from Iran back in 1918, so the application was rejected.[42]

Members were disciplined about other matters, too: a memo was circulated criticizing members who attended a meeting without a notepad, or others who sat inappropriately cross-legged – they were reminded that the leader himself had denounced the latter habit as indicative of lack of party discipline.[43] Another habit that was held in utter contempt was card playing, and members were warned "that those tempted to engage in this abhorrent phenomenon will be punished severely."[44] Some habits were hard to change or were resisted; for instance, when a member of the RCC

[39] Party Secretariat to Secretary General, April 1, 1980, *BRCC*, 003-1-1 (526).
[40] *BRCC*, 003-1-1 (528).
[41] Party Secretariat to the President's Secretary, "Information," April 12, 1987, *BRCC*, 003-3-3.
[42] *Ibid.*
[43] Al-Karkh Branch, Baghdad to All Party Secretaries, "Guidance," September 30, 2001, *BRCC*, 004-1-3 (122).
[44] Party Secretariat, Suleimaniyya Branch to Members, "Information," December 22, 1987, *NIDS*, PUK 040, Box 242 (020054).

recommended that Ba'th Party members should celebrate without firing their guns in the air because this made the people of Iraq look like an "uncivilized society," Saddam Hussein turned the suggestion down, as he believed this activity allowed members the ability to express themselves.[45]

For Saddam Hussein, discipline was not only about adhering to party rules and ideology. On an order from the president, physical fitness became a criterion, and all members had to undergo a fitness test. They had to have a medical checkup to confirm their physical fitness, and if they did not pass the second time, they were demoted by one rank in the party. Similarly, no member was allowed to be promoted to a higher rank unless he or she was deemed physically fit.[46]

Like other authoritarian regimes, party discipline was used to get rid of political enemies. The regime wanted to control and know everything there was to be known about its members or, for that matter, all citizens. For example, an order was issued that the presidential *diwan* should be informed if any member or official, at any level from head of department all the way to minister, was to enter a hospital or undergo surgery.[47] Party discipline was also used to enforce the personality cult of Saddam Hussein (see Chapter 6).

Membership and Recruitment

When the Ba'th Party came to power in 1968, it was determined to increase its membership dramatically to compete with other ideological parties, in particular the widely popular Communist Party. As in Ba'thist Syria, it became evident to the new leadership that "the more participants and the more intensely mobilized they are, the more potential power" the party would have.[48] Saddam Hussein was very frank in discussing his strategy: in the mid-1970s he declared that "it should be our ambition to make all Iraqis in the country Ba'thists in membership and belief or in the latter only."[49] This stood in sharp contrast to the 1990s, when adding

---

[45] Audiotape of a meeting of the RCC, 1991, *CRRC*, SH-SHTP-A-000-633.

[46] Presidential *diwan* to Party Secretariat, "Decision," May 12, 1987, *BRCC*, 003-3-5 (14).

[47] Presidential *diwan* to Party Secretariat, "Government Cadres," October 3, 2001, *BRCC*, 004-3-1 (089).

[48] Raymond A. Hinnebusch, *Authoritarian Power and State Formation in Ba'thist Syria: Army, Party, and Peasant* (Boulder, CO: Westview Press, 1990), p. 13.

[49] Speech delivered by Saddam Hussein at the meeting of the General Federation of Iraqi Youth, February 15, 1976, in Saddam Hussein, *Social and Foreign Affairs in Iraq*, translated by Khalid Kishtainy (London: Croom Helm, 1979), p. 57.

FIGURE 2. Party Membership Hierarchy. *Source:* Ninewa branch's form for the hierarchy of party personnel, *BRRC*, 005-3-3 (180).

members took priority over believing in the Ba'th ideology. In fact, two concepts developed during that period: *intisab* (affiliation) and *intima'* (membership); under the former, masses of Iraqis became affiliated but only a small percentage were active members.

Like any large organization, the party membership was very hierarchical (see Figure 2) and was based on depth of commitment and years of service. At the lowest level, the *mu'ayyid* (sympathizer) was only required to attend weekly meetings, and as this group made up the solid core of new recruits, they received intense political education to prepare them for the next stage: becoming a *nasir* (supporter). Progressing through the ranks meant devoting significant time and effort to serving the party, and it could take five to ten years to become an *'udhu 'amil* (active member). At the top of every branch, section, and division, there was a secretary general who was in charge of running the unit and handled all correspondence with the Party Secretariat. In northern Iraq potential members had to pass through an additional layer, *al-nashat al-watani* (national activity), before even joining the ranks of sympathizers, and sometimes it took two to three years to become a *mu'ayyid.*[50]

---

[50] *NIDS*, KDP 016, Box 2176 (040045) and KDP 017, Box 2182 (010036).

Yearly evaluations and obedience to the party were essential to reach a higher rank. The evaluations give a clear indication of what was expected from members wishing to climb the hierarchical ladder: loyalty, abiding by party rules and regulations, hard work, modesty, and, last but not least, following the example of *al-qa'id* (the leader) in bravery and carrying out the responsibility of being a Ba'thist.[51] In addition to displaying these qualities, an active member wishing to progress to *'udhu firqa* (division member) must possess leadership and organizational abilities, as well as being a good exponent of the Ba'th's ideals.[52] Needless to say, numerous forms had to be filled out by the applicant and by several referees before any promotion could be given. Details about the applicant's political work, commitment to the party and its leader, participation in battles or missions for the regime, voluntary activities in one of the popular militias, and ability to recruit new entrants were all assessed before a decision was reached.[53] According to one of the forms, an applicant's promotion was delayed six months because he did not attend party meetings or would arrive late with "lame" excuses.[54] In essence, "it is not sufficient for a member just to believe in the idea of the party, but what is required is total commitment and not simply a political affiliation."[55]

Once a member fulfilled all the conditions and managed to reach the rank of *murashih* (candidate), he or she had to go through political education courses followed by the ceremony of *tardid al-qasm* (oath reiteration) in front of a group of senior Ba'thists. This was a rite of passage for all members, and, akin to Stalinism, being part of the Ba'th "involved considerable symbolism and ritual."[56] The personal files of each applicant held the names of the senior members who had witnessed his or her swearing of allegiance to the party, and this was a vital feature of a member's record. Interestingly, it played a role in deciding the future of those who joined the party before the 1968 revolution but then stopped being active.

[51] Party Secretariat, "Evaluation of a Comrade," January 14, 1980, *BRCC*, 003-3-7 (169–172).

[52] *Ibid.*

[53] Zacho Section, "Form for Evaluating Members," June 1984, *NIDS*, KDP 009, Box 2092 (220031); *BRCC*, 006-2-5 (170).

[54] Party Secretariat, "Form for Evaluating Promotion," January 28, 2003, *BRCC*, 004-3-5 (026).

[55] Hizb al-Ba'th al-'Arabi al-Ishtiraki, *al-Taqrir al-siyasi lil mu'tamar al-qawmi al-'ashir* [The Political Report of the Tenth National Conference] (Baghdad: The Party, 1970), p. 47.

[56] J. Arch Getty and Oleg V. Naumov, *The Road to Terror: Stalin and the Self-Destruction of the Bolsheviks, 1932–1939* (New Haven, CT: Yale University Press, 1999), p. 78.

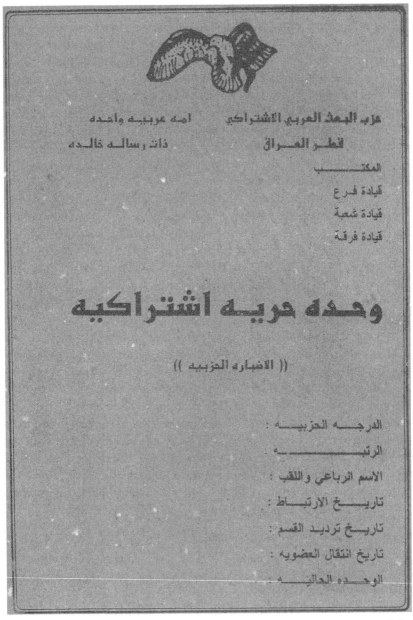

FIGURE 3. a. An Example of a Party File Cover. b. Translation. Courtesy of the Iraq Memory Foundation.

Arab Socialist Ba'th Party
Iraq Region

One Arab country
with an eternal message

Bureau
Branch Headquarter
Section Headquarter
Division Headquarter

Unity Freedom Socialism
(Party File)

Party grade:
Rank:
Full name and title:
Date of joining:
Date of swearing allegiance:
Date of transfer:
Current unit:

Enrolling new recruits was a major aspect of the Ba'thification of Iraq. Known in Ba'th jargon as *al-kasb al-hizbi*,[57] it was part and parcel of the work of branches and sections (see also Chapter 3). The documents provide ample data about this process, as each section and division had to file a form detailing its success in recruiting for the party. For instance, one *shu'ba* (section) in Baghdad, with its numerous *firaq* (divisions), recruited 672 people in the six weeks from the end of September to mid-November 2002. Because the statistics state the profession and workplace of those recruited, we can see that a majority of those enlisted in this section in Baghdad were university students, doctors, and engineers, and that educational institutions and hospitals (particularly university hospitals) were fertile areas for recruitment.[58] In this case the high level of those recruited could be attributed to being in central Baghdad, but it also illustrates the nature of the Ba'thification of Iraqi society by targeting the educated middle class.

Given that one section in Baghdad managed to enroll 672 people in six weeks, what does this tell us about the number of active party members and the extent of recruitment? The party headquarters collected statistics on a regular basis as part of the control process. Unfortunately, much of the time, data are not consistent and do not allow statistical analysis. However, there are detailed statistics from September 2002 that are used in this text to give a "final" picture of the regime a few months before its collapse in April 2003. Appendix II provides detailed data about membership within each structure and by division, section, and cell. The number of party affiliates reached about 4 million by the end of 2002, including more than 400,000 attached to the military bureaus. It is also important to underline that women's branches had their own statistics but were included in the overall number (see Table 6 and the discussion about the Ba'th and women in Chapter 8). Thus, out of an estimated population of 25 million in 2002, those affiliated with the Ba'th Party constituted about 16.5 percent, a very high number indeed. But, a close look at the table shows us a fundamentally different conclusion: the upper echelons of the party represented only 14.5 percent of the overall affiliates and about 2.4 percent of the overall population in 2002. It should also be highlighted that only a relatively small percentage carried party

---

57 The translation of *al-kasb al-hizbi* is "to gain or attain for the party," but *recruitment* will be used, as it is more appropriate in this case.
58 Baghdad Section to Party Secretariat, "Party Recruitment," BRCC, 003-5-3. The file contains the report of each division and the affiliation of the recruited.

cards, as these were designated for individuals working full time for the party, whereas the majority, at all levels of the party hierarchy, continued with their regular jobs. Obviously, in certain areas, the percentages were higher; within the Baghdad area, this figure ranged from 5.5 percent in al-Zuʿfraniyya to only 3.3 percent in al-Battawin.[59] It would be safe to assume, therefore, that even with the intensified Baʿthification of the 1990s, the percentage of Baʿth members who were active and carried out functions in the party was no more than 4 percent of the total population. Iraqi officials told journalists in 2003 that 2 million citizens were affiliated with the party, a number that seems not to have included the lowest echelon of sympathizers.[60]

How accurate are these statistics? It is hard to make a definite conclusion in light of the exaggeration that frequently prevailed in the documents. Although the number of those recruited at the lower levels was probably embellished, it would have been risky for any branch to fabricate numbers related to the rank of *ʿudhu ʿamil* (active member) and above. For example, in a study prepared in April 2002 for the Baʿth calendar year (which always started on April 28 – the birthday of Saddam Hussein – and ended on April 27 the following year), the writer quoted the party's deputy secretary as telling a group of senior members that "recruitment this year [2001] was approximately 1.5 million recruited, and this recruitment is a birthday gift to the leader: 1.5 million Baʿthists."[61] The deputy secretary affirmed that "it is not appropriate to give material gifts to the leader, but this gift will resonate with him deeply." This number is almost certainly a hyperbole, but it gives some indication of the extent of enrollment in the party.

Nevertheless, there is no doubt that the growth in the party cadre had been nothing short of spectacular. A comparison of membership between 1986 and 2002 (see Table 1) shows an increase of more than 140 percent in those sixteen years, at a time when the population increased by about 56 percent (from 16 million to 25 million).

Many have argued that the party weakened after the 1991 uprising, but the statistics clearly illustrate that recruitment continued at an intensified pace. Unfortunately, data for 1991, 1996, and 2002 cannot be matched,

[59] Bureau of Baghdad *tandhim*, "Suggestion," October 10, 1989, *BRCC*, 021-1-4 (082–085).
[60] Michael Slackman, "Baath Party Is Bedrock of Hussein's Power Base," *Los Angeles Times*, April 5, 2003.
[61] Al-Samawa Branch, "Plan Framework for the Calendar Baʿth Year April 2002 to April 27, 2003," April 26, 2002, *BRCC*, 003-5-5 (130–158).

TABLE 1. *Comparison of Countrywide Membership between 1986 and 2002*

	1986	2002
Bureau Members or Secretary Generals	82*	76
Branch Members	234	1,027
Section Members	1,179	6,128
Division Members	6,235	45,537
Active Members	32,655	223,622
Apprenticed Members	20,347	254,081
Supporters	589,004	1,113,211
Sympathizers	987,708	2,328,080
TOTAL	**1,637,444**	**3,971,762****

* The 1986 number includes secretary generals of the bureaus of the professional unions.

** The total here is different from Appendix II, as some categories were excluded in order to make a more accurate comparison with the 1986 statistics.

Source: For 1986: Ninth Regional Conference, BRCC, 164-3-1 (087); For 2002: BRCC, 108-4-6 (004–025).

but by taking data from the same categories during the three different periods, we still can observe the dramatic expansion. As Table 2 indicates, division members, for instance, grew by almost 500 percent between 1991 and 2002 and by roughly 60 percent even in the first five years after the 1991 events.

Interestingly, Saddam Hussein claimed as early as 1983 that the Ba'thists constituted 10 percent of the total Iraqi population, arguing that this was very high compared to the Communist Party in either the Soviet Union or Yugoslavia. This could have been a political ploy against other political parties, because in the same speech he warned that the number should go down, given that "the Iraqi people are bigger and

TABLE 2. *Increase in Membership between 1991 and 2002*

	1991	1996	2002
Branch Members	222	324	1,027
Section Members	1,305	1,717	6,128
Division Members	7,661	12,163	45,537
Apprentices	64,043	108,693	254,081
Supporters	272,486	352,958	1,113,211
TOTAL	**345,717**	**475,855**	**1,419,984**

Source: For 1991 and 1996: Party Secretariat, November 7, 1996, BRRC, 136-1-5 (001–036); For 2002: From Appendix II.

wider than the Baʿth Party, and that the party, in all conditions, should be only a small percentage of the population."[62]

It is important to point out that in spite of the fact that there was a lot of pressure on citizens to join the party and although some indeed found themselves in the ranks of the Baʿth through duress, many Iraqis voluntarily wanted to be part of the system because they either believed in its ideology or could benefit from being a Baʿthist. The documents reveal abundant evidence of citizens applying to join or rejoin the party. In one example, a doctor wrote asking to be reaccepted after more than eleven years of not being involved in party activities while he was busy pursuing his specialization as a neurosurgeon.[63] Another example was a twenty-four-year-old man who wrote asking to be allowed to join and serve the party because of his deep belief in its principles.[64]

In its recruitment policy the party was concerned about two issues: one was the percentage of women members, and the second, more important concern was the aging of the party's cadre and its inability to attract enough young men and women.

Age and Gender in the Baʿth Party

In 1992, acting on Saddam Hussein's instructions, the party decided to launch a study of *al-fiʾat al-ʿumriyya* (the age structure) within its cadres. This was due to the leadership's concern that not enough young people were being attracted and that the party was aging. Five main branches were chosen to undertake this study: two from Baghdad and one from each of the central, northern, and southern structures. Over a few months, each branch did some in-depth research and presented its study, accompanied by graphs and tables. Unfortunately, not all branches used comparable methods, and this explains why the statistics in Table 3 are not consistent. For instance, although the Saʿad bin Abi Waqqas branch in Baghdad did the most detailed analysis and attached a computer analysis projecting age structure over the next ten years, it did not use percentages like the other branches but instead used average and median figures.[65]

---

[62] Saddam Hussein, *al-Mukhtarat* (Baghdad: Dar al-Shuʾun al-Thaqafiyya al-ʿAmma, 1988), vol. 4, p. 19.

[63] Party Secretariat, Baghdad, "Request for Resumption of Activity," November 8, 2001, *BRCC*, 004-3-1 (006–008).

[64] Party Secretariat, Baghdad, "Request for Joining," October 8, 2001, *BRCC*, 003-5-3 (177).

[65] Saʿad bin Abi Waqqas Branch to Headquarters of *tandhim* Baghdad, February 14, 1992, *BRCC*, 174-3-2 (339–359).

TABLE 3. *Age Formation within the Ba'th Party, 1992*

Branch Name	No. of Affiliates*	Percent of Affiliates				
		35 & below	36–40	42–45	46–50	51–55
Basra	3,171	14	25	28	25	8
Khalid bin al-Walid	3,796	52	21	27		
Mosul	3,860	25	12	27	23	13
Salah al-Din	2,091	51	39	10		
Sa'ad bin Abi Waqqas	4,366	Average Age: 50 Average for Apprenticed & Active Members: 43				

* The statistics apply to each branch, its sections and divisions, and include the leadership, all full members, and, in addition, apprenticed and active members.
Source: BRCC, 174-3-2.

The Party Secretariat was duly worried after collating these statistics. First, it became clear that the forty-one to fifty-nine age group was the largest one among members. Second, the party was aware that, with time, the age structure would deteriorate further. For example, according to the analysis of the Sa'ad bin Abi Waqqas branch, which covered the areas of al-A'dhamiyya, Saddam City, and a number of educational institutions in Baghdad, the average age of branch affiliates was expected to increase from fifty years in 1993 to more than fifty-two in 2003. Third, among the leadership of the divisions, the forty-one to fifty-nine age group comprised almost 70 percent.[66]

Time and again, Saddam Hussein spoke about attracting the young generation to the party: "Let us capture the youth, so we can capture the future." As far back as 1979 he had criticized the party's activities among young people, arguing that that its message was far from clear and that it was not providing "romantics for youth" in its ideology.[67] Because of a strong belief within the party that a true Ba'thist should begin political involvement at an early age (see Chapter 8), the conclusions from the age structure studies were obvious:

1. Concentrate on the eighteen to thirty age group.
2. Continue the focus on students not only at university levels but also in high school, and hasten the membership process among them.

[66] Party Secretariat to Heads of All *tandhimat*, November 23, 1992, BRCC, 174-3-2 (299).
[67] Saddam Hussein, *al-Mukhtarat*, vol. 3, p. 276.

3. Create genuine competition in party elections so as to encourage the younger group to assume leadership roles.

4. Encourage more retirement of members of sections and divisions, and allow them to keep their fringe benefits.

5. Introduce age group quotas so as to reduce the number of members aged forty-five or more.[68]

To emphasize the importance of students, ʿUday, the elder son of Saddam Hussein, was appointed to head the National Student and Youth Union in the late 1990s, and reports talked about him personally overseeing the campaign to enlist Iraqi students to the party.[69]

Following these recommendations, the party began to focus on adolescents from the age of fifteen onward and during the next ten years placed more emphasis on recruiting university students. In fact, one main purpose of the School Register, which encompassed lists of middle school and high school students (aged fifteen to eighteen), was the potential recruitment of these students.[70] The party also made it very difficult for new recruits over the age of fifty to become candidates for membership unless there was an order from a higher authority (i.e., Saddam Hussein). This led to so many requests imploring Saddam Hussein to rescind the ruling that he refused to deal with these applications unless they were related to very high-ranking military officers.[71] Already in the late 1980s, an association called *munadhammat al-munadhilin* (the Organization for Party Veterans) was created to cater to retiring senior members who had assumed, at one point or another, a leadership role and had spent at least twenty-five years in the service of the party. This was part of the strategy of allowing younger members to assume responsibilities within the party structure. The organization was also used as a reservoir when the regime needed more experienced members to oversee activities in ministries, or write studies on topics about which they were knowledgeable.[72] Another organization catering to old or frail members was created as a pensioners' group and was called *munadhammat al-sabirin* (the Organization for

---

[68] Party Secretariat to Heads of All *tandhimat*, November 23, 1992, BRCC, 174-3-2 (300).

[69] *Al-Sharq al-Awsat* (London), "Campaign to Enlist Iraqi Students in the Ruling Baʿth Party," January 8, 2000, FBIS-NES-2000-0108.

[70] See Chapter 7 for more details on the School Register.

[71] Party Secretariat, November 22, 1989, BRCC, 003-3-2 (057).

[72] Party Secretariat to All *tandhimat*, "Decision," December 5, 1989, BRCC, 003-3-7 (139–147). The memo details the reasons for setting up the organization, qualifications for joining it, and duties of its members. The literal translation of *munadhammat al-munadhilin* is the "Organization for the Strugglers."

Party Pensioners).[73] Some, however, were shifted to this association due to "their slow comprehension or increased loss of memory."[74] Needless to say, many were affronted by this and wrote numerous letters to the party leadership detailing their actions and contributions to the party.[75]

The other aspect of membership on which leaders focused was gender. The subject of the Ba'th and women is discussed in detail later (see Chapter 8), but it should be mentioned that Saddam Hussein championed the women's movement in the 1970s, emphasizing the need to give women a role in society similar to that of men, which necessitated granting women full rights. In essence, Saddam Hussein wanted and needed the support of women for his regime. However, when he launched the religious campaign in the 1990s, he changed his stance. Although continuing to recruit women to the party, he began talking about finding a balance between a woman's political activities, on one hand, and "her devotion to her house and family so she can play the role expected from her by society,"[76] on the other. As a result, by the 1990s women were being separated from the regular cells as part of the religious campaign. For example, in one *shu'ba* in Baghdad, there were nine women-only cells under the command of a male member of a *firqa*.[77]

The emphasis, therefore, continued to be on female students, and on increasing the percentage of both women and young people among the membership. In the early 1990s, on average, 25,000 male and female students were admitted to Iraqi universities in each academic year, with females representing between 38 and 42 percent.[78] One *shu'ba* in Baghdad had a total membership of 3,812, of whom 46 percent were women, and among the sympathizers and supporters (the two lowest ranks in the membership pyramid), women comprised more than 52 percent. However, there were no women in the leadership of sections; only 2 percent were members of *firaq*, and just 20 percent were full members.[79] (See Table 6 for more details on women in the party.)

[73] The literal translation is the "Organization for the Tolerants."
[74] Party Secretariat, January 10, 1988, BRCC, 021-1-4 (408–409).
[75] Party Secretariat to Deputy Secretary of the Party, July, 22, 1987, BRCC, 021-1-4 (441–442).
[76] Baghdad Section, Division of al-Fawz al-'Adhim (The Great Victory) to Headquarters, "Organizational Structure," May 23, 2002, BRCC, 004-4-6.
[77] *Ibid.*
[78] Sa'ad bin Abi Waqqas Branch to Headquarters of *tandhim* Baghdad, February 14, 1992, BRCC, 174-3-2 (347).
[79] Baghdad *shu'ba, firqa* of al-Qa'id al-Muntasar (The Victorious Leader) to Headquarters, November 11, 2002, BRCC, 004-5-6.

Life of a Member

Each member was required to complete a detailed questionnaire recording his or her personal life and family. All were warned that those details would be checked thoroughly and would remain on their personal files throughout their careers. There were thirty-six questions, among them topics such as education; hobbies; how the candidate was introduced to the party ideology and how he or she responded to those ideas; who were the people responsible for the first cell that the candidate joined; the time and place of swearing allegiance to the party; activities on behalf of the party at every stage; attendance at party conferences, particularly who participated and what left a lasting impression; an exhaustive history of where the candidate was during the events of 1958, 1959, 1963, and after November 1963 (including any imprisonment); and finally, the role played, if any, during the July 1968 coup d'état. The duties of each member were extensive, including total commitment to party policy without arguing about orders and instructions issued; payment of membership fees; joining of the organization or the union related to the member's profession; putting the member's interests below those of the party; and the practice of self-criticism. Whereas there were fifteen duties, there were only five rights for the member, such as voting in party elections and participating in its meetings.[80]

The documents contain many personal files of members, and it is instructive to examine the party career path of a typical member, whom I shall call Muhammad.[81] Born in Tikrit (like his leader, who was born south of Tikrit), which is part of the province of Salah al-Din, to a blacksmith father in 1945, Muhammad epitomized the true Baʿthist. He joined the party at the young age of thirteen, and at eighteen, he joined *al-haras al-qawmi* (the National Guard – the Baʿth militia when the party was in power between February and November 1963) and was imprisoned for a week after the collapse of the Baʿth regime at that time. Between 1965 and 1968 he worked for the Railways Company and was active in its labor union. He received his full party membership in 1974 at the age of twenty-nine. True to party ideals, he did not take any break from political activity, and became a member in a *firqa* in 1980, a member in a *shuʿba* in 1986, and finally a *firʿ* member in 1992.

---

[80] *CRRC*, SH-BATH-D-000-144.
[81] Muhammad's file is about 140 pages long and covers the years from 1970 to 1997, *BRCC*, 017-1-6 (001–142).

الجانب التنظيمي			

المستوى والالتزام

ماهي المسؤوليات التنظيمية للمرشح تذكر :
- ١
- ٢
- ٣

ممتاز	جيد	وسط	ضعيف	ماهو مستوى ادارته للاجتماع الحزبي
☐	☐	☐	☐	
☐	☐	☐	☐	ماهو التزامه بالحضور في المواعيد المقررة
☐	☐	☐	☐	ماهي درجة التمتع بثقة واحترام المنظمة الحزبية
☐	☐	☐	☐	ماهو مستوى تنفيذ التعليمات الحزبية

الكسب الحزبي (يذكر بالتفاصيل)

تاريخ الكسب	مستواه الثقافي والاجتماعي والوظيفي	اسم الشخص الذي قام المرشح بكسبه

FIGURE 4. a. A Typical Organizational Form from a Member's File. b. Translation. Courtesy of the Iraq Memory Foundation.

The Organizational Section
Level and Commitment
What are the organizational responsibilities of the candidate 1. 2. 3.

	Weak	Average	Good	Excellent
How well does he manage a party meeting	☐	☐	☐	☐
What is his commitment to attending meetings according to schedule	☐	☐	☐	☐
How much does the person inspire the confidence and respect of the party organization	☐	☐	☐	☐
How well does he implement party instructions	☐	☐	☐	☐

Party Recruitment (give details)		
Name each individual that the candidate recruited	Educational, social, and employment level of those recruited	Date of recruitment

Muhammad's educational background is the only part of his file showing contradictions: in the early 1970s, he stated that he finished only
middle school, but the file later stated that he completed high school. He
did not master any foreign language, although the file indicated that he
aspired to learn English. The paper that he presented as part of his political training to become a full member, entitled "The Importance of the
Revolutionary Party to the Public," was not exactly riveting; he repeated
time and again how the Ba'th was the only party capable of meeting the
revolutionary needs of the people in every sphere of life.

Although he did not have a military education, Muhammad participated in special infantry courses designed for political commissars, which
in turn allowed him to join the party's military bureau. He was given
the rank of infantry colonel, similar to many of those who worked in the
military bureaus. As a political commissar, Muhammad was injured during the Iran–Iraq War, and even though his file does not provide details
of his injury or the circumstances, one could assume it was during an
Iranian bombardment, given his lack of military duties. He was awarded
three bravery awards during 1984–86, and in 1985 he received *sharat
al-hizb* (Party Insignia), which entitled its holder to many benefits. During the Gulf War of 1991 he received another bravery award (no details
provided).

Muhammad was a committed active member: he worked his way
up through different military units until the mid-1980s, when he was
attached to the military bureau affiliated with the Special Republican
Army. By 1988, he became *amin sir* (secretary general) of the military
bureau in one of the units stationed in the presidential palace and was
also given responsibility for cultural affairs (i.e., political education) for
the section.

In his yearly evaluations, Muhammad scored highly for being a true
believer in party ideals; he was good at keeping secrets, praised for his
teamwork and balanced attitude, and never disciplined. He regularly
passed the fitness test and was not overweight (he was five feet six inches
and weighed 154 pounds). Not only did none of his larger family belong
to any other political movement, but one of his brothers was an active
member of the party. Muhammad easily received his security clearance
each year, given that he had no contact throughout his life with any
political movement other than the Ba'th, had never left Iraq, had "neither
an Arab nor a foreign friend," and had no relative residing outside Iraq or
married to a citizen of an Arab or a foreign country. Even his hobbies were
analogous to Saddam Hussein's: reading and hunting. He lived modestly,

and his family life was stable: he was married (his wife never worked and was a housewife) with four children, and he supported his mother, who lived with them. Yet, for some unknown reason, his file indicated in 1988 that the party's future plans for him were limited. Before that, the yearly recommendations were that he was "fit" or ready for a promotion.

Somehow, it seems that once Muhammad became a *fir'* member in 1992, his career languished, either due to his limited capabilities or because his sponsor was removed in one of the numerous purges that Saddam Hussein inflicted on senior party members. In 1997, his file ends abruptly with a directorate from the Party Secretariat declaring that "approval has been obtained from the comrade[,] the struggling leader[,] and the secretary general of the party (May God Protect him) to transfer comrade Muhammad... (member of headquarters of the military *fir'* al-Faris) to *munadhammat al-munadhilin* based on his request."[82] We have no way of knowing whether it was really Muhammad's request to be moved to the veterans association because he realized he had few prospects, or whether he ended up having a political enemy who organized his transfer. Whatever the circumstances, Muhammad retired at fifty-two, the optimal age of retirement for the party, thus helping to open the way for a cohort of younger, enthusiastic Ba'thists.

Party Political Education

As discussed in the Introduction, the Ba'th's ideology, with its three mottos of unity, freedom, and socialism, lost its real allure, and Iraqi patriotism was given more prominence. The party fostered archeological work "to make the Iraqi people aware of the importance and relevance of the country's ancient history – including the pre-Islamic era."[83] The historical inheritance of Mesopotamia, Nebuchadnezzar (king of Babylon), the ancient culture of the Sumerians and Babylonians, and local folklore were all harnessed to serve the party's ideology and to underscore the uniqueness of Iraq, past and present, in the Arab and Muslim world. The documents rarely show any serious debates or thorough examination of ideological issues, and by the early 1990s, most research work by the party cadre centered on the personality of Saddam Hussein and his achievements. Political indoctrination of members was a central

---

[82] Party Secretariat to Deputy Party Secretary, "Transfer to *munadhammat al-munadhilin*," March 16, 1997, BRCC, 017-1-6 (001).
[83] Baram, *Culture, History and Ideology*, p. 25.

concern of the party and its branches. The indoctrination had an impact on culture in two ways: through *al-thaqafa al-hizbiyya* (political education) and *al-thaqafa al-'amma* (general culture). Ba'thification of the masses was no less important than indoctrination of party members, and the party paid special attention to "educating the masses in general and the youth in particular about the national culture . . . , and immunizing them from foreign theories and ideas that do not fit our [the Ba'th] national and humanitarian goals."[84] Similar to other authoritarian regimes, the intention was to create a "new man" and a "new society,"[85] whereby the ideal Iraqi citizen would be a Ba'thist, ideologically committed and loyal to the party's leaders.[86]

The Ba'thist cultural policy was run by the Ministry of Culture and Information, which played an important part in the *tawjih fikri* (intellectual guidance) of the population through the media, as well as through Saddam Hussein's copious speeches and special education and cultural programs targeting different sections of society. The issue of culture has been covered extensively by certain scholars,[87] and the emphasis here is on understanding how the regime dealt with political education within the party structure. Needless to say, the two were closely connected, especially in the educational sphere. As in the Soviet Union and similar regimes, Iraqi school curricula were full of political content, and the writing of history became a major focus for Saddam Hussein and his officials.[88] Thus, political education, historical books, and new interpretations of history were prominent in the training of the Ba'th political cadre.

The correlation between the "intellectual guidance" of the population and the indoctrination of party members was clearly expressed in a study prepared in 1984 for the "mobilization of the people to clearly understand the principles of the party." It made six recommendations:

1. Deploying the media (television, radio, and newspapers) to explain the party's principles.

---

[84] Eighth Regional Conference, January 1974, p. 50. See also Bengio, *Saddam's Word*, pp. 50–51.

[85] Makiya, *Republic of Fear*, p. 69.

[86] Sami Zubaida, "Une société traumatisée, une société civile anéantie, une économie en ruine" [A Society Traumatized, a Population Crushed, an Economy in Ruins], in Kutschera (ed.), *Le Livre Noir*, pp. 601–27.

[87] Two important books deal with this issue: Eric Davis, *Memories of State: Politics, History, and Collective Identity in Modern Iraq* (Berkeley: University of California, 2005) and Baram, *Culture, History and Ideology*.

[88] Davis, *Memories of State*, pp. 203–07. Poetry was another focus of the regime.

2. Communicating with the masses via professional unions (labor, women, and students).
3. Making use of videos (which became popular in the mid-1980s) of conferences and lectures by senior party members.
4. Utilizing Saddam Hussein's speeches and his various life experiences.
5. Capitalizing on youth centers in small villages and towns to attract more people, by taking advantage of poets, writers, and artists to deliver the party's message to the crowds.
6. Using all forms of popular expression or entertainment such as cinema, murals, sport, folklore music, paintings, etc., to mobilize the people.[89]

Internally, although indoctrination was spread through all the preceding approaches, it was epitomized most of all in courses in the *madrasat al-i'dad al-hizbi* (the Party Preparatory School), which was set up to develop party cadres. Clear targets for political education were established for each level of the party hierarchy. Hence, for sympathizers, the courses were more a general overview of the party's history, its principles, and the internal application of party terminology and discipline. For supporters, the courses were geared more toward the party's structure and their own capabilities in carrying out party principles, as well as Iraqi and Arab history through a Ba'thist lens, with an emphasis on Saddam Hussein's role. For both categories – sympathizers and supporters – the courses were also aimed at finding the most suitable cadre for the party.[90]

These schools began on a small scale but developed with the expansion of party membership[91] and became more professionally run as time went by. The school charter declared that its aim was "to raise the cultural level of party comrades and deepen their understanding of the party's ideals and its history."[92] The teachers had to be, at minimum, members of *shu'ba* leadership, hold a university degree, and be full-time teachers. Originally the courses lasted four months, but as a result of the rapid expansion in recruitment, this became unfeasible given the urgent need for swift, practical training. The length of the courses was therefore

[89] Al-Furat *tandhim* to Party Secretariat, "Study," March 22, 1984, *BRCC*, 021-1-5 (645–649).
[90] Al-Samawa Branch, "Plan Framework for the Calendar Ba'th Year April 2002 to April 27, 2003," April 26, 2002, *BRCC*, 003-5-5 (130–158).
[91] Matar, *Saddam Hussein*, p. 204.
[92] Cultural Bureau to Party Secretariat, "*al-Madaris al-hizbiyya*," November 11, 2001, *BRCC*, 014-5-7 (036–039).

shortened to two months, and each school would run four courses a year. Discipline was strict: no one was allowed to withdraw from a course without written approval from the Party Secretariat, and anyone who missed three consecutive days, or five days in total, would be dismissed.[93]

The school aimed at creating a sense of camaraderie among participants, and each tutor was expected to develop strong relations with the attendees and get a good sense of their future potential in the party.[94] In theory, attendees were free to criticize the party and suggest new ideas. Saddam Hussein, like Stalin, encouraged self-criticism, and in 1974 he told a meeting of party cadre at a preparatory school that, "as a Ba'thist, free and honest speech, rather than finding excuses, is a necessity," and that members should not shy away from criticizing existing structures and roles.[95] His advice to the participants was to be daring and innovative, to "take the tradition of the party to the state apparatus but do not borrow the state's tradition into the party."[96] However, in both Stalinism and Ba'thism, self-criticism and critique of the party were, in numerous cases, used against members after they had made their critical remarks.

By the late 1980s, these schools had to deal with significant numbers of candidates. One stumbling block, particularly outside Baghdad, was the high percentage of illiteracy and the low educational level of some of the new recruits. The Ba'th Party, like the Communist Party under Stalin, regarded literacy as "a necessary pre-requisite for further political education."[97] In 1999, for instance, in the Baghdad *tandhim*, 4,079 attended the indoctrination course, representing 29 percent of the total registered in the seven *firu'* (branches).[98] It seems that this was the average of those attending courses within the Baghdad structure.[99] The supporters and junior members were not the only ones who periodically had to go through those courses. From time to time, senior party members had

93 *Ibid.*
94 Al-Fawz al-'Adhim *firqa* to Party Secretariat, "Ideological Quality in Recruitment," May 28, 2000, *BRCC*, 004-4-3 (010).
95 Saddam Hussein, *al-Mukhtarat*, vol. 7, pp. 10–11.
96 *Ibid.*
97 Catherine Merridale, *Moscow Politics and the Rise of Stalin: The Communist Party in the Capital, 1925–32* (New York: St. Martin's Press, 1990), p. 143.
98 *Tandhim* Baghdad to Party Secretariat, "Course for Candidates," January 21, 1990, *BRCC*, 003-3-3 (012).
99 For the years 1988 and 1989 respectively, see Party Secretariat to Supervisor of Courses, "Course," July 11, 1988, *BRCC*, 003-3-2 (034) and Head of Information and Documentation to Party Secretariat, "Opening a Course," November 10, 1989, *BRCC*, 003-3-2 (112).

to take a two-week course with an emphasis on recruitment, public relations, the dangers of bureaucracy and corruption, and, of course, lessons
in history using examples from Saddam Hussein's activities.[100] A different group needing political guidance was the returning prisoners of war
who were accepted back into the party, in order to make sure that "their
connection to the party" stayed strong.[101]

The programs of these courses were relatively limited. They were orga-
nized along four major themes: ideology (such as concepts of unity and
freedom), organization (the internal structure of the party and the eti-
quette of writing political reports), history of the party (the life of Saddam
Hussein and his epic battles), and national and regional topics (such as
Palestine or *qadisiyyat Saddam*, the euphemism for the Iran–Iraq War).[102]
In the mid-1990s another theme was added: the party and religion.[103]
During the courses, candidates had to write essays on topics chosen by
the supervisors from these themes. One list of forty topics included the
commands of the leader and their impact on the Ba'th personality; the
development of an ideal Ba'thist leader; the Ba'th and the Palestinian
problem; America and Zionism; international terrorism and resistance
against occupiers; who benefits from sanctions against Iraq; and the role
of women in the Mother of All Battles (the First Gulf War).[104] Interestingly, the party emphasized essay writing and circulated a memo on
writing research papers: how to read secondary and primary sources; how
to define and approach the subject; the style of writing and how to use
quotes, and so on.[105]

In addition to essays, candidates had to take a written examination.
In what was probably the last course held, given that the exam was on
February 3, 2003, each candidate had to answer four out of six questions.
Among them were the following: what is the essence of a successful party
meeting; how does the party see religion; why does the leader insist on
recruiting the young; why was Iraq targeted by America and Zionism; and

---

[100] "Spheres of Culture in Course for Secretaries of Branches, June 10 to June 25, 2002,"
BRCC, 014-1-3 (147–149).
[101] Party Secretariat to Structure Bureaus, "Party Connectivity to Returning Prisoners of
War," October 10, 1990, *BRCC*, 003-3-7 (056).
[102] The name was taken from the battle of al-Qadisiyya in 636 A.D., when the invading
Arab Muslim army defeated the Sassanid Persians in a three-day battle, ending their
rule over Iraq.
[103] Baghdad Section, "Program for Candidates," June 1, 2002, *BRCC*, 003-5-6 (065–066).
[104] Baghdad Section to Cultural Committee, "Style of Writing a Study," March 3, 2002,
BRCC, 004-3-2 (183).
[105] *Ibid.*, (173–182).

what are the rights and duties of a member?[106] It should be noted that passing these courses was far from automatic; candidates were graded on their participation, their essays, and the final examination. At least 2 percent failed to complete the training successfully. Some were given a pass with a note attached declaring that the candidate passed "by a ruling," but we do not know the reasons for this.[107]

Whereas course topics were limited in scope, the attendees came from every walk of life. The list for one of the party courses, attended by fifty-three comrades, was truly varied: army and police officers; government officials from all levels, including heads of departments; merchants from the private sector; an ambassador at the foreign ministry; university teachers and students; and even a candidate from Sudan.[108] For the *murashih* (candidate), the pinnacle was the swearing of allegiance ceremony at the end of the course, signifying that he or she could become a full member and serve the party. Many of these ceremonies took place on national days, particularly April 28, the birthday of Saddam Hussein.[109] As time went by and as the country faced further military attacks, there were more national days to celebrate those occasions. Among them were *yawm al-raya* (the Day of the Banner), to commemorate the American attack on the presidential palaces in February 1998, and *yawm al-zahf al-kabir* (the Day of the Big March), to celebrate the day of referendum for the leadership of Saddam Hussein in October 1995.[110]

As mentioned, party members had also to undergo, as part of their courses, guidance in *al-thaqafa al-'amma* (general culture). These cultural courses were not, however, much different in content from the political education. In the program of one of the cultural education courses, the emphasis was still on the wars with Iran and Kuwait and how Saddam Hussein had led the country to victory in both wars; Arab unity, its history, and its importance in the doctrines of the Ba'th; the struggle against

106 Party Secretariat, "Examination," February 3, 2003, *BRCC*, 014-4-4 (044).
107 Party Secretariat to Supervisor of Courses, December 3, 1989, *BRCC*, 003-3-2 (008).
108 Party Secretariat, "List of the Attendees of the 47th Course," October 10, 1999, *BRCC*, 009-2-3 (095–096). The duration of this course, like many of its kind, was about two months.
109 Party Secretariat, "Swearing Ceremony," May 18, 2002, *BRCC*, 003-5-6 (051).
110 For a list of national days and their explanations, see *CRRC*, SH-BATH-D-000-144.

America and Zionism; and so on. Some courses included historical topics, such as Iraq's history from its independence in 1932 until July 1968 (when the Ba'th came to power), and the economic system during that period.[111] For each topic, historical or political, the sources consulted were, again, comparable to the material used in political education: Saddam Hussein's speeches and interviews, reports of the different Ba'th Party conferences, and the pamphlets published by the party.[112]

The party and its different organizations invested tremendous effort into building and running these cultural events. For instance, *maktbat al-talaba wa al-shabab* (the Bureau for Students and Youth), which was part of the party's cultural committee, claimed that it had arranged during one year 4,868 seminars, 6,261 lectures, and hundreds of poetry readings, as well as participating in almost 15,000 publications and studies and sponsoring more than 1,000 magazine articles.[113]

Party publications played an important role in the indoctrination not only of Ba'th cadres but also of the Iraqi people in general. Between 1998 and the end of 2002, the Bureau for Information and Studies, under the directorship of the Party Secretariat (see Appendix I), published 117 publications ranging from three to fifty-two pages in length. Among the topics covered were confronting America, globalization, dialogue with the Russian Communist Party, the events of 9/11: what changed and what did not change, and numerous studies on the Ba'th and Saddam Hussein.[114]

The party also devoted significant resources to opening libraries in branches across the country and donated a wide range of books. In 2001, Saddam Hussein authorized an additional sum of ID42 million (equivalent to $15,000) to the party's budget, to be spent by the branches solely on expanding their libraries and purchasing new books.[115] As mentioned, there was a constant process of amalgamation and creation of new branches. One such branch created in early 2001, called al-Zubair bin

---

[111] Arbil Section to Headquarters, "Cultural Week," August 23, 1990, *NIDS*, PUK 001, Box 3006.

[112] Party Secretariat, "Details of the Cultural Program for Members," June 23, 1999, *BRCC*, 003-4-1 (183–189).

[113] Central Bureau for Students and Youth to Party Secretariat, "Cultural Activities during the Period April 1, 2001, to March 31, 2002," May 7, 2002, *BRCC*, 014-1-3 (370).

[114] Party Secretariat to All Party Organizations, "Index of Publications," February 17, 2003, *BRCC*, 008-1-4 (004–016).

[115] Bureau of Information and Studies to Party Secretariat, "Party Libraries," January 14, 2002, *BRCC*, 012-2-5 (005–007).

al-ʿAwam,[116] boasted owning roughly 18,000 books housed in its thirty-four libraries across its sections and divisions.

The library holdings of this branch were categorized according to subject. The largest category was historical books, which contained a wide variety of books on Iraq and the Middle East, some of which were translated from foreign languages, whereas others were strictly Baʿth propaganda and histories about Saddam Hussein. The second-largest group was literature books, primarily poetry and novels, with a subsection of books and novels written by Iraqi prisoners of war about their experiences. The library also had a collection of political and military books, some of which were published by the party, while others were written by specialists analyzing Iraq's numerous wars with emphasis on wars won by the party's leader. Other categories included religious and legal books.[117] Many books were published under the party's auspices; for instance, a decision was made in 2002 to print a biography of ʿAdnan Khairallah Tulfah, the brother-in-law and first cousin of Saddam Hussein, to honor his role in the Iran–Iraq War.[118]

Saddam Hussein's personal interest in culture and poetry cannot be underestimated. Saddam saw himself as a writer and a poet, and thus he felt a kinship toward artists of all kinds. By the year 2000, artists in Iraq were divided into three groups depending on their output and seniority and were given monthly stipends according to the category to which they belonged. In addition, Saddam Hussein was extremely generous with any poet who adulated him and paid between $100 to $500 for those poets, a large sum in those days of economic hardship.[119] A case in point for his interest in literature and language was when Saddam Hussein was watching television one evening in September 2000 and heard the reader making grammatical mistakes when reading the leader's commands.

---

[116] Al-Zubair bin al-ʿAwam was one of the ten Sunnis believed to have been promised paradise while living. Saddam Hussein used some of their names to name party branches, for example: Abu Bakr al-Saddiq, ʿUthmann bin ʿAffan, Saʿad bin Abi Waqqas, and Abu ʿUbaida bin al-Jarrah.

[117] Al-Zubair bin al-ʿAwam Branch to Party Secretariat, "Party Libraries," September 29, 2001, *BRCC*, 010-2-5 (049–061).

[118] Party Secretariat to Deputy Secretary of the Party, March 20, 2002, *BRCC*, 014-1-4 (004). ʿAdnan Khairallah was the minister of defense during the 1980s, but Saddam Hussein became suspicious that that there were plots to replace him with his cousin. Khairallah was killed in May 1989 in a helicopter crash, which many believed was not wholly accidental. For more details, see Tripp, *A History of Iraq*, pp. 249–50.

[119] Saman Abdul Majid, *Les années Saddam: Révélations exclusives* [Saddam's Years: Exclusive Revelations] (Paris: Fayard, 2003), pp. 141–42.

He immediately called the minister of culture and information; a special committee was formed to investigate the matter; tapes were studied; and it was decided that the reader would reread accurately the same commands two days later. Afterward, the announcer was punished by being suspended from his work for six months.[120]

Saddam also freely volunteered advice to writers on how to write and regularly advocated reading books. In one meeting with the Republican Guard, he advised that their commander (his son Qusay) and all the officers should read one book every month, because it would add to their general knowledge, stimulate their minds, modify how they communicated orally and in writing, and more importantly increase their fighting capability by 50 percent.[121] Saddam Hussein spent inordinate time with writers who were given the "task" of writing for the regime; lists of writers were discussed, and drafts of stories and poems were sent to the presidential *diwan* to be reviewed before being published.[122] Indeed, scholars have written about the fact that artists in Iraq during the Ba'th era had to "walk a tightrope between selling one's soul and preserving artistic freedom."[123] Others have argued that Iraqi artists did not have much choice: either to collaborate with the regime or to go into physical or inner exile.[124] In reality, many artists were marshaled to serve the regime and the president's cult. Naziha Selim, from the famous family of Jawad Selim, the doyen of Iraqi sculpture, won a drawing competition in 1996. Her drawing was called "The Referendum" and showed the word "yes" to electing Saddam Hussein proclaimed in different languages. The competition was part of the Babel art festival, which took place on the occasion of the referendum.[125]

As part of cultural education, the house of Ahmad Hasan al-Bakr, the president who preceded Saddam Hussein, was turned into a museum for the party as a historical symbol of its struggle. Candidates were regularly

---

[120] Minister of Culture and Information to My President Leader, May God Glorify You, Protect You and Bless You, September 26, 2000, Ministry of Information Dataset, 003–004.

[121] Audiotape of Saddam Hussein with top leadership of the party and the army, October 1995, *CRRC*, SH-SHTP-A-000-758.

[122] Press secretary to the president, April 29, 2001, advising him that eighty writers of novels, stories, and scripts who met with the president recently "have begun to write the works they were tasked with." *CRRC*, SH-PDWN-D-000-499.

[123] Rohde, *State–Society Relations*, p. 156.

[124] Salam 'Abboud, *Thaqafat al-'unf fi al-'Iraq* [The Culture of Violence in Iraq] (Köln: Al-Kamel Verlag, 2002), pp. 238–39.

[125] *Alif Ba*, issue no. 1427, January 31, 1996.

taken there for visits and lectures about the party's history, both before and after the 1968 revolution that brought the Ba'thists to power.[126] Another medium used to indoctrinate not only party members but also people in general was the *jidariyyat* (murals). The regime invested vast amounts of money in creating murals and then had to go to the trouble of safeguarding each of them in case they would become a target for any of the regime's opponents. A committee that included representatives of the Party Secretariat, the Ministry of Culture and Information, the Ministry of Interior, and the Special Security Organization was responsible for protecting the murals from defacement.[127] These *jidariyyat* had the dual purpose of spreading the message of the Ba'th and reinforcing the personality cult of the president, by "showing the love of the people for its leader in an artistic and elegant manner that befits his Excellency's position and his role in the renaissance of our people."[128]

In conclusion, the Ba'th Party played a critical role in governing Iraq from 1968 to 2003. Although at times, such as after the 1991 uprising, the party lost some of its credibility in the eyes of Saddam Hussein, it nevertheless managed to reorganize itself and strengthened its stronghold over the population. It should also be noted that although the party's activities might not have been always well-organized and seamless, given its hierarchical and bureaucratic nature, overall it was run relatively efficiently and managed to control the country for thirty-five years.

The focus of this chapter has been on understanding how the party headquarters, *maktab amanat sir al-qutr*, functioned and its structure. The party's branches, which were spread throughout every city and town across Iraq, carried out the tasks of the leadership and were its eyes and ears in every corner of the country, as discussed in the next chapter.

---

[126] Party Secretariat to Presidential *diwan*, "Repairing the Museum of the Party," January 24, 2002, *BRCC*, 005-4-6.

[127] *Ibid*. Based on a memo by the Intelligence Services: "Defacing the *jidariyyat*," July 20, 1996.

[128] From the television program *dhaw'* (light), based on a memo by the minister of culture and information, November 20, 1990.

3

The Baʿth Party Branches

Away from the center of power, the party operated effectively on a regional and local basis. A rare insight into almost every aspect of regional life is provided by the archives of the *NIDS*, which cover the three northern governorates of Arbil, Duhok, and Suleimaniyya.[1] Together with the *BRCC*, these archives enable us to understand how these party branches functioned and their structure, activities, finances, membership, and internal elections. Certain important branch functions, such as recruiting informers, building the cult personality of the president, or managing the local economy, are elaborated on in other chapters. Although the branches were the roof organization for the sections and divisions, the cells were the grass roots, which had to spread and expand so as to provide the cadre for the hierarchical organs of the party. Among the cells' numerous tasks were to implement the party's policies; supervise candidates and educate them politically and culturally; collect donations from candidates, supporters, and friends; and establish ties with the local population to gauge their needs and convey them to the party.[2]

Branches were continually evaluated and compared with one another by using information collated from their own reports of their efforts in five different categories: organizational activities, cultural events,

---

[1] These archives are not dissimilar from the Smolensk archives in the Soviet Union. Smolensk is about 260 miles southwest of Moscow. In mid-July 1941 German army units invaded the city and shipped back to Berlin a trove of Communist Party documents covering the period 1917–38. At the end of the war the documents fell into the hands of American troops and were transferred to the United States. See Merle Fainsod, *Smolensk under Soviet Rule* (Cambridge, MA: Harvard University Press, 1958).
[2] *CRRC*, SH-BATH-D-000-144.

relations with the public, political and security operations, and financial procedures.

Tasks of Branches

1. Organizational Activities

Following Party Secretariat guidelines, party branches placed emphasis on the organizational aspects of their responsibilities. Among those were recruitment, creation of new cells and divisions, election of members to branch committees, visits to other branches, and organization of conferences and meetings to spread the party's doctrine.

Recruitment was repeatedly highlighted, and there were constant demands from the leadership for updated statistics on new members. As we have seen, the Ba'th leadership felt insecure unless those holding positions in government and security organizations were affiliated with the party in some way. In one example, the chief of *al-amn al-'am* (General Security)[3] in Suleimaniyya warned that quite a number of employees had no party affiliation, while others either dodged filing their application forms or avoided party meetings. In his opinion, this situation was undermining the secrecy and security of the party organization.[4] Endless pressure was exerted to recruit new members, to the extent that the senior leadership instructed branches that each party affiliate should recruit at least two new people each year, and that those associated with the party should try to recruit their own children and relatives.[5]

Although recruitment activities among the young and students were a high priority, there was also a strong emphasis on enlisting women, particularly in northern Iraq. Files of female members in the north show that many were young, aged twenty to twenty-five; had finished high school; and, for the most part, were sympathizers or supporters, the lowest levels in the party pyramid. Some of these young women worked in factories, whereas others were housewives or employees in schools or government offices.[6] Interestingly, the files of men involved with the party

---

[3] *Al-amn al-'am* is abbreviated to *al-amn*, as most Iraqis know the organization by the first name.

[4] Suleimaniyya *amn* to All Heads of Sections, "Party Affiliations," May 25, 1980, *NIDS*, PUK 012, Box 50 (130102).

[5] Al-Qi'qa' Division, "Organizational Plan for the Period April 7, 2002, to April 6, 2003," April 2, 2002, *BRCC*, 003-2-3 (228).

[6] Files of members in Suleimaniyya dating back to 1991, *NIDS*, PUK 046, Box 293 (420000–420100). See also *NIDS*, KDP 021, Box 2229.

indicate a completely different profile; most were in their forties and very few had been educated beyond primary school. Many, in fact, were only graduates of organized party courses to eradicate illiteracy.[7]

Whether men or women, Kurds or Assyrians, Muslims or Christians, all had to fill in the cumbersome and detailed questionnaires and swear allegiance to the party and its leadership. Even those in northern Iraq who were simply joining the rank below that of a sympathizer, *al-nashat al-watani* (the national activity), had to sign a declaration based on a resolution by the RCC that anyone who joined the Ba'th Party but had hidden other political affiliations would be hanged. In addition, anyone who severed their relationship with the Ba'th Party and later became active in another political party would be liable for a seven-year imprisonment.[8]

It is hard to pinpoint why the party was relatively successful in recruiting so many Kurds; possible reasons include the privileges and rewards that came with the affiliation[9] (a topic discussed in Chapter 7), or the subtle pressure applied, such as the threat of losing a job or of collective punishment for the family if a relative had left Iraq or, even worse, had joined the enemies of the regime.

Adding new members necessitated the creation of new cells and the spinning off of divisions to absorb new recruits. In some cases, new cells were geared to tackle the needs of recruits from colleges or hospitals. For example, within the Baghdad University Hospital, a sixth cell was added in 2002 by transferring affiliates from the existing five cells, to cater to the members of the medical staff who were being recruited.[10] In other cases, dividing one section into two was dictated by geographic coverage or the needs of a specific group of potential recruits.[11]

Election of members to branch committees was another organizational duty. Following Saddam Hussein's instructions that "democracy must flourish among us [the party cadres]," the branches invested a lot of time

---

[7] Files of members in Suleimaniyya dating back to 1991, *NIDS*, PUK 039, Box 239 (550001–550025).

[8] See, for example, application form to join *al-nashat al-watani*, Arbil Section during 1980, *NIDS*, KDP, Box 2176 (040005).

[9] Among the most important privileges was receiving a piece of land. See, for example, Barazan Division to Headquarters, May 13, 1989, *BRCC*, 021-2-3 (370).

[10] There were 775 affiliated with the existing five cells within the different ranks, and although the overall number stayed the same, the average cadre per cell dropped from 155 to 129. See Baghdad Section, "Creation of a New Cell," August 12, 2002, *BRCC*, 003-2-2 (026).

[11] Baghdad *tandhim* to the Victorious Leader Branch, "Dividing the Section," December 31, 2002, *BRCC*, 003-2-2 (014).

and energy into running elections for different positions.[12] There had to be a quorum, and it often took a few rounds of balloting before a majority vote was reached to elect branch members.[13] Part of the election effort was to push forward the young cadre and reduce the party's dependency on older members.

Organizing internal conferences and meetings was another important yardstick for measuring the success of each branch. "Party conferences form the central hub where the party mechanism in all its components meets to experience life within the party, and where ideas and plans are mooted."[14] Hence, attendance was critical for the cadre, and endless statistical reports were prepared after each conference to record the number of attendees and absentees. One report by a branch in Baghdad concluded that 76 percent came regularly to all meetings and conferences, 21 percent attended infrequently, and the balance rarely turned up.[15] Efforts were made to schedule meetings to maximize the number of attendees, and frequent surveys were conducted to find the most convenient time and meeting place for the majority of the cadre. During some meetings, cash was raised for the party, and it seems that subtle pressure was exerted on attendees to contribute to whatever causes the Ba'th Party was currently endorsing.[16] Needless to say, attendance or lack of it was recorded in each member's personal file. For instance, when one housewife did not show up to any party meetings for a whole year, her cell leader visited her at home to convince her to attend, but neither his call nor visits from representatives of the women's organization in the area were heeded. As a result, the woman was dismissed from the cell.[17]

Interestingly, according to one branch survey, only 35 percent of members were fully satisfied with the political content of these conferences, whereas 56 percent thought that the meetings were partially interesting.[18]

---

[12] Duhok Branch, "Organizational Activities for 1989," *NIDS*, KDP 009, Box 2096 (110039). For elections in different branches see, for example, Kirkuk Branch, "Minutes of Election Meeting," April 12, 2001, *BRCC*, 021-1-6 (052).

[13] Khanaqin Branch, "Minutes of Election Meeting," December 6, 2001, *BRCC*, 006-4-3.

[14] Al-Rashid Branch, Baghdad, "Organizational Plan for al-Rashid Branch for 1992," *BRCC*, 005-1-2 (404–434).

[15] *Ibid*. The statistics relate to the year 1990 for al-Rashid branch.

[16] Misan Branch Secretariat to the Southern *tandhim*, "A Study," October 13, 1992, *BRCC*, 003-5-1 (091–100).

[17] Women's Organization in Sarsank to Party Headquarters, "Lack of Attendance," October 13, 1987, *NIDS*, KDP 029, Box 2305 (0080038).

[18] Al-Rashid Branch, Baghdad, "Organizational Plan for al-Rashid Branch for 1992," *BRCC*, 005-1-2 (404–434).

Across the branches, it was felt that the subjects discussed in these party seminars were too theoretical and not related to the practical issues facing society. Theorizing was an issue that Saddam Hussein himself had addressed when he told the party in 1992 that it should focus on the practical matters at the center of people's lives rather than on general discussions and political theories.[19] Another concern that kept emerging in branch reports was the quality of the speakers, and seminar organizers were called on to provide more articulate and interesting speakers.[20] In a study by one of the branches, fifteen characteristics were required of those running a seminar; among them were the ability to influence others, to be presentable and not suffer from any physical disability, to be able to create friendships with the attendees, and to be well versed in the Baʿth ideology.[21]

Party visits and hosting affiliates of other branches constituted another organizational requirement. Visits were an important tool to consolidate party efforts and to learn from other branches about their work and political activities. They were also used as an instrument "to check on the performance of the party mechanism."[22] Hosting other branch members was also used to learn, mostly from senior cadre, about developments within the party, and both those visiting and those hosting were supposed to encourage self-criticism, as advocated by the party leadership.[23]

Finally, disciplinary and contentious issues among members occupied the time and energy of senior branch and division leadership. In one instance, one senior member wrote to the Party Secretariat and the president complaining about the secretary general of the Mosul branch for "his pessimism, poor organizational experience and bad reputation... and [because] he was spreading adversary news and point of views that he had heard from enemy broadcasts."[24] Needless to say, such letters led to the creation of investigative committees, which lasted until the bureaucracy machine reached a decision about the merit of those complaints.

---

[19] Misan Branch Secretariat to the Southern *tandhim*, "A Study," October 13, 1992, *BRCC*, 003-5-1 (094–095).

[20] *Ibid.*

[21] Branch of the Victorious Leader to Party Secretariat, "A Study," June 5, 2002, *BRCC*, 003-2-4 (153).

[22] Al-Rashid Branch, Baghdad, "Organizational Plan for al-Rashid Branch for 1992," *BRCC*, 005-1-2 (404–434).

[23] Duhok Branch, "Organizational Activities for 1989," *NIDS*, KDP 009, Box 2096 (110042).

[24] T.T. (full name withheld) to the President and the Party Secretariat, October 14, 1990, *CRRC*, SH-BATH-D-000-441.

2. *Cultural Activities*

Ideological education aimed at molding the beliefs of the party cadre was intertwined with the general cultural education of the Iraqi people, and both were a major function of the Party Secretariat and the branches around the country. Cultural activity was seen as a major stage in the building of the Ba'thist character, just as the Stalinist system had emphasized learning the Communist Party's mores and rituals.[25] Most of these cultural gatherings used the speeches of Saddam Hussein, the party's political reports, and publications endorsed by the Ba'th leadership.[26] Cultural education within branches came in different formats: attending seminars, writing research papers, taking part in cultural competitions, exchanging cultural visits with other branches, participating in cultural conferences, joining Iraqi book fairs held in Arab capitals, and replenishing branch libraries with appropriate reading material.[27]

Analogous to political education, cultural efforts varied from one group to another depending on each group's party rank. Whereas the program for sympathizers focused on explaining the Ba'th ideology and encouraged attendees to delve into its literature, the seminars for supporters centered on political issues and how individuals could be instrumental in protecting the country and ensuring its security.[28] For both sympathizers and supporters there was an examination at the end of their courses, and those who excelled were rewarded. In one exam, for instance, the five questions to be answered asked the participants to discuss the following topics: Security Council Decision no. 598,[29] the party's attitude toward the national liberation movements in the world, the reasons behind the Khomeini regime's conspiracies against Iraq, the factors threatening political independence since the 1968 revolution, and the important

---

[25] For an interesting comparison with the Soviet system, see how the Communist Party functioned in Magnistogorosk city, located by the Ural River, in Stephen Kotkin, *Magnetic Mountain: Stalinism as a Civilization*, paperback edn. (Berkeley: University of California Press, 1997).

[26] Al-Rashid Branch, Baghdad, "Organizational Plan for al-Rashid Branch for 1992," *BRCC*, 005-1-2 (404–434).

[27] See, for example, Sarsank Division to Party Secretariat, "Decisions," February 17, 1988, *NIDS*, KDP 029, Box 2305 (080006–080009).

[28] Branch of the Victorious Leader, "A Study," June 5, 2002, *BRCC*, 003-2-4 (151–156).

[29] Resolution 598 was adopted in July 1987 and called for a ceasefire in the Iran–Iraq War. Although this resolution was rejected by both sides, it ultimately formed the basis of the ceasefire that took effect in 1988.

settlements that were created in Duhok province for those displaced from their houses.[30]

An integral part of cultural undertakings was building the personality cult of Saddam Hussein. His slogans were repeated in meetings, and quotes from his writings and speeches were used as subjects for seminar research papers. When the book *rijal wa madina* (Men and a City) was published by "its author," that is, Saddam Hussein, branches had to order hundreds of copies and distribute them to members, given that the book "carries the meaning of basic masculinity that would immune the party apparatus from the malaise of the epoch."[31] Thus, branch libraries were well stocked with this book, and whenever a book of Saddam Hussein was published, it immediately became the "book of the month" for discussion in cultural meetings across the branches.

Given the enormous number of slogans and speeches by Saddam Hussein, the branches had no problem choosing ones appropriate for any occasion. Whenever the branches had to prepare for a celebration, such as woman's day or child's day, the leader's slogans would be written on banners for these occasions.[32] Whether celebrating the anniversary of the revolution, the Day of the Martyrs, or Saddam Hussein's birthday, the party apparatus handled these occasions extremely seriously and planned every step of the celebration meticulously. For all branches, these festivals provided important occasions to outshine other branches and attract the attention of the party's senior leadership. For instance, during the celebrations for the anniversary of the 1968 revolution, one Baghdad section prepared a week of activities that included political lectures on the revolution and Jerusalem; a seminar about the role of the great leader in the revolution; the opening of an art exhibition; the hosting of other cells and sections; a cultural competition between two cells; and an inspection of the various arms of the branch by the military advisor of another party division.[33]

---

[30] Sarsank Division to Party Branches in Duhok, "Cultural Initiative," May 26, 1988, *NIDS*, KDP 029, Box 2305 (080070). Many families were deported from their villages as part of the Arabization of Kurdistan during the 1980s.

[31] *Ibid.*

[32] For a detailed list of some of Saddam Hussein's slogans that were used to celebrate the July 17–30, 1968, revolution, see Victorious Leader Section to *fir'* Headquarters, "Exhibition," July 22, 2002, *BRCC*, 003-5-7 (105–122).

[33] Victorious Leader Section to *fir'* Headquarters, "Activities," July 18, 2002, *BRCC*, 003-5-7 (076–079).

3. Relations with the Public

The Ba'th Party, realizing that it could not rule the country through its members alone, needed to enlist the support of the public. Its leadership knew that this was an "arena where it is not only the source of recruitment for the party, but where negative hostile ideas and actions could develop."[34] The guidelines for branch activities were that the only discrimination among people should be based on their contribution to the party, both qualitative and financial, and that personal connections should be developed and continuity encouraged in relationships. Strengthening ties with different groups of people involved participating in their happy and sad occasions and in social activities in the local area.[35] Improving relations with the public took many forms during the regime's thirty-five-year rule and, more importantly, also depended on the geographical area covered by the branch in question. After the war with Iran began in the early 1980s, for instance, the party leadership had to confront the important issue of martyrdom (see Chapter 5). The branches became responsible for the task of taking care of martyrs' families and visiting them regularly, "to create a humanitarian example of the party's dealings with the public."[36]

In certain areas, such as 'Amara city, dealing with the various tribes and building bridges with their leaders were essential functions. It was felt that regular meetings with tribal elders would help the branch to understand the issues faced by different tribes, in order to solve them in the spirit of the Ba'th.[37] In urban areas, on the other hand, there was an emphasis on establishing cordial relations with the academic and scientific communities. Given that Saddam Hussein was always in awe of scientists, because of his belief in their vital contribution to building a strong modern Iraq, scientists were continually honored and rewarded by the party.

Both in rural and urban areas, there was an emphasis on nurturing strong ties with students and with the youth in general. While the party prioritized recruitment of the young, it also tried hard to have good relationships with those who were not yet recruited. University students

---

[34] Al-Rashid Branch, Baghdad, "Organizational Plan for al-Rashid Branch for 1992," *BRCC*, 005-1-2 (404–434).

[35] Duhok Branch, "Organizational Activities for 1989," *NIDS*, KDP 009, Box 2096 (110051).

[36] *Ibid.*

[37] Misan Branch Secretariat to the Southern *tandhim*, "A Study," October 13, 1992, *BRCC*, 003-5-1 (097).

affiliated with the party were told time and again by the branch leadership about the importance of being exemplary both academically and in behavior. Party members were strongly advised not to abuse their powers within the academic community, so as to enhance a positive image of the party. Ba'th activists in universities were encouraged to pay attention to other students who excelled in their studies, to attend poetry and literature meetings on campus, to discuss the party's ideology with other students, and to convince them of the importance of joining the party by studying its ideology and that of its leader.[38] One method of getting closer to the youth was via sporting activities such as football matches and bodybuilding. Similar to the stress placed on the role of sports in communist states, the Ba'th Party supported athletic activities to attract the youth to its ideals.[39] At some point, Saddam Hussein's son 'Uday was appointed head of the Iraqi Olympic Committee and turned it into another vehicle of the regime.

Whatever the target, the Ba'th Party was very fond of organizing public meetings, conferences, and symposiums to discuss the role of the party and to gauge trends among the public. The number of these public meetings was staggering; in Ninewa, 637 meetings were held during 1999, whereas in the two branches of Misan and Wasit, 411 public gatherings took place in a single month in 1997.[40] Although we have abundant statistics on the number of symposiums (which might easily had been overstated), there is little information about their content, unlike the detailed agendas of party member gatherings, and there is also no hint of how many nonaffiliated members of the public attended. It seems that in some meetings, decisions by the Ba'th leadership or speeches of Saddam Hussein were explained to the public, particularly those with economic implications for them.[41] Some of these meetings involved charity works such as collecting clothes for the poor and, during the sanctions in the 1990s, food distribution.[42]

---

[38] Al-Rashid Branch, Baghdad, "Organizational Plan for al-Rashid Branch for 1992," *BRCC*, 005-1-2 (404–434).

[39] Division of the Arab Glory, Baghdad, to Party Secretariat, "Activities for the Period January 1, 2001, to August 25, 2001," *BRCC*, 011-4-4 (072).

[40] Party Secretariat of Ninewa, "Activities for 2001," March 21, 2001, *BRCC*, 007-4-5 (151); Party Secretariat of Misan and Wasit to Regional Command, "Monthly Activities," November 9, 1997, *BRCC*, 08-4-6 (178–179).

[41] See, for example, meetings to explain the economic embargo on Iraq after the 1991 invasion of Kuwait, in Misan Branch Secretariat to Southern *tandhim*, October 19, 1992, *BRCC*, 003-5-1 (093).

[42] Victorious Leader Section to *fir'* Headquarters, "Exhibition," September 15, 2001, *BRCC*, 003-5-7 (428).

Certain branches volunteered their doctor members to devote part of their time to treating without charge patients who lived in the area, whereas other branches paid for the medical care of citizens who were not affiliated with the party.[43] This was part of the overall strategy of rewards and punishment that is discussed later (Chapter 7).

Beginning in the 1990s, after Saddam Hussein had changed his stance in regard to religion from being secular to launching *al-hamla al-'imaniyya* (the faith campaign), the party began to give prominence to religious occasions and pushed for greater piety in Iraq as an Islamic nation.[44] Hence, the branches became involved in the faith campaign and organized meetings to explain the importance of religion for Iraq and its citizens.[45] Based on instructions from Saddam Hussein, some branches hosted special luncheons, and food was distributed to a large number of families on the day commemorating the martyrdom of Imam Hussein.[46] In general, the branches took part in all celebrations, religious or national, by arranging meetings and orchestrating festivities. They were responsible for planning demonstrations and parades on national occasions and making sure that large crowds attended.[47]

Another important public relations task for the branches was organizing the venues for referendums and national censuses. There was an intense flurry of activity whenever a referendum for electing a president was held. Although there was only one candidate – Saddam Hussein – it was important to mobilize the largest possible number of voters to demonstrate the people's belief in the party and its leader, particularly for the referendum of October 15, 2002, when Iraq and its leader were in the international spotlight.[48] In a detailed memorandum written four months ahead of polling, the secretariat of the Victorious Leader *fir'*, which was part of the al-Karkh *tandhim* of Baghdad, described

---

[43] Party Secretariat of Ninewa, "Activities of 2001," n.d., *BRCC*, 007-4-5 (132); Division of the Arab Glory, Baghdad, to Party Secretariat, "Activities for the Period January 1, 2001, to August 25, 2001," *BRCC*, 011-4-4 (072).

[44] Bengio, *Saddam's Word*, pp. 176–202.

[45] Party Secretariat of Ninewa, "Activities of 2001," n.d., *BRCC*, 007-4-5 (149).

[46] Division of the Arab Glory, Baghdad, to Party Secretariat, "Activities for the Period January 1, 2001, to August 25, 2001," *BRCC*, 011-4-4 (072). Imam Hussein is known among the Shi'is as *sayyid al-shuhada'* (the master of martyrs) because he was killed in a famous battle in Karbala in 680 A.D. See Yitzhak Nakash, *The Shi'is of Iraq* (Princeton, NJ: Princeton University Press, 1994), p. 21.

[47] Misan Branch Secretariat to the Southern *tandhim*, "A Study," October 13, 1992, *BRCC*, 003-5-1 (091–100). The Misan branch, for example, organized twenty-seven public festivities during the month of November 1997. See *BRCC*, 008-4-6 (179).

[48] Victorious Leader Section to *fir'* Headquarters, "Visit," September 19, 2002, *BRCC*, 003-5-7 (001).

preparations for this referendum. The document called for enlisting tribal leaders, religious personalities, students, women's organizations, and other professional unions to encourage their members to vote, and to understand the importance to the country of having high participation as a rebuke to America and Zionism. Among the mottos for the referendum were, "Yes, yes to the leader Saddam Hussein," and "Saddam Hussein is all of Iraq, and all of Iraq is Saddam Hussein."[49]

The branch's plan specified how to raise public awareness of this event by displaying new posters and murals describing the leader's qualities, having musical bands parade in the streets to inject a spirit of excitement and create a joyful atmosphere, and decorating the neighborhood to show happiness and confidence in the leadership. The memorandum also called for the preparation of a large cadre of "presentable" women and men who would explain to the crowds where and how to vote. Administratively, the branch arranged cars and buses to transport voters to polling booths and provided refreshments on referendum day. Finally, the branch made all the security arrangements and called on its members not to wear military uniforms that day and to carry only light guns that could be concealed in their clothes.[50]

Another task that fell within the category of dealing with the public and that was related to security was encouraging people, particularly the youth, to enlist in the various parallel armies, such as *al-jaysh al-shaʿbi* (the Popular Army) and later on *fidaʾiyyu Saddam* (see Chapter 5). Some branches organized the training of recruits and supervised the inspection of arms for militia members.[51] The Popular Army was seen as a military training vehicle for all kinds of people, including party members, and large numbers were cajoled into joining this militia.[52] At different times during the regime, these parallel armies were seen as instrumental in providing the security and political backing for the Baʿth leadership.

4. Political and Security Activities

Security activities were vitally important for the branches throughout the Baʿth's reign of power. The branches were the eyes and ears of the regime, and the lines between the security forces and the activities of branches

---

[49] The Victorious Leader Branch to the Party Secretariat, "Mechanism of Referendum Day," June 27, 2002, *BRCC*, 004-3-2 (103–109).

[50] *Ibid.*

[51] Rawanduz Division to Party Secretariat, "Third Quarter of 1987 Organizational Plan," August 23, 1987, *NIDS*, KDP 021, Box 2225.

[52] Duhok Branch, "Organizational Activities for 1989," *NIDS*, KDP 009, Box 2096 (110051).

were quite blurred when it came to dealing with the "enemies" of the regime, or carrying out the party's political/military plans, such as the Arabization of northern Iraq. Maintaining the regime's stability was seen as a core task for party branches, and they were responsible for doing what was necessary to perpetuate Ba'th rule.[53]

Given the importance of this task, branches were encouraged to select only the most loyal and devoted members to serve on their security committees. These committees were charged with mapping strategies for gathering and establishing efficient sources of information among certain sectors of the local population, for dealing with the enemies of the regime in their areas, for checking rumors, for keeping appropriate files and documents on individuals, and for coordinating with the security forces in their area.[54]

Gathering information was indeed a priority, and the next chapter discusses the recruiting of informers and how the security services used their information. Monitoring suspicious elements and all non-Ba'th political movements was high on the list of all branches. Brochures and leaflets of parties such as Da'wa or the KDP were regularly collected and sent for analysis to the Party Secretariat and the security agencies. Members of those parties and their families were followed, and reports about their movements and meetings were recorded meticulously.[55] In northern Iraq, field reconnaissance was considered vital for any branch: the need to know the strength of the enemy in each branch's geographical area, the type and amount of arms under its control, its ammunition supply routes, and its weak points.[56] Branches kept an eye not only on their opponents but on activities among the youth in their areas. For instance, schools had to prepare lists with the names of all teachers and their qualifications, as it was imperative that the majority of teachers were believers in the party's ideology.[57] Similarly, there was continual monitoring of professional groups such as nurses and doctors.

[53] Al-Qi'qa' Division, "Organizational Plan for the Period April 7, 2002, to April 6, 2003," April 2, 2002, *BRCC*, 003-2-3 (230).
[54] Al-Rashid Branch, Baghdad, "Organizational Plan for al-Rashid Branch for 1992," *BRCC*, 005-1-2 (404–434).
[55] Arbil *amn* to Political Section, "Telegram," August 5, 1989, *NIDS*, PUK 013, Box 052 (020034).
[56] Party Secretariat to *tandhim* of Salah al-Din and al-Anbar Provinces, "Analytical Symposiums," September 20, 1994, *BRCC*, 033-1-6 (084).
[57] Sarsank Division to All Party Organizations, "Schools," January 1, 1986, *NIDS*, KDP 021, Box 2223.

Depending on the importance of the information gathered, some reports were sent to the security agencies, but in many instances, if deemed sensitive, they were delivered directly to the secretary of the president. Examples include reports of attacks in southern Iraq against government installations and buildings or important intelligence about the intentions of opponents of the regime.[58] In the southern region of ʿAmara and the marshes, there were almost daily attacks during the period following the invasion of Kuwait and the uprising that took place in 1991 at the end of the First Gulf War, and these continued throughout 1992.[59]

As in the south in the early 1990s, so it was in the north for most of the 1980s, where the branches played a critical role in the campaign against the Kurds. The Arabization of Kurdistan was coordinated by a special committee for northern affairs within the RCC, but the branches carried out that policy. Displacing many Kurdish families and replacing them with Arab families from other regions to change the demographic balance in northern Iraq was a policy initiated by the Baʿth regime in the late 1970s and pursued throughout the 1980s.[60] In the province of al-Taʾmim, peasants were relocated and given land on condition that it would not be sold or transferred. Party officials had the responsibility of moving these peasants from their old dwellings to their new land and had authority to arrest anyone trying to return to their own villages. In addition, branch officials were ordered to make sure that the new arrivals severed all connection with their previous areas of residence. Branches were told to be on the lookout for Arab families willing to settle in the area and, when such families were found, to make their transfers smooth.[61] Not only Kurdish families were displaced; families with Iranian roots were also uprooted, unless they were part of the Iranian opposition to the Khomeini regime.[62]

---

[58] See, for example, Party Secretariat to Secretary of the President, "Information," August 18, 1992, *BRCC*, 003-5-1 (063). This information is based on a report sent by the Misan branch to the Party Secretariat a couple of days before.

[59] Misan Branch to Party Secretariat, "Daily Situation from August 27, 1992," *BRCC*, 003-5-1 (139).

[60] For the resistance among the Kurds against the Baʿth regime in the 1980s that culminated in the *al-anfal* campaign in April 1987 see Tripp, *A History of Iraq*, pp. 243–46.

[61] RCC, Secretary for Northern Affairs to Presidential *diwan*, "Transfer of Arab Citizens to al-Taʾmim Province," October 23, 1985, *BRCC*, 006-2-6 (032–033). Al-Taʾmim is the province of Kirkuk, but after the nationalization of oil in June 1972, its name was changed to al-Taʾmim, which means "nationalization."

[62] Suleimaniyya *amn*, "Committee Meeting," December 7, 1988, *NIDS*, PUK 045, Box 283 (030042).

Party officials were also encouraged to settle in al-Ta'mim province; they were given incentives such as new homes and financial rewards on condition that the official would live there for a minimum of five years, if he did not settle permanently.[63] Given the sensitivities of their duties, it was decided that only party members should engage in implementing the leadership's policy in the autonomous region in the north. Priority was given to bachelors, but if they were married, their children should be of primary school age, and ideally the member should be a teacher or a clerk. Serving in the autonomous region was considered equivalent to serving in the battle of *al-qadisiyya*, and each member was therefore entitled to all the rewards associated with it. Significant rewards were heaped on party officials willing to serve in the north, both during and after their assignments.[64]

In addition, branches were instrumental in coordinating economic affairs in the north. They policed the distribution of food and took steps to combat the enormous amount of smuggling that took place across the Iranian and Turkish borders.[65] Some party branches were also involved in major projects such as the rebuilding of Fao city in southern Iraq after it was destroyed during the war with Iran. The local branches raised contributions, recruited volunteers for the project, and marshaled contractors and builders to contribute to the effort of rebuilding the city.[66]

Northern branches played a role not only in tracing the source of rumors, but also in spreading counter-rumors that served the regime's interests. For instance, in 1988, it was decided to spread rumors that Turkey might sever diplomatic relations with Iran, and that there were serious disagreements between Iran and Pakistan because Iranian intelligence was behind the attempt to assassinate the president of Pakistan, and thus Pakistan was planning to launch a revenge attack against Iran.[67]

Those involved in security functions on behalf of the branches carried weapons, and as a result, the inspection of arms and receiving proper training and information about the storage of weapons and ammunition were all part of a branch's security operations. In fact, registration

---

[63] Party Secretariat to All Headquarters, "Decision," April 27, 1980, *BRCC*, 006-2-6 (059).

[64] Party Secretariat to Presidential *diwan*, "Proposals," November 27, 1986, *BRCC*, 021-2-6 (156–158). These proposals were reviewed by the president, who gave his full approval, and they thus became effective by 1987.

[65] Committee for Resistance of Enemy Activities, Arbil to Northern *tandhim*, December 3, 1988, *NIDS*, PUK 008, Box 32.

[66] See *BRCC*, 046-4-7, regarding "Participation in Reconstructing Fao."

[67] *Amn* Shaqlawa to All, "Rumors," November 13, 1988, *NIDS*, PUK 016, Box 064.

of guns owned by party members presented a major bureaucratic headache. The branches had to regularly update these records, and they sometimes deregistered owners of guns who were traveling abroad or had been demoted.[68] Party members needed their weapons in case they had to arrest opponents of the regime or, in the 1980s and 1990s, to arrest deserters from military service, which became a serious problem. Given their local knowledge, branches were best suited to arrange for a group of party members to track down deserters and arrest them.[69]

Finally, the branches were part of the strategic plans against the American-led invasion. They were given the responsibility, in addition to all other security and political tasks, of overseeing the strategic storage of oil and other basic commodities. Some branches even promised full guerilla warfare against the Americans and assured the military they were ready for such an event.[70] Obviously, once the party headquarters disintegrated as the invading forces neared Baghdad, the branches descended into total paralysis.

5. Branch Finances

Taking care of a branch's finances was no less important than managing its relations with the public. Branches were expected to be financially sound, which meant collecting members' fees on time, keeping within the budget, and fulfilling other duties such as maintaining their buildings and ensuring that all documentation and filing were in order.

The main source of income, apart from allocations from party headquarters, was membership fees. These were collected on a monthly basis and were correlated with the person's rank; lower ranks paid very little compared to others. The fees were relatively moderate, yet branches had difficulty collecting them on time, and many members had to be reminded repeatedly of the need to pay their dues promptly.[71] In one division called the Arab Glory, there were 3,554 affiliates, about 83 percent of whom were in the lower ranks of sympathizers and supporters. During the first

---

[68] Branch of Abu Ja'far al-Mansur, Baghdad to Party Secretariat, "Party Weapons," November 11, 2002, *BRCC*, 020-1-6 (003).

[69] Spring Section to Headquarters, "Setting Up a Unit," March 4, 2002, *BRCC*, 018-2-7 (028).

[70] See, for example, memo by Fallujah branch to Party Secretariat, December 30, 2002, *CRRC*, SH-BATH-D-000-689.

[71] Duhok Branch, "Organizational Activities for 1989," *NIDS*, KDP 009, Box 2096 (110047).

seven months of 2001, affiliates paid a total sum of about ID1.25 million (less than $1,000). This translates into about ID50 per person per month, a paltry sum in 2001, given the low value of the Iraqi currency at the time.[72] In 1988, before the devaluation of the currency, a supporter earning a monthly wage of ID110 had to pay 300 fils a month.[73] As a result, there was constant pressure on those associated with the branches to contribute to the party. Contributions were considered a key point in a member's file and were discussed with each member during his or her review.[74] Conferences and party symposiums were also used to raise cash for the party.

In their annual reports, branches emphasized the need to control and reduce their spending to be commensurate with their income. An important item in expenditure was payments to needy members. As part of what became known as *al-takafful al-hizbi* (party responsibility), and based on Saddam Hussein's guidelines, party affiliates were told that they must take care of other members, both active and retired, who were in need of help.[75] Emoluments were paid monthly to those in the category of "friend" or *mukarram* (venerated) individual, and these payments assumed further importance with the economic deterioration in Iraq after the invasion of Kuwait.[76]

In looking at the balance sheet of the Ba'quba branch in the province of Diyala, honorariums and bonuses made up about 30 percent of total spending, whereas in another branch in the same province, they constituted the largest budget entry.[77] The next leading outlay was "miscellaneous," and although there was rarely an explanation, items such as payments to encourage early marriages per the instructions of the party leadership were included in this category. Buildings, gardens, and

---

[72] Division of the Arab Glory, Baghdad, to Party Secretariat, "Activities for the Period January 1, 2001, to August 25, 2001," *BRCC*, 011-4-4 (070; 073). The Arab Glory section was part of the Sa'ad bin Abi Waqqas branch, which was within al-Rusafa *tandhim* in Baghdad.

[73] Rawanduz Division to Party Secretariat, "Fees for the Month of April 1988," May 20, 1988, *NIDS*, KDP 036, Box 2362. One dinar equals 100 fils.

[74] See, for example, lists of contributions and fees for the division of Rawanduz during different months in 1988, *NIDS*, KDP 029, Box 2308.

[75] Al-Qi'qa' Division, "Organizational Plan for the Period April 7, 2002, to April 6, 2003," April 2, 2002, *BRCC*, 003-2-3 (231).

[76] In al-Miqdad branch, about 600 people were on the payroll for different amounts during the year 2000, *BRCC*, 017-2-5 (002–017).

[77] *Tandhim* of Diyala Province to Party Secretariat, "Budget for the First Nine Months of 2002," October 28, 2002, *BRCC*, 008-3-6 (002–037).

maintenance were the next-largest expense. Other payments included cultural activities and the cost of security patrols carried out by members. Later in 2002, preparing emergency plans for the invasion took up a big portion of the budget.[78]

On the income side, "the fund" was the most important entry, and one could assume that it represented the allocation from headquarters. The Party Secretariat allocated funds to hundreds of branches across the country in an elaborate and calculated way by creating yardsticks for measuring each and every branch and compelling branches to compete.

Competition among Branches

Saddam Hussein encouraged competition among branches and party members, and the reviews of all branches were carried out annually in a systematic and businesslike manner. Branches were asked to present their achievements in the five areas of activity discussed previously and were graded proportionately as follows:[79]

1. Political and security activities: 25 percent
2. Organizational activities: 25 percent
3. Cultural activities: 20 percent
4. Relations with the public: 15 percent
5. Finances: 15 percent

Within each category there were evaluations for subsections. For example, arresting enemies of the regime was worth 4 percentage points, while catching thieves earned only 3 points. Recruitment was part of the organizational activities, and it received the highest grading (6 percentage points), not only within this activity but across all the five tasks. Cultural events such as conferences and symposiums were allocated 3 percentage credits, whereas visiting martyrs' families and encouraging young people to join the Popular Army or other parallel armies each received 4 percentage points.[80]

Competition was taken very seriously by the party leadership, and all results were usually announced on national holidays, especially on

---

[78] *Ibid.* See the budget of al-Miqdad branch (036).
[79] *Tandhim* al-Karkh, Baghdad to Party Secretariat, "Evaluation Measurements," March 5, 2002, *BRCC*, 003-5-7 (336–343).
[80] *Ibid.*

Saddam Hussein's birthday.[81] Within each category there was national coordination, whereby committee members in charge of each activity met with their counterparts in other branches and with the party's senior leadership to discuss how to improve their performance.[82] The detail and thoroughness of the forms for reviewing the achievements of each branch are truly remarkable. Every cell, division, section, and branch had "planned" activities that were compared with "executed" ones. For example, in 2002, the branch of the Victorious Leader in Baghdad was comprised of 8 divisions, 57 cells, 108 groups for supporters, and 132 groups for sympathizers, with a total of 3,672 affiliates. During six months in 2002, this branch organized 248 party meetings (versus 416 planned), 56 organizational symposiums (versus 82 planned), and 156 party visits to other branches (versus 162 planned). Interestingly, 915 members were recruited during those six months, versus a plan calling for 1,532.[83]

In the cultural sphere, the number of gatherings, seminars, visits, hosting of other members, discussion groups, and book-of-the-month events was overwhelming. For instance, according to the Victorious Leader branch's records, 286 cultural activities took place during six months of 2002, compared to a much higher number planned. There were also unplanned activities, such as organizing an exhibition of pictures and posters celebrating the anniversary of the 1968 revolution, arranging the circumcision of children within their district, and erecting ten murals extolling the country's leadership. In regard to security, a total of 106 meetings and symposiums took place, and numerous research papers were published on the topic in the same six months. According to the report of this branch, 150 associates were trained militarily and were ready to serve as a reserve unit for the branch in the geographical area it covered.[84]

Whether divisions and branches exaggerated their activities in order to win accolades from the party leadership is difficult to judge. What is clear is that all branches were under tremendous pressure to perform. A case in point is that all of them needed to report, in addition to the competition forms, other activities such as the number of people arrested

---

[81] Party Secretariat to All *tandhimat*, "Appreciation," June 16, 1990, BRCC, 003-3-7 (106).

[82] Party Secretariat to All *tandhimat*, "Timetables for Meetings," May 11, 2002, BRCC, 014-5-7 (050).

[83] Victorious Leader Branch to Party Secretariat, "Competition Forms between the Sections for the Period April 7, 2002, to October 6, 2002," BRCC, 003-2-3 (001–005).

[84] *Ibid.*

during each period, the number of arms captured, and the value of confiscated assets (including cars) of the regime's opponents.[85] Forms submitted by the branches were reviewed and criticized. A memo by a senior party member who studied them indicated that most of the information provided was unsubstantiated. According to his critique, branches mentioned the number of visits they made or the number of occasions in which they hosted other branches, but none of them stated how many people attended those meetings or the topics discussed. On security matters, the memo called on branches to provide more detailed information, such as the map of the area they covered, showing clearly the cell responsible for security in each street and neighborhood. The same note criticized the way rumors were analyzed and the failure to ascribe them properly according to the nature of their instigators. Finally, the memo underlined the failure of many branches to collect membership fees on time and the lack of discipline in spending.[86] Another memorandum underlined the need for better forward planning, instead of just mentioning the number of activities desired; advised that successful execution required allocating responsibilities to members in a clear and defined way; emphasized the need for a perceptible system of rewards and punishments for members in carrying out their tasks; and last but not least, advised that the branches' operations would be successful if they were to rely on the guidance of the leader Saddam Hussein.[87]

The pressure was not only on the branches but also on the senior individuals running them. The man in charge of the Misan and Wasit *tandhimat*, who happened to be also a member of the party Regional Command, had to file a list of his daily activities. For instance, during November 1997, this comrade had thirty-eight engagements ranging from attending political gatherings to meetings with tribal leaders, students, and security coordinators in the area. In addition, he visited Baghdad to report on his two branches, met with the cadre of the party in his *tandhim*, and attended graduation ceremonies for *fidaʾiyyu Saddam*.[88]

---

[85] Baghdad *tandhim*, al-Karkh to Party Secretariat, "Appraisal on the Occasion of the Birthday of the Leader Comrade (May God Protect Him)," July 12, 2002, *BRCC*, 004-3-2 (076–088).

[86] Secretary of Abu Jaʿfar al-Mansur Branch to Party Secretariat, "Observations," May 2, 2000, *BRCC*, 004-4-3 (119–122).

[87] Duhok Branch, "Organizational Activities for 1989," *NIDS*, KDP 009, Box 2096 (110052).

[88] Member of the Regional Command of Iraq and Overseer of *tandhimat* Misan and Wasit to Party Secretariat, "Activities," December 1, 1997, *BRCC*, 008-4-6 (037–038).

Frequently, members and supporters sent suggestions for increasing the efficiency of operations or for initiatives that were intended to strengthen branch operations and increase the incentives to fulfill their plans. Some of these suggestions focused on the relationship of the party with the public and how to improve communication, whereas others dealt with ways of helping sick or needy party members.[89] Sending memos to senior leadership was one way for associates to be noticed and probably led to promotion, given the importance placed by Saddam Hussein on taking initiative. It seems also that there was some kind of competition among branches in sending lists of initiatives to impress the senior leadership. Among the initiatives mentioned by one branch was the fact that a member made copies of a letter written by Saddam Hussein and distributed them to all affiliates, whereas another member attended funerals in his neighborhood to show his concern for the local people.[90] As part of this competitive ethos, self-criticism by members and heads of branches became an essential element in increasing pressure on the overall system to achieve its goal.

In conclusion, there was competition at all levels of the party, from the lowest to the highest rank in the Ba'th hierarchy. Saddam Hussein and the leadership encouraged this spirit of competition among affiliates, members, and all branches to increase efficiency and commitment in serving the party and its ideals. This constant pressure no doubt helped the party to reign more than three decades in spite of wars, sanctions, and numerous coup d'état attempts.

Life of a Party Unit

In the previous chapter we examined the life of a member throughout his long membership in the party, and here we will look at one unit of the party in the small town of Shorsh, in northern Iraq. The documents provide insight into a group of active members who, as part of their political job, met on a weekly basis to discuss issues in their area. Each party cell had to submit regular reports and information to regional leadership. These fascinating minutes, which are neatly handwritten and cover a period of about four years from 1982 to the end of 1985, allow us

---

[89] See, for example, a memo by a sympathizer to the headquarters of the Abu Ja'far al-Mansur branch, May 14, 2000, *BRCC*, 004-4-3 (119).

[90] Victorious Branch to Party Headquarters, "Initiatives for the Month of September," September 30, 2001, *BRCC*, 003-5-7 (428).

to reconstruct what one small Ba'th Party group faced, how it dealt with the five categories of activities discussed previously, and how it confronted the problems facing it, considering that Iraq was embroiled in a war with Iran and there was great tension with the local Kurds.

Shorsh is situated near Gamgamal, between Arbil and Suleimaniyya, and unlike the regular Ba'th structure of cells, sections, and so on, the meetings were held by a *munadhamma* (organization) of a group of members, some of whom were responsible for overseeing cells and groups of supporters. In essence, they were at the level of a *shu'ba* (section).[91] The meetings took place in the office of the section, but on a few occasions the group met in the offices of *al-amn* in their area. Interestingly, a logbook of meetings of all party units within the Suleimaniyya area during one month in 1991 indicates that meetings were held in a wide variety of places, including schools, government offices, police or fire brigade stations, factories, or the homes of some comrades. Most of the meetings took place at the same time every week, but for smaller and less important groups such as the sympathizers, they were held twice a month.[92]

Throughout 1982 and 1983, seven comrades were part of Shorsh unit, but by the end of 1985 the number had increased to eighteen. Notably, the position of *amin sir* (secretary general) of the group was held by the same person until April 1985, when his name disappeared from the minutes, but there is no record of his promotion or demotion. Interestingly, on his departure, attendees stopped signing their names on the minutes, and the new secretary adopted a new format, either by mentioning only the names of absentees, or by having two lists of attendees and absentees (with the reason for their abstention). On average, one or two members did not join the meeting, and they tended to be different people each week. The meetings took place at the same time every Monday afternoon but later shifted to Tuesday evenings. The topics on the agenda were similar: approval of the previous meeting's minutes, cultural affairs, updates on the activities of political movements in the region, conversations and trends among the public, party recruitment, preparations for celebrations, volunteers for the Popular Army, and organizational issues such as launching new courses for sympathizers or supporters. Often the discussion was curt and to the point; in one session, when the topic of *ahadith*

---

[91] The file, containing 268 pages, relates to the period from January 25, 1982, to December 3, 1985. Each weekly set of minutes for the meeting was about 1–3 pages, depending on the number of issues raised. See *NIDS*, PUK 043, Box 271 (150001–150268).

[92] Suleimaniyya Section, "Times and Places of Meetings for the Branch," July 1991, *NIDS*, PUK 030, Box 149 (041003).

al-muwatinin (conversation among the public) began, it was summed up quickly: "There is nothing important, and anyway citizens do not talk in front of us as [they realize] that the majority of the party apparatus are affiliated with *al-amn*."[93] Hence, comrades were called on to redouble their efforts in building bridges to the public and gaining their trust.

With regard to celebrations, the organization decided that, given the region's circumstances whereby anti-Ba'th slogans were always shouted during parades, security organizations should therefore be given a free hand to handle these "situations." In addition, the group decided that only "schools where we have support for our operations should be asked to join in any celebration."[94]

Some of the members were in charge of cells for sympathizers and supporters, and one or two of them were in charge of multiple cells comprising more than sixty affiliates at different levels of the hierarchy.[95] There is not much information about the members of this group, but one entry in the minutes indicated that a comrade was made responsible for the Office of Roads and Bridges, whereas another was appointed to be in charge of the Office for Food Provisions. There is no indication of the qualifications of these comrades or what their previous assignments had been.[96]

Security and political affairs were mooted most weeks; for example, members discussed how to deal with relatives of members of the Da'wa Party and how to approach families of deserters to warn them of the consequences of the action of their sons and brothers.[97] In certain meetings, the group felt the need to ask for studies about Kurdish tribes in the area or about members of the KDP, but the minutes of subsequent meetings do not indicate any follow-up.[98] Within the security realm, items appear without much explanation or detail and were sometimes summed up in a single sentence: "It was noted that there were disturbances among students."[99] Common topics discussed were requests for information about certain citizens and preparation of volunteers from

---

[93] Shorsh Organization, "Minutes of Meeting," January 11, 1982, *NIDS*, PUK 043, Box 271 (150007).

[94] *Ibid.*

[95] See, for example, Shorsh Organization, "Minutes of Meeting," March 24, 1982, *NIDS*, PUK 043, Box 271 (150009).

[96] *Ibid.*, August 3, 1982, *NIDS*, PUK 043, Box 271 (150037).

[97] *Ibid.*, July 5, 1983, *NIDS*, PUK 043, Box 271 (150091).

[98] *Ibid.*, March 12, 1985, *NIDS*, PUK 043, Box 271 (150212–150213).

[99] *Ibid.*, July 6, 1982, *NIDS*, PUK 043, Box 271 (150033).

within the sympathizers and supporters either to enlist in the Popular Army or to join the regular army that was fighting on the Iranian front.[100]

Recruitment was on the agenda during most of the period reviewed. It was noted in the minutes whenever sympathizers or supporters were added, and sometimes their names were mentioned. There was a definite feeling of pride among the group when one of their comrades managed to recruit new people. Files of sympathizers and supporters were passed on to the members of the Shorsh organization to review and decide who would be eligible for promotion within the party.[101] The group was also involved in arranging courses for political education and coordinating the distribution among party members of pamphlets and speeches of the president about current issues and Baʿth ideology. Also on the agenda were hosting different cells and sections from other regions, preparing for elections in the Student Union, and collecting statistics about party affiliation.[102] Financial matters such as collecting membership fees, raising the level of contributions for the party, and balancing the budget were on the agenda most weeks.

Criticism and self-criticism showed up occasionally. Intriguingly, the only time the minutes carried details about criticism was when one comrade was absent, and it was recorded that the organization criticized him for leaving Shorsh without permission, for being frequently late to party meetings, and for not fulfilling his duties with the cells for which he was responsible.[103] Another comrade who missed a few meetings was criticized for notifying the group that he was sick, because they later found out that he had gone to his office as usual.[104]

In spite of the serious economic problems gripping the country, particularly in the north, and given that the economic management of the area was complicated by the vast amount of smuggling along the border with Iran, it was remarkable that the economic situation in the area was rarely discussed during those four years of weekly meetings.

---

[100] See, for example, Shorsh Organization, "Minutes of Meeting," February 21, 1984, *NIDS*, PUK 043, Box 271 (150131).

[101] See, for example, Meeting of September 10, 1985, *NIDS*, PUK 043, Box 271 (150248).

[102] Shorsh Organization, "Minutes of Meeting," May 25, 1982, *NIDS*, PUK 043, Box 271 (150025). The week before, the minutes indicated that the same comrade also did not show up and a note was sent to him expressing the need to attend those meetings. See (150023).

[103] *Ibid.*, May 25, 1982, *NIDS*, PUK 043, Box 271 (150025).

[104] *Ibid.*, March 29, 1983, *NIDS*, PUK 043, Box 271 (150074).

The life of this party unit was probably not exceptional when compared to other sections and divisions. Files of other units, although often not as comprehensive and well arranged as Shorsh's, indicate that similar topics turned up on the weekly agenda. In general, the location and period affected the items discussed by any branch; if the branch was not in northern Iraq, more emphasis was placed on dealing with members of and sympathizers with the Da'wa Party and local Communist Party than on dealing with the Kurdish insurgency. Also, it seems that cultural activities became more highlighted, given that sections had to deal with the ramifications of the end of the war with Iran.[105]

It is evident that the branches were the backbone of the Ba'th; they allowed the party to spread its control by recruiting new members and acted as the eyes and ears of the leadership. After the 1991 uprising in southern Iraq, Saddam Hussein criticized the branches in the region for failing to warn the leadership of these trends among the insurgents. This created more pressure and competition, which in turn led those branches to become more engaged with their communities and to expand their activities. One subject high on the leadership's agenda was the security of the regime, and in addition to the work of the major security organizations, it is important to remember that party branches played a crucial role in collecting information and enforcing Ba'th rule over Iraq.

---

[105] See, for example, the file containing the minutes of al-Faris al-'Arabi (the Organization for the Arab Knight), which took place at the headquarters of the Hattin section, deals with the period from May 1988 to April 1989, and is more fragmented than the Shorsh file. See *NIDS*, PUK 002, Box 006 (350006–350058).

4

Security Organizations during the Ba'th Era

The survival of the Ba'th Party and its leadership under Saddam Hussein can be largely attributed to the party's ability to expand and control its security apparatus. This system was established long before 1968, but Saddam Hussein perfected its working arrangements and utilized it in ways previously unknown in the history of Iraq. The security agencies were designed to overlap and were structured so as to ensure that no one agency would become strong enough to threaten the regime.

During the years 1968–2003 four main agencies operated in Iraq:

1. *Al-amn al-'am* (General Security) was the oldest agency, dating back to the British mandate in 1921. It underwent dramatic changes in 1973 after its head, Nadhim Kazzar, attempted a coup against both President Hasan al-Bakr and the then Vice President Saddam Hussein.[1] The failed plot led Saddam Hussein to rethink his strategy for the security apparatus, which was part of his responsibility. The eighth regional conference of the Ba'th Party in 1974 admitted that *al-amn* had made many mistakes, such as lack of real control over the security system, and that it was not enough to rely on party members in these organizations.[2] *Al-amn* monitored domestic

---

[1] For details of the plot, see the memoirs of the head of the *mukhabarat* at that time, Barazan al-Tikriti, *Muhawalat ightiyal al-Ra'is Saddam Hussein* [Attempts to Assassinate the President Saddam Hussein] (Baghdad: Arab Publishing House, 1982), pp. 91–161.

[2] Hizb al-Ba'th al-'Arabi al-Ishtiraki, *Thawrat 17 Tammuz: al-Tajriba wa al-afaq* [The 17 July Revolution: The Experience and the Horizons], (Political Report of the Eighth Regional Conference of the Arab Ba'th Socialist Party–Iraq Region) (Baghdad: The Party, 1974), pp. 139–40.

opposition groups, ethnic minorities, and religious factions; it was responsible for patrolling Iraq's borders, particularly in the north, and it kept an eye on illegal economic activities such as currency trading and dealings in the black market.[3]

2. *Al-istikhbarat al-'askariyya al-'amma* (General Military Intelligence) was also established when Iraq became independent in 1932 but was reorganized after Saddam Hussein became president in 1979. This agency collected intelligence on the military capabilities of countries bordering Iraq, as well as on Kurdish forces. Besides gathering information, it acted as an internal force to detect enemy "infiltration" of the army by placing intelligence officers in every military unit down to battalion level.[4] In addition, it gathered information on Iraqi political dissidents abroad and monitored the activities of foreign military attachés in Iraq. In Kurdistan, the agency had unlimited authority to combat Kurdish insurgents.[5] Although headquartered in the Ministry of Defense, the agency reported directly to the president.[6]

3. *Jihaz al-mukhabarat al-'Iraqiyya* (the Iraqi Intelligence Service [IIS]) evolved from the internal security apparatus of the Ba'th that was created after the party rose to power in 1963 and was originally called *jihaz hunain*. Saddam Hussein, then deputy secretary of the party and vice president as well as in charge of all security agencies, dissolved *jihaz hunain* in 1973 and set up the IIS.[7] According to Kanan Makiya, the IIS was distinctly different from other security organs in that it was more of a "political body" and its first members "combined professional inexperience with political knowledge, not mere loyalty."[8] The organization kept tabs on Ba'th Party members, monitored the activities of Iraqi students abroad, targeted operations against foreign intelligence services,

---

[3] For a full list of its functions and its structure, see Central Intelligence Agency, *Iraq: Foreign Intelligence and Security Services*, Report no. 276, August 1985, MORI DocID: 1127938, pp. 16–19.

[4] Iraq Survey Group, *Regime Strategic Intent*, vol. I, p. 83.

[5] Isam al-Khafaji, "State Terror and the Degradation of Politics in Iraq," *Middle East Report (MERIP)*, no. 176 (May–June 1992), p. 16.

[6] For a full list of its functions and its structure, see Central Intelligence Agency, *Iraq*, pp. 12–15.

[7] Aburish, *Saddam Hussein*, pp. 64 and 76. Aburish points out that most writers mistakenly referred to the organization as *jihaz haneen* (Instrument of Yearning), but in fact *jihaz hunain* was named after the battle of Hunain in the early days of Islam.

[8] Makiya, *Republic of Fear*, p. 15.

and from 1997 was used for illegal procurement for the Military Industrial Commission.[9] The IIS's regional offices in nine provinces carried out miscellaneous functions for its directorates.

4. *Jihaz al-amn al-khass* (the Special Security Organization [SSO]) was set up by Saddam Hussein after he became president and was in essence the leadership's eyes and ears. It was the most powerful of all the agencies and reported directly to Saddam Hussein. Hussein Kamil al-Majid, Saddam's son-in-law and nephew of 'Ali Hasan al-Majid (known as Chemical 'Ali), was instrumental in its organization, and Saddam's son Qusay became its director sometime in late 1991, thus strengthening the SSO's direct access to the president. The documents of the *BRCC* provide an unprecedented insight into the workings of this organization.

In addition to the main four, there were other agencies, such as *al-amn al-'askari* (Military Security), which was established in 1992 by Saddam Hussein in response to potentially threatening events within the military, following the First Gulf War and the uprising in the south. Some of its responsibilities overlapped with the General Military Intelligence, such as detecting dissent in the armed forces and investigating corruption and embezzlement within the army.[10] As we saw in previous chapters, the Ba'th Party itself was deeply involved in security matters through its own security forces and intelligence gathering, particularly in the provinces outside Baghdad. By 1998, it had its own intelligence unit, called *shu'bat al-istikhbarat al-'askariyya* (Section of Military Intelligence), which was part of the Baghdad military bureau to oversee intelligence activities, and more importantly to keep an eye on employees of other intelligence services. *Shu'bat al-istikhbarat* operated as any other party section, and its hierarchy was exactly the same, but it had the added responsibility of being part of the intelligence community.[11]

When the intifada of 1991 took place, rebels focused their attacks on the symbols of the regime and its power, especially the party's

---

[9] Iraq Survey Group, *Regime Strategic Intent*, has a detailed chart of the different directorates of the *mukhabarat* and their functions. See vol. I, pp. 74–83.

[10] Ibrahim al-Marashi, "Iraq's Security and Intelligence Network: A Guide and Analysis," *Middle East Review of International Affairs (MERIA)*, vol. 6, no. 3 (September 2002), p. 10.

[11] Section of Military Intelligence Command to Baghdad Branch, 2002 (no specific date), CRRC, SH-BATH-D-000-313. By 2002 there were 3,413 affiliates of the party at all levels working within this section. It was evaluated as any other unit of the party and participated in cultural debates and political education.

installations.[12] In addition, the fact that the two sets of files studied here, the *BRCC* and *NIDS*, contain tens of thousands of secret documents of the security organizations that were copied to the Party Secretariat demonstrates the symbiosis between the party and the security agencies. Speaking as the director of the SSO, Qusay told his officers that "an affiliate of the SSO must be a Ba'thist and a believer in the principles of the Arab Ba'th Socialist Party."[13] In addition, the party held information, such as political and party background, about most senior officers in the intelligence services.[14]

In spite of the overlapping created by Saddam Hussein, there was a forum for coordination between the different organizations called *majlis al-amn al-qawmi* (National Security Council). According to the Iraqi Survey Group, 'Izzat Ibrahim al-Duri, at the time vice president and the vice chairman of the Revolutionary Command Council, acted as chairman of the National Security Council, which consisted of the directors of the four security and intelligence services. The presidential secretary, who had a lot of power, attended the meetings, screened all reports sent to the president, and decided what should be brought to his attention. The council did not have regular meetings, and in fact all directors of the agencies, irrespective of the council's meetings, brought important matters to Saddam Hussein directly.[15]

The two sets of documents used in this study, the *NIDS* and *BRCC*, provide ample information on how the four main agencies worked in northern Iraq prior to 1991 and across the whole country during the Ba'th regime. Most of the *NIDS* documents relate to *al-amn al-'am*, whereas the *BRCC* holds copies of the correspondence by the four main agencies that was sent to the Ba'th Regional Command or its branches. The *BRCC*, however, has a special section of 1,917 files relating to the SSO, which are the basis for the next topic discussed.

Jihaz al-amn al-khass (the Special Security Organization [SSO])

The security organizations' main task was to gather information through monitoring, surveillance, and an extensive network of informers. Among

---

[12] Marr, *The Modern History of Iraq*, p. 245.

[13] Commandments and Guidelines by Qusay Saddam Hussein, Director of SSO, to Employees of the Organization, compiled July 21, 1994, *BRCC*, B 002-3-6 (060).

[14] See, for example, Head of General Military Intelligence to Party Secretariat, September 27, 1984, "Information," *BRCC*, 170-1-6 (195–253). The information contained background details on 142 officers from the rank of major upward. A senior party official had to endorse the appointment of every officer: "Marching in the path of the revolution."

[15] Iraq Survey Group, *Regime Strategic Intent*, vol. I, p. 86.

the long arms of the state, the SSO was the most powerful security agency in Iraq from 1980 until the U.S.-led invasion in 2003.

The SSO consisted of eleven departments and directorates reporting to the SSO director (see Figure 5). According to the Iraq Survey Group, there was also a scientific branch that reported directly to the director, Qusay Hussein, in the 1990s, but the documents show that the scientific branch – which operated, inter alia, a laboratory to test the president's food – was part of the Directorate of Security Affairs.[16] This directorate was the most important department of the SSO. In its first decade it was responsible for the protection of the president. But in the late 1980s, this responsibility was removed from the SSO, and a special group known as the *himaya* (Protection), made up of the presidential bodyguards, became the first tier of security closest to Saddam Hussein. In fact, a detailed study about the history of the Directorate of Security Affairs and its functions pointed out that there was so much turmoil during the late 1980s, with three different directors holding the helm over a short period of time, that the department almost faced closure.[17] Eventually, the Directorate of Security Affairs, which according to the Iraq Survey Group had more than 1,700 personnel (out of the 5,500 personnel in the whole SSO), became the second tier of protection for the president and the senior leadership of the Ba'th Regional Command. Among its duties were checking and monitoring all employees of the palaces and those traveling with the president.[18]

Many of the other departments had the task of monitoring the loyalty of officers and employees working in various organizations affiliated with the party or the army. For example, the Directorate of Republican Guard Security focused on the loyalty of military commanders within the Republican Guard, whereas the SSO Security branch monitored SSO personnel except for those working directly with the president.[19]

---

[16] Iraq Survey Group, *Regime Strategic Intent*, vol. I, p. 89. According to this report, when confronted by UN inspectors, Qusay refused to acknowledge that the laboratory belonged to the SSO, p. 91.

[17] Directorate of Security Affairs, SSO, "The Directorate of Security Affairs from a Personal Point of View," October 13, 1991, *BRCC*, B 003-4-6 (399–420). The report was written by a veteran employee who was with the SSO almost from its beginning. Consistent with this book's policy, no names are mentioned, unless they were well-known senior officials during the period under study.

[18] Iraq Survey Group, *Regime Strategic Intent*, vol. I, pp. 88–90.

[19] Director of SSO Security Branch to Director of SSO, "Information," April 13, 1996, *BRCC*, B 002-1-5 (039–041). According to this memo, there were 1,305 personnel working in this department, comprising 494 in the Special Surveillance Group and 811 in the housing and logistics affairs related to the president.

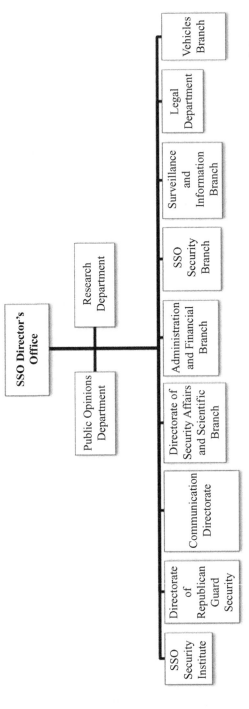

FIGURE 5. The Structure of the Special Security Organization (SSO). *Source:* Iraq Survey Group, *Regime Strategic Intent,* vol. I, p. 89.

This intentional overlap with other departments meant that everyone kept an eye on everyone else. The Surveillance and Information branch had the responsibility of watching senior Iraqi officials and preparing files on any official prior to his or her being promoted or assigned to a new senior job.

Protecting the president was by far the SSO's most significant function, and everything else in the working of the organization was subordinated to that responsibility. On one occasion the director of the SSO told his employees that "the duty of the SSO is not simply guarding [the president], but the underlying security concept means [that] protecting the President Leader (May God Protect him) is protecting Great Iraq."[20] Whenever the president left one of his palaces, the whole system swung into action. Elaborate details were planned ahead of any visit he made, and all other security agencies had to follow the SSO's orders in that regard.[21] Celebrations for national holidays or Saddam Hussein's birthdays involved not only worries about his route and the people he would meet, but also concerns about the food and drink that would be offered to him and his escorts. For birthdays, for example, orders were given to bakers as to which ingredients and decorations they could use, and they could only go ahead after these had been analyzed at the SSO's laboratory.[22] In an interesting memo by the SSO Security branch, the director of the department explained that the "special section" part of the branch was responsible for surveillance of the "close circles to the great leader, May God Protect and Bless him." Among these close circles were workers in the presidential palaces such as electricians, butchers, tailors, the special group that ironed the clothes of the president and his family, drivers, and photographers. Surveillance took many forms: installing secret listening devices in the homes of employees, telephone tapping at work and home, personal monitoring of after-work activities, and continual gathering of information about those in the inner circles and their families.[23]

---

[20] Commandments and Guidelines by Qusay Saddam Hussein, Director of SSO, to Employees of the Organization, compiled July 21, 1994, *BRCC*, B 002-3-6 (060).

[21] See, for example, a visit made by Saddam Hussein to inaugurate a new bridge in Baghdad in March 1995, *BRCC*, B 001-2-1 (364–366). This is probably similar to many other countries, including some democratic ones.

[22] Director of the Security Affairs to the Director of SSO, "Duty," May 15, 1994, *BRCC*, B 002-1-5 (232–234).

[23] Director of SSO Security Branch to Director of SSO, "Plans of Operation of the Special Section," January 12, 1994, *BRCC*, B 002-1-5 (257–260). For some reason, the group that ironed and pressed Saddam Hussein's clothes and shirts was a category of its own,

All employees working in any presidential palace or installation had to sign written commitments and acknowledge that they would face serious punishment if they ever contravened these rules:

1. Employees were required not to chat about what they saw or heard in their place of work, even with other employees or ex-employees of the same department.
2. Employees had to pledge not to establish any relationship with foreigners, Arabs, or traders.
3. Employees had to commit to divulge to the SSO any information regarding the president and any negative talk that permeated the workplace.
4. Employees also had to agree not to use their mobile phones in the offices or to discuss work matters from their home telephones.[24]

One problem that faced the Security branch and was referred to a number of times in the documents was that most of the workers in the presidential palaces, who totaled more than 1,300 in 1995, were Christians. Because these employees spoke among themselves and with their families in the Assyrian and Chaldean languages, it was very hard for the SSO to monitor their telephone calls or to understand conversations that went on at their bugged homes.[25] In one intriguing case, the SSO found out through its informers that the wife of Saddam Hussein's personal chef (also a Chaldean Christian) was addicted to gambling and in one evening lost the sum of ID30,000 (about $300), which obviously made her a security risk. Saddam Hussein was unhappy with the way the SSO wanted to deal with the issue: by immediately arresting the chef and his wife. In one of his rare handwritten comments in the margins of the memo, he stated, "Shouldn't you be more patient, and instead of just arresting them, you should plant one of your employees or informers to play cards at the

---

as it seems that Saddam, who was always immaculately dressed, put a lot of emphasis on the crispness of his attire.

[24] *BRCC*, B 028-3-5 (001–015). The file contains the personal file of one such employee who was assigned to work in a warehouse attached to the office of the senior *murafiq* (adjutant) of the president. There is no explanation why employees could not have any relationships with traders.

[25] Deputy Director of Security Branch to Director of SSO, "A Study," September 5, 1995, *BRCC*, B 002-1-5 (179–180). The memo warned that, in many cases, it took three days to decipher and translate those conversations, which meant a serious risk in case of a plot. More resources were allocated by hiring more native speakers of Assyrian and Chaldean, which are two old languages spoken by many of the Christians in northern Iraq.

[chef's] house so he could report on what is being discussed during those evenings?" A week later, a report to the president indicated that one of the SSO's employees had indeed begun playing cards with the wife, but no security issues were raised.[26] One might assume that the matter was closed, but the chef and his wife were kept under even more vigilant observation. The practice of hiring ethnic minorities in palaces and security organizations was not an invention of Saddam Hussein's; Stalin realized that ethnic minorities, even in senior positions, cannot constitute a threat for the regime, given their lack of a power base.[27] In Iraq, as Assyrians have the reputation of being tidy and punctual and of having no political ambitions, they were a natural group to employ.

Security for the president and his family involved checking anyone who was close to them or to members of their families. When Qusay's children were about to start kindergarten, his deputy asked for information about the six teachers who worked in his children's school.[28] Sometimes the documents give the sense that the SSO was a private family company. Memos indicate that ʻUday, Saddam's older son, would call and ask for information about someone without specifying the reason. Immediately the organization was put to work and background checks were made, not only through the SSO but also via requests sent to the Party Secretariat and other security organizations to fill any gaps in the information.[29] ʻUday's boats and yachts also enjoyed the full protection of the SSO; crews and technicians had to undergo detailed background checks before being approved, and SSO men were on board every vessel.[30]

The real concern for the country's leadership was the people who were on the inside, whether in the army or in the security organizations, including the SSO, and this applied to those in senior positions as well. "The insecurity of the masses must be supplemented by the insecurity of the governing elite who surround the dictator."[31] The files of the SSO are rampant with examples of SSO employees being monitored, arrested,

---

[26] Director of SSO to the Secretary of the President, "The Cook A.Y.A," March 16, 1995, *BRCC*, B 002-1-5 (002–009). His full name was mentioned in the original document but is initialized here.

[27] Paul Gregory, *Terror by Quota: State Security from Lenin to Stalin (An Archival Study)* (New Haven, CT: Yale University Press, 2009), pp. 62–63.

[28] Deputy Director of SSO to Director, "Request for Information," January 2, 1992, *BRCC*, B 003-1-3 (27).

[29] Director of SSO Security Branch to ʻUday Saddam Hussein, "Information," December 21, 1989, *BRCC*, B 003-4-4 (199–201).

[30] SSO Directorate, "Addition of Security," May 8, 2001, *BRCC*, B 024-4-9 (007).

[31] Fainsod, *How Russia Is Ruled*, p. 441.

and punished. Many had their telephones tapped, and their families were closely watched.[32] Under direct orders from Saddam Hussein, a special prison was set up within the General Security organization to hold SSO employees who were suspected of disloyalty, and senior SSO directors were instructed to be involved in their interrogation.[33] A deputy director of the SSO, however, complained that not enough pressure to confess to their crimes was put on SSO staff who had been arrested, and he asked for permission to use tougher interrogation measures, which was immediately granted.[34] Directors of departments were later given authority to imprison any employee for seven days if the director felt that the employee was not carrying out his or her job properly.[35] Employees who had illicit relationships were also reported to the heads of departments. In one case, it was reported that an employee who was separated from his wife brought women to his apartment late at night. His case was exacerbated by the fact that his brother was married to a Syrian woman, which meant that he fell into the category of a possible "foreign" threat (see the following discussion). Concern about romantic affairs was widespread: for example, when an SSO official stationed in northern Iraq formed a liaison with a Kurdish woman, his supervisors were extremely worried about the security implications.[36]

Controlling the employees of the SSO took many shapes and forms. Like army officers, officials had to apply for approval to get married. This obviously gave the organization a free hand to collect information on prospective spouses.[37] Numerous files indicate multiple requests for

[32] Tapping the telephones of SSO employees was frustrating, as they were naturally more aware than anyone else of the workings of their organization. In one instance, an employee's telephone calls were either related to business or of a general nature, which seems to have annoyed those listening to his calls. Their superior officer advised patience and continual monitoring. Report to Director of Security, "Telephone Monitoring," September 4, 1994, *BRCC*, B 001-2-1 (319).

[33] SSO Director to Secretary of the President, "Update," April 13, 1995, *BRCC*, B 002-1-5 (001).

[34] Deputy SSO Security Branch to SSO Director, November 20, 1985, *BRCC*, B 003-4-4 (187). The director just wrote in the margins: "Yes."

[35] Head of Legal Department to All Directors, "Order," April 15, 2001, *BRCC*, B 002-3-2 (161).

[36] Iraqi Intelligence Service to SSO, "Information," February 22, 2003, *BRCC*, B 001-5-7 (022).

[37] Deputy Director of SSO to Religious Court, "Marriage Approval," March 15, 1989, *BRCC*, B 002-4-4 (070); Deputy Director of SSO to Religious Court, "Marriage Approval," January 8, 1992, *BRCC*, B 003-1-3 (13). It seems that religious courts were ordered not to allow marriages of officials without the prior approval of the party or the SSO.

information about employees; mostly without giving the reason why these officials became suspect, but many of them were put under surveillance if a member of their family fled abroad or was arrested for an activity against the regime.[38] The most potent source of information was in an employee's personal file. The sixteen-page questionnaire given to applicants requested exhaustive personal and family details. In addition to the usual personal questions, each applicant was asked in depth about his political beliefs and activities, hobbies, trips abroad, assets, and loans outstanding. Furthermore, there were questions such as the following: "Do you smoke? And if you do, state two kinds of cigarettes you smoke"; "Do you drink? And if you do, state the brand of alcohol you consume, quantity and its impact on you"; "Do you attend night clubs?"; and "Do you have enemies?" Questions about relatives spanned the entire extended family of the spouse, uncles, aunts, and cousins of the candidate and their political affiliation. Some candidates, however, knew how to manipulate the system; in one file, in answer to the question of whether he had any enemies, a candidate replied, "Yes, I do. The enemies of the Ba'th Party are my personal enemies."[39]

Even employees who had left the SSO remained under surveillance, particularly if they or one of their family members were associated with Kurds; prisoners of war; those with a connection to the 1991 uprising – called in the Ba'th jargon *safhat al-ghadr wa al-khiyana* (the page of betrayal and treachery)[40] – employees who had been dismissed; and those who became linked to other political movements.[41]

In the report of the Directorate of Security Affairs mentioned previously, the writer put forward two reasons for the success of the SSO's operations: total loyalty based on kinship and the substantial rewards enjoyed by employees.[42] This frank analysis was based on the fact, clearly indicated by the origins of the directors of the different departments and many of their employees, that belonging to a limited number of trusted families and tribes was paramount in tests of loyalty. The nine heads

[38] See, for example, files requesting information about employees: Secretary of the President to SSO, "Request for Information," November 1, 2000, *BRCC*, B 004-1-1 (23).

[39] Personal File of Employee A.M., *BRCC*, B 002-3-1 (001–016); B 002-3-1 (312–313).

[40] In the parlance of the Ba'th, "the page of treachery and betrayal" refers to the fact that the period of the 1991 uprising is merely one page in the large book of the Ba'th history.

[41] SSO Security Branch, "A Study on Monitoring and Surveillance of Pensioners and Removed Personnel," October 25, 1999, *BRCC*, B 002-2-1 (012–015).

[42] Directorate of Security Affairs, SSO, "The Directorate of Security Affairs from a Personal Point of View," October 13, 1991, *BRCC*, B 003-4-6 (410).

TABLE 4. *Clan Affiliation of Senior Specialists in the Directorate of Security Affairs, SSO*

Tikriti	Duri	Nasiri	'Ajeli	'Azzawi	Hadithi	Misc.*	Total
33	13	36	4	4	4	35	129

* Within the miscellaneous category there were a couple belonging to al-'Ubaidi and two from al-Qaisi.
Source: August 1, 2001, BRCC, B 001-5-6 (129–132).

of the important departments (excluding the Research Department and the Public Opinions Department), together with the director of Qusay's office, belonged to five different tribes and extended families. In 2001, the ten departments' heads comprised three Tikritis, four Nasiris, one Duri, one Alusi, and one 'Ajeli.[43] Many were interrelated; for example, the head of the SSO Security branch was a first cousin of Qusay. Data about 129 senior employees of the Directorate of Security Affairs showed a similar trend, as Table 4 indicates.

Although a reliance on families and clans close to the regime was essential for the preservation of power, sometimes it could be a double-edged sword; once a particular clan was considered too powerful or dangerous, the authorities had to purge the system of all its members. At one point in 1996, an order was issued to single out all those from the al-'Ani clan. As a result, eighteen members of the Special Republican Guard and seventy-one members of the Republican Guard were earmarked by the authorities, but the records do not tell us what happened to them.[44] A similar fate befell the al-Janabis and many from their clan, whether in the army or in the intelligence services.[45] In a similar vein, it seems that the leadership of the SSO was worried about the high number of siblings working in the SSO. For example, there were eleven pairs of brothers working in the Directorate of Security Affairs, twenty-one pairs in the Vehicles branch, and four pairs in the Communication Directorate.

---

[43] Directorate of SSO, "Timetable for Special Shifts of the Directors of Departments for the Period July 21, 2001, to July 30, 2001," July 18, 2001, BRCC, B 001-5-6 (159).
[44] Director of SSO Security to Director of SSO, "Sect," June 4, 1996, BRCC, B 001-2-1 (114–115).
[45] See the story of General Kamel Sachet al-Janabi in Wendell Steavenson, *The Weight of a Mustard Seed: The Intimate Story of an Iraqi General and His Family During Thirty Years of Tyranny*, paperback edn. (New York: Harper, 2010).

According to this study, many were transferred outside their brothers' departments or completely out of the SSO.[46]

The report of the Directorate of Security Affairs was also correct in its analysis of the importance of rewards to the organization's success (see Chapter 7 for more on rewards). First and foremost, many employees were granted land and offered loans to build houses. Others had apartments that were fully paid for or subsidized by the organization, with the rent directly deducted from the officials' salaries.[47] Removing these property benefits was among the punishments imposed by the SSO if an employee was sentenced to five or more years in prison. Although owning homes or being given subsidized rentals in Baghdad were considered among the highest rewards, there were other fringe benefits. Many employees were able to enroll in universities based on their affiliation to the party and the SSO, and in numerous cases the SSO paid for their education.[48] Other benefits were free cigarettes or parties organized by the SSO to celebrate the circumcision of employees' children.[49]

In addition to formal education, employees at the SSO had to participate in specialized training courses. A mandatory course for employees at all levels was *hasana amniyya* (security awareness), which included measures to protect documents and instructions on what to do if a document was lost; instructions on "combating spying"; procedures against "penetration" of the system; and, as in all military or Ba'th Party courses, special lessons based on the "commandments of the President leader."[50] Among these were phrases such as the following: "The thief will not sneak in unless the guard is asleep and you are the guards"; "Accuracy, I command you; accuracy in work"; and "The most important aspect of a security officer is to love his work and feel that he can excel in his area of expertise."[51] The Special Security Institute, which was responsible for

---

[46] Director of SSO Security Branch to Director of SSO, "Brothers," May 17, 1990, *BRCC*, B 001-4-4 (035–036; 044).

[47] The SSO files had dozens of these files with lists of rents paid and monthly deductions. See, for example, *BRCC*, B 004-4-4; B 004-3-2; B 002-5-3.

[48] SSO to Baghdad University Law School, "Support for a Candidate," October 1, 1997, *BRCC*, B 002-1-2 (067).

[49] SSO Directorate, August 11, 2001, *BRCC*, B 002-1-6 (008); Administrative and Financial Branch to All Directorates, "Circumcision Celebrations," May 15, 2001, *BRCC*, B 001-5-6 (040).

[50] Deputy Director, Special Security Institute, to All Directors, October 8, 1993, *BRCC*, B 001-1-6 (006); B 002-1-7 (027).

[51] From the "Security Commandments of the President Leader (May God Protect Him)," compiled July 21, 1994, *BRCC*, B 002-3-6 (057–059).

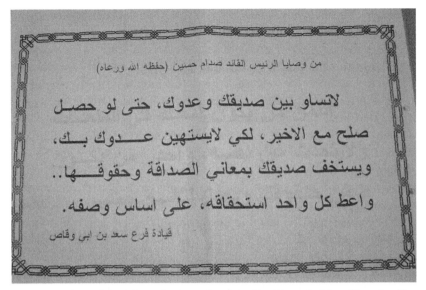

من وصايا الرئيس القائد صدام حسين (حفظه الله ورعاه)

لاتساو بين صديقك وعدوك، حتى لو حصـل

صلح مع الاخير، لكي لايستهين عــدوك بــك،

ويستخف صديقك بمعاني الصداقة وحقوقـــها..

واعط كل واحد استحقاقه، على اساس وصفه.

قيادة فرع سعد بن ابي وقاص

FIGURE 6. One of the Many Commands of the President, Saddam Hussein. The text reads: "From the commands of the President Leader Saddam Hussein (may God protect him and bless him) / Do not treat your friend and enemy equally even if you make peace with the latter. You do not want to allow your enemy to scorn you or your friend to belittle your friendship and its meanings. Give each their due, based on their status. / Headquarters of branch of Sa'ad bin Abi Waqqas." Courtesy of the Iraq Memory Foundation.

training SSO officers, offered a three-month basic training course consisting of physical security training, personnel security, search techniques, and methods of debriefing casual contacts.[52] An annual physical fitness test was part of the curriculum, but it appears that many employees did not pass it.[53] In addition, the institute decided in 1995 that all employees had to learn to swim.[54]

Not all courses were related to security and physical fitness; intriguingly, officers with university degrees were encouraged to take a ten-day course in parapsychology to increase "expertise in this field." Unfortunately, there are no documents indicating why SSO officers needed to

[52] Iraq Survey Group, *Regime Strategic Intent*, vol. I, p. 91.

[53] In one year, 1995, 376 officials failed the fitness test; see *BRCC*, B 001-2-2 (244). Interestingly, heads of sections and general directors were exempted from fitness tests, *BRCC*, B 001-1-3 (008).

[54] Deputy Director, Special Security Institute, to All Directors, October 8, 1993, *BRCC*, B 002-4-1 (130).

study the existence and causes of psychic abilities and life after death.[55] Most likely this was because similar courses were taught in the Soviet Union and the United States as part of the preparation for elite security forces.[56] In addition, both Saddam Hussein and his close associate, ʿIzzat al-Duri, were believers in the power of magic and of dervishes.[57]

In addition to rewards and education, for those working in the SSO, the feeling of power must have been intoxicating. The SSO was omnipresent; it had a say in any significant promotion or demotion within the system. For example, when a senior officer in the General Military Intelligence was on the verge of being promoted in the chief of staff's office, the SSO decided to block this promotion by delving into all the files and information collected during the officer's career. Sure enough, his promotion was suspended.[58] Indeed, the SSO's authority was all-encompassing; documents indicate that it was involved in appointments of doctors in hospitals and of scientists in universities, property allocation, religious activities, archeological digs, and even "Arabization" of Latin words.[59] Requests for information and responses to those requests occupy a large portion of the SSO files; the "insecurity of the elite" was shown by the fact that information on many senior party and army officials was passed on to the presidential *diwan*.[60] Even ministers had to get approval from the SSO before traveling abroad, and files of senior officers' family members were constantly being recalled by the SSO or the presidential *diwan* to be used against any official suspected of opposing the regime. This applied to family members of even those who had been executed to ensure the tight grip of the regime.[61]

---

[55] Ministry of Education and Scientific Research to SSO Directorate, "Courses in Parapsychology," August 18, 1991, *BRCC*, B 001-1-6 (039–041).

[56] See, for example, Jon Ronson, *The Men Who Stare at Goats* (New York: Simon & Schuster, 2009), about the recruitment of gifted minds into special courses within the U.S. army. The book was made into a movie.

[57] Interview with two Iraqis, a general and a senior diplomat, June 15, 2010.

[58] Director of SSO to Presidential *diwan*, "Transfer of an Officer," January 12, 1996, *BRCC*, B 001-1-7 (333–340).

[59] See *BRCC*, B 001-1-7. On inaugurating work for building a hospital, the SSO prepared lists of specialized doctors whom it recommended; three out of eight doctors had an al-Tikriti surname and one an al-Duri. SSO to Presidential *diwan*, "Nomination of Doctors," October 2, 1994, *BRCC*, B 001-5-3 (187–189).

[60] See, for example, a request for information about a senior member of the Baʿth Party from *tandhim* al-Karkh, March 8, 1994, *BRCC*, B 001-2-1 (323–325).

[61] *BRCC*, B 002-3-7. The SSO provided information to the presidential *diwan* about the brother of the "buried criminal," Health Minister Riad Ibrahim Hussein, who was executed in June 1982 after daring to challenge Saddam Hussein during the war with

Needless to say, possessing such power led to its abuse by many SSO officers. Some citizens were brave enough to complain of such abuses, and in many cases officers were disciplined. Both Saddam Hussein and his son Qusay warned against the misuse of power by security officers who took advantage of their positions: "Do not exploit the name of this office and brag about your identity card using it as a tool of control and power."[62] Although many such instances went unnoticed, there was a mechanism of discipline and punishment. The essential element was whether a complaint reached Saddam Hussein himself; if it did, this usually triggered an investigation.

In one complaint, a citizen wrote that members of the SSO entered her house after midnight and punched her son, returning a few hours later to repeat the maltreatment. The police refused to interfere, and she felt obliged to write a complaint to the president. Interestingly, as with other complaints, it was dealt with because the letter asked for a meeting with the president, thus setting the process in motion.[63] A special committee was formed to look into cases of officers demanding bribes from citizens, and the committee found that some had abused their positions. In a different case, an SSO unit that raided a casino showing pornographic movies confiscated the films and kept them rather than handing them to the authorities.[64] Members of the SSO carried weapons and entered night clubs against all regulations, which led the Ministry of Interior to write to the SSO asking them to put a halt to that practice.[65] Firing in the air during ceremonies was another manifestation of power abuse; after a football match between Iraq and Yemen, five people were killed and about fifty injured, mostly from firearms carried by members of the security forces.[66]

Of course, it was not just SSO staff who abused their power under the Ba'th regime; a memo indicated that officers of *al-himaya* (the special presidential protection unit) forced their way into a night club, beat the bartender, and forced the club manager to recall the club's singer from

---

Iran and suggesting that the president should step down. *BRCC*, B 002-5-6 (141). For more information on the incident, see Tripp, *A History of Iraq*, p. 236.

[62] From the Security Commandments of the President and the Director of the SSO, compiled July 21, 1994, *BRCC*, B 002-3-6 (057–059).

[63] "Citizen M. to the President Leader (May God Protect You and Bless You)," n.d., *BRCC*, B 001-3-7 (042).

[64] SSO, "Minutes of Committee," December 1, 1996, *BRCC*, B 002-2-6 (032–038).

[65] Directorate of SSO, "Entering Night Clubs," April 7, 1993, *BRCC*, B 003-1-5 (464).

[66] Presidential *diwan* to Party Secretariat, "The Phenomenon of Firing in the Air," June 30, 1993, *BRCC*, B 002-5-5 (019).

his home at three in the morning to perform for them. Saddam Hussein ordered the creation of a committee to look into the matter, which later sentenced two of the bodyguards to brief terms of imprisonment (not more than three months) and imposed fines on the others.[67] In a different case, a woman complained that Saddam Hussein's son ʿUday had raped her, and although she was granted a piece of land and was awarded some money by the minister of interior, she began showing up in front of the SSO building and shouting about how she was sexually abused by ʿUday. Here, no action was taken, and the woman was arrested for "attacking" a member of the president's family and was admitted to a psychiatric hospital.[68]

Other abuses were within the organization itself; one official claimed, in a complaint sent to his Baʿth branch, that he was humiliated by his senior officer and denied promotion due to personal conflicts.[69] The SSO had to engage in disciplinary action in scores of incidents of corruption; theft; breaking of security rules, particularly telephone and wireless violations; and lack of follow-up in investigating certain matters. Reports received by the organization about its employees loitering or disturbing neighbors in the subsidized apartments occupied by party and SSO officers were also met with reprimands and punishments.[70] Romantic liaisons within the organization were another problematic issue; in one instance, a female clerk working in the Communication branch had numerous affairs with other officers and began blackmailing them. This came to an end when she was caught naked with an officer in his office. She was demoted and transferred to the Ministry of Health, and her son, who also worked in the SSO, was transferred to the Military Industry Organization.[71] In fact, each week, there was on average a list of about fifteen employees who were arrested for different abuses and violations.[72]

---

[67] Minister of Interior to Secretary of the President, "Attack," September 8, 1993, *BRCC*, B 001-2-2 (253).

[68] SSO Directorate, "Insult by a Citizen," September 20, 1995, *BRCC*, B 002-4-3 (157–158).

[69] Al-Faris Branch to Director of SSO, "Report," September 26, 2001, *BRCC*, B 002-3-7 (031–033). Bizarrely, the complainant argued that his superior did not like people who came from Tikrit, and this was the reason for the discrimination against him.

[70] See *BRCC*, B 001-1-1 (0033–009); B 002-5-6 (245); B 003-1-6 (091). Violations of telephone and wireless rules were dealt with harshly, particularly if the unauthorized calls were made in the vicinity of the presidential palaces. See B 001-3-7 (079–080).

[71] Director of Security Branch to Director of SSO, "Information," January 8, 1989, *BRCC*, B 001-4-4 (135–142).

[72] See, for example, the weekly ledger of internal arrests for the week of April 4, 1990, *BRCC*, B 003-4-7 (83).

The influence of the SSO was due mostly to its ability to use information against its enemies. All security services realized that information was power and those who controlled it were the most powerful – hence the tremendous attention paid by systems such as the Ba'th to collecting information, whether through informers or by other means.

Gathering Information

In order to penetrate, monitor, and control the state and society, the Ba'th regime used every possible source of information. All government offices were supposed to assist the security services in gathering information. In a cabinet meeting, Saddam Hussein ordered all ministers to cooperate with and facilitate the work of the intelligence community, and to "give them whatever required to achieve their mission."[73]

The regime, and in particular its leader, Saddam Hussein, had clear ideas about security and intelligence gathering: "The security man must be knowledgeable about his local environment, whether it is a lake [*sic*], a mountain or a city, and he must gather all details, large and small about his surroundings."[74] A memo written in northern Iraq describing ways and means of infiltrating different levels of society to collect information and monitor "enemies" emphasized that the security officer needed to have a good education in order to absorb information within the political, economic, military, and social spheres. "Understanding how opposition parties and movements inside and outside the country are structured" and "how these movements recruited and how they transferred information to their followers" was essential to the success of the security personnel.[75] Along those lines, the director of the IIS discussed the approach that should be taken by an intelligence officer: how to choose the source of information, how to approach him, and how to orient the relationship; the characteristics needed in an officer, such as

[73] Cabinet Secretariat to Minister of Higher Education and Scientific Research, "Students Studying Abroad," November 19, 1998. The memo about utilizing Iraqis studying abroad for gathering information was copied to all heads of intelligence services, *BRCC*, 021-2-7 (583).

[74] From the "Security Commandments of the President Leader (May God Protect Him)," compiled July 21, 1994, *BRCC*, B 002-3-6 (057–059).

[75] This draft of a memo was written on the stationery of the Ministry of Agriculture and Irrigation in northern Iraq, without the name of the author or the recipient. There was also no date, although the file in which this memo was found was dated 1988. *NIDS*, PUK 007, Box 025 (120002–120009).

understanding the local culture; the importance of patience, persistence, and teamwork; and finally the need for specialization.[76]

Obviously, not all security officers were well versed in politics and economics, and in certain instances in which the regime could not muster enough officers, the criteria changed. In one case, the head of *al-amn* in Suleimaniyya in the early 1980s allowed the appointment of security officials in different government offices as long as the official was a Ba'th member with at least five years of service, had a good reputation and a reasonable working relationship with other employees in the ministry.[77] The reason for this scarcity of security officers was the huge extent of the network required to cover every government department, factory, or industrial installation regardless of its size; one list of *al-amn* officials in Suleimaniyya shows the scope of this network, and many of the offices and factories included more than one security officer.[78]

Any government official not cooperating with the security organizations was harshly reprimanded, and his file carried that stigma. In one case, the head of "popular culture" in Suleimaniyya refused to provide the security officer with the employment records of all employees in his department. As a result, memos and notes were circulated until he was summoned by the head of *al-amn* and warned about the consequences of his actions.[79]

In the eyes of the regime, there were many enemies inside and outside Iraq. One of the Ba'th Party documents identifies at least eight opposition movements inside the country, among them the Communist Party, the two Kurdish parties (the Kurdish Democratic Party [KDP] and the Patriotic Union of Kurdistan [PUK]), the Da'wa Party, the Muslim Brothers, any movement that had "a religious cover," groups that had split from the Ba'th Party, and any movement that pretended to be "nationalistic."[80] Thus, the regime needed to gather enormous amounts of information

---

[76] IIS to Field Operations Base Directors, "IIS Director Instructions," July 30, 2000, in Kevin M. Woods with James Lacey, *Iraqi Perspectives Project: Saddam and Terrorism: Emerging Insights from Captured Iraqi Documents* (Alexandria, VA: Institute for Defense Analysis [IDA], 2007), vol. 2, pp. 203–07.

[77] Director of *al-amn* Suleimaniyya to All Deputies, "Characteristics and Requirements from Security Officers," October 30, 1983, *NIDS*, PUK 030, Box 147 (090057–090058).

[78] Director of *amn* Suleimaniyya, "Evaluations of Security Officers in the Province," February 21, 1983, *NIDS*, PUK 029, Box 141 (52B000.005; 52B000.000–52B000.003).

[79] Head of *amn* Suleimaniyya to the Governorate of Suleimaniyya, "Information," November 25, 1984, *NIDS*, PUK 029, Box 141 (520007).

[80] Party Secretariat, "Statistics of Opposing Political Moments," January 16, 1990, *BRCC*, 003-3-7 (187). This form was part of the annual review of party members.

about the country's citizens. Much like the Soviet system, it used censuses, detailed questionnaires, and a wide range of personal files to amass details about almost every individual in Iraq.[81] Among the personal records used were applications to obtain an identity card, in particular *shahadat al-jinsiyya* (a certificate of nationality),[82] documentation from places of work, educational records, membership lists of associations and clubs, and health records, particularly for those who served in the army or the parallel militias.[83] Information was collected about citizens from every level of society, including the most senior within the regime. Among the *BRCC*'s documents there is a very thick file on Taha Yasin Ramadan, then the vice president, a member of the RCC, and a close associate of Saddam Hussein throughout his years in power. The more than 300-page file begins with a 1992 presidential decree awarding Ramadan three medals of courage, and contains biographical sketches dating back to his childhood and an autobiographical report that he wrote.[84] The regime did not hesitate to use any source irrelevant of the circumstances; for instance when members of the Daʻwa Party attacked officers from *al-amn* around Najaf, the Minister of Interior wrote to the President that the doctor treating one of the injured attackers was told to befriend the assailant and while treating him, the doctor managed to gain information about the assailants who had avoided arrest.[85]

---

[81] For a discussion of collecting information in the Soviet system, see Peter Holquist, "State Violence as Technique: The Logic of Violence in Soviet Totalitarianism," in David L. Hoffmann (ed.), *Stalinism: The Essential Readings* (Malden, MA: Blackwell, 2003), pp. 129–56. For using censuses to know about families under surveillance, see *BRCC*, 004-4-3. Given that each employee in the public sector had a file containing all his details, the security organizations used these files widely; see, for example, the file of an official in the Iraqi Railways containing hundreds of pages of information about his family, education, and employment, *BRCC*, 005-1-6 (001–220) and 005-4-5.

[82] All Iraqis needed to get a certificate to prove their origin; without it, the doors of the army and higher education were closed. Throughout the country's history, governments utilized this certificate for political reasons, none more so than the Baʻth regime, which exploited it to target Iraqis of Iranian origin. For a comprehensive historical study of the issues surrounding nationality, see ʻAbd al-Hussein Shaʻban, *Man huwa al-ʻIraqi? Ishkaliyat al-jinsiyya wa alla-jinsiyya fi al-qanunayn al-ʻIraqi wa al-duwali* [Who Is Iraqi? Complexities of Nationality and Lack of Nationality in Iraqi and International Laws] (Beirut: Al-Kanuz Publishing House, 2002).

[83] From the file of an employee transferred from the Ministry of Industry and Military Industrialization to a party branch in al-Anbar. It contains about fifty pages of forms; see "List of Documents and Types of Information," *BRCC*, 002-4-2 (117–167).

[84] "Taha Yasin Ramadan," *BRCC*, 002-3-7 (001–347).

[85] Minister of Interior to President of the Republic, "The Reactionary Daʻwa Party," February 20, 1980, *BRCC* 021-2-7 (311).

Saddam Hussein fully understood the potential of information about possible enemies. When the SSO sent him a report advising that the son of Tariq 'Aziz (who was at the time foreign minister and a close confidant of the leader) was taking advantage of his father's position and negotiating with foreign companies (although many of those deals had already been embarked upon by the Ministry of Industry), Saddam Hussein wrote in the margins: "I reviewed, no interrogation of [the son] but more information to be collected about him."[86] In other words, Saddam Hussein realized that this damaging information could be used against Tariq 'Aziz if he strayed from fully supporting the President. Gathering information and acting on it even included children; in one instance, the children of four officials living in subsidized apartments constantly played with the elevator, causing it to malfunction, and amazingly, a memo was sent from no less than the presidential *diwan* to the Ministry of Finance to deduct fines from the salaries of the children's fathers.[87] So much information, from such diverse sources, flowed to the security organizations that in many cases they admitted they were arresting and interrogating the wrong people; in one memo the director of *al-amn* urged security officers to be more thorough in their investigations before rushing to arrest innocent citizens.[88] Of course, in an indirect way, these arbitrary and faulty arrests helped to heighten the state of fear and the pervasive sense of unpredictability.

Hostile activities in northern Iraq by the Kurds took up much of the energy and resources of the security forces, particularly during the 1980s. The documents contain hundreds of files portraying in graphic terms how suspects were followed, arrested, investigated, sent to prison, or even executed in the pursuit of gathering information. The operations of the two groups led by Barazani and Talabani, both inside or outside the country, occupied many of the security officers and their informers. Movements and meetings held by any senior member of PUK and KDP received top priority, because the regime was at war with the Kurds for most of its time in power.[89]

---

[86] Director of SSO to the Secretary of the President, "Top Secret and Personal," June 11, 1995, *BRCC*, B 002-4-5 (079–081).

[87] Presidential *diwan* to Ministry of Finance, "A Fine," September 4, 1992, *BRCC*, B 004-3-6 (046).

[88] Director of *amn* Arbil to All Security Officers, "Guidelines," January 2, 1983, *NIDS*, PUK 011, Box 046 (550028).

[89] See, for example, *NIDS*, PUK 006, Box 021; Box 022; and PUK 001, Box 001.

In addition to monitoring those who were active against the regime, such as the Kurds, the security system needed to collect information about the economy, religion, education (see Chapter 8), and, last but not least, Iraqis living abroad. In the economic sphere, the security organizations – primarily *al-amn* – needed to know about market manipulation, particularly when related to food imports and the currency market. From the 1980s until the invasion of 2003, smuggling was an important element of the economy, hence the emphasis on information about the black market and sources of smuggling.[90] Moreover, the regime kept a watchful eye on religious activities; there was constant surveillance of ceremonies and prayers in mosques to make sure that no one overstepped the boundaries. A memo called on all security agents never to reprieve members of Islamic movements, even those who were investigated and released.[91] Memoirs of Iraqi Shi'is confirm that the Ba'th authorities targeted not only members of the Da'wa Party but also Islamic charitable foundations, religious processions, and gatherings.[92] Education was another vital area of observation, both of teachers and students. Time and again, the documents record how lists of teachers or professors from the primary school level to the university level were sent to the intelligence community for vetting, based on the teachers' political activities.[93] Students were also investigated, and many were arrested for allegedly belonging to one of the factions opposed to the regime.[94]

Foreigners and Iraqis abroad loomed large in the minds of the authorities throughout the thirty-five-year rule. Fear of anything foreign, or the impact of foreigners, was not unique to the Ba'th system; Václav Havel explains that systems such as the Ba'th show their "most essential characteristic to be introversion."[95] Whether in Romania under Ceauşescu

---

[90] *Amn* Shaqlawa to *amn* Arbil, "Weekly Economic Report," November 4, 1988, *NIDS*, PUK 017, Box 071 (320004).

[91] Head of *al-amn*, Arbil to All Directors of Security in Province, "Instructions," August 30, 1989, *NIDS*, PUK 005, Box 019 (11086). Attached to the memo is a study of the structure of the bureau of *al-thawra al-islamiyya* (the Islamic Revolution), which was a movement calling for an Islamic system similar to Iran's.

[92] Salah al-Hadidi, *Qabdhat al-huda: Hussein Jalukhan tarikh wa rihla* [The Guiding Hand: Hussein Jalukhan's History and Journey], 2nd edn. (Karbala: al-Hadidi Center for Studies and Research, 2009), p. 103.

[93] See, for example, a list of primary school teachers vetted by the SSO, in Head of SSO to Presidential *diwan*, "Information," July 29, 1992, *BRCC*, B 004-2-5 (007–008).

[94] See, for example, the investigation of three women teachers in northern Iraq, all studying at the Teachers' College, October 24, 1985, *NIDS*, PUK 005, Box 016.

[95] Václav Havel et al., *The Power of the Powerless: Citizens against the State in Central-Eastern Europe*, 2nd printing (New York: M.E. Sharpe, 1990), p. 30.

or in Iraq under Saddam Hussein, "anyone belonging to associations with links abroad" was watched carefully for any sign of "treacherous behavior."[96] The Iraqi regime frequently used the term *shuʿubiyya* to refer to non-Arabs, but after the 1991 uprising this term became derogatory and was mostly used to describe the Shiʿis.[97] Saddam Hussein consistently branded any political opponent as "foreign" and called for "extinguishing the fires of *shuʿubiyya* and communism," as both were foreign. Describing the Communist Party in his book *rijal wa madina*, he wrote, "Communism is foreign: Fahd is originally Farsi, Marx is Jewish, and Lenin was married to a Jewess.[98] This is the reason the Soviet Union was the first country to recognize the Zionist entity."[99] In Saddam Hussein's eyes, politicians who were Jewish or thought to be Jewish were tainted and not to be trusted; an example was his distrust of Boutros Boutros Ghali, who was secretary general of the United Nations (1992–96) and foreign affairs minister in Egypt during the period when Anwar Sadat negotiated the peace treaty with Israel. In fact Boutros Ghali's mother was not Jewish, as Saddam Hussein was convinced, but rather a Coptic Christian; his wife, however, is Jewish.

Immediately after coming to power, the Baʿth began to imbue the population with the fear of spies everywhere and warned that people should be vigilant and inform about anyone they suspected of spying. Conspiracies were constantly discovered and announced on radio and television, and the public was ordered to be careful of the "fifth column" living inside the country.[100] Saddam Hussein told a group of Baʿthists from other Arab countries that "it turned out that the number of Iranian agents within our people and army could not be underestimated," because Iraq had become a land where foreigners were fighting to gain influence over its people.[101] The focus on guarding the country from foreign influence or monitoring Iraqis abroad is an excellent example of the tightly interwoven relationship between the Baʿth Party and the security

---

[96] Dennis Deletant, *Ceauşescu and the Securitate: Coercion and Dissent in Romania, 1965–1989*, 2nd impression (London: Hurst, 2006), p. 341.

[97] Bengio, *Saddam's Word*, pp. 103–06.

[98] Fahd is the *nom du guerre* of Yusuf Salman Yusuf, who was the first secretary general of the Communist Party in Iraq. Fahd actually was a Christian Assyrian, and it is not clear why Saddam referred to him as Persian. Fahd was hanged in 1949 during the Hashemite monarchy.

[99] Saddam Hussein, *Rijal wa madina*, p. 166.

[100] For details about the public hangings of "spies" in January 1969, see Makiya, *Republic of Fear*, pp. 46–52.

[101] Saddam Hussein, *al-Mukhtarat*, vol. 3, p. 124.

forces: both were in the business of collecting information about Iraqis abroad, recruiting students, and monitoring any kind of interaction with foreigners.

Marriage to a foreigner or even to a non-Iraqi Arab was seen by the party and the security organizations as a dangerous sign (see Chapter 2 for a description of the appraisals and security clearances that were obligatory for party members). This semiofficial ban included senior officials and government employees; an aeronautical engineer working in the Institute of Civil Aviation was dismissed for marrying a foreign woman, even though he was an active Ba'th member and had been so during his studies abroad.[102] It was therefore natural for a regime with a phobia of foreign spouses to extend this opprobrium to those traveling abroad or coming into contact with foreigners, as did the Stalinist authorities. Irrespective of position and status, every Iraqi had to go through an elaborate approval process before leaving the country. Whether they were ministers attending Arab summit meetings, senior officials going abroad to negotiate deals, or mandarins invited by other governments, all had to get clearance from the different security organizations.[103] Indeed, there were very strict rules for sending delegates abroad, with many dos and don'ts, such as avoiding making long telephone calls and having at least one member of the intelligence community accompanying every delegation. Under these regulations, Iraqi women married to foreigners could not be included on official missions, any dismissed member from the Ba'th Party was prohibited from representing the country, and anyone "having hostile feelings towards the party and the revolution" would be banned from traveling in an official delegation.[104]

Many officials who worked in sensitive positions before their retirement were prohibited from traveling; directors of government departments were barred from going abroad for three years, and even manual workers from the presidential palaces who had left their jobs had to wait at least a year before being allowed to leave the country, assuming that

---

[102] Presidential *diwan* to Party Secretariat, "Dismissal," August 24, 1985, *BRCC*, 119-5-6 (295–298).

[103] See, for example, a memo about the delegation attending the emergency meeting for Arab foreign ministers in Cairo, December 15, 2001, *BRCC*, B 002-3-7 (011); a note regarding a senior official, B 002-2-5 (003).

[104] Presidential *diwan* to All Ministries, Higher Education Council, Central Bank, Tourism Board, and al-Thawra Publications House, "Delegations," November 11, 1983, *NIDS*, PUK 030, Box 147 (090016–090034).

their files were clean.[105] Iraqi students returning home were obliged to undergo a detailed security scrutiny before receiving permission to apply for employment in the public sector.[106] Iraqis were also ordered "not to enter in any commercial or financial relations with Iraqis living abroad if they held a hostile attitude towards the country [i.e., the regime], and any such existing relations should be re-evaluated."[107] Finally, government officials could not be stationed abroad in the party's foreign bureaus or diplomatic service if they had a relative (first or second degree) living permanently abroad.[108] It seems that Saddam Hussein himself was very wary of anything foreign, even issues that his advisors thought would promote Iraq in the international arena. For instance, in 1998, when *Vanity Fair* magazine offered to send one of its accomplished photographers to take pictures of Saddam Hussein as part of a story about Iraq, both the Iraqi ambassador to the United Nations and the minister of culture and information endorsed the idea and saw it as a great opportunity "to show the human and bright side of the personality of the leader." However, without any explanation, the response from the presidential palace was a curt refusal – "approval was not obtained" – and the matter was closed.[109]

Although there was fear and suspicion of Iraqis traveling abroad or married to foreigners, the Baʿth Party marshaled its resources to recruit Arab students studying in Iraq. Together with the intelligence services it kept an eye on Iraqis abroad, especially students. Within the party structure, a special *tandhimat* dealt with Arab and foreign countries where the party was operating. The budget of the party outside Iraq for 1988 shows allocations to 68 countries, ranging from $500 for countries such as Portugal, Brazil, Nigeria, and Finland to $37,000 for France and $85,000 for the United Kingdom. It should be emphasized that this funding included maintenance of buildings and cars in each location rather than the full

---

[105] SSO Directorate to Security Organizations, "Rules for Travel Ban," August 18, 1997, *BRCC*, B 002-4-6 (037). See also the letter of a woman who worked in the hospitality palaces, who even three years later was not allowed to leave the county, *ibid.* (213).

[106] Secretary of President to Military Intelligence, *al-amn*, and SSO, "Inspection and Scrutiny," July 26, 2000, *BRCC*, B 001-3-7 (058).

[107] Presidential *diwan* to All Ministries, Governorates, and Public Entities, "Dealing with Iraqis Abroad," May 12, 2000, *BRCC*, 004-4-3 (025).

[108] Party Secretariat to Secretaries of Branches, "Candidates for Working Abroad," October 14, 2001, *BRCC*, 003-2-6 (463).

[109] Ministry of Information Dataset, Correspondence in July and August 1998, 003–103 to 109.

extent of operations, such as surveillance.[110] Furthermore, the lines sep-
arating the Ba'th's activities from those of Iraqi embassies or intelligence
operations outside Iraq were blurred. The party helped to organize visits of students to Iraq; each year a few hundred students, mostly from
across the Arab world but some from Asian and European countries,
were invited to be guests of the Iraqi government and learn about the
regime's achievements.[111]

Each *tandhim* had responsibility for dealing with a specific country and
its citizens. For example, *tandhim Misr* (Egypt's structure) had a bureau
in Cairo and was also responsible for Egyptian citizens and students
residing in Iraq. There was a strong emphasis on attracting Arab students
to study in Iraq. Some were recruited while attending Iraqi universities;
others became active in the Ba'th Party abroad and thus managed to get
accepted to Iraqi higher education institutions even if their grades were
lower than required.[112] Among Arab students there was an important
contingency of Palestinians, and many were very active in the students'
organizations within the party.[113] The regime did not hesitate to take
severe measures with Arab students if there were reports of "hostility" to
the Ba'th; many were not allowed to reenter the country on return from
their summer holidays, and others were arrested and questioned about
their activities.[114] In one instance, the authorities arrested a number of
Egyptian students for distributing pictures of Jamal 'Abdul Nasser and
Husni Mubarak, whereas a Palestinian student was detained for being
a member of the Popular Front for the Liberation of Palestine.[115] Arab
students active in the party went through the same appraisal procedure

---

[110] Bureau for Party's Organizations outside the Country to the Party Secretariat, "Proposed Budget for Party Bureaus Abroad for the Year 1988," February 13, 1988, *BRCC*,
021-1-3 (105–112).

[111] Party Secretariat, Visits of Arab Students to the Country," March 3, 1984, *BRCC*,
021-1-5 (219–220).

[112] Head of *tandhim Misr* to Party Secretariat, "Recruiting Arab Students," January 15,
1990. In this memo, the author complained that there was too much pressure on
Egyptian students to enroll in the party; otherwise they would be rejected from higher
education. *BRCC*, 128-1-3 (041–046). See also a note about accepting an Egyptian
student whose grades were below the required standard: Party Secretariat to Presidential
diwan, "Request," June 5, 1985, *BRCC*, 021-5-5 (031).

[113] See the file regarding nine Palestinian students in *NIDS*, PUK 025, Box 111 (020003).

[114] Deputy Director of *al-amn* to Ministry of Interior, "Preventing Re-Entry of Students,"
August 11, 1980. The memo banned 126 students from Egypt, Syria, Palestine, Bahrain,
Sudan, Tunisia, Lebanon, Yemen, and Morocco from reentering Iraq, *NIDS*, PUK 025,
Box 111 (020025–020029).

[115] *Amn* Suleimaniyya, July 12, 1986, *NIDS*, PUK 004, Box 013 (570046); PUK 025, Box
111 (020024).

as party affiliates, were ordered to take the same secrecy precautions on visiting their countries, and were asked to engage in propaganda warfare against their regimes if necessary.[116]

The Ba'th Party also organized visits of other Arab Ba'thists to Iraq, to expose them to the experience accumulated by the Iraqi Ba'th Party in spreading its political education and building up its organization. This system, called *al-mu'aisha* (cohabitation), was intended to increase Iraq's influence over Ba'th parties in other parts of the Arab world, in an attempt to weaken the influence of the Syrian Ba'th and to assert the Iraqi Ba'th as the only genuine Ba'th Party of the Arab world.[117]

Party and intelligence activities outside Iraq received much attention from the leadership.[118] The focus on activities in Syria is a classic example of the distorted lines between Iraqi intelligence and Ba'th activities, given the animosity between the Iraqi and Syrian wings of the Ba'th Party that existed for most of the period under study.[119] The intelligence services of both Iraq and Syria tried to plant spies and double agents in each other's systems.[120] One of the ploys used by the regime to track down its opponents outside the country was enlisting Arab students to monitor their Iraqi brethren. At one point, the heads of the Arab student unions in Britain and Italy were both full members of the Iraqi Ba'th Party, and their files indicated their devotion to party ideology.[121] Another tactic

---

[116] See, for example, some evaluations in 1985 of Yemeni students in the party, in *BRCC*, 006-2-2; a memo to Moroccan students about taking precautions when returning to Morocco, 006-2-5; and correspondence of 1985 about Syrian students helping in the commemoration of the "massacre of Hama" and the "crimes of the Asadi [*sic*] regime," *NIDS*, PUK 005, Box 020 (130026–130029).

[117] Special Secretary to the President for Party Affairs to Party Secretariat, "Cohabitation with Sudanese Ba'th Party," September 26, 1988, *BRCC*, 021-1-3 (053–058).

[118] See, for example, a talk by Saddam Hussein to a group of Ba'thists working undercover in their countries, August 1983 in *al-Mukhtarat*, vol. 3, pp. 119–31.

[119] For the deteriorating relations between Syria and Iraq after 1979 and their mutual subversive activities, see Kienle, *Ba'th v Ba'th*, pp. 153–69.

[120] See, for example, the correspondence regarding a Syrian student returning to Syria from his studies in the Soviet Union, where he was recruited by the Iraqi Ba'th. The recruit filed a report from Damascus about an Iraqi Ba'th member meeting with Iraqi dissidents in the Syrian capital. The Iraqi party assured the intelligence services that this was a plot by Syrian intelligence to sow doubts about the operations of the Iraqi branch in Damascus. See Party Bureau in the Soviet Union to Party Secretariat, November 10, 1983, *BRCC*, 006-2-4 (022). In 1985, one document showed that there were 111 Syrian students in Iraq active in the Ba'th at all levels of membership, 40 percent of whom were women. See *BRCC*, 001-5-7 (207–208).

[121] Party Secretariat, "File of Comrade H.S." and "File of Comrade A.M.," *BRCC*, 021-1-4 (264–265).

similar to many regimes worldwide was to appoint officials to the country's embassies abroad whose main task was intelligence gathering; one example from the documents relates to a deputy press attaché in Tunis who wrote in a memo that his official job was "only a cover in order to reduce the attention of the Tunisian authorities."[122]

Whether gathering information about people living in Iraq or about its citizens resident abroad, the regime had to use a critical source of information: informers.

Informers

Iraq was no different from other tyrannical regimes in its reliance on informers and collaborators to ensure the loyalty of the populace. The terms *mu'tamin* (trusted) or *muta'awan* (collaborator) were given to people providing information to the authorities; the latter were sometimes also called "friends." Most informers were paid, although others supplied information on a quid pro quo basis, as is discussed below. Usually, an *al-amn* officer would collate information from his informers and send two copies of his report to headquarters for review.[123] Before being enrolled, each informer would have to sign a *ta'hd khatti* (written commitment), which stated, inter alia, that the applicant must guard the principles of the Ba'th Party; commit to keep secret anything that he or she would see, hear, or read; never expose his or her identity as an informer; and provide any information gathered or heard that might affect security.[124] Once an informer had been hired, a weekly evaluation was filed by his or her officer containing seven items: the number of reports presented about rumors; reports about specific information; the number of "friends" acquired during the week; initiatives taken by the *mu'tamin*; comments by his or her direct officer and the security officer of the district; and finally, his or her overall evaluation.[125]

There are no statistics on the number of informers and collaborators. They were not all hapless, illiterate, or coerced into providing

---

[122] Party Secretariat, "Report," September 9, 1985, *BRCC*, 001-5-7 (193–196).

[123] Arbil *amn* to *al-amn* Directors (in Governorate), "Activities," March 6, 1988, *NIDS*, PUK 005, Box 019 (070067).

[124] See, for example, *ta'hd* by an informer in northern Iraq, *NIDS*, PUK 003, Box 0008, (010042); an informer in Baghdad, in *BRCC*, 007-3-5 (004).

[125] "Weekly Evaluation Form," February 1, 1986, *NIDS*, PUK 002, Box 004 (310002–310004).

information;[126] a review of dozens of informers' files clearly shows that they came from a broad range of socioeconomic strata and educational backgrounds. Some were obviously driven to inform in return for an approval or license; in one instance, a teacher agreed to become a *mu'tamin* in order to receive a license to open a bookshop, whereas a technical school graduate sought an approval to buy a photocopying machine so he could provide copying services to commercial offices. A housewife who had finished primary school not only was willing to inform but also donated gold to the war effort against Iran.[127] The informers were drawn from all religions and nationalities (the majority in the north were Kurds), and some belonged to opposition political movements and became informers under threat or in response to persuasion.[128] A threat was made either during the forceful interrogations that took place after someone was caught or by influencing the prospective collaborator by threatening his family.[129] One father broke down during his interrogation and provided information about his two sons who had absconded from their military service and four relatives who were with the KDP.[130] In some instances, pressure was put on families to get them to ask their relatives to return to Iraq or surrender themselves to the authorities.[131] It should be noted that sometimes, in regimes such as Iraq's Ba'th, denouncing a relative or a spouse was the only course of action for somebody who wanted to survive once they were in the hands of the security forces.

Nevertheless, there were informers who supplied information out of a conviction that the regime's policies were correct and should be supported; in one instance, a housewife volunteered information because she

---

[126] See an example of an informer given by al-Khafaji in his article, "State Terror," *Middle East Report (MERIP)*, no. 176, p. 16.

[127] There are numerous files on informers in *NIDS* and some in *BRCC*; see, for example, *NIDS*, PUK 038, Box 227, which is a whole file devoted to this subject.

[128] See, for example, how one informer was put to work within the Communist Party in Halabja in 1986, *NIDS*, PUK 038, Box 229 (320003–320008); an informer who was in the PUK and "returned to the national front" was debriefed and sent back to report on his cell, PUK 017, Box 069 (340013–340016).

[129] The informer was asked to write a report on the KDP and its connections with the Communist Party in the region. In addition, he was told to bring any pamphlets or brochures that either party distributed, see *NIDS*, PUK 008, Box 031 (410003–410020). *Al-amn* report does not specify what "pressure" was exercised over his family (410024–410025).

[130] *Amn* Arbil to Headquarters, October, 8, 1985, *NIDS*, PUK 008, Box 031 (410028).

[131] In one case, the father of a Kurd from Suleimaniyya was forced to contact his son in Holland to seek his return. See Director of *amn* Suleimaniyya, "Information," October 2, 1988, *NIDS*, PUK 045, Box 283 (030058).

believed that the PUK's policies were detrimental to the interests of the region.[132] Some informers volunteered information because of a grudge against a friend or a neighbor or to settle a score, which is akin to practices in regimes such as Ceauşescu's Romania. One anonymous citizen sent a letter to *al-Thawra* newspaper (the party's official paper), which in turn forwarded it to the SSO, with information about the connection of an employee in the presidential palace to the Da'wa Party. This led the SSO, after investigating the matter, to place the employee under permanent surveillance.[133]

It should be noted that in Iraq, much like the Soviet Union, citizens were encouraged to write letters to newspapers, as these constituted an important data source on economic, social, and cultural aspects of life in the country. In fact, 'Uday Saddam Hussein founded and edited a daily newspaper called *Babil* that became very popular for publishing letters from citizens attacking government bureaucracy outside the political sphere, which was acceptable as long as the letters contained no hint of criticism of the president or the top leadership.[134] Intriguingly, Saddam Hussein opined that the "best source of accurate information" was his regular meetings with the Iraqi people, which took place almost on a daily basis.[135]

The Ba'th regime, realizing the importance of informers as a source of information, took steps to protect its agents around the country. A law promulgated in July 1979, called Protecting *al-mu'taminin* in Defending the Revolution, defined *al-mu'tamin* as any individual working for or without pay for any of the security agencies, according to their directions. The law outlined the benefits of an informer, which included pension rights and compensation for disability or death in the course of action,

---

[132] Letter from B. to *amn* Suleimaniyya, January 19, 1988, *NIDS*, PUK 038, Box 227.

[133] SSO Directorate, "Information," October 9, 1989, *BRCC*, 003-4-4 (009–011). For comparison with Romania, see Deletant, *Ceauşescu and the Securitate*, pp. 392–95.

[134] For an understanding of how the Soviet system used those letters, see Sheila Fitzpatrick, *Everyday Stalinism: Ordinary Life in Extraordinary Times: Soviet Russia in the 1930s*, paperback edn. (Oxford University Press, 2000), p. 165.

[135] U.S. Department of Justice, Federal Bureau of Investigation, "Saddam Hussein Talks to the FBI," National Security Archive Electronic Briefing Book No. 279, www.gwu.edu/~nsarchiv/NSAEBB/NSAEBB279/index.htm (accessed February 25, 2010). Twenty interviews and five casual conversations were conducted with "Detainee no. 1" during 2004, after his capture by American forces. The interrogation of Saddam Hussein was conducted by an Arabic-speaking FBI agent, George Piro, who managed to establish a rapport with Saddam Hussein to the extent that the former head of state wrote him a poem thanking him and comparing him to a son. See, Casual Conversation, May 10, 2004.

on condition that the individual was deemed valuable by the security organization responsible for him or her. According to the law, there were three levels of payment for informers; the amount paid at each level was decided by the director of the security agency.[136] Thus, informers were not only protected but rewarded financially or, as indicated previously, in the form of licenses or approvals for their requests. Some informers who were caught by "the enemies of the revolution" were rewarded on their release, or their families received a special payment if they were killed.[137]

The vast majority of informers were paid monthly wages, which were correlated to the value of their input. The *NIDS* documents in particular contain dozens of files pertaining to the payment of informers and their acknowledgment of receiving the monthly payment. Most of the receipts do not include the full name of the *mu'tamin*, and in many cases an alias was used in the correspondence between the different *amn* directorates.[138] Interestingly, *al-amn* officers in charge of payments for informers also distributed the salaries of the village *mukhtars* (mayors) in the region, clearly illustrating the extent to which the security forces permeated every aspect of life in Iraq.[139]

Providing information to the regime about its political opponents was paramount, and all political movements in the country were included in this category. The files are full of reports about activities within those political parties, their publications, and the movements of their senior affiliates. In all countries under dictatorship regimes, clandestine political movements are continually engaged in a blind and dangerous struggle against security infiltration, and Iraq was no different. Reports by informers included all the enemies of the state previously mentioned: the Kurdish movement and its two main parties (KDP and PUK), the Communist Party, the Da'wa Party, and any splinter groups of nationalists and others who were not committed to the Iraqi Ba'th ideology.[140] Political activists who were arrested but refused to confess were sometimes

---

[136] *Al-Waqa'i' al-'Iraqiyya* [Iraqi Official Gazette], no. 2,720, July 9, 1979, pp. 785–88.

[137] SSO Directorate to Presidential *diwan*, "Citizen R.," December 1, 1995, *BRCC*, B 001-2-1 (174). The memo indicated that a Kurdish woman who was very helpful to the SSO was arrested by Kurdish forces and tortured; hence it was recommended to allocate her an apartment to live in.

[138] See, for example, *NIDS*, KDP 013, Box 2143, and PUK 044, Box 279.

[139] *Amn* Arbil to All Directorates, "Salaries for *mukhtarin* and *mu'taminin*," September 26, 1989, *NIDS*, PUK 008, Box 031 (1260033). According to one list, twenty-two mayors were on the payroll of *al-amn* (1260018–1260019).

[140] See, for example, a report about a senior member of the Communist Party sent by the informer to *amn* Sarjanar in northern Iraq, November 16, 1990, *NIDS*, PUK 030,

confronted with the informers who had reported on them, to try to force them to confess.[141] Given that the regime was fundamentally wary of religious tendencies (see Chapter 8), any individual or group who subscribed to a religious ideology or held strong Islamic beliefs was also under the spotlight; informers reported on men who frequented mosques and distributed religious books or pamphlets, and details of Friday sermons were sent by informers to their security officers.[142]

Dealing with deserters from the army and military service, whose numbers increased dramatically throughout the war with Iran and later in the 1990s, was another major area in which the role of informers was significant, specifically in supplying information to the authorities about deserters' whereabouts, a task made easier because the informers were living in the same localities as the deserters.[143] Needless to say, denigrating military service also met with a harsh reaction; in one meeting of a group of women, one participant said that "anyone serving the military is a loser," and this was immediately reported by another woman participant.[144] Similarly, instances of demeaning or swearing at the president or his family were immediately reported by informers.[145]

The economy was another fertile area for informers, who were supposed to report on black market activities or related topics such as counterfeit currency. In one example of how informers worked, a taxi driver in Baghdad managed to get his passenger to discuss economic affairs and found out that he was involved in dealing in forged currency.[146] Any manipulation of fruit and vegetable prices was also recorded by informers and sent to the officers in charge of economic affairs.[147] Saddam Hussein was a believer in the idea that informers should be everywhere; for instance, when a citizen wrote to a newspaper complaining about the

Box 149, (750005–750007); a report on the activities of members of the Da'wa Party in Basra, November 12, 1986, *BRCC*, 003-2-7 (019–022).

[141] Al-Hadidi, *Qabdhat al-huda*, pp. 124–25.

[142] See, for example, Party Secretariat to Intelligence Service, "Information," October 11, 1992, *BRCC*, 005-1-2 (192) and (307).

[143] Branch of Khalid bin al-Walid, Baghdad, "Death Incident of a Deserter," September 6, 1992, *BRCC*, 033-1-6 (047).

[144] Al-Karrada Section, "Report," August 30, 1992, *BRCC*, 005-1-2 (313–314).

[145] Branch of Khalid bin al-Walid, Baghdad, "Death Incident of a Deserter," September 6, 1992, *BRCC*, 033-1-6 (047).

[146] Security Officer to *al-amn*, "Information," September 2, 1992, *BRCC*, 005-1-2 (309–310).

[147] Party Secretariat to General Headquarters of *al-amn*, "Information," September 22, 1992, *BRCC*, 005-1-2 (281).

increased number of stolen cars, the leader was baffled that there were not enough agents among car dealers who would report on stolen cars.[148]

Informers were also given the task of reporting on rumors, as these were an important source of information for the Ba'th about people's feelings on current issues.[149] Like other authoritarian regimes, the Ba'th collected information on public opinion through "snooping by its agents" whether on the streets or in offices or shops.[150] An informer's skill in reporting about rumors was essential to his or her evaluation and the determination of his or her wage. For each rumor, the informer had to file a form stating details about the rumor, the location and milieu of its dissemination, and the date it began to be spread. The officer in charge would then "analyze" the rumor and recommend how to deal with it.[151] Informers were rarely asked to spread rumors on behalf of the regime, as this lay more within the realm of party affiliates who could be relied on to execute such a mission properly.

In systems such as the Ba'th in Iraq, almost every citizen was forced to be a watchdog and informer for the regime, because not reporting a "suspicious" act by anyone, including a family member, was considered to be a crime. Society became brainwashed into believing that only the vigilance of its citizens would protect the regime from the plots of those who sought to harm it. In one interesting story from the files, a loyal employee of the SSO who had participated in its so-called secret missions, including missions in his own neighborhood, reported to his superiors that his brother, sent to England to study aeronautical engineering, did not return to the country in spite of having completed his studies and that he had married an English woman and had two children with her. The employee was put under surveillance, but no signs of disloyalty were uncovered. The matter was raised to the highest level, and President Saddam Hussein decided that, given the fact that he had a relative of the first degree living abroad and in spite of the utter loyalty of the employee

---

[148] Presidential Secretary to Ministry of Interior and Party Secretariat, August 23, 1998, BRCC, 021-2-7 (617–618). This complaint is additional proof that the regime took seriously letters to the newspapers. In addition, the interference of Saddam Hussein was a classic example of his micromanagement style.

[149] For an interesting discourse on rumor as a source of information, see Pierre Darle, *Saddam Hussein maître des mots: Du langage de la tyrannie à la tyrannie du langage* [Saddam Hussein the Master of Words: From the Language of Tyranny to the Tyranny of Language] (Paris: L'Harmattan, 2003), pp. 135–43.

[150] Fitzpatrick, *Everyday Stalinism*, p. 164.

[151] See file, BRCC, 005-3-3 of 1993, containing many rumors, forms for those rumors, and comments by security officers.

and his record of serving the party and the SSO, he would be transferred outside the SSO and be monitored by the security agencies. The employee, under pressure from the SSO, wrote to his brother, urging him to return to Iraq to serve his country, but the brother refused.[152] This story shows us two things: how members of families were forced to inform on and denounce one another to protect themselves and the level of the regime's paranoia about anything foreign that might "contaminate" even loyal officers of the regime.

Insecurity, unpredictability, and fear of the unknown were all phenomena that permeated Iraq and other tyrannical systems. In his classic *Bread and Wine*, Ignazio Silone eloquently described the atmosphere in Fascist Italy in the early 1930s:

> It is well known that the police have their informers in every section of every big factory, in every bank, in every big office. In every block of flats the porter is, by law, a stool pigeon of the police. In every profession, in every club, in every syndicate, the police have their ramifications. Their informers are legion, whether they work for a miserable pittance or whether their only incentive is the hope of advancement in their careers. This state of affairs spreads suspicion and distrust throughout all classes of the population. On this degradation of man into a frightened animal, who quivers with fear and hates his neighbor in his fear, and watches him, betrays him, sells him, and then lives in fear of discovery, the dictatorship is based. He who has had the misfortune to succumb to this shame is condemned to wishing that the dictatorship may endure.... The real organization on which the present system in this country is based is the secret manipulation of fear.[153]

The Ba'th regime's remarkable success in remaining in power for thirty-five years was due partly to its ability to instill fear in the population to such an extent that Iraqis came to believe that collaborators and informers were ubiquitous. The security organizations in Iraq were "as much a state of mind as the instrument of state terror," similar to the Securitate in Romania and the KGB in the Soviet Union.[154] It is, however, misleading to ascribe that success simply to "a republic of fear." Other vital factors kept the regime in control for such a long time, as we will see in subsequent chapters.

[152] Director of SSO to the President, "M.A.," January 22, 1990, *BRCC*, B 001-4-4 (072–076).

[153] Ignazio Silone, *Bread and Wine*, translated by Gwenda David and Eric Mosbacher (New York: Harper & Brothers, 1937), pp. 260–61.

[154] Deletant, *Ceaușescu and the Securitate*, p. 393.

5

The Ba'th Party and the Army

The Iraqi army was created in 1921 during the British mandate of Iraq, and by the early 1930s the Iraqi Military Academy had opened its doors to the sons of the lower middle class. From that point on, the army was the best opportunity for these youths to be educated and climb the ladder of power. Officers played a political role from those early times, and many of Iraq's different political ideologies were expressed within the army's ranks. A revolt by nationalist officers in 1941 left a deep impression on Iraq's future leader, Saddam Hussein, and its heroes became for him symbols of nationalism and bravery. Although there was no coup between 1941 and 1958, political activities never entirely ceased. The toppling of the monarchy in 1958 was followed by other coups d'état in the 1960s, and all were engineered by army officers.[1] Thus, when the Ba'th Party returned to power in July 1968, Saddam Hussein understood the task facing his party, and coup-proofing became a top priority.[2] In 1971, he told a British journalist that "with party methods, there is no chance for anyone who disagrees with us to jump on a couple of tanks and overthrow the government."[3]

---

[1] For historical background on the role of the army in politics, see Mohammad Tarbush, *The Role of the Military in Politics: A Case Study of Iraq to 1941* (London: Routledge and Kegan Paul, 1982); Ahmed Hashim, "Saddam Husayn and Civil–Military Relations in Iraq: The Quest for Legitimacy and Power," *Middle East Journal*, vol. 57, no. 1 (Winter 2003), pp. 9–41.

[2] James T. Quinlivan, "Coup-proofing: Its Practice and Consequences in the Middle East," *International Security*, vol. 24, no. 2 (Fall 1999), pp. 131–65.

[3] David Hirst, "The Terror from Tikrit," *Guardian*, November 26, 1971.

Thus, at an early stage, Saddam Hussein began orchestrating how to coup-proof his regime. Throughout its first decade in power, many purges were carried out to get rid of the regime's enemies.[4] By the early 1980s, at the ninth regional congress, this mission was clearly stated:

> To consolidate the party's leadership of the army, and disseminate in its ranks Ba'thist principles as well as nationalist and socialist culture; to strengthen the military and the principled criteria and discipline which enable the army to fulfill its duties satisfactorily; to protect it against deviation and error; to ensure its correct and effective contribution to revolutionary construction and the fulfillment of national tasks.[5]

Coup-proofing was intertwined with the infiltration of the army by party ideologues. The Ba'th, similar to the regimes of communist China, the Soviet Union, and North Korea, needed to subjugate the army to the party. In essence, the party controlled the army by penetrating the system with its "political commissars" and making sure that only loyal Ba'thists entered the officer corps. The system operated by utilizing an intricate and effective system of rewards and punishments, by monitoring soldiers and officers on a regular basis, and by the creation of parallel armies to reduce the influence of the regular army. These parallel armies are discussed in detail at the end of this chapter.

Al-makatib al-'askariyya (Military Bureaus)

In pursuing its aim of establishing and maintaining power over the armed forces, the Ba'th Party charged *al-makatib al-'askariyya* (military bureaus) with the task of infiltrating and controlling every aspect of military life. These bureaus permeated every military unit and were directly accountable to the Party Secretariat. The hierarchy within these bureaus was identical to the party's hierarchy, and those belonging to the bureaus were part and parcel of the party's structure. Along the lines of Stalinist Russia, the party leadership in Iraq developed a complex and highly integrated system of controls to contain the army. Similar to the Red Army, the system was composed of "two hierarchies which operate side-by-side

---

[4] Amatzia Baram, "Saddam Husayn, the Ba'th Regime and the Iraqi Officer Corps," in Barry Rubin and Thomas A. Keaney (eds.), *Armed Forces in the Middle East: Politics and Strategy* (London: Frank Cass, 2002), pp. 208–09; Tripp, *A History of Iraq*, pp. 139–46.

[5] Hizb al-Ba'th al-'Arabi al-Ishtiraki, *al-Taqrir al-markazi lil-mu'tamar al-qutri al-tasi'*, *Huzairan 1982* [Central Report of the Ninth Regional Congress, June 1982] (Baghdad: The Party, 1983), p. 200.

with the professional military command."[6] One hierarchy consisted of the political workers within the network of the Ba'th Party, whereas the other was formed out of the security organs whose duties were to root out disaffection and disloyalty. Already by 1974, the party reported its success in "cleansing the army from suspicious, conspiring and adventurous elements."[7] A book commemorating the sixtieth anniversary of the creation of the Iraqi army defined the specific mission of "the Political Guidance" as "to take part in the creation of the new person in the Armed Forces. A person of the Revolution and its principles, the creation and upkeep of the struggling Baathist [sic] person, the creation of the revolutionary combatant, believer in the objectives and principles of the ABSP [Arab Ba'th Socialist Party]."[8] Eric Nordlinger described such a system as the "penetration model":

> Civilian governors obtain loyalty and obedience by penetrating the armed forces with political ideas... and political personnel. Throughout their careers officers (and enlisted men) are intensively imbued with the civilian governors' political ideas. In the military academies, training centers, and mass-indoctrination meetings, and in the frequent discussions that take place within the smallest military units – at these times and places intensive efforts are made to shape the political beliefs of the military.[9]

These bureaus mushroomed, and as Appendix II shows, there were more sections, divisions, and cells in these bureaus than in any of the other branches around the country, including Baghdad. The number of those affiliated with the bureaus reached more than 500,000 by 1990 but dropped to about 432,000 by 2002, a decline of about 18 percent. This could be explained, as mentioned before, by the shrinkage of the army after the 1991 war.[10] However, as Table 5 indicates, the number of those fully committed (members and division and section members) increased significantly between 1991 and 2002, and the drop in the total number occurred mostly among supporters and sympathizers. Again, this table is not totally accurate, as many of the categories we have for 2002 are

---

[6] Fainsod, *How Russia Is Ruled*, pp. 489–90.

[7] Hizb al-Ba'th, *Thawrat 17 Tammuz*, p. 138.

[8] Ministry of Defense, the Political Guidance Bureau, *The Iraqi Army Sixtieth Anniversary 6th January 1921–1981* (Baghdad: Al-Adeeb Press, 1981), p. 68.

[9] Eric A. Nordlinger, *Soldiers in Politics: Military Coups and Governments* (Englewoods Cliffs, NJ: Prentice-Hall, 1977), p. 15.

[10] "The Structural Organization," *BRCC*, 134-4-3. See also Appendix II.

TABLE 5. *Changes in Numbers of Party Affiliates in Military Bureaus between 1991 and 2002*

	1991	1996	2002
Members	33	61	92
Section Members	337	275	782
Division Members	1,740	2,871	8,215
Apprentices	18,441	28,567	71,342
Supporters	104,480	90,335	99,551
TOTAL	125,031	122,109	179,982

Source: Party Secretariat, November 7, 1996, BRRC, 136-1-5 (001–036) and Appendix II.

nonexistent for the other two periods, which explains the vast differences between the totals mentioned in Table 5 and Appendix II. Still, the table gives an idea of the changes in the military bureaus between 1991 and 2002. The high ratio of commissars in the units could be attributed to two reasons: first, many new recruits began volunteering to work in the military bureaus to avoid active military duty; second, the endless stream of meticulous reports that needed to be filed in the vast, sprawling bureaucracy required hiring more administrators. Nevertheless, the vast majority of those affiliated with *al-makatib al-'askariyya* continued their regular duties as officers and soldiers while being registered within the party military mechanism. In other words, one has to distinguish between full-time political commissars and the rest of the military who were merely associated with the party at one level or another.

The bureaus, similar to other party organs, conducted elections regularly. As the documents clearly indicate, these elections were taken very seriously by the party, and sometimes those not elected were demoted. For example, in the elections within the Ba'quba *firqa*, which was part of al-Yarmuk military branch, 100 out of the total 115 members attended the meeting, and 34 stood for the election of four commissars. The vast majority of the 34 candidates were officers who belonged to different units within the branch, whereas others were solely members of the party who had received military titles.[11] The names of those not attending were put on a separate list with the reasons for their nonparticipation.[12] It is difficult to know whether these elections were democratic or whether the names were decided beforehand.

[11] "Election Proceedings," BRRC, 003-3-1 (079), May 31, 1992.
[12] "Election Proceedings of *shu'bat* Tariq Bin Zaid," BRRC, 003-3-1 (003), June 3, 1992.

Although the primary focus of the military bureaus was to keep an eye on the armed forces and ensure they stayed faithful to the party's principles, they also had other activities. Eliminating illiteracy among soldiers became an important mission of the bureaus from the mid-1970s. Soldiers were forced to attend literacy courses, and libraries were opened on most military bases. The Ba'th Party realized that its recruitment reservoir could be enlarged by eradicating illiteracy, as there were frequent complaints that even some highly politically motivated soldiers were incapable of passing through the party's special courses because of their inability to read or write.[13]

The bureaus were involved in every aspect of military life. Their members sat on military committees, and they felt at ease criticizing officers and the military headquarters. In one example, during the infiltrations by anti-regime Iraqi Kurds across the border with Iran during the 1980s, the officer in charge of the military bureaus within the armed forces wrote a detailed report to the chief of staff on how to stop the infiltration and increase protection measures in collaboration with the security organizations.[14]

This situation begs the question of how these "political commissars" affected military decisions. In my interviews with senior Iraqi military officers, they indicated that it depended on the relationship between the professional officer and the party official. In one case, for example, the political official was himself an army officer in the intelligence corps before joining the party military bureau and thus had respect for military professionalism.[15] In many other cases, however, there was friction, and as discussed in this chapter, the relationship between the party and the military had a critical impact during the Iran–Iraq War, and even more so during the 2003 invasion of Iraq.

Military Colleges and Ba'thification

To ensure the Ba'thification of the army and to prevent other competing political ideologies such as communism from taking hold among the officer corps, the Ba'th regime knew that it had to control all military education establishments.[16] Saddam Hussein paid a great deal of attention

---

[13] "Eradicating Illiteracy in the Armed Forces," April 15, 1992, *BRRC*, 003-4-7 (12–13).

[14] Secretary of Bureaus to Chief of Staff, "Committee Report," December 15, 1985, *NIDS*, PUK 047, Box 302 (050095–050098).

[15] Interview with General Ra'ad al-Hamdani, November 29, 2009.

[16] Hashim, "Saddam Husayn and Civil–Military Relations," pp. 16–23.

to military education and believed strongly that "the military commander who has no fundamental general knowledge should be resolutely
banished from all commanding positions," and that "military education
is part and parcel of the general education."[17] There was a substantial
increase in doctrinal writing and rewriting between 1982 and 1987, and
Saddam Hussein actually reviewed all draft military doctrine. Within the
Revolutionary Command Council (RCC), Saddam Hussein appointed an
overseer to all military training courses within the army to coordinate
these courses and report directly to him.

The *BRCC* documents provide an extraordinary insight into the admission of students to these military establishments. Each candidate had to
complete, as usual, many forms to get the necessary clearance from the
different security organizations (the Special Security Organization was
crucial in this process), and the final say was left to the party mechanism.
The process, from a party perspective, consisted of the applicant filling
in a detailed form of sixteen questions. The most important question
was number nine: "Did you belong to any political movement except the
Arab Ba'th Socialist Party?" At the bottom of the form, there were two
remarks: "1. Anyone who concealed information regarding question nine
will be hanged" and "2. Anyone who has given false information in the
other questions will be dismissed from college."[18] Once the candidate
had completed this form, the secretariat general of the party in charge of
military courses sent his own form to the candidate's local branch,
requesting information about the applicant and his family. The branch, in
turn, provided details about the candidate and his family (their political
leanings, reputation in the area, connection to the party, and whether any
member of the family carried the card of "Friends of the President," etc.).
Usually, the verdict came in one simple sentence: "We have no objection
to his acceptance." Three party affiliates always had to sign the form,
including the secretary generals of the *firqa* and *shu'ba*, in addition to the
branch member who checked all the information.[19] In certain cases in
which it turned out that the information gathered was inaccurate, investigation committees were formed, and the party members in charge of
collating the data were punished.[20] It is interesting to note that in the

---

[17] Saddam Hussein, *al-Mukhtarat*, vol. 6, p. 141.
[18] "Form for Acceptance to Saddam Military University," March 4, 2002, *BRRC*, 008-3-2
(004).
[19] *Ibid.*, (005–006).
[20] See, for example, correspondence that took place between June and September 1999
regarding how one candidate, a committed Ba'thist, hid the fact that his cousin was

1970s and early 1980s, these military colleges took a few "independent" applicants whom the party felt could be "good material for conversion." But by the late eighties, anyone who was not a committed Ba'thist was denied.[21]

Entering the military establishment continued to be a high priority for many families and their sons, as it had been in the period prior to Ba'th rule. The documents contain numerous appeals by fathers whose sons were rejected by military colleges in spite of the fact that they themselves had been officers in the army. Many of those fathers had participated in *qadisiyyat Saddam* or *umm al-ma'arik* ("the Mother of All Battles," a euphemism for the First Gulf War in 1991), and some even carried the badge of "Friends of the President." Mostly, these applicants were turned down due to their low average grades, or just because the competition for a specific course, such as the Military Engineering College, was too great.[22] These appeals were taken seriously by all concerned, and copies were sent to the Ministry of Defense, the officer in charge of military courses, and of course the Party Secretariat. Sometimes parental pressure paid off and decisions were reversed, whereas in other cases there were simply too few places to satisfy all contenders. Overall, in the beginning of the regime, the system of evaluating applicants, and, more importantly, the cadets, was pretty egalitarian. By the 1980s, however, loyalty to the Ba'th became more critical in the cadets' assessment, and by the 1990s, the quality of the recruits, and subsequently the officer corps, deteriorated significantly, as entering and graduating from those colleges was no longer based on capabilities and personal achievements.

As the war with Iran dragged on, the Iraqi army expanded dramatically – almost quadrupling in size – during the 1980s,[23] reaching more than one million, but by late 2002, its land forces and paramilitary forces

hanged fourteen years earlier before he applied to the military college. As a result an investigative committee was formed to analyze how this information was not checked by the party branch and the other security organizations, *BRCC*, 012-3-6 (003–076).

[21] Director of the Military Training Courses to Comrade Member of the Regional Command and Overseer of Military Courses, August 23, 1997. In his report, the director recommended that two applicants to the naval academy who were independent should be rejected from the course, although they met all other requirements. *BRCC*, 003-1-4 (004–006).

[22] *BRCC*, 003-1-6 contains many of those appeals and correspondence. One request was from a mother whose husband was killed in *qadisiyyat Saddam*, but her son's results fell well below the college standard.

[23] Shahram Chubin and Charles Tripp, *Iran and Iraq at War* (Boulder, CO: Westview, 1988), p. 294.

shrank and were estimated to be about 500,000, excluding reservists.[24] Iraq had two military colleges, a staff college, a technical military college, a reserve officers college, and al-Bakr University for Higher Military Studies. The latter comprised two colleges: the College of War and the College for National Defense Studies. In addition, there were the naval and air force colleges. Al-Bakr University was considered one of the two leading academies in military studies in the Arab world (the other was in Cairo).[25] The Ba'th regime managed to make sure that these colleges could cope with the increasing demand for officers in all fields while maintaining a strong grip on their ideological education.

Saddam Hussein kept pushing to improve the level of studies in these colleges but continued to emphasize the Ba'thification process. For instance, when it was noticed that the standard of English among the officers corps had deteriorated in the early 1970s, courses for teaching English were launched, and the officers were ordered to attend.[26]

In an interview with a senior military officer who was responsible for al-Bakr University during the late 1980s, and who later taught there as a professor of strategy and national defense, the officer assured me that the party did not get involved in setting the curriculum of this university or the military colleges, although all candidates had to go though "political guidance" sessions.[27] Although military strategy studies may not have been affected by the party's intervention, strategic reports were. Lieutenant General Ra'ad al-Hamdani, a professional soldier, felt that the political influence had in many cases led to the burying of basic facts in military reports to please the political leadership. He gives an example of how, in 1995, the air force military intelligence adjusted a report it had prepared indicating that it had suffered most from the sanctions imposed after 1991, and that by 1996 its combat ability would be near zero. The new report showed the air force continuing to strengthen, and

---

[24] See, for example, the estimate of one million in Ibrahim al-Marashi and Sammy Salama, *Iraq's Armed Forces: An Analytical History* (London: Routledge, 2008), p. 192. There are some who estimated the army on the eve of the invasion to be much less, around 500,000, including 120,000 Republican Guards.

[25] Pesach Malovany, *Milhamot Bavel ha-Hadashah* [The Wars of Modern Babylon] (Tel Aviv: Ma'rakhot, 2009), p. 769. The book, which is more than 900 pages long, is based mostly on newspapers and published memoirs and discusses in detail all the wars in which Iraq participated.

[26] "Opening English Language Courses for the Officers," September 6, 1975, *NIDS*, PUK 008, Box 32 (270066–270067).

[27] Interview with General M., November 30, 2009.

fictitious data had been put in to justify its revised report.[28] Needless to say, this was due to the overpowering personality of Saddam Hussein and his interference in military affairs.

Saddam Hussein as a Military Leader

Saddam Hussein's relationship with the army and its officers was very complex and difficult to generalize. It is worth noting that he himself was not accepted into the military college, and his frustration about being unable to pursue a military career led him to be active in the Ba'th Party from an early age. Some scholars argue that his relationship with the military was "animus-ridden,"[29] and that the Ba'th regime had a phobia of army officers when it came to power in 1968.[30] Although both statements are correct, Saddam Hussein realized that he had to have a strong army to fulfill his objective of becoming a powerful country in the region. Thus, the relationship was rife with contradictions. On one hand, Saddam Hussein could be "quite open and flexible when adapting to difficult military situations." On the other hand, he "had little understanding of military issues or what made for effectiveness in military institutions."[31]

There is no doubt that Saddam Hussein saw himself as a true military leader. After he had elevated himself all the way to the rank of field marshal, the party began extolling his military abilities and military genius. One of its reports stated that "the leader Saddam Hussein is an exemplary model for a leader in this battle [Iran–Iraq War]."[32] Saddam Hussein devoted a lot of attention to describing the qualities of a leader. Throughout the ten volumes of *al-Mukhtarat*, which contain his speeches and meetings with different groups, including the officer corps, he exhaustively described what makes a good military leader, how the leader should behave, how decisions are made by successful leaders, and so on.[33] Saddam Hussein undoubtedly fancied himself as a military strategist and never hesitated to censure or challenge military studies or

[28] Ra'ad Majid al-Hamdani, *Qabla an yughadirana al-tarikh* [Before History Leaves Us] (Beirut: Arab Scientific, 2007), pp. 262–63.

[29] Hashim, "Saddam Husayn and Civil–Military Relations," p. 27.

[30] Baram, "Saddam Husayn, the Ba'th Regime and the Iraqi Officer Corps," p. 207.

[31] Kevin M. Woods, Williamson Murray, and Thomas Holaday with Mounir Elkhamri, *Saddam's War: An Iraqi Military Perspective of the Iran–Iraq War*, McNair Paper 70 (Washington, DC: National Defense University, 2009), pp. 16–17.

[32] Hizb al-Ba'th, *al-Taqrir al-markazi lil-mu'tamar al-qutri al-tasi'*, p. 217.

[33] See, for example, Saddam Hussein, *al-Mukhtarat*, vol. 6.

reports. Writing to the Directorate for Warfare Development, he harshly criticized their research report on an "abortive attack" as confusing and not based on proper military strategy.[34]

Many of his generals, however, felt that Saddam Hussein had no understanding of military strategy. "His centrality as a political leader extended to the process of making strategic military decisions by being the chief commander of the armed forces, but he did not have the necessary military education for this unique position."[35]

Saddam Hussein also had a habit of micromanaging, whether in regard to major military operations or simple bureaucratic decisions. For instance, he sent an order to all frontline units during the war with Iran stating the exact dimensions of the trenches to be dug.[36] In another example, an order was issued without any explanation by the Minister of Defense, bluntly informing all units that according to the orders of the leader, there would be no reassignment or transfer of any member of the Republican Guard or the Special Republican Guard to any ministry without the approval of Saddam Hussein or the RCC.[37]

Saddam Hussein's strength and longevity could be attributed to his ability to adapt himself quickly to new situations. In the 1980s, after a string of losses during the Iran–Iraq War, he allowed the military more flexibility in conducting the war without constantly intervening.[38] He was also a fast learner, and in certain cases his decisions did help the military command to cope with loss of control in the field.[39]

In essence, Saddam Hussein was more preoccupied with the risk of a coup d'état than any other issue. During the Iran–Iraq War, he prohibited generals from communicating directly with the air force as "one of his pillars of coup-proofing."[40] This preoccupation gathered even more

---

[34] Saddam Hussein, "Letter to the Directorate for Warfare Development," December 25, 1982, in *al-Mukhtarat*, vol. 6, pp. 129–35.

[35] Al-Hamdani, *Qabla an yughadirana al-tarikh*, p. 244.

[36] Interview with al-Hamdani, January 10, 2010.

[37] ʻAbd al-Jabbar Shanshal to the Palace *diwan*, December 10, 1990, BRCC, B001-4-4 (055).

[38] There are many comprehensive accounts of the Iran–Iraq War, see Dilip Hiro, *The Longest War: The Iran-Iraq Military Conflict* (New York: Routledge, 1991); Woods et al., McNair Paper 70; al-Marashi and Salama, *Iraq's Armed Forces*, pp. 129–73.

[39] General al-Hamdani mentions Saddam Hussein's positive impact on the night of September 13, 1982, when Iraqi forces suffered serious losses. In his opinion, Saddam Hussein's personal impact prevented the defeat from becoming a major disaster, *Qabla an yughadirana al-tarikh*, p. 82.

[40] Al-Marashi and Salama, *Iraq's Armed Forces*, p. 164.

momentum after the invasion of Kuwait and the intifada of 1991.[41] Senior officers whom I interviewed, although they supported the Iran–Iraq War, felt that the invasion of Kuwait was an unmitigated disaster for the country. After 1991, Saddam Hussein's confidence in his generals eroded, while his self-confidence as a military leader rose to such an extent that he began to issue an endless stream of banal instructions and to give detailed training guidance.[42] Less and less consultation was taking place, particularly after Hussein Kamil fled the country in summer 1995. In one of the meetings held to discuss the Gulf War of 1991 and the uprising that followed it, Hussein Kamil was relatively open, but of course exonerated Saddam Hussein from any responsibility: "*Umm al-ma'arik* revealed to us weakness in our military leadership.... Also there are political leaders who clearly failed in their responsibility, when the President asked them to be involved."[43]

Rewards and Punishment

A carrot-and-stick policy toward the military was another method of keeping the army under the control of the Ba'th Party and ensuring the regime's survival. The tactic of promotions and rewards was counter-balanced by severe punishment of those disloyal to the regime (see also Chapter 7). Most of the promotions and appointments to senior jobs were based on political loyalty rather than ability. People who served Saddam Hussein well were promoted to the highest military ranks, and some, like his deputy, 'Izzat Ibrahim al-Duri, who was made deputy commander in chief of the armed forces, had never actually served in the armed forces. Another promotion that was resented by many generals was that of Saddam Hussein's second cousin, and later his son-in-law, Hussein Kamil. There was a widespread sense of schadenfreude when Kamil defected to Jordan. Wafiq al-Samarra'i, the ex-director of the military intelligence services, argued that Saddam Hussein's promotions of

---

[41] For a comprehensive study of the Kuwait invasion and the decision-making process, see Kevin M. Woods, *The Mother of All Battles: Saddam Hussein's Strategic Plan for the Persian Gulf War* (Annapolis, MD: Naval Institute Press, 2008).

[42] Kevin M. Woods with Michael R. Pease, Mark E. Stout, Williamson Murray, and James G. Lacey, *The Iraqi Perspectives Report: Saddam's Senior Leadership on Operation Iraqi Freedom from the Official U.S. Joint Forces Command Report* (Annapolis, MD: Naval Institute Press, 2006), p. 46.

[43] Audiotape of discussion about lessons from the 1991 war (no date but most probably 1992), *CRRC*, SH-SHTP-A-000-832.

"those with low capabilities and suffering from limited education and experience" were wholly based on loyalty and sycophancy toward the leader.[44] Saddam Hussein encouraged the intrigues that were rife among senior officers whose main ambition was to achieve a closer relationship with the leader because a closer relationship meant higher positions, and these translated into more rewards.[45] Some promotions, however, were based on achievements such as participation in battles or killing enemies of the regime.[46] Al-Samarra'i tells how when he was in favor with Saddam Hussein because of the successes of his intelligence apparatus, he was given a new Mercedes car, a medal (and with a medal, other rewards flowed, see Chapter 7), and his department was given the resources to expand.[47]

The rewards included pay rises, lavish housing facilities, and other benefits to the officers' families. Economic stagnation and inflation generally have negative consequences for middle-class salaried employees, and this included soldiers and officers. In some countries, coups take place when the army acts to protect its interests. Saddam Hussein not only understood this but also was a master of providing rewards and incentives to his loyal officers and his army in particular. As inflation began to gather momentum in the 1990s, and Iraq's economy was severely damaged as a result of the invasion of Kuwait, officers' salaries were raised dramatically to cope with inflation. When orders to raise salaries or bestow grants were issued, the notifications always stated that the leader and president, rather than the RCC, had ordered them.[48] Pensions were another form of reward: military men who were active in the party and were members of the command of a *firqa* or above were excluded from the age requirement to retire unless they wished to do so.[49] Senior officers were also granted

---

[44] Wafiq al-Samarra'i, *Hutam al-bawwaba al-sharqiyya* [Ruins of the Eastern Gate] (Kuwait: al-Qabas Publishing, 1997), pp. 393–94.

[45] *Ibid.*, pp. 228–30.

[46] Head of *al-amn*, Suleimaniyya Province, "Administrative Order," August 10, 1980, *NIDS*, PUK 041, Box 255 (130022). The order was to promote a sergeant who participated in a battle that led to the killing of five "terrorists" and the capture of their arms.

[47] Al-Samarra'i, *Hutam al-bawwaba al-sharqiyya*, p. 103. Luxury cars later became common gifts to senior military.

[48] Head of Presidential *diwan* to Ministry of Defense, "Income for the Armed Forces," December 30, 2002, *BRCC*, B 001-2-3 (24). Three months before the invasion of Iraq, salaries for all armed forces were raised by 25 percent.

[49] Head of Presidential *diwan* to Ministry of Defense, "Decision," August 14, 1998, *BRCC*, 183-4-1 (118).

plots of land, and many of those plots were prime agricultural or river-front lots.[50] Fringe benefits to officers were also utilized: those ranked major or above did not have to pay for domestic air travel.[51] Free credit in shops was also given to officers and senior noncommissioned officers, although the intelligence services were worried that too much debit was accruing, particularly in the accounts of senior noncommissioned officers, and that overall many officers were lagging behind in paying their debts.[52]

Officers' families were an important part of the rewards system: by the late 1970s, health coverage was extended to all family members of serving officers, including parents and siblings who were economically dependent on the officer. The coverage included all treatments and even preventive checkups.[53]

Saddam Hussein also understood that increased defense expenditure could affect the self-perception of officers. Part of the coup-proofing, as Nordlinger explains, was achieved by supplying the army with sophisticated weapons, building large bases, and even providing high-quality uniforms, all of which could have an impact on the morale of the officer corps.[54] General al-Hamdani confirms that the large resources dedicated to the military establishment, especially during the period of severe sanctions that began after the First Gulf War and lasted until the 2003 invasion, boosted the Iraqi army's morale.[55]

Parallel to the carrot, there was a stick to overwhelm any disloyalty or sign of treachery. Officers were executed whether they were real participants in conspiracies against the regime or merely suspected of being conspirators. Many studies have dealt extensively with the officers who were executed or tortured during the Ba'th Party's thirty-five-year rule, using practices similar to regimes such as Stalinist Russia, and it is not

[50] The ownership of many of those properties continues to be a divisive issue in post-Ba'thist Iraq, as many of those plots were originally confiscated by the state from opponents of the regime and then redistributed.

[51] Presidential *diwan* to Ministry of Defense, "Travel inside Iraq," August 16, 1975, *NIDS*, PUK 008, Box 32 (270099).

[52] Head of Intelligence Services, North Region, to All Intelligence Branches in the North, "Credit for the Officers," November 18, 1975, *NIDS*, PUK 008, Box 32 (270034).

[53] Ministry of Defense, "Treatment of Families of Armed Forces Personnel in Military Hospitals," January 16, 1979, *NIDS*, PUK 012, Box 50 (130034).

[54] Nordlinger, *Soldiers in Politics*, p. 69.

[55] Al-Hamdani, *Qabla an yughadirana al-tarikh*, pp. 260 and 264.

the intention of this text to examine this further.[56] It seems, however, that Saddam Hussein felt that punishment was just another aspect of life, and those who crossed him had to be punished. In an interview with a foreign journalist who asked him about the hanging of senior officers during the Iran–Iraq War, Saddam Hussein replied, in a very natural manner, that in a war it is hard to conceive that soldiers and officers would not be punished, and he confirmed that three senior officers were hanged because they carried the responsibility for losing the battle of al-Muhamarra.[57]

In addition to mass purges, executions, assassination of senior officers, retirement of large groups of officers, arrests, and torture, the Ba'th – and similar regimes – used another method of control: rotation to prevent officers from building up a base of support among fellow officers. In fact, rotation was the "most benign tool of control" among officers.[58] The documents show many transfers but rarely give the reason. However, from the information attached to each transfer, one can deduce whether or not it was an "upward" move, yet it is still hard to judge if the purpose of the rotation was to reduce the officer's influence or for efficiency reasons.[59] Some rotations were due to Saddam Hussein's capricious nature, and because no one dared to ask the leader for reasons behind the transfers of generals or divisions, many of these decisions will continue to be shrouded in mystery.[60]

Aside from ensuring the loyalty of military personnel, the regime had to deal with punishments for mundane criminal acts and abuses of power within the armed forces. There was a wide range of abuses: officers used their military cars to ferry their families and children to such an extent that the chief of staff ordered a halt to it, and some officers were reprimanded. A more serious offence was when the intelligence services discovered that many soldiers, in one of the units stationed in northern Iraq, were selling their leave forms or forging entries in their military service records about nonexistent service.[61] Once these illicit sales spread throughout the army,

---

[56] See, for example, Makiya, *Republic of Fear*, Appendix I, pp. 291–96; al-Marashi and Salama, *Iraq's Armed Forces*, pp. 144–49.
[57] Saddam Hussein, *al-Mukhtarat*, vol. 5, p. 167.
[58] Hashim, "Saddam Husayn and Civil–Military Relations," p. 19.
[59] Office for Republican Guards Affairs to SSO, "Transfer of Officers," May 20, 1991, BRCC, 003-5-2 (115). The transfer related to three relatively senior officers. Each transfer described the resume of the officer and a summary of the information about him and his family.
[60] Interview with a senior military officer, January 10, 2010.
[61] Head of *istikhbarat* for the North Region to Headquarters of Intelligence Services, "Information," September 2, 1988, NIDS, PUK 011, Box 48 (11005; 110035).

the regime dealt with it in the way it knew best: "The RCC decided that anyone committing forgery of a military service record will be hanged."[62]

In the 1990s, as the economic situation deteriorated, the number of soldiers caught selling their weapons increased dramatically, and the SSO became involved in rooting out this serious problem.[63] Another form of punishment was that once a member of a family committed an offence, the entire family became vulnerable to other acts of retribution such as rejection from military and police academies.

In order to keep the system of punishment working efficiently, a well-oiled monitoring machine was needed, and the Baʿth Party, similar to other tyrannical systems, closely monitored military personnel.

Surveillance and Monitoring

As discussed in Chapter 4, Iraq had multiple military intelligence services, which were "maintained to cancel each other out in terms of power and influence," and much of the "intelligence effort goes to gather information on the military itself, including officers' attitudes and any dissent that might exist in the ranks."[64] General al-Hamdani told me that the fear of internal conspiracies eclipsed everything after 1991, and that Saddam Hussein became obsessed with the possibility of a coup d'état or another intifada to an extent that made life unbearable for professional soldiers in their daily jobs. In 1993, in a seminar on the lessons of the First Gulf War, al-Hamdani gave a lecture entitled "*al-amn lana wa lais ʿalina*" (Intelligence for Us and Not on Us). Needless to say, this talk sent shock waves through the system, but al-Hamdani was fortunate in having the protection of Qusay Hussein, who, back in 1983, had served under al-Hamdani's command and got to know him and to respect his professionalism.[65]

Saddam Hussein was quite open about the need to "keep an eye on the army." In addition to the vigilant military bureaus in every military unit, the regime used other methods of surveillance. All army movements

---

[62] RCC, "Decision," October 8, 1994, *BRCC*, B 001-2-1 (008).

[63] Head of *mukhabarat* to SSO, "Transfer of Arrested Officials," July 25, 1995, *BRCC*, B 001-2-1 (289). Some of those arrested were trapped by the *mukhabarat* while trying to sell two rocket launchers.

[64] Barry Rubin, "The Military in Contemporary Middle East Politics," in Rubin and Keaney (eds.), *Armed Forces in the Middle East*, p. 5.

[65] Interview with al-Hamdani, November 29, 2009. See also al-Hamdani, *Qabla an yughadirana al-tarikh*, p. 93, with regard to ʿUday and Qusay's service in al-Hamdani's unit.

and transfers of arms or ammunition were reported daily to the SSO by the *mudiriyat al-harakat al-'askariyya* (Directorate of Military Logistics), and special attention was paid to any tank or heavy equipment transfer.[66] In an interview with a journalist, Saddam Hussein said that although the people of Iraq should be proud of their army's achievements, "I would like to warn the people of any weakness they might find by any member of the military ranks... it is just a possibility, but it is a warning," for in his opinion, fear could strike any military man of any army in the world, and thus one had to be on guard against such a possibility.[67] In other words, he was asking people to inform about military personnel who were out of line with the regime.

Monitoring the officers not only involved being watchful of their political leanings and activities; it went much further than that. Akin to other systems, officers in Iraq had to receive approval before marrying, in case the prospective wife might endanger the security of the regime. In fact, the custom of approving marriages dated back to the British mandate; a military man needed approval before his wedding to ensure that his prospective wife was "suitable." This process continued following the mandate era, but after 1968, the Ba'th regime expanded suitability checks to include security aspects.

The documents clearly demonstrate the amount of time and effort that the Ba'th mechanism invested in checking and deciding about these marriages. In each case, the officer filed an application with details about the prospective spouse. The system then went into action: the local *amn* and the local branch of the party prepared reports that were later sent to party headquarters. For instance, in one case the initial report indicated that the prospective spouse was independent (i.e., not attached to any political party) and that her and her family's reputations were good. But it was discovered that one of her brothers had been a communist who was killed (no details are provided). The verdict of the director of the Party Secretariat was to the point: "She is not suitable for an army officer."[68] It took almost two months of internal correspondence until the decision was reached and communicated to the officer. One can just imagine the tension during the waiting period, followed by the pain and disappointment each negative decision brought to these couples. We also

[66] Controlling Headquarter, SSO to Director of SSO, "Movements," July 8, 2001, *BRCC*, B 002-1-1 (306–308).

[67] Saddam Hussein, *al-Mukhtarat*, vol. 3, p. 79.

[68] Military Intelligence to Secretary of the Regional Party, "Marriage of Miss T," December 9, 1984, *BRCC*, 002-4-4 (185–195).

have no idea what happened to the prospective wife, as it became obvious that she would not be eligible for marriage to any other officer or member of the party.

Requests for marriage were turned down for other reasons, including having a relative who was at some point active in the Daᶜwa Party or even the fact that one or more siblings of the prospective wife lived abroad.[69] In one case in which an officer married without consent but was later discovered by the SSO through an informer, the officer was arrested immediately to face trial under military law, which dictated that the penalty for marriage without consent was three to seven years in prison.[70]

What is truly remarkable in looking at the documents is the seniority of the officers involved in approving or rejecting marriage requests. In all these files, there are at least one or two items of correspondence by the head of military intelligence. No wonder, then, that the intelligence services were not doing their real job of collecting information about the enemy. General al-Hamdani recounts in his book an episode during the 1990 invasion of Kuwait when, on receiving his orders to prepare an attack, he found to his total shock and dismay that the military intelligence had no detailed maps of the area concerned, and he had to use a tourist map of the city of Kuwait.[71]

Special Armies

In addition to monitoring and surveillance, the regime set up parallel militias to reduce the influence of the regular army. Many such special armies were created during the Baᶜth era: *al-jaysh al-shaᶜbi* (the Popular Army); *jaysh al-quds* (the Jerusalem Army); *fida'iyyu Saddam* (fedayeen Saddam); and most importantly, as a parallel army, the Special Republican Guard. As Quinlivan comments:

> Regimes create parallel militaries to counterweight the regular armed forces – forces that can be used against the regime in a coup. Parallel militaries also permit the creation of much larger regular military forces that regimes can use to project power abroad with greater confidence. Because the purpose of a parallel military is to protect the regime, it must be bound to the regime through special loyalties and social relationships.[72]

---

[69] *Ibid.*
[70] SSO, "Information," December 16, 1989, *BRCC*, 003-4-4 (004).
[71] Al-Hamdani, *Qabla an yughadirana al-tarikh*, p. 199.
[72] Quinlivan, "Coup-proofing," p. 141.

Saddam Hussein believed, particularly during the war with Iran in the 1980s, that Iran's numerical superiority had to be countered by enlisting large numbers of men to Iraq's military apparatus. He reiterated that the larger the number of men in the armies and militias, the better it would be for the country. His motto, *al-rajul qabla al-silah* (Man before Arms), explains one reason for creating the numerous parallel armies.

The Popular Army

Created in 1970 by the Ba'th, the Popular Army was the first special military organization established after the party came to power. Military men saw it as purely "the army of the party," because it was supplied with light arms to protect essential buildings and services in major cities and towns. The training for it was rather short, and many members were relatively old.[73] In charge of the Popular Army was Taha Yasin Ramadan al-Jazrawi, who lacked any military experience and, according to al-Samarra'i, was a sycophant par excellence who could never rid himself of his sense of inferiority for being originally Kurdish.[74] It seems that Taha Yasin began to aggrandize his position, as evidenced from a report he sent to almost every ministry and security agency to organize a festival celebrating the sixteenth anniversary of the Popular Army in a way that "befits such an army on the national level."[75]

There appears to have been an issue of lack of discipline, not only with the Popular Army but with other parallel military structures, except the Special Republican Guard. The chief of staff of the Popular Army complained in a memo that many affiliates of the militia were carrying temporary identity cards, many of which were forged and even sold outside the Popular Army.[76]

In northern Iraq, as part of the war against the Kurdish militias, collaborators with the regime were organized into military units called *al-mafariz al-khassa* (special squads) and annexed to the Popular Army to fight against Kurdish rebels. These squads had many negative attributes, and the documents are full of complaints by all concerned. The Bureau for Northern Affairs within the RCC called for members of the squads

---

[73] Al-Hamdani, *Qabla an yughadirana al-tarikh*, p. 273.

[74] Al-Samarra'i, *Hutam al-bawwaba al-sharqiyya*, pp. 313–14.

[75] Taha Yasin Ramadan to Chief of Staff of the Popular Army, "Anniversary of the Creation of the Popular Army," July 30, 1985, *BRCC*, 006-2-6. The celebration was to take place six months later on February 8, 1986.

[76] Chief of Staff of Popular Army to All Army Units, "Temporary Identity Cards and Documents for Carrying Arms," *NIDS*, PUK 007, Box 28 (030035).

to be prevented from guarding depots, given the high incidence of theft. The minister of interior sent a memo urging the police and *al-amn* to be on their guard, to increase political guidance among those squads, and finally to find military camps that were distant from city centers to house the members of the special squads.[77]

During the First Gulf War, the Popular Army was split into five administrative regions in order to improve its efficiency and functionality. But it seems that neither during the war with Iran nor during the Gulf War was the Popular Army truly effective, and the military leadership viewed it with disdain and did not believe in its value. Soon after the end of the First Gulf War, an order was issued to dissolve the Popular Army, and the Ministry of Defense was given the responsibility of taking over all its buildings and assets.[78]

The Jerusalem Army

After the intifada of 1991 and the failure of both the Popular Army and Ba'th units to crush it at an early stage, Saddam Hussein decided to create the Jerusalem Army to quash any disorder. Officially, this parallel army was created to "liberate Jerusalem." Iraqis were called on to join special camps and devote part of their time to training to achieve this historic mission. In October 2000 it was announced that 7 million volunteers had joined this army. This number seems much exaggerated, and although the documents are not specific, they do indicate the numbers of volunteers joining training camps in the larger provinces, and these were far from millions. Based on interviews of Iraqi officials, Woods estimated the army to be around 500,000.[79]

The Jerusalem Army represented a good opportunity for retired military personnel who were asked to train the new recruits and thus were able to earn extra money to add to their pensions in a period of high

---

[77] Secretary of Northern Affairs to *diwan* of Ministry of Defense, "Special Squads," November 18, 1984, *NIDS*, KDP 035, Box 2354; Minister of Interior to Police and *al-amn* Headquarters, "Special Squads," *ibid*. In addition, a pro-Ba'th military, the *fursan*, was formed in the 1970s to fight the Peshmerga. However, during the intifada of 1991, the *fursan* joined the rebellion. See Marr, *The Modern History of Iraq*, pp. 158 and 248–49.

[78] RCC, "Decision," April 24, 1991, *BRCC* 041-3-7 (060). The dissolution of the army took effect on June 30, 1991. *Al-jaysh al-sha'bi* was described by many in Iraq as "neither very popular nor much of an army." See Woods, *The Mother of All Battles*, p. 100, and Hashim, "Saddam Husayn and Civil–Military Relations," p. 24.

[79] Woods et al., *Iraqi Perspectives Report*, p. 48.

FIGURE 7. Iraqi Volunteers March during the Jerusalem Day Parade in Baghdad, November 20, 2000. © Reuters/Corbis.

inflation.[80] In fact, Saddam Hussein declared that there should be no retirement age, and *yawm al-nakhwa* (the Day of Military Training) was launched, whereby a special directorate was set up to recruit pensioners for training the young militias.[81] There was, however, a lot of pressure on party activists to reach the necessary quotas decided on by the senior party leadership. Students were cajoled to join and train for two months during the summer. For many, this meant lost earnings during this period of hard physical training.

Once again, huge efforts were diverted to recruit, train, and manage the logistics of providing ammunition and equipment and keeping an updated register of hundreds of thousands of "volunteers." A large number of documents deal with finding places for training, special training camps for women, the light arms to be used in each training session, and the political guidance necessary for the new recruits, in addition to their military training.[82] Also, the party had to be vigilant about prospective officers

[80] David Baran, "Iraq: The Party in Power," *Le Monde Diplomatique*, December 2002.
[81] In the Ba'th parlance, the word *nakhwa*, which means chivalry, refers to April 18, 1998, when large numbers of people "volunteered" to receive military training for one day.
[82] BRCC, 004-4-1; 033-2-2; 132-5-4.

of the Jerusalem Army whose details showed "discouraging information about them or their families."[83]

Many problems faced this militia, especially when there was so much need for the regular army to get ready for another war or cope with a possible invasion by the Americans and their allies. In a detailed study, the chief of staff of the Jerusalem Army sent the presidential *diwan* his suggestions to improve and solve many of the obstacles facing his army. The chief of staff had many concerns – most importantly the lack of permanent officers, which prevented continuity in training and running the courses. He opposed extending the training from two to three months given the lack of facilities and personnel. He called for more resources to be given to the Jerusalem Army and emphasized the need for increased political guidance to ensure that only "good elements" were recruited.[84]

By the end of 2002, and with the leadership aware that the country was on the verge of another war, the emphasis shifted from focusing only on internal threats to dealing with external ones, and plans were drawn up for civil defense and fighting the invading helicopters.[85] Woods, in his *Iraqi Perspectives Report*, quotes the minister of defense, Sultan Hashim Ahmed, who was interviewed after the fall of Baghdad, as saying:

> The Quds [Jerusalem] force was a headache, they had no equipment for a serious war, and their creation was a bad idea. The Ministry of Defense was required to give them weapons that were taken from the real army. But the army had no control of them. Their instructions came only from the President's office and not from normal military channels.[86]

Fidaʾiyyu Saddam

This militia was also created in reaction to the intifada of 1991 after the disappointment with the local Baʿth branches and the Popular Army for not crushing the uprising. Set up in late 1994, *fidaʾiyyu Saddam* (roughly translated as "those who are willing to sacrifice themselves for Saddam") was not just another state police structure; it was involved in

---

[83] Director of Training Courses to Ali Hasan al-Majid, Member of the Regional Command, August 23, 2001, *BRCC*, 033-2-2 (009–015).

[84] Chief of Staff, *jaysh al-quds*, to Presidential *diwan*, June 19, 2002, *BRCC*, 003-5-5 (175).

[85] Baʿth Regional Command to All Party Headquarters, "Volunteers of *jaysh al-quds*," December 10, 2002, *BRCC*, 003-3-5. The file contains many of these plans and related correspondence.

[86] Woods et al., *Iraqi Perspectives Report*, p. 50.

numerous small military operations and "extermination" of enemies.[87]
Unlike the Jerusalem Army, its officers were permanent and came from
the regular army and the Republican Guard. Documents show that they
were involved in assassination of those labeled as *al-ru'us al-mu'affana*
(the rotten heads) under directives from senior leadership.[88]

The idea of *fida'iyyu Saddam* originated in a memo by an ex-general
of the Iran–Iraq War, Hisham Subhi al-Fakhri, sent to 'Uday Hussein
suggesting the creation of a military unit that would sacrifice itself to protect the president. Interestingly, Saddam Hussein's second son, Qusay,
asked two other generals (including General al-Hamdani) to study the
proposal. Both generals rejected the idea as one that could complicate
relations with existing security organizations and might have negative
repercussions. However, their counterproposal was rejected, and 'Uday
was appointed head of the new militia. The members of *fida'iyyu Saddam* had a bad reputation among the Iraqi people as thugs who took
advantage of their positions and were mostly unemployed youths from
Tikrit and the neighboring villages.[89] Their uniforms, incredulously, were
based on *Star Wars*, with helmets, black shirts, and ski masks to conceal
the soldiers' faces. The only difference was that each helmet featured
Saddam Hussein's face in profile, surrounded by the words, "Allah, the
Homeland, and the Leader."[90] Al-Hamdani believes that this organization, known for its brutality, was used by 'Uday Hussein to settle
scores with his personal enemies and engage in grand public activities
such as the beheading of prostitutes in Baghdad.[91] Also, corruption
permeated these forces, and in 2001 there were reports that members
of this organization were smuggling arms to the Saudi border to sell
them.[92]

---

[87] *Ibid.*, pp. 51–55. Woods and Lacey in *Iraqi Perspectives Project: Saddam and Terrorism*
bring to light many documents about *fida'iyyu Saddam*. See, for example, vol. 3 and vol.
5.

[88] For a list of those to be assassinated and their backgrounds, see "Plan for Assassinating
the Rotten Heads in the Southern Region," November 6, 2000, *CRRC*, SH-FSDM-D-
000-693.

[89] Ibrahim al-Marashi, "The Struggle for Iraq: Understanding the Defense Strategy of
Saddam Hussein," *Middle East Review of International Affairs (MERIA)*, vol. 7, no. 2
(June 2003), pp. 1–10.

[90] For an interesting comparison, see "Strike the Empire Back," by Michael Rakowitz, an
exhibition at Tate Modern (London, 2010).

[91] Al-Hamdani, *Qabla an yughadirana al-tarikh*, pp. 272–73.

[92] Kevin M. Woods, James Lacey, and Williamson Murray, "Saddam's Delusions: The
View from the Inside," *Foreign Affairs*, vol. 85, no. 3 (May/June 2006), pp. 2–26.

Special Republican Guard (SRG)

Al-haras al-jamhuri al-khass (the Special Republican Guard) was a spinoff from the Republican Guard. In 1982, as Saddam Hussein needed to mobilize more units of the Republican Guard for the war against Iran, *siraya al-himaya* (the Palaces' Protection) was created. This later became known as *quwwat al-tawari'* (the Emergency Force), and by 1988, it became known as the SRG. Its primary task was to protect the president, his palaces, the strategic buildings in Baghdad, and all access roads. This was, in many ways, Saddam Hussein's private army. As concern over the reliability of the Republican Guard rose following news that some of its senior officers were implicated in an attempted coup d'état, the SRG's importance in protecting the president grew.[93] Both the SRG and the Republican Guard were made to feel superior to the rest of the army.

Akin to the praetorian guards of the Roman Empire, the Republican Guard was originally established in the 1960s, before the rise of Saddam Hussein, as a special military unit for the protection of the regime from the regular army, and it continued to be so after 1968 and even after the purges of 1992. "The loyalty between Hussein and the Guard was ensured through the common regional origins and sectarian affiliation of its men, predominantly Sunni Arabs from the north of Baghdad."[94] It was well equipped and its soldiers and officers were well motivated – in fact, they were probably the most effective soldiers in the Iran–Iraq War. In 1992, following the First Gulf War, a presidential decree announced that 28,178 Republican Guards who participated in the Mother of All Battles would receive three stripes of bravery.[95]

The Special Republican Guard was relatively small, estimated at about 15,000 men, but it enjoyed a sense of elitism that was reflected in the semiannual evaluation forms created for the SRG's officers. The form had a balance sheet of "positives and negatives" with regard to administration, training, technical ability, behavior, and leadership. In addition, there was a section about the psychological characteristics of the officer, such as his emotional state, work-life balance, and attitude toward his superiors and juniors. Needless to say, the form has all the other comparable aspects of questionnaires developed by the Ba'th regime: the officer's political leanings, the opinion of the party commissar in his unit, his contribution to major battles, and whether he had participated in the

[93] Hashim, "Saddam Husayn and Civil–Military Relations," p. 24.
[94] Al-Marashi and Salama, *Iraq's Armed Forces*, pp. 156–57.
[95] Republican Decree no. 106, February 27, 1992, *BRCC*, 017-3-2 (004).

"treachery and betrayal page" of 1991.[96] Woods argues that the United States and its allies considered the Special Republican Guard "the elite of the elite," but that view turned out to be wrong.[97]

Deserters, Prisoners of War, and Martyrs

No discussion of the Iraqi army can be complete without analyzing the three topics of deserters, prisoners of war, and martyrs. All occupied the attention of the regime, given the large numbers involved and the repercussions of these three categories of soldiers on the morale and political atmosphere of the army and the people in general.

Deserters

The issue of desertion was a major problem, particularly in the 1990s, for the army, the party, and the leadership. It started as a serious issue in the previous decade during the war with Iran. Desertion during the war carried a death sentence, but there are no statistics or information on the numbers sent to their death for deserting their units. It took place also among security agency personnel and the police force.[98] The regime, although admitting to the phenomenon, pretended that it was mostly Kurds, and in 1983 Saddam Hussein said that there were 48,000 deserters, mostly Kurdish. "Not only did these desertions drain the numbers of the Iraqi military,"[99] but also many of those deserters joined the Kurdish guerillas. The regime changed its tack and in early 1985 pardoned all deserters if they would rejoin their units within thirty days of the promulgation of the law.[100] After the end of the war the problem declined, although in northern Iraq it continued to worry the authorities, as many deserters found refuge in villages and towns controlled by the Kurdish guerrillas.[101]

The First Gulf War and the intifada of 1991 changed the magnitude of the problem and troubled the senior leadership, as the documents indicate.

[96] SSO to Bureau for the Affairs of the Republican Guard, "Evaluation Form," August 23, 1993, *BRCC*, B 001-2-2 (408).

[97] Woods et al., *Iraqi Perspectives Report*, p. 57.

[98] Interior Ministry to the Presidential *diwan*, "Escapees from Internal Security Forces," December 1985, *CRRC*, SH-PDWN-D-000-603.

[99] Al-Marashi and Salama, *Iraq's Armed Forces*, p. 150.

[100] RCC, Order no. 209, February 11, 1985, *BRCC*, 001-5-1 (007–008).

[101] Political Assistant, Headquarters of *al-amn*, Suleimaniyya to *al-amn* Headquarters, November 5, 1988, *NIDS*, PUK 001, Box 001 (330103).

It seems that desertions reached such a level that the Ba'th leadership sought to resolve this disquieting phenomenon in the way it knew best: severe punishments and rewards. In August 1994, after a pardon was reissued for a limited period, the RCC and the Regional Command of the party decided on the following:

1. Anyone who arrests a deserter from military service will be rewarded with ID10,000.
2. Anyone who provides information about a deserter will receive ID5,000.
3. Any deserter who is caught will be punished as follows:
   a) The auricle of the right ear will be cut for first-time deserters.
   b) For those who deserted more than once, the auricle of both ears will be severed, and a minus sign will be etched on the forehead of the deserter.[102]

The preceding list is a classic example of the Iraqi Ba'th system that helps us to understand its longevity: the balance between bribing some people and severely punishing others. This was followed by another decision by the RCC whereby anyone attempting to help with reconstructive surgery would have his hand or his whole ear cut off. Similarly, those helping to remove a deserter's mark would be punished in the same manner.[103] Interestingly, Saddam Hussein told his cabinet that "I have tried many times to dissuade the leadership from resorting to these measures of cutting off ears and hands, because I know that we will kill five to six thousand people in this operation.... But I have agreed recently ..."[104]

In fact, once the decision was made, Saddam Hussein took a personal interest in this matter and asked his *murafiq* (an adjutant or aide-de-camp) to report to him daily about the arrests and punishments. In a memo sent by the party headquarters to the president's *murafiq* two weeks after the RCC's decision, it was reported that 13,273 deserters had surrendered and 83 were arrested. In one of the few documents that Saddam Hussein annotated in his own hand, he asked, "And how many of those are punished by severing the ear and etching the sign on the despicable forehead?" The same day, he was assured that this was only the first

---

[102] Bureau of Secretariat of the Regional Command to All Military Bureaus and Headquarters of the Party Branches, August 15, 1994, *BRCC*, 033-6-1 (748).
[103] RCC, Decision no. 117, August 25, 1994, *BRCC*, 033-1-6 (617).
[104] Audiotape of a Cabinet meeting, February 21, 1994, *CRRC*, SH-SPPC-D-000-448.

day after the law had been enforced. The following day, another memo reported that the number of deserters who surrendered had jumped to an incredulous 220,027 by August 31, 1994, and that 269 deserters had their ears cut. The *murafiq* sent the memo to the president and commented in the margins that he was attaching this information but would like to bring to the leader's attention that the Ba'th branch of Saddam in Baghdad did not cut any ears, despite the high number of deserters. Once again, Saddam Hussein, a diligent reader of all memos, asked irritatingly, "Who is in charge of Saddam branch? He should be asked why he did not execute the orders and an answer should be provided to us."[105] By mid-September, Basra branch reported that in its territory alone, 709 deserters were caught, of whom 240 had their ear's auricle cut off and 317 were whipped.[106]

Absconding from active military service did not take place only among soldiers and low ranks of the military. One report indicated the arrest of a Republican Guard officer who carried an identity card of the palace and a second card issued two years before his arrest identifying him as one of the "Friends of the President."[107] Another account dealt with the desertion of an army captain who happened to be the son of a major general. The father informed the security services, and they discovered that he had absconded and escaped to Turkey.[108]

In many cases, desertion carried with it tragedies for deserters' families and put them in an intolerable position. In one instance, a unit of the party in Baghdad raided a house in Baghdad to capture a deserter. On arriving at the house, the mother of the deserter scolded her son and called him a coward if he would not return to his unit. A heated argument between mother and son ensued, and the son ran to his room, pulled out his gun, and committed suicide. After giving details of the incident, the secretary of the branch recommended to the president's aides "to honor the mother

[105] Secretariat of the Party to the *murafiq* of the President, R. A. G., August 30, 1994. Saddam Hussein's comments are dated August 31 and September 1, 1994, BRCC, 033-1-6 (507–512).

[106] Secretary of Basra Branch to Secretariat of the Regional Command, "Deserters from Military Service," September 14, 1994, BRCC, 033-1-6 (529). For ramifications of cutting ears, see John Leland, "Iraq Mends a System to Treat Trauma," *New York Times*, January 30, 2010.

[107] Secretariat of the Party to Bureau of Affairs for Republican Guard, "A Fugitive," BRCC, 033-1-6 (291).

[108] *Al-amn* Directorate to SSO, "Information," July 6, 2000, BRCC, B 002-5-6 (122–123).

for her positive stand."[109] In another case, a man was pardoned for killing his brother, who had absconded from his military unit, because his act of murder indicated his patriotism and willingness to defend his country's honor.[110]

Studies were prepared by the party about the sociological reasons for desertion, and the minister of defense, 'Ali Hasan al-Majid, sent a handwritten memo to the chief of staff and all senior directors of the ministry and the intelligence services, calling on them to treat this issue with the utmost importance, as this phenomenon "has begun to affect the great Iraq," and "we should not allow those deviates to contaminate the spotless achievements of this great army."[111]

The problem of desertion did not go away, even in the last year of the regime. In April 2002, for example, just in the province of Diwaniyya, sixty-nine deserters were arrested by the special Ba'th Party units that had been established to capture deserters. However, no mention was made of the total number for that period.[112]

Prisoners of War

Prisoners of war were another major concern for the regime, particularly those captured by Iran. As discussed previously, the Ba'th Party had difficulty trusting anyone who fell into Iranian hands, on account of the paranoia about the Shi'is after the 1991 intifada. Prisoners of war were categorized as *asir murtadd* (turncoat prisoner) and *asir samid* (steadfast/loyal prisoner). From the latter, some were also given the title of *asir mutamayyiz* (distinguished prisoner of war), which carried with it numerous rewards. There are no accurate statistics on the number of prisoners of war during the war with Iran or the First Gulf War, but it was hundreds of thousands. After years in captivity and suffering at the hands of the Iranians, they returned home only to be heavily mistrusted; many were followed by the security services and not allowed to go back to their previous jobs, in exactly the same manner that Stalin dealt with Soviet prisoners of war captured by Nazi Germany. Many were arrested

---

[109] Secretariat of the Party to Special Assistant of the President, "Suicide," September 17, 1994, *BRCC*, 033-1-6 (404).

[110] RCC, Decision no. 898, December 17, 1988, *BRCC*, 021-5-6 (129).

[111] Minister of Defense to All Headquarters and Directorates, "Letter," September 5, 1994, *BRCC*, 033-1-6 (650–654).

[112] Diwaniyya Branch to Party Secretariat, "Honoring Party Units," April 10, 2002, *BRCC*, 019-4-4 (009).

on suspicion of working for the Iranians, and when they later completed applications for jobs or universities, the security services had to clear their names before these could be processed. Both the party and the security agencies were considerably occupied with this issue given the complexities of checking the facts surrounding the prisoners' imprisonment. In one case three prisoners who were originally exonerated and received important jobs in the government were found to have cooperated with the Iranian army.[113]

However, other prisoners of war who proved "their distinguished stand in captivity" were allowed to return to military service, and their time spent in captivity was considered as part of their service.[114] There are no statistics on those with a "distinguished stand" status, but the process was clear: prisoners of war would file with their local party branch to be classified under this category. The local branch, in turn, wrote to military intelligence in case it had any information about the specific prisoner. Although there were no clear definitions of the *asir mutamayyiz*, the files contain numerous letters of prisoners of war who claimed they deserved to be included in the category of the distinguished because of their actions, which included, inter alia, preventing other prisoners from joining the Da'wa Party, refusing to participate in any anti-Ba'th action, chanting slogans in praise of Saddam Hussein and celebrating his birthday and other national days, and continuing to be active in creating more cells for the Ba'th Party.[115] Given the ambiguity of the distinction, a memo by the Party Secretariat advised on splitting the prisoners of war into two groups: party members and non-party members. The former group was subdivided into three categories: those who withstood the enemy's coercion; those who collapsed under pressure; and finally, those who lost their lives in the struggle against the enemy. A similar categorization of non-party members took place, but ultimately there was considerable arbitrariness in determining who distinguished themselves during captivity.[116]

---

[113] Party Secretariat to General Military Intelligence, September 22, 1997, *BRCC*, 088-4-3 (035). The whole file deals with this issue.

[114] RCC, Decision no. 125. July 24, 1999, *BRCC*, 017-1-17 (121). The decision was retroactive to October 21, 1990.

[115] See an example of the file of one prisoner of war and the related correspondence in *BRRC*, 022-1-2 (019–025).

[116] Secretariat Headquarters to Secretaries of Party Branches, "Suggestions," December 24, 1991, *BRCC*, 174-3-2 (283–287). See also lists of "Distinguished Prisoners of War" in *BRCC*, 174-3-2 (259–261).

Martyrs

For regimes such as the Ba'th, martyrdom for the leadership and its wars had to be made sacred, to encourage more sacrifices. The process was multilayered: lavish rewards, medals, ceremonies, symbols, and slogans to ensure that martyrs' families continued to be part of the system. "The martyrs are more honorable than all of us," was one of the most powerful slogans that Saddam Hussein created with regard to martyrs. Many ministries and army units had this motto printed on their stationery, and it appeared in all ceremonies honoring the martyrs.

Saddam Hussein seemed blasé about the number of martyrs. For him, martyrdom was an act of bravery and, more importantly, a way of achieving the targets determined by the regime. When talking about the period from 1974 to 1979, he mentioned casually that about 16,000 of the Iraqi army had been killed or maimed in the *ridda* (fight against rebellion) battles in northern Iraq. What was important, he emphasized, was that this was a heroic generation, and he wondered whether any generation could be heroic without sacrifices.[117]

The rewards for martyrs and their families were abundant. A "martyrs' fund" was created to help the families of those who fell fighting in the north against the Kurds.[118] After the Gulf War of 1991, a decision was made to grant posthumously to all martyrs who fell in "*qadisiyyat Saddam* and the Mother of All Battles" the title "Friends of the President Leader."[119] In 1999, another decision was made to reward anyone killed in "fighting the enemy" with ID2 million (about $2,000), and anyone injured would receive ID1 million (roughly $1,000). No explanation was given about who the enemy was, but the rules applied to all members of the security forces as well as to the armed forces.[120]

The rewards were commensurate with the number of martyrs that families sacrificed to the regime. Saddam Hussein was very proud of families who had given a large number of martyrs. Taunting Syrian president Hafiz al-Asad about the loss of the Golan Heights, he said,

> Isn't it something that makes us proud that thousands of Iraqis have been martyred fighting the Persians, while you, brother Hafiz, lost in 1967 only 137 Syrian martyrs, but Syria lost the Golan.... We will

---

[117] Saddam Hussein, *al-Mukhtarat*, vol. 4, p. 361.

[118] Director of *amn* Suleimaniyya to Suleimaniyya Treasurer, "Funds for Martyrs and Needy among the Police," January 10, 1976, *NIDS*, PUK 001, Box 2 (490019).

[119] RCC, Decision no. 212, December 24, 1993, *BRCC*, 008-4-6 (390).

[120] Secretariat of the Party to All Headquarters, "Order," August 15, 1999, *BRCC*, 003-4-1.

not give thousands but will give millions, brother Hafiz, because it is a [matter of] pride for us.... The important loss is not losing the blood of martyrs but losing territories and losing the national sovereignty and dignity.[121]

As a result, the more martyrs given per family, the higher the rewards they received. Families that gave three or more martyrs were known as "distinguished families," and Saddam Hussein met many of these and bestowed personal gifts on them. The party was asked in the late 1980s to conduct a countrywide survey of these families and to make sure that the martyrs were indeed directly related (father, son, or brother). In a summary report addressed to the president himself, the statistics indicated that during *qadisiyyat Saddam* there were 337 families with three martyrs, 29 with four martyrs, 7 with five martyrs, and 2 with six martyrs. These numbers included families who had lost relatives in the Iranian bombing of Iraq's cities, in addition to those killed on the battlefield.[122]

Combining awareness of his cult personality, his pride in those families, and his desire to justify wars and purges, Saddam Hussein told an Arab journalist:

> Here in this office I received during the last two months thousands of elderly people and children who were consoling me for the loss of their fathers and sons ... [and saying to me] you are our father ... Iraq is our father ... the army is our father.... I wonder who taught these people [to have] this mighty spirit? And my answer is that it is the revolution, the grandest teacher of all. Anyone can say whatever [they want], that we are bloodthirsty but [it is acceptable] as long as necks are severed to cleanse the country from the filth of deviation, conspiracy and betrayal.[123]

There were many ceremonies to celebrate martyrdom, and *yawm al-shahid* (Day of the Martyr), which fell on December 1 of every year, was an official holiday.[124] These ceremonies were planned meticulously to the last detail and combined prayers, speeches, visits by party officials to

---

[121] Saddam Hussein, *al-Mukhtarat*, vol. 3, p. 94.
[122] Director of Secretariat Bureau for the Region to Comrade Leader, Struggler and Secretary of the Region, July 30, 1989, *BRCC*, 004-2-2 (001–003).
[123] Saddam Hussein, *al-Mukhtarat*, vol. 3, p. 88. The interview was with Nasr al-Din al-Nashashibi and took place on January 19, 1981.
[124] December 1 was chosen because on December 1, 1981, the Iranians executed an unknown number of Iraqi prisoners of war. See Military Bureau, "*Yawm al-shahid*," January 16, 1982, *NIDS*, PUK 003, Box 007 (050044).

the families of martyrs, and a procession carrying the slogans of Saddam Hussein and the Ba'th Party. Apart from remembering the dead, the party wanted the day to remind people of the need to continue their sacrifices for the country and its leadership.[125]

The 2003 Invasion

As it became more plausible by the summer of 2002 that a war or invasion would take place, the army and the party began to make serious preparations. Hundreds of documents show clearly the thorough preparation at every level for the military encounter. The Ba'th Party was supposed to play a critical role in fighting the American invaders, particularly in the inner cities, and to protect essential installations. Already in August 2001, a detailed plan was prepared for combating the invasion.[126] By October 2002, emergency plans were drawn up, and the role of the military bureaus was clearly defined: to instill more discipline within military units during the expected invasion.

Party branches were given most of the responsibilities for air defense, resisting the invading helicopters, and "controlling the internal enemies."[127] Whereas each branch had its emergency plan for the invasion, it seems there was very little coordination with the army, although the plans were synchronized with the security organs of the regime. For instance, in a fifteen-page plan of one branch of the party in Baghdad, there was not even one mention of the armed forces or any kind of coordination, even where it discussed air defense and civil defense for the city.[128] Studies were made of different scenarios of the invasion and how to cope with an airdrop versus an attack by land forces. Preparations were also made for strategic storage of oil and essential commodities.[129]

The fundamental question that needs to be addressed is why, given all the preparations and the regime's obvious awareness of the intentions of the Americans and their allies, did so few of these preparations translate

---

[125] Presidential *diwan* to All Ministries and Municipalities, "Celebrating *yawm al-shahid*," November 20, 2001, *BRCC*, 004-3-1 (001–004).

[126] Under-Secretary of al-Karkh, Baghdad Branch to Headquarters, "Recommendations for Combating Invasion," August 15, 2001, *BRCC*, 004-4-6 (185–189).

[127] Security Officer of al-Karkh, Baghdad Branch to the Victorious Leader Branch, Baghdad, October 5, 2002, *BRCC*, 003-2-6 (001–008).

[128] Secretariat of the Victorious Leader Branch, Baghdad to All Branches, "Emergency Plan," February 21, 2002, *BRCC*, 003-2-6 (372–388).

[129] *BRCC*, 003-2-6 (249), mostly from April and May 2002.

into real action, and when they did, why were they so ineffective? Historians and strategists will continue to discuss this question for a long time. Woods, a military historian, attributes part of the collapse to Saddam Hussein's decision-making process.[130]

The president himself had a different take on it, of course. Talking from his prison cell to his lawyer, Saddam Hussein gave twelve reasons why the invasion was swift and successful. Among those reasons were the thirteen years of sanctions that weakened the country, the "inhumane" bombing of cities, the Americans' accurate knowledge of all the strategic installations, and the breakdown of communications between military headquarters and units in the field. (Actually, communications continued unabated for the first couple of weeks of the war and were even filed systematically.)[131] He felt that "Iran's double-crossing" was an important factor in facilitating the entry of American and British forces into Iraq. Interestingly, Saddam Hussein admitted that subjugating military leaders to the political leadership might have led to the collapse of the defense, but he argued that he felt this was a battle for "our destiny" and thus it was necessary for the political arm of the regime to control the armed forces.[132]

A different view of the regime's rapid collapse is provided by Saddam Hussein's translator, who worked with him closely until the invasion. In his memoirs, he talks about the betrayal of many of the senior army and intelligence officers, including the head of *istikhbarat* (military intelligence), who was blamed for tipping off the Americans about the whereabouts of Saddam Hussein on April 7, 2003, when American rockets were fired toward a house where the president had been a few minutes before the attack. According to this account, Saddam Hussein told a close friend just before he escaped that "the people of the south [of Iraq – meaning Shi'is] are more courageous than those close to me who betrayed me; they are not much better than the sole of my shoes."[133] When asked by his lawyer about these betrayals, Saddam Hussein was in denial; he argued that treacheries do take place in the heat of the battle but none was

[130] Woods et al., "Saddam's Delusions," pp. 2–4.
[131] See, for example, a memo dated March 29, 2003, and another one dated April 7, 2003, in *CRRC*, SH-PDWN-D-000-329.
[132] Khalil al-Dulaimi, *Saddam Hussein min al-zanzana al-Amrikiyya: Hadha ma hadath!* [Saddam Hussein from the American Cell: This Is What Happened!] (Khartoum: al-Manbar Printing Company, 2009), pp. 133–38.
[133] Abdul Majid, *Les années Saddam*, p. 41.

committed by any senior army or intelligence officer.[134] It is certain – not just from a military point of view – that a combination of factors led to the swift collapse of the regime.

In conclusion, there is no doubt that Saddam Hussein and the Ba'th regime succeeded in dominating and controlling the armed forces; the party leadership remained united, which made it almost impossible for the military to emerge as an independent political force. The civil control and the penetration of the army (as well as of the civil service) was enormously effective in preventing any coup d'état or change of regime from within for a long thirty-five years.

[134] Al-Dulaimi, *Saddam Hussein min al-zanzana al-Amrikiyya*, pp. 139–40.

6

The Personality Cult of Saddam Hussein

To understand the Ba'th Party in Iraq between 1968 and 2003 in greater depth, one has to focus on its most dominant personality, Saddam Hussein. The party devoted an enormous amount of energy and resources to building up the image of its leader, and from the mid-1980s the Ba'th's philosophy and political education came to embody a cult rather than a political ideology. Spectacular monuments to Saddam Hussein, such as the Arch of Victory, formed by two sabers anchored in large models of his hands, dotted the Baghdad cityscape and became international symbols of his regime. Given his crucial role after taking over the presidency in 1979 until he was overthrown in April 2003, one could legitimately call those twenty-four years a period of Saddamism, similar in form to Stalinism or Maoism.

Saddam Hussein: The Man and the Leader

Numerous academic biographies and analyses of Saddam Hussein's life and personality have been published,[1] and it is not my intention to repeat those details. Rather, I intend to examine how the Ba'th system became intertwined with its leader's personality cult and how this impacted the governing of the country. How did Saddam Hussein become omnipotent and omnipresent to the extent that he, personally, could make any

---

[1] Among those biographies are Efraim Karsh and Inari Rautsi, *Saddam Hussein: A Political Biography* (New York: The Free Press, 1991); Aburish, *Saddam Hussein: The Politics of Revenge*; Shiva Balaghi, *Saddam Hussein: A Biography* (Westport, CT: Greenwood Press, 2006); Jerrold M. Post and Amatzia Baram, "Saddam Is Iraq: Iraq Is Saddam" (Maxwell Air Force Base, AL: USAF Counterproliferation Center, Paper No. 17, 2002).

decision he wanted, unconstrained by any group or institution? To understand how the cult was created, it must be placed into a wider cultural, economic, and political context.

Since independence, Iraq had become accustomed to strong men, beginning with Faisal I and continuing after the toppling of the monarchy in 1958, when 'Abd al-Karim Qasim became *al-za'im al-awhad* (the sole leader). The Iraqi people suffered long periods of instability and numerous coups d'état that affected the country's growth and development. Saddam Hussein gave Iraq a certain sense of stability, and the economic boom jump-started by increased oil revenues and the nationalization of oil in the early 1970s provided him the opportunity to establish control over the regime and the country as a whole. Iraq advanced in all areas – particularly in the 1970s – and Iraqis who were not opponents of the regime or politically active benefited from the overall economic, educational, and social improvements.

Saddam Hussein's personality cult had many prototypes in world history and is unlikely to be the last of its kind. Stalin, Hitler, Ceauşescu, Kim Il-sung, Saparmurat Niyazov of Turkmenistan, and Syria's Hafiz al-Asad were all exemplars that Saddam Hussein read about, and the last four were his contemporaries. Comparisons to all these personality-driven dictatorships show strong parallels to Saddam's accumulation of power and control.

Born in the small village of 'Oja, south of Tikrit, on April 28, 1937, Saddam Hussein was involved from his youth in political activities, and at the age of twenty-two, he participated in a failed assassination attempt against 'Abd al-Karim Qasim. In 1968, when the Ba'th Party came to power, Saddam Hussein was well placed as a cousin of the then president Ahmad Hasan al-Bakr. He began to build a network to cultivate power for himself and in July 1968, aged only thirty-one, was appointed vice president. The fact that Saddam Hussein, unlike the previous leaders of the country, never attended military college did not hinder his progress. His childhood became mythologized: how he loved to study; how he overcame the obstacles of living in a small, undeveloped village; and how he had an "awareness about the national fate" from early childhood.[2]

There is no doubt that Saddam Hussein was both intellectually astute and extremely talented at manipulating different situations to his own

---

[2] *CRRC*, SH-BATH-D-000-775. This file contains pictures and anecdotes about Saddam Hussein's life and schooling. Some of the papers belonged to the party's archives, others to the Ministry of Culture and Information.

ends. He "understood what motivated people at their basest level"[3] and
knew how to use his charisma on friend and foe alike. A number of people
who worked with Saddam Hussein and whom I interviewed in summer
2010 reminisced that he could be extremely charming, kind, generous,
attentive, and caring. "He is not impulsive, he acts only after judicious
consideration, and he can be extremely patient; indeed, he uses time as
a weapon."[4] As his associates came to know all too well, he could also
be capricious, ruthless, evil, and unwilling to listen to anyone. He always
claimed that he understood the psyche of the Iraqi people and could
anticipate their behavior. In his most revealing book, *rijal wa madina*
(Men and a City), he tells the story of a tribal sheikh who rode his mule
for days from his remote village to send a telegram to the army officers
who, in 1941, had engineered a coup d'état against the monarchy by
taking advantage of the British administration's weakness. Arriving at
the post office in the nearest town, the sheikh dictated his telegram of
support for the officers but found out that since he had left his village,
the British and the regent were back in power. Without hesitation, he
sent the same telegram of support to the regent instead of to the officers.[5]
The story's significance lies in Saddam Hussein's belief from an early age
that people respect only one thing: power. In the same book he recounts
numerous stories to underline his strength, both physical and mental,
in confronting larger and stronger opponents until he gained the upper
hand, and how those around him, whether they were children or later
party members, were made to respect and fear him.[6]

The principle of being strong at all times and at any cost accompanied
Saddam Hussein throughout his life. Whether in *rijal wa madina* or in
one of the "ordered" biographical books about himself, called *al-ayyam
al-tawila* (The Long Days), which was based on the attempted assassination of 'Abd al-Karim Qasim in 1959, the heroes in these books never
succumbed to fear or lost control, even when a doctor operated on the
hero (i.e., Saddam Hussein) to remove a bullet shot by one of Qasim's

[3] Charles Duelfer, *Hide and Seek: The Search for Truth in Iraq* (New York: Public Affairs,
   2009), p. 386. Duelfer was a special advisor in Iraq looking for weapons of mass destruction, and his book contains interesting anecdotes about Saddam Hussein and the people
   who worked with him.
[4] Jerrold M. Post, "Saddam Hussein of Iraq: A Political Psychology Profile," in Jerrold M.
   Post (ed.), *The Psychological Assessment of Political Leaders: With Profiles of Saddam
   Hussein and Bill Clinton*, paperback edn. (Ann Arbor: University of Michigan Press,
   2005), p. 342.
[5] Saddam Hussein, *Rijal wa madina*, pp. 75–76.
[6] *Ibid.*, pp. 136 and 189.

bodyguards.[7] This story of Saddam Hussein's "heroism" in the attempted assassination entered the mythology of the Ba'th Party. Even the motorcycle that he had used with another comrade during their escape to Syria was retrieved two decades later and placed in the party's museum.[8]

His determination not to show any weakness is also the key to understanding why he refused to tell the Americans and UN inspectors that there were no weapons of mass destruction in Iraq, thus allowing the country to suffer from sanctions and providing the pretext for the U.S.-led invasion. Compounding this obsessive need to demonstrate strength were Saddam Hussein's stubbornness once he reached a decision and his reluctance from the mid-1980s until his demise to accept negative news. (Although, as discussed later, he was willing to change his views on fundamental issues to suit his purpose.) In a symposium to analyze the 1991 war attended by senior military officers, he snubbed those presenting a dim view of Iraq's military, saying, "I will not permit pessimistic views, only positive ones."[9]

This need to show strength probably stemmed from his constant paranoia, founded or unfounded, that he was surrounded by enemies. There were many attempts on his life; his chief of military intelligence recorded seven attempted assassinations by 1982, and in the following two decades, there were scores of other attempts on him, his family, and his close associates.[10] He did not show fear or weakness; his facial expressions rarely gave a clue about his state of mind, and he would intimidate people who met him by insinuating that he could read their minds and would

---

7　'Abd al-Amir Mu'alla, *al-Ayyam al-tawila* [The Long Days] (Baghdad: Wizarat al-I'lam, 1978), pp. 74 and 110. The book, based on the attempted assassination of 'Abd al-Karim Qasim, was made into a lengthy movie. The actor was none other than Saddam's cousin, also named Saddam Kamil, and the brother of Hussein Kamil. When the two fled to Jordan on August 7, 1995, with their wives, who were Saddam Hussein's daughters, the film was banned and a new version produced. For details of the intrigues surrounding the making of the film, see https://www.kassemhawal.com/wesima_articles/ articles-20070806–63.html (accessed April 26, 2010). See also Saddam Hussein, *Rijal wa madina*, pp. 247–51. For details of Kamil's flight, see Tripp, *A History of Iraq*, p. 267.

8　For the story of how the motorcycle was retrieved and its significance for the party, see a memo written to 'Ali Hasan al-Majid, June 25, 2001, BRCC, 005-4-6 (513–514).

9　Interviews with General al-Hamdani, June 16, 2010, and July 11, 2010. Saddam Hussein's words in Arabic were: *"La-asmah lil jawanab al-sawdawiyya illa al-jawanab al-mushriqa."* The seminar took place on November 27, 1995.

10　Al-Tikriti, *Muhawalat ightiyal al-Ra'is*. Saddam's son 'Uday suffered an assassination attempt in December 1996 that left him paralyzed from the waist down. See Amatzia Baram, *Building Toward Crisis: Saddam Husayn's Strategy for Survival* (Washington, DC: Washington Institute for Near East Policy, Policy Paper No. 47, 1998), pp. 17–20.

know if they were with him or against him. Like Stalin, he watched everyone, as is the "habit of a predator understanding its prey."[11] Hence, Saddam Hussein trusted no one, not even his closest family. His paranoia and lack of trust were exacerbated by two events: the 1991 uprising and the fleeing of his sons-in-law to Amman in summer 1995.

In a review of the 1991 uprising with his military commanders in 1992, Saddam Hussein admitted – unusually – that he bore some responsibility for underestimating the popular reaction:

> The main factor, which probably I contributed to, was the trust in our people. In other words, what happened could not be expected, and thus we were not prepared to face such a factor.... I never expected that some of our people, a small number, would betray us and unite with those who came across from Iran. I thought that it would never happen. However, things that you do not expect to happen probably will happen.[12]

The sudden departure of his son-in-law Hussein Kamil was a severe blow to Saddam Hussein, who always had a soft spot for him, had relied on him, and had trusted his judgment. Kamil, the quintessential sycophant, knew – to the annoyance of generals and senior party officials – how to charm the president and say all the right things in front of him. Deep distrust and fierce competition for the president's attention prevailed between Kamil and Saddam's son 'Uday, and Kamil was one of the very few who dared to inform Saddam Hussein about 'Uday and criticize his activities. In one letter he sent to the president, he complained that 'Uday was using his newspaper *Babil* to attack the regime and the economic committee of which Kamil was a member. He urged Saddam Hussein to take action, as 'Uday "knows that no one will stand up to his face, and that is why I would like you to forgive me from doing this task in the economic committee, which annoyed 'Uday and gave us pain and humiliation."[13] Indeed, 'Uday's problems and misbehavior occupied a lot of the president and his entourage's time and energy throughout most of this period.

Saddam Hussein constantly played political chess with his friends and enemies; in one example he dismissed his minister of agriculture and irrigation, announcing publicly that he had failed to stem the floods in

---

[11] Overy, *The Dictators*, pp. 10–11.
[12] Iraqi Revolutionary Command Council, "Saddam Hussein and His Military Commanders," February 1992, *CRRC*, SH-RVCC-D-000-610.
[13] Letter from Lieutenant General Hussein Kamil to Mr. President, the Commander, December 27, 1992, *CRRC*, SH-SPPC-D-000-235.

the late 1980s, only to tell him later that this was a ploy to get his opponent at the presidential *diwan* to believe that the president was fully behind him. He later reinstated the minister and hanged the senior official at the *diwan* in charge of agriculture.[14] His ruthlessness and intimidation of generals, ministers, and even of his immediate family knew no bounds.

A minister, whom I interviewed, told a chilling story about how Saddam Hussein ordered him to confiscate some land belonging to a company called al-Sajid. A few weeks after the order was given, the director of his ministry was contacted and threatened that if the ministry continued in its plans to confiscate the land, "his body and the minister's body will be found in the rubbish dump." It turned out that the land belonged to some members of Saddam Hussein's family, and to this day the minister does not know whether or not he was set up by the president. The minister was obviously in a tough spot: on one hand he had an order from the president, but on the other hand he and his senior official were threatened indirectly by members of the leader's family.

A number of telephone conversations took place between the minister and some of his senior staff about this issue, and at the same time he wrote to the president's secretary, who controlled Saddam Hussein's daily schedule, asking for a private meeting. Three more requests were sent to the presidential *diwan* with no answer, followed by a direct request at the end of the weekly cabinet meeting. The minister said that he knew he was in trouble and felt utterly helpless, as the president was not willing to meet him to hear his explanations.

In a weekly cabinet meeting in December 1994, the minister walked into the room to find security men present with large tape recorders. In trepidation, he sat motionless, like all the ministers, waiting for the president to begin. Saddam Hussein informed the cabinet that he would like them to hear the telephone conversations of one of their colleagues. The security men began playing taped conversations of the minister with his officials, but their own voices were blocked, so that those in the room heard only what the minister said. In one of the conversations, when his director told him of the repeated threats he was receiving, the minister, in a moment of rage, cursed the system and said that Qusay, 'Uday, and Hussein Kamil (who were among those behind the company) were

---

[14] Interview with the minister, June 15, 2010. The minister was an active Ba'th member from an early age, a governor of a province, and twice a minister. The *diwan* officials competed with the different ministers for the attention of the president, as discussed in Chapter 8.

"a bunch of gangsters," but fortunately for him, he did not mention the president by name. In another taped conversation, he told his son, who worked in the intelligence services, that even as a minister he had no power and no influence.

Utter silence prevailed in the room when the tapes stopped, and one could imagine the state of terror in the hearts not just of this minister but of all his colleagues watching this humiliation. The president turned to the minister and asked him if he had anything to say. The minister replied that he had asked five times to see the president to no avail, and he would now like five minutes in private with him. Saddam Hussein refused and said that he could say anything in front of all those present. Obviously, the minister realized that he would face death if he were to divulge the true story about the land and its owners. Saddam Hussein turned to his legal advisor and asked whether the incident came under *qanun al-tahajjum* (the law of assault) and whether the minister should be hanged.[15] The advisor, to his credit, informed the president that, as the minister had not attacked the president directly or personally, he could not be sentenced under this law. The minister was taken away by the security men, blindfolded, and thrown into a cell for several weeks.

Later he was transferred to Abu Ghraib prison, and after a few months a court sentenced him to fifteen years of imprisonment. He spent two years in prison until his release in 1996, but his troubles did not end there. His oldest son had committed suicide, but he did not hear about it until the day that a car whisked him from the prison to the presidential palace. The minister was not a favorite of Hussein Kamil, and after Kamil fled to Jordan, Saddam Hussein decided to bring back Kamil's enemies from the cold, one of whom was this minister. On arriving at the palace, Saddam Hussein greeted the minister by embracing him, telling him that he loved and respected him, and saying that he was more than right about Hussein Kamil, who had proved to be not only a criminal but also a traitor.

The minister, who did not yet know about the death of his son, suddenly found himself being consoled by the president, who told him, "Your son was also my son." Devastated, he went home to grieve with his family. A month later, Saddam Hussein sent a message telling him that he should forget the past, because he would like him to become a minister again, but when the minister refused, citing reasons of grief and health, the president became very angry. The minister was placed under house

[15] As discussed in Chapter 4, this 1986 law made it a criminal offense to curse or verbally attack the president and his leadership.

arrest for two more years and prevented from leaving the country. This not untypical story conveys the atmosphere prevailing at senior levels and explains why the vast majority of people acquiesced to Saddam Hussein's overwhelming power and domination.[16] "There is about Saddam Hussein a peculiar ruthlessness, an almost calculated cruelty, perhaps even an interest in pain."[17]

Among Saddam Hussein's greatest strengths, however, was his ability to be flexible and even to reverse certain decisions he had made, in both internal and external policy. Sometimes, when he felt that he had miscalculated, he would change his mind, but he never admitted that he had erred in judgment. For example, he reversed his position on Iran in 1975 and gave up control of the Shatt al-Arab waterway in return for Iran's withdrawal of support for Kurdish guerillas. Later, he launched the war against Iran after canceling the 1975 treaty with Tehran. In domestic policy, Saddam Hussein made dramatic volte-face with regard to tribalism, religion, and the status of women (see Chapter 8). Even with regard to issues such as his family, nepotism, and corruption, he held contrasting views: on one hand he tolerated corruption and encouraged nepotism, but on the other hand he reprimanded his associates by telling them (and interestingly here he consistently used the third person when talking about himself) that

> Saddam Hussein is not concerned to make the Ba'th Arab Socialist Party a tool or a ladder for his relatives so they could sneak into authority one after the other.... Saddam Hussein is the son of the party ever since he was a student in the school until now. There was not a day he imagined that he is favoring himself over the party or over the nation, despite the fact that he is ruling the nation and he is ruling the party.... They [his family members] are in the service of the Ba'th and not in the service of themselves. They may obtain a title when they provide a service for [the country].... Most of my relatives have become part of the authority because they excelled during the period of betrayal [during the 1991 uprising].... I deal with them on the basis of the Ba'th's needs.... Do you think I am happy when you give my relatives land? Don't you understand that this is an insult to Saddam?... Do not grant anything illegal to my relatives and to the officers working with me, and do not ever be scared from anyone [if you reject them].[18]

---

[16] Interview with the minister, July 11, 2010.

[17] Robert Fisk, "Saddam Hussein: The Last Great Tyrant," *The Independent*, December 30, 2000.

[18] Audiotape of a meeting of the top leadership, no specific date, but it took place after Hussein Kamil fled in August 1995. His strong words have to be taken in context of

Observers and associates of Saddam Hussein noted that he underwent dramatic changes over time, like other leaders such as Mao Tse Tung. In the early 1970s he was mostly a listener and a gatherer of information and ideas, but by the early 1980s he had begun to speak out more in the RCC and cabinet meetings instead of listening to the views of others, and disagreement with him or serious discussion rarely took place in these meetings.[19] Mao, known as an intent listener in the 1940s, changed a great deal by the time he became the "exalted leader" in the 1960s.[20] After Hussein Kamil fled to Jordan, Saddam Hussein became very introverted and began devoting a lot of time and energy to writing books and reading poetry.[21] Throughout his presidency, in fact, he devoted immense effort and resources to writing books, and some of them, such as *al-qal'a al-hasina* (The Immune Castle), published in 2001, were more than 700 pages long (like his other books, it was published not under his own name but as "a novel by its author").[22] As the war of 2003 was approaching, Saddam Hussein was busy trying to finish his novel *ikhruju ayyuha al-shayatin* (Be Gone, Demons), which, according to one of the translators, Saman Abdul Majid, dealt with ancient prophets and modern issues and was an attack on the Jews, who were portrayed in the novel as the demons.[23] Another literary-minded dictator was Niyazov, whose associates claimed that his first book, *ruhnama* (Book of the Soul), contained answers to "all of life's questions." He too produced one book after another.[24]

the fact that Kamil exploited being Saddam Hussein's son-in-law to accumulate large amounts of wealth. See *CRRC*, SH-SHTP-A-000-837.

[19] Fakhri Qadduri, *Hakadha 'araftu al-Bakr wa Saddam: Rihlat 35 'aman fi Hizb al-Ba'th* [This Is the Way I Knew al-Bakr and Saddam: A Journey of 35 Years in the Ba'th Party] (London: Dar al-Hikma, 2006), p. 180.

[20] Interview by *The Economist* with the journalist Sidney Rittenberg, who knew Mao well during his many years in China. See www.economist.com/mode/21010257 (accessed September 3, 2010).

[21] Interview with a senior Iraqi diplomat who, before becoming an ambassador, acted as a translator for Saddam Hussein from English to Arabic.

[22] Saddam Hussein, *al-Qal'a al-hasina* [The Immune Castle], *riwaya li-katibiha* [a Novel by Its Author] (Baghdad: al-Huriyya Publishing House, 2001). The story begins at the end of the Iran–Iraq War and ends in the late 1990s. Its hero, Sabah, falls into the hands of Iranians and becomes a prisoner of war. On his release, he meets the heroine, Shatrin, a Kurdish woman, while studying at the law school in Baghdad. The book delves into the history of many Iraqi cities near the Tigris River.

[23] Abdul Majid, *Les années Saddam*, pp. 130–34. Most of the copies of the novel were destroyed, as they were published just as the invasion began, but some survived, see *The Telegraph*, "Saddam the Great Dictator of Fairy Tales," December 17, 2003.

[24] David Lewis, *The Temptations of Tyranny in Central Asia* (New York: Columbia University Press, 2008), pp. 81–82.

Increasingly, Saddam Hussein had no tolerance for dissent, and the party itself became extremely intolerant of any opposition to the Ba'th. This was exacerbated by two factors: the functioning of Saddam Hussein's inner circle and his personal capabilities. A systemic feature of dictatorships such as Saddam's Iraq, Stalin's Soviet Union, or Ceauşescu's Romania was the creation of "a close circle of loyal colleagues and subordinates who formed a leadership corps of which the dictator remained unquestionably the master."[25] In Iraq, the inner circle was a quartet comprised of 'Izzat al-Duri, Taha Yasin Ramadan, Tariq 'Aziz, and 'Ali Hasan al-Majid (an uncle of Hussein Kamil), who all remained dedicated to Saddam Hussein to the very end. Although personally competent, they were primarily a group of yes-men who played a significant role in building the president's personality cult, while simultaneously advancing their own careers via the Saddam-glorifying enterprise.[26] They became completely acquiescent and never functioned as a sounding board in the face of their leader's arbitrary dominance. This state of affairs was aggravated by Saddam's unshakeable belief in himself as a true military leader and planner, and he relied less and less on professional military strategists. He was also a master of playing his colleagues against each other and of exploiting the competition between senior mandarins for promotion and power.

The second factor, which cannot be underestimated, was that Saddam Hussein was very capable, worked very long hours, had a photographic memory, read daily hundreds of memos sent to him, and – at least in the first decade – was extremely well prepared for important meetings or decisions. This was evident, for example, in the nationalization of the Iraq Petroleum Company. A review of the president's activities published by *al-Thawra* newspaper indicated the numerous meetings, conferences, and ceremonies he attended, in addition to meeting foreign dignitaries and Iraqi citizens.[27] He never hesitated to ridicule ministers and senior officials if they were ill prepared, thus increasing their fear and awe of him and making them very reluctant to express an opposing opinion even on trivial matters.[28] Having witnessed what Saddam Hussein did to other members in the infamous party meeting in 1979 and in other

---

[25] Overy, *The Dictators*, p. 77.

[26] For a comparison of the inner circle surrounding Stalin and their role in building the cult, see Robert C. Tucker, "The Rise of Stalin's Personality Cult," *American History Review*, vol. 84, no. 2 (April 1979), pp. 362–63.

[27] *Al-Thawra*, no. 10453, January 1, 2002.

[28] For example, as head of the Planning Council in the mid-1970s, while he was vice president, Saddam Hussein humiliated the then minister of health, 'Izzat Mustafa, for

cabinet meetings, few officials or ministers were willing to dissent. His untrammeled power extended to any individual in society, and like Stalin or Mao, Saddam Hussein "could have members even of his immediate entourage incarcerated or killed without his needing to inform, let alone consult, the others."[29]

Decision making therefore became mostly concentrated in the president's hands and epitomized by lack of consultation, and by the 1980s, the official statement "An order from the leader the President" eliminated all discussion and became a law in itself. Party documents give a dramatic insight into how Saddam Hussein's orders became, in effect, the law of the land and penetrated into every sphere of civil and official life. Among these orders were the regulation of office hours for all security officials (from 8 A.M. to 3 P.M.), the ruling that any security official responsible for investigating the activities of the Da'wa Party or those associated with Wahhabism must study the history and the development of these movements, the allocation of food stipends to all workers in the Baghdad municipality according to their positions, instructions to all senior party members to wear military uniform,[30] and orders regarding cleanliness.

Saddam Hussein was obsessed with sanitation and personal hygiene; in a meeting in Kut recorded by a French journalist, he was seen telling two senior officials:

> It's not appropriate for someone to attend a gathering or to be with his children with his body odor trailing behind him emitting sweet or stinky smell mixed with perspiration. It's preferable to bathe twice a day, but at least, once a day. And when the males bathe once a day, the female should bathe twice a day. The reason is that the female is more delicate and the smell of a woman is more noticeable than the male. If the son does not remember his father's nice scent, this will take away some of his son's love toward his father.[31]

---

not reading the technical reports and for coming unprepared to the meeting. See Hashim, *Mudhakkarat wazir 'Iraqi*, pp. 323–25.

[29] Rigby, "Stalinism and the Mono-Organizational Society," p. 60.

[30] Secretary to the President to All Security Organizations, May 30, 1994, *BRCC*, B 002-2-2 (061); Presidential *diwan* to All Security Organizations, November 16, 1994, B 002-2-2 (025); Presidential *diwan* to Baghdad Municipality, April 11, 1994, 021-2-7 (115); and Baghdad *tandhim* to All Party Secretariats, March 23, 2002, 004-4-1 (323). Many appointments were made directly by Saddam Hussein in different ministries and institutions. See, for example, the appointment of a senior official in the Organization for Military Industrialization, January 11, 1993, *BRCC*, 017-2-7 (308).

[31] Joel Soler Film, *Uncle Saddam*, Xenon Pictures and Frog Entertainment, 2003. No date was given for this speech.

Along the same lines, all ministries and government institutions such as the Central Bank, utility companies, municipalities, and so on, were informed in 2002 that the leader had discussed in cabinet meetings the issue of cleanliness, and all ministers were now categorically ordered that it was not enough to take care of their own hygiene. It was incumbent on them that all their subordinates be clean, and it was the responsibility of every minister, if he wanted to stay a minister, to enforce this rule.[32]

In all these orders the wording is similar: "Mr. the President Leader (May God Protect him) ordered the following." Everyone without exception had to obey. Nonetheless, there were a few recorded cases in which Saddam Hussein would heed different advice even if it angered him. In one example told to me, he considered reinvading Kuwait in September 1994, in a desperate move to break the blockade against Iraq and stop the frequent American and British bombardments of Iraqi installations. This was discussed with the inner cabinet, and as usual no one opposed the idea. However, when the subject was brought for discussion to the senior military leadership, who had to begin preparing for the invasion, one general, Ra'ad al-Hamdani, argued that this could be military suicide. The next day he was summoned to a private meeting with Saddam Hussein, who was enraged that a general had expressed an opposing view in front of other generals and began to reprimand him for refusing to obey an order. Al-Hamdani was convinced that this was his last day before being executed, but he explained to the president that he did not disobey an order; on the contrary, he felt it was his duty to tell his leader the truth, and that in essence what he saw was "one plus one equals two." Saddam Hussein shouted at him, "You might think one plus one equals two but I have a *risala* [message from God] and sometimes I can see that one plus one equals ten." To Saddam's credit, the meeting ended without al-Hamdani being punished, and the plan was shelved.[33] This profound sense of destiny and inner belief in being chosen by God to lead the masses is not, of course, unique to Saddam Hussein's dictatorship.[34]

Yet the aberrations in decision making did not create limitations for Saddam Hussein even when his power was supposedly weak, such as during the war with Iran and, most importantly, during the uprisings in southern and northern Iraq after the invasion of Kuwait. His overwhelming

---

[32] Council of Ministers to All Ministries, "Order," June 15, 2002, *BRCC*, 010-2-3 (038–041).

[33] Interviews with al-Hamdani, June 16, 2010, and July 11, 2010.

[34] For a comparison with Hitler and Stalin, see Overy, *The Dictators*, pp. 21–22.

control of the party and the security organizations remained intact; thus there was no serious diminution of the power he was able to exert. As with Stalin and Hitler, a principle was tacitly observed that, except for Saddam Hussein, no one should know any more than they needed to know, a principle that strengthened the hands of all these tyrannical rulers.[35]

For Saddam Hussein, the importance of legacy was critical. This came across in numerous presidential interviews and even during his interrogation after he was captured by the Americans. He saw himself as one of the world's great leaders, similar to those whom he greatly admired, such as Stalin, De Gaulle, Nasser, Tito, and Nelson Mandela. Each year he compiled long lists of books, mostly biographies, to be purchased for his private library.[36] He was dismissive of most of his contemporary Arab leaders. Discussing with his comrades the state of Arab diplomacy in the mid-1990s, he chastised the Arab leaders:

> The Arab leaders since 1947 to this day have given concessions [to Israel] with nothing in return... there is a chasm between the people and the leaders. How is the leader to lead? Rule by his height and length [sarcastically]? When you separate the governor from the people, the battle is over. When the governor becomes in the weakest of positions, he begins asking what he could do... apart from surrendering, and so he surrenders.[37]

Saddam Hussein saw himself as engaged in a long, epic struggle to lead Iraq to modernity and regain its past glory. He told his American interrogator, George Piro, that one of his favorite books was Ernest Hemingway's *The Old Man and the Sea*, and he clearly identified with its hero, a fisherman who struggled alone to bring in a fish despite the attacking sharks.[38]

Whether under the Ba'th regime or similar dictatorships, hegemony is sustained because the populace comes to assume, based on "the myths

---

[35] *Ibid.*, pp. 67–68.

[36] His translator, Saman Abdul Majid, tells that Saddam purchased roughly 300 books a year. See *Les années Saddam*, p. 140. See also U.S. Department of Justice, "Saddam Hussein Talks to the FBI."

[37] Audiotape discussing Arab diplomacy and the sanctions in the mid-1990s (exact date unknown), *CRRC*, SH-SHTP-A-000-714.

[38] The sayings of the book's hero, Santiago, must have served Saddam Hussein well in his captivity after the collapse of his regime. Santiago said, "But man is not made for defeat"; "A man can be defeated but not destroyed." Ernest Hemingway, *The Old Man and the Sea*, paperback edn. (London: Triad Grafton, 1988), p. 89. For details of this specific conversation between Piro and Saddam Hussein, see Duelfer, *Hide and Seek*, p. 401.

of infallibility and omniscience generated by the cults of personality,"[39] that their leaders are making the right decisions.

Building the Personality Cult

Saddam Hussein played an active role in developing his personality cult even before he became president. Articles extolling him and promoting the need for a true *qa'id* (leader) were published as early as 1975. Saddam had understood very quickly the importance of the media and writers in developing a personality cult and fully exploited them to his own advantage. His 1977 biography (*The Long Days*) cleverly helped to pave the way for his emergence as the *qa'id*.[40]

After Saddam took over the presidency from Ahmad Hasan al-Bakr in 1979, the rhetoric about his achievements and his role as a leader increased markedly. This culminated in 1982 with the publicly staged *bay'a* (pledge of allegiance), in which 4 million Iraqis participated.[41] It was the first of many such massive gatherings organized by the well-oiled machine of the Ba'th Party. Interestingly, just as in Syria with Hafiz al-Asad, the contract of allegiance was signed in the blood of members of the national assembly. In both cases, the *bay'a* was intended to be personal, binding, and lifelong.[42]

"All cults of personality are more or less fiction."[43] By invoking historical, religious, and cultural factors, the images of the leader are exaggerated to set him above the state and the people. In Saddam Hussein's case, this mythical image "was created in poetry, prose, and the arts, all of which were made subservient to this aim."[44] As in other cults, symbols and spectacles were prominent, and Iraq had hundreds of these.[45] A defining feature of Saddam Hussein's cult was the systematic adulation expressed through every medium, projecting him as superhuman and

---

[39] Overy, *The Dictators*, p. 125.

[40] For a discussion of the concept of the leader and its connotations, see Bengio, *Saddam's Word*, pp. 70–74.

[41] The *bay'a* is a covenant between the ruler and the ruled and dates back to the time of the Prophet Muhammad. For more details, see Bengio, *Saddam's Word*, pp. 74–77.

[42] Lisa Wedeen, *Ambiguities of Domination: Politics, Rhetoric and Symbols in Contemporary Syria* (Chicago: University of Chicago Press, 1999), p. 38.

[43] Overy, *The Dictators*, p. 109.

[44] Bengio, *Saddam's Word*, p. 77.

[45] Kanan Makiya, *The Monument: Art and Vulgarity in Saddam Hussein's Iraq* (London: I.B. Tauris, 2004). For examples in Syria and a comparison with Nazi Germany, see Wedeen, *Ambiguities of Domination*, pp. 10–11.

capable of doing all things perfectly. In the novel *The Long Days*, the author emphasized that the hero (i.e., Saddam Hussein) should not go to prison, given that "he is capable of doing many things" for the party.[46] The Iraqi media worked assiduously to present the leader's great achievements on every front: his nationalization of oil, his defense of Palestine, and his outstanding leadership of a kind rarely seen in modern history.[47] One editorial stated, "We cannot think of any human society at any time or place without having a leader or president who is responsible for the state," and continued by describing how fortunate the Iraqi nation was to have found "the heroic leader Saddam Hussein, May God Protect him and Bless him...as he [has] an innovative mind and a belief stemming from the spirit of the nation and its culture."[48]

Before the referendum to choose the president, called *al-zahf al-kabir* (the Big March), all media were marshaled to get as many people as possible to vote for the president. There was no opposition, and the voters had to tick "Yes" or "No" on a voting slip. An editorial in *al-Qadisiyya*, under the headline, "Why do we love Saddam Hussein?" delivered lofty praise of his qualities, particularly his courage in leading the nation from one victory to another, and ended with the famous motto, "Yes, Yes to Saddam."[49] A senior Iraqi official who was present at a meeting after the 1996 referendum told me that Saddam Hussein could not understand why only 99.9 percent voted for him. He asked how many people the 0.1 percent represented and then answered immediately that it was probably 5,000 to 6,000 voters. He blamed the party's organization for not explaining him well enough to those few thousands and added that if he had had the opportunity to talk to those people, they would have voted for him.[50] Sure enough, in the next referendum, in October 2002, the vote was 100 percent, and he was sworn in for another seven-year term.[51]

Similar to the cult of Stalin, Saddam Hussein's writings in philosophy and history were used to build up his stature as leader.[52] His ten-volume collection of articles, speeches, and interviews, *al-Mukhtarat*, was

---

[46] Mu'alla, *al-Ayyam al-tawila*, p. 136.
[47] *Al-Jumhuriyya*, no. 10962, October 13, 2002.
[48] *Al-Qadisiyya*, no. 7564, October 16, 2002.
[49] *Al-Qadisiyya*, no. 7560, October 12, 2002.
[50] Interview on file, June 15, 2010.
[51] For the swearing-in ceremony and the president's speech, see *al-Qadisiyya*, no. 7566, October 19, 2002.
[52] Tucker, "The Rise of Stalin's Cult," pp. 352–53.

published in attractively bound volumes in 1988. A long list of booklets and pamphlets detailing his philosophy and opinions on important issues were produced, including his books *Education and the Revolution* and *About Writing History*, both published before he became president.[53] Many court writers (including non-Iraqis) were ready to serve the president and write hagiographies and articles about his unique qualities as a leader.[54] At the same time, Saddam Hussein's personal interest in culture and poetry cannot be underestimated, as discussed in Chapter 2.

Religion was also used to consolidate the personality cult. As Overy states, "Cults are conventionally religious rather than political phenomena," and he adds that both in Stalin's Soviet Union and Hitler's Germany the distinction between the two became blurred.[55] In Iraq, Saddam Hussein and his court writers began tracing his origins to the tribe of the Prophet Muhammad and equated him to 'Ali bin Abi Talib, the Prophet's son-in-law. Later on, he used the Caliph al-Mansur to enhance his Arab Islamic image.[56] As discussed in Chapter 8, one of the reasons for launching his "faith campaign" was to counterbalance the possible spread of Khomeinism among the Iraqi people, particularly its Shi'is. Akin to the description of Hitler "either as God himself, or a gift from God,"[57] *fida'iyyu Saddam* – the president's personal paramilitary – boasted the motto that "those who swear allegiance to Saddam are swearing allegiance to God."[58] Letters addressed to Saddam Hussein requesting a meeting began placing him after God and before any of the prophets. One tribal leader wrote that Saddam Hussein "is the sole patron after God . . . to anyone who needs help."[59] Another letter from a medical doctor in a Basra hospital declared, "My noble leader: Our love and loyalty

---

[53] Saddam Hussein, *al-Thawra wa al-tarbiya al-wataniyya*; and *Hawla kitabat al-tarikh* [About Writing History] (Baghdad: Dar al-Huriyya, 1979).

[54] One such biography is Amir Iskander, *Saddam Hussein: The Fighter, the Thinker and the Man*, translated by Hassan Selim (Paris: Hachette Réalités, 1980).

[55] Overy, *The Dictators*, p. 120.

[56] Caliph al-Mansur was an Abbasid leader who established his new capital in Baghdad. For more details on Saddam Hussein's role models, see Bengio, *Saddam's Word*, pp. 79–85. It was said that he could not understand how the Shi'is in Iraq revolted against him in 1991, given his alleged connection to Imam 'Ali.

[57] Overy, *The Dictators*, p. 120.

[58] This motto was written on the stationery of *fida'iyyu Saddam*; see, for example, Woods and Lacey, *Iraqi Perspectives Project: Saddam and Terrorism*, vol. 5, ISGQ, 2003-00002541, pp. 3–6.

[59] The letter asking for a meeting with the president was, as procedure dictated, sent to the SSO to check its sender and the details it contained, before a decision was made whether to grant the meeting. *BRCC*, B 001-2-1 (192).

to you is the same love and loyalty that [we give] to the great leaders of our nation, such as the Prophet Muhammad . . . and the Caliph Omar al-Khattab . . . and the Imam 'Ali bin Abi Talib."[60]

An important feature differentiating Saddam Hussein from other personality cult dictators was that he met with a dozen ordinary Iraqis almost daily right up until 2002, when security fears prevented such meetings. Rarely did Stalin or Hitler meet members of the general public in their presidential offices. But Saddam Hussein saw it as another way of controlling events; it allowed him to hear directly from ordinary citizens and created an additional check on senior officials, because many of those citizens had problems with the government or with the party's bureaucracy. For Iraqis, it was like winning the lottery; Saddam Hussein's translator revealed that no one would leave the meeting empty-handed, as Saddam Hussein would give each person an envelope of money.[61]

In the mid-1980s a new law, *qanun al-tahajjum*, was promulgated, stating that any offense such as swearing at or cursing the president or his family was considered an attack on the regime, and special courts were set up to deal with these "attacks" (see Chapter 4). Over the years, Saddam Hussein became an almost sacred figure, and any criticism or hint of hostility was considered to be heresy. In a memo sent to all Party Secretariats, one senior member laid down guidelines that on public occasions, party members or announcers should not use the same descriptions of the president as they use to describe other senior persons, given the leader's uniqueness. The memo further advised that although other senior party members should be accorded a warm welcome, the chanting and reciting of poems should be done only for "the leader of the nation, humanity and Arabs."[62]

---

[60] Letter from Dr. A. J. to the Leader, "Letter from a Son of Basra," December 31, 1988. A copy of the letter was sent to the party branch in Basra, *BRCC*, 005-3-7 (151–155). It is interesting to note that the writer had abbreviated all the prayers and the blessing for the Prophet and the Caliphs into just an acronym, whereas for Saddam, the ritual sentence asking God to protect and bless him were written in full and repeated several times in the five-page letter.

[61] Abdul Majid, *Les années Saddam*, pp. 101–02. According to the memoirs, on some days Saddam Hussein met with sixty people in groups of four. Most of the meetings centered on complaints, and the president rarely asked the supplicants for their political views. The one issue on which he would not budge, as confirmed by his translator, was his refusal to grant non-Baghdadis land to build a house in Baghdad, because a law had been passed stating that anyone who had not lived in the capital since 1977 had no right to own a house or apartment there.

[62] Senior Member of *tandhim* al-Karkh to All Party Secretariats, "Guidelines," August 7, 2001, *BRCC*, 004-3-1 (121–122).

Wasaya al-ra'is (the commands of the president) became, in time, almost like those of a prophet or spiritual leader. They permeated every aspect of life and were routinely taught in schools, universities, and of course at all party events, becoming part and parcel of the Ba'th cadre's "cultural education" and of the political/religious culture at large. One of Saddam Hussein's promulgations was featured on the letterhead of every government ministry or security organization. Some of these were simply wise advice, such as, "Always remember that you might regret saying or doing something in some situations, but you will never regret being patient." Others had more subtle angles that served the regime, such as, "Watch out for yourself from your enemy and from your friend before your enemy," and – hypocritically for someone who was notorious for not accepting the blame for anything that went wrong during a thirty-five-year rule – "As a leader, do not choose those who take credit for success and deny their responsibility for failure."[63] A party memo dictated that each branch should select a number of these commands and hang them in their section, divisions, and cells, so that everyone attending meetings could benefit from them.[64] A book published in early 2001, called *Studies in the Commands of the Struggling Leader Saddam Hussein*, inspired one journalist to comment that these commands were "a lamp that enlightens the way for the writer, the critic, and the researcher."[65]

In the established tradition of extolling dictators and tyrants, the cult created for Saddam Hussein showered him with titles and metaphors expressing his supposed characteristics. Two such titles seem to be perennial favorites, whether applied to Stalin, Ceauşescu, Kim Il-sung, or Asad: leader and father. In the Soviet Union, Stalin was portrayed in a stream of "paternal poses" to show his care for children and workers; in Romania, Ceauşescu was given the title of "Conducător" (leader) and "Genius of the Carpathians"; Kim Il-sung was known as the "Fatherly Leader"; and Hafiz al-Asad was depicted in Syrian political discourse as "Father," "Leader Forever," and "First Teacher."[66] Wedeen explains that "family

---

[63] The documents contain hundreds of those commands. One batch is in *BRCC*, 183-4-1 (484–501).

[64] Party Secretariat to All Party Bureaus, "Commands of the Comrade Leader (May God Protect Him)," August 26, 2000, *BRCC*, 183-4-1 (592).

[65] *Al-Jumhuriyya*, no. 10953, October 2, 2002.

[66] Overy, *The Dictators*, p. 117; *Nicolae Ceauşescu: The Genius of the Carpathians* (Milton Keynes: Filiquarian, 2008), p. 23; Bradley K. Martin, *Under the Loving Care of the Fatherly Leader: North Korea and the Kim Dynasty*, paperback edn. (New York: Thomas Dunne, 2006), pp. 11–28; and Wedeen, *Ambiguities of Domination*, p. 1.

metaphors operate in the official narrative to represent the idealized relations of domination and membership," and implicit "in the metaphor of
the father is also love and connection between ruler and ruled."[67] Capitalizing on the father metaphor, Saddam Hussein told tribal sheikhs who
called him their father that sometimes "the father becomes angry and infu-
riated with his brothers and children," and that thus he had the fatherly
right to be incensed for their lack of support during the uprising.[68]

Indeed, sycophancy in Iraq knew no bounds. A senior teacher in the
College of Physical Education at the University of Baghdad wrote to 'Uday
Hussein, as chairman of the Olympics Committee, requesting his help in
procuring pictures and producing a new book titled *Saddam Hussein the
Athlete and the Hero*. According to the author, Saddam Hussein was the
"first leader in the world" who gave high priority to sports, applied the
rule of fitness to all his people, and most importantly, was "an inspi-
ration for all athletes who achieved huge victories for their country."[69]
Another citizen wrote to the minister of culture and information asking for permission to construct statues of Saddam Hussein and his son
'Uday on his private land, at his own expense, "to show the heroism
of these two." Among the reasons for this endeavor, he said that Saddam Hussein had smiled at him twenty years ago at one of the major
rallies in 1979, and this smile had never left him.[70] One senior officer
wrote, "It is impossible to get to the level of your Excellency's brain
power and your exceptional planning."[71] Even foreign companies realized that an efficient way to gain a foothold in Iraq was to exploit the
cult. An Indian export company based in Mumbai offered to print, at
its own expense, one thousand copies of a book called *Saddam Hussein
and Men of Civilization in Iraq*, and to distribute it throughout India on
Saddam Hussein's birthday.[72] The audiotapes of the RCC and the party

---

[67] Wedeen, *Ambiguities of Domination*, p. 51.
[68] Audiotape of a meeting with the tribal leaders in Saddam City after the 1991 uprising,
    CRRC, SH-SHTP-A-000-891.
[69] Correspondence with Minister of Culture and Information and Approval from 'Uday
    Hussein, December 31, 2000, and February 20, 2001, Ministry of Information Dataset,
    003–0033/0034.
[70] Mr. A. to the Minister of Culture and Information, February 9, 1998, Ministry of
    Information Dataset, 003–0180 to 003–0185.
[71] Head of Department of Political Affairs to the President, September 24, 1989, *CRRC*,
    SH-PDWN-D-000-469.
[72] Export Manager to Zuhair Sadiq al-Khalidi, Ministry of Information Dataset, 003-421-
    423. In fact, it was not a book, but rather a booklet written by Zuhair al-Khalidi with
    an introduction by Taha Yasin Ramadan.

leadership accentuate the reverence in which Saddam Hussein was held by his associates and subordinates; their obsequiousness in those meetings was limitless and far more extreme than what the documents ever could indicate.

As we have seen, Saddam Hussein focused particularly on the role of children and youth as the upcoming cadre of the Ba'th Party. Anyone born after 1979 was known as part of *jil Saddam* (Saddam's generation). Likewise, children called him *baba Saddam* (Daddy Saddam) in kindergartens and schools, and the organization *ashbal Saddam* (Saddam's Cubs) was created for youths under sixteen to train them militarily and ideologically. Saddam Hussein's cult went further than that of most dictators: "Iraq is Saddam and Saddam is Iraq" was a motto used on banners and in speeches, echoing Louis XIV's famous epithet, "L'état c'est moi" (I am the state).[73] The ritual affirmation of Saddam Hussein as the great leader continued unabated at all public and political events. Jawad Hashim underlines this phenomenon by indicating the exponential growth in utilizing Saddam Hussein's name in the party's conferences: in 1974 the Ba'th regional conference mentioned Saddam Hussein's name only once and that was under his picture, but by 1982, the party's 366-page report referred to him more than one thousand times.[74] The absence of such references, whether deliberate or accidental, invited punishment. As one ex-minister and ex-ambassador recounted in his memoirs, praising Saddam Hussein's greatness had become, by the early 1980s, an important part of diplomatic protocol for all embassies, and the security organizations watched carefully for any deviation from this formula.[75] Writers and poets extolled the Iraq of Saddam Hussein in phrases such as, "Saddam is the peak of the mountains and the roar of the seas," and "Saddam in this country is the country."[76]

Naming towns, mosques, streets, theaters, bridges, and rivers after Saddam Hussein was another time-honored form of expanding the cult. The large city of al-Thawra, built by Qasim in a suburb of Baghdad to accommodate rural migrants, was renamed Saddam City (after 2003

---

[73] Louis XIV was called the Grand Monarch or the Sun King. His seventy-two-year reign was the longest in modern European history. "I am the state" expressed the absolutism of his authority.

[74] Hashim, *Mudhakkarat wazir 'Iraqi*, pp. 347–48.

[75] Qadduri, *Hakadha 'araftu al-Bakr wa Saddam*, p. 365.

[76] Ghazy Dir' al-Ta'i, *al-Bahr al-akhdhar* [The Green Sea] (Baghdad: Cultural Affairs Department, 1988), p. 7. This line is taken from a poem called "Saddam's Valley." Others in the same collection include "The Eagle" and "'Oja the Land of Heroes."

it was renamed Sadr City, after the Shi'i leader Moqtada al-Sadr). In
addition, many sections and divisions of the party were named after
Saddam Hussein or one of his variants, such as, "Section of the Winning
Leader," "Section of the Hero of Liberation," and "Section of the Pride
of Arabs." Likewise, new units and army battalions were named after
him. Calling the eight-year war between Iran and Iraq *qadisiyyat Saddam*
emphasized publicly the president's importance and his critical role in
that war.[77] In 1992, a new canal 351 miles (565 km) in length was dug
from Baghdad to the Gulf to reduce the country's reliance on the Shatt
al-Arab waterway. The program for inaugurating Saddam's new canal
showed how the cult was structured at every step. First, a memo was sent
to all cabinet and RCC members stating that by presidential order all
should attend the ceremonies. Second, the ceremony agenda was packed
with different aspects of the cult: it began with a speech by Hussein
Kamil, who was in charge of the project, followed by numerous activities
praising the president – some poets recited their poems, a mural and statue
of Saddam Hussein were unveiled, telegrams congratulating the president
on this achievement were read out, music and songs abounded, and finally
the ribbon was cut. As was customary on those occasions, all banner
slogans were preapproved: in this case, eighteen slogans were prepared,
among them, "Saddam's River is a great challenge to the embargo,"
"If Saddam said . . . Iraq said," and "Saddam's River is a gift from all
mujahidin [strugglers] to their great leader."[78] Saddam Hussein devoted
ample time to these ceremonies; documents show us the numerous drafts
and revisions he made to his speech, which praised the Iraqi people, in
particular the six thousand individuals who were involved in the canal's
construction, for their strength during the sanctions.[79]

Saddam Hussein's face adorning stamps, notes, and coins helped
to reinforce his ubiquitous presence. "[Saddam] Hussein exploited the
stamps to foster a cult of personality";[80] in 1990, the Iraqi Red Crescent,
among other agencies in the country, issued a set of three stamps featuring

---

[77] See Makiya, *Republic of Fear*, pp. 270–76.
[78] Presidential *diwan* to All Members of the Revolutionary Command Council, "Inaugurating Saddam's River," December 4, 1992, *BRCC*, B 003-4-6 (162–168). Interestingly,
the program for the inauguration, which took place on December 7, 1992, did not
mention the attendance of Saddam Hussein for the usual security reasons; the president
made his plans at the last moment to thwart any assassination attempt. Copies of all
such ceremonies were always sent to the SSO and the Party Secretariat.
[79] *CRRC*, SH-SPPC-D-000-244, December 6–7, 1992.
[80] Donald Malcolm Reid, "The Postage Stamp: A Window on Saddam Hussein's Iraq,"
Middle East Journal, vol. 47, no. 1 (Winter 1993), p. 79.

the president as "the icon of victory and peace."[81] Visual images were essential in communicating the cult to the Iraqi people; colossal monuments, statues, murals, and posters were put up throughout the country.[82] Interestingly, in neighboring Syria, the somewhat lower-key al-Asad did not erect grandiose monuments comparable to Baghdad's Arch of Victory or to Nazi architectural excesses in Germany.[83]

Portraits and posters of Saddam Hussein were everywhere; it was said that large pictures or cardboard statues of him were at the entrance of every village in Iraq. His photograph was not only in offices but also in homes, where people put the photographs up to demonstrate to informers that they were loyal citizens and admirers of the president.[84] Words and pictures of the leader had to be omnipresent to have impact; when the Internet started to spread in Iraq and government offices began to use it, the presidential *diwan* ordered all ministries to have Saddam Hussein's picture as their screen saver.[85]

In fact, a joke circulated in the late 1980s that the country's population was 34 million – 17 million people and 17 million portraits of Saddam Hussein. Not having a picture of the president in a prominent place, preferably on the wall, towering over everyone, led to severe repercussions. One major general, a highly decorated veteran of Iraq's wars, told me that in late 1994, while away from his office on a visit, officers from the intelligence services took photographs of his room. A few days later, the chief of staff called him to a meeting and reprimanded him for not having Saddam Hussein's picture on the wall. He explained that he had placed Saddam Hussein's picture on a table rather than on the wall, for fear that Allied air raids at that time would cause the picture to be smashed and injure those close by. He was investigated for almost three months, but given that military law did not prescribe punishments for not hanging pictures, the accusation centered on his "mistreatment" of some of his subordinates. He was sentenced to four years in prison but served only one year, was discharged from his job, and was demoted to brigadier general. The portrait's position was almost certainly not the

[81] *CRRC*, SH-PDWN-D-000-247. See stamp on the front cover
[82] For some of the large monuments and their significance, see Makiya, *The Monument*.
[83] Wedeen, *Ambiguities of Domination*, pp. 28–29; Overy, *The Dictators*, pp. 115–16.
[84] Arnold Hottinger, "Personality Cult and Party in Iraq," *Swiss Review of World Affairs* (June 1984), p. 13.
[85] Minister of Information to Presidential *diwan*, "Pictures of Mr. President Leader, May God Protect Him and Bless Him," August 6, 2002, Ministry of Information Dataset, 003-0164.

main issue, and he probably had enemies in the army, but this story shows how the issue was exploited to plant fear in the hearts of soldiers and civilians.[86] This example was not unique; one document recorded that an artist whose work was rejected by a gallery complained to the party that he was "emotionally upset and deeply affected" by the gallery owner's refusal to accept pictures of the president printed on postcards as a form of art. No information was given about the ramifications for the gallery owner.[87]

Another common visual were the *jidariyyat* (murals) discussed in Chapter 2, which were used to spread the political and cultural education of the population, and to enhance the personality cult of Saddam Hussein. For example, among the murals erected in 2002 on the occasion of the reelection of the president was one of Saddam Hussein in traditional Arab robes, accompanied by the slogan, "Yes, Yes, Yes, to the Leader Saddam Hussein (May God Protect and Bless him), and Death to America and Zionism."[88]

Saddam Hussein's birthday on April 28 became a major celebration for the party and the entire country. Streets were decorated, ceremonies were held in all government institutions, and all party members were involved in celebrating the occasion. In some aspects it was comparable to the birthday of the Prophet Muhammad, in that all religious institutions had to mark the occasion; it was given the title *al-milad al-maymun* (the Auspicious Birthday), and the date became sacred in the Iraqi calendar. No expense was spared, either by party branches or by the government, even during the depressed economic climate of the 1990s.[89] The Party Secretariat, in consultation with the presidential *diwan*, would decide each year on the nature of the festivities, but these usually included a military parade followed by a carnival in which thousands of schoolchildren and members of professional unions participated. The celebrations lasted for three days, filled with poetry competitions and speeches by party and government officials; the diplomatic corps in Baghdad was invited

[86] Interview with Major General Bashar Mahmud Ayyub al-Sa'ig, June 15, 2010. Al-Sa'ig is convinced that two men who reported to him were behind the accusation; interview February 13, 2011.
[87] Al-Faris Branch to SSO, "Information," November 22, 1995, BRCC, B 001-2-1 (122–124).
[88] Intisar Section to Bagdad Division, "Initiative," October 11, 2001, BRCC, 004-3-2 (001–003).
[89] See, for example, the preparations by the Great Victory Branch for the birthday in 2000: BRCC, 004-4-3. See also Bengio, *Saddam's Word*, pp. 83–85.

to lavish dinners; and last but not least, a special bonus was paid to all party members.[90] In addition, every year, prisoners – including political prisoners – were released on this day.[91]

As part of the cult, slogans would be created for each birthday. In 1993, for example, among twenty-two such slogans were, "All the Iraqis swear allegiance to you on your birthday"; "All Iraq is chanting: Saddam is the glory of our nation"; and "Saddam Hussein is the leader for whom this nation waited for a long time."[92] As noted in Chapter 2, the Ba'th calendar was adjusted to begin each year on April 28. Budget and annual reports had to coincide with this date, and swearing-in ceremonies for party members took place during these festivities. Even so, Saddam Hussein fell short of Turkmenistan's Niyazov, who changed the names of the calendar months to his and his family's names.[93]

To perpetuate the name of Saddam Hussein, dozens of prizes and medals were given annually to honor individuals in the fields of humanities, social sciences, science, and art. In 1996, the RCC issued a law whereby eleven of Saddam's prizes and medals were to be distributed annually to scientists, academics, and writers. In all categories, the monetary reward accompanying the prizes was at the president's discretion.[94]

Saddam Hussein took a particular interest in science, in addition to his love of literature and poetry. He seemed to be in awe of scientists, and people who worked with him said that they were the only category of academics whom he could not tell how and what to produce. Under such relatively lenient conditions, many scientists continued to work in Iraq even though they were not Ba'thists. Numerous documents underline Saddam Hussein's fascination with science and how protective he was of scientists. In 1999, for instance, he expanded the hiring of scientists and granted them better terms, as well as encouraging science students to continue graduate studies.[95] Time and again, he emphasized the

[90] Party Secretariat to All Party Secretaries, "Celebrations for the Auspicious Birth of Comrade the Leader (May God Protect Him)," March 25, 1999, *BRCC*, 004-4-3 (088); Head of al-Karkh *tandhim* to All Branch Secretaries, "Invitations to the Diplomatic Corps," April 19, 2000, *BRCC*, 004-4-3 (139).
[91] In one Kurdish town, twenty-six political prisoners were released in 1986. See *NIDS*, PUK 033, Box 171.
[92] For a list of the slogans for 1993, see *BRCC*, 004-5-4.
[93] Lewis, *The Temptations of Tyranny*, p. 82.
[94] Republic of Iraq, "Law for Saddam's Prizes for Science, Humanities, and Art, No. 6 for 1996," *BRCC*, 119-4-8 (94–99).
[95] Presidential *diwan* to President, "National Program for Preparing Scientific Cadre," January 1, 1999, *BRCC*, 021-2-7 (025–026).

importance of "planting nationalistic feelings in the hearts of scientists and of [students] who excel and connecting them romantically [to the cause] of Iraq."[96] Obviously, Saddam Hussein's interest in science was not wholly altruistic but was an integral part of his efforts to counteract sanctions and to strengthen Iraq technologically and militarily. He insisted in one cabinet meeting that "we have to develop the theoretical with the practical and the practical with the theoretical...so that university professors do not become only philosophers of ideas."[97]

The Role of the Party

The creation of a personality cult, either in Iraq, China, Nazi Germany, or the Soviet Union, could not have been achieved without the prominent role of the party and its overweening influence on society. Even in authoritarian regimes, it is difficult to see how a personality cult could be efficiently built up in the absence of a dominant political party. The Ba'th political indoctrination became more and more centered on the cult of Saddam Hussein as its ideology became fused with the exalted idealization of him. As discussed in Chapter 2, the courses in the party's preparatory school became largely devoted to studying Saddam Hussein's biography, his historic battles, speeches, and writings. At least half of the questions in every exam or essay competition in any party branch related to the leader and his achievements. As part of this cultural education, members regularly received press cuttings of editorials about Saddam Hussein selected by the Information and Studies Department, which reported to the office of the director of the Party Secretariat. These were circulated among different branches and used for discussions about different aspects of the leader.[98] Saddam Hussein's commands were treated as sacred; one memo advised all members, as part of their cultural education, to "read daily two commands of Comrade the Leader (May God Protect him and Bless him)."[99]

---

[96] Council of Government Cabinet to All Concerned Ministers, "Cathodic Prevention," April 13, 1999, *BRCC*, 021-2-7 (124–125).

[97] Party Secretariat to All Party Secretaries, "Execution of an Order," October 2, 2000, *BRCC*, 021-1-5 (045–046).

[98] See, for example, a batch of press cuttings about Saddam and his battles dated mid-February 2002, in *BRCC*, 016-5-3.

[99] Minutes of Meeting of the Victorious Leader Branch, November 17, 2002, *BRCC*, 004-5-6 (246).

As mentioned, Saddam Hussein's books were high on the ideological agenda. They were summarized and discussed, and members attending special courses held by the party had to write essays on these books and their significance for the people of Iraq. In one such essay, a woman member of a divisional headquarters who was also responsible for a cell analyzed *Zabiba wa al-Malik* (Zabiba and the King), a novel that was later produced as a play and, like others, was published as "a novel by its author."[100] She concluded that "the author is an ardent innovator" and, without naming Saddam Hussein, posited that he gave a lesson in modesty to the Iraqi people by publishing anonymously.[101] By orders of the president himself, his books were presented as gifts to all Arab delegations visiting Iraq, and Iraqi delegations visiting Arab countries were instructed to carry a few copies to give to their hosts.[102]

Preparations for referendums, Saddam Hussein's birthdays, and demonstrations in support of the president would not have been possible without the elaborate party machine at all levels. For the referendums, party members scoured the country, distributing examples of the ballots to explain to educated and illiterate people alike how to vote. They organized transportation for large numbers of voters and galvanized all local cells in universities and offices. Some branches went to the extent of sending their allegiance to the president written in their own blood. This got the attention of the Party Secretariat, who swiftly forwarded these extreme manifestations of loyalty to the president.[103] The party also enlisted those who supposedly had mastery of English to write banners that could be used on national occasions. For the public celebration

---

[100] Saddam Hussein, *Zabiba wa al-Malik* [Zabiba and the King], *riwaya li-katibiha* [a Novel by Its Author] (Baghdad: al-Bilad Publishing House, n.d.). The novel was probably published late 2000 or early 2001. The story is set in Tikrit, Saddam Hussein's hometown. Zabiba's husband is a cruel and unloving man who rapes her. Although on the surface a novel, the book was intended to be read as an allegory. Zabiba represents the Iraqi people, and the hero is Saddam Hussein. The vicious husband is the United States, and his rape of Zabiba represents the American invasion of Iraq. The book was later published in 2002 in Cairo by Dar 'Ashtar and translated into French and published in 2003 by Editions du Rocher. It was also made into a play. For a detailed analysis of the book, see Ofra Bengio, "Saddam Husayn's Novel of Fear," *Middle East Quarterly*, vol. 9, issue 1 (Winter 2002), pp. 9–18.

[101] Head of al-Karkh *tandhim* to Party Secretariat, "A Cultural Effort," September 17, 2001, *BRCC*, 011-2-6 (017–026).

[102] Head of Presidential *diwan* to Minister of Culture, "Order," March 2, 2002, *BRCC*, 011-1-2 (016).

[103] Party Secretariat to Presidential *diwan*, "Contract of Allegiance in Blood," November 27, 1992, *BRCC*, 005-1-2 (111). The allegiance document was from the Great Victory division.

of Saddam Hussein's birthday in April 2003, which obviously did not take place due to the invasion, banners had been prepared proclaiming, "Saddam = Our Choice," and "Lead on Saddam: Quitting is NO Option."[104] The party also documented and commended some citizens for initiatives they took during the presidential referendum. For example, on referendum day in 2002, the following voters were congratulated: a man and his wife who insisted on voting in their blood (according to one memo, in certain areas so many people wanted to vote with their blood that a first aid station was set up to deal with emergencies); many citizens who had held their weddings on referendum day; and a few citizens who were extremely ill or had lost a family member but still insisted on voting. In each case, the name of the individual and his or her address were noted and his or her local party informed.[105]

The extensive planning for the annual birthday ceremonies meant that the party had to call on all its members. The documents describe in detail how much time and effort were devoted by all branches throughout the country, either to prepare or to celebrate. There was clearly a competition between different cells and divisions as to which could shine most in the celebrations and attract the attention of their superiors, and the Party Secretariat actively encouraged branches to come up with new initiatives to engage the crowds and not to repeat the same speeches and lectures. Some branches began organizing chess matches and sporting activities, whereas others stayed with traditional arrangements such as lectures on the party's history or lessons about the president's achievements.[106] Indeed, the efforts of certain branches or members were highlighted by senior party officials, and notes of appreciation were sent to them and put on their files.[107] One of the tough tasks facing the party machine every year was the choice of presents for the leader; in 2002 this was relatively easy, as the party was galvanized into getting a 100 percent participation in the referendum. The importance of the birthday and preparations for it were summed up by one senior official, who said simply, "April festivities

[104] Secretary of the Victorious Leader Division to Headquarters of Party Secretariats, "Banners of Prayers for Iraq and Its Leader," February 25, 2003, *BRCC*, 004-5-7.

[105] Headquarters of Ba'quba Branch to Party Secretariat, "Initiatives and Special Cases during Referendum Day," October 17, 2002, *BRCC*, 002-2-4 (026–029).

[106] See, for example, a memo by the headquarters of the al-Ta'mim branch, "Central Program for the Celebrations of the Eternal April Festivities," April 11, 2002, *BRCC*, 009-2-2 (056); Babil Branch, *BRCC*, 009-2-2 (059).

[107] *Tandhimat* Baghdad to Members, "Thanks and Appreciation," May 11, 2002, *BRCC*, 003-2-6. The note was sent to seven male and two female members with copies to their files.

FIGURE 8. Mural of Saddam Hussein in Baghdad, 1998. © Shepard Sherbell/ Corbis.

are special for all Iraqis because the birth of the leader meant the birth of the nation."[108]

Whatever the occasion, the party was involved in erecting portraits and murals of the president everywhere. Sensitivities about how and which words should be used when discussing Saddam Hussein or his murals reached such an extent that the Party Secretariat issued an order to replace the word *'uziha* (displaced or withdrawn) by *raf'* or *kashf* (lift or unveil) in regard to removing the curtain from murals, as *'uziha* was not an appropriate term for the president, given its political connotation.[109] The party saw itself as the guardian of the cult; in one instance, the Secretariat wrote to the Ministry of Information complaining that Iraqi soap operas shown on television were not displaying pictures of Saddam Hussein in the background sets. The minister immediately concurred and sent a note to the head office of the television corporation to remedy this deficiency.[110]

---

[108] Secretary of al-Karkh Branch, "Birthday of Comrade the Struggling Leader (May God Protect Him and Bless Him)," April 13, 2002, *BRCC*, 009-2-2 (076).

[109] Party Secretariat to All Headquarters of Party Branches and the Military Bureau, "Executing an Order," October 25, 2002, *BRCC*, 020-1-5 (001).

[110] Party Secretariat to Minister of Information, January 27, 2002, Ministry of Information Dataset, 003-0186.

Nevertheless, domination by a one-party government is not enough to explain the rise of a powerful personality cult. To succeed in any country, a cult has to grow in a fertile political environment where the citizens accept it or at least acquiesce in it. In Iraq, the seeds of tyranny were cultivated long before Saddam Hussein came to power. In his analysis of why Qasim, then prime minister, began changing after the 1958 revolution and encouraged the idea of becoming the sole leader, Batatu quoted an Iraqi minister who worked with Qasim at that time: "Qasim got the taste of being the only man in the country. In other words, we built a dictator.... Our people are in truth builders of dictators."[111]

In Nazi Germany and the Soviet Union, the success of personality cults "relied on [the] active and willing participation of millions, who suspended their disbelief and endorsed and magnified the overblown personalities constructed by the authorities."[112] In Syria, Hafiz al-Asad resorted to "utilitarian and coercive strategies to some degree, since the failure to perform may result in economic hardships, or punishment, and performing well helps promote security and possibly enhances economic and political opportunities."[113]

In Iraq, the success of the personality cult relied on a combination of all these factors. True believers and cynical opportunists behave outwardly in the same way. Indeed, it is hard to explain what motivated the artist whose art was turned down or the enemy of the general who complained that his superior officer did not have Saddam Hussein's portrait on the wall. There is no doubt, however, that many party officials or government bureaucrats realized that the cult could be exploited for their own interests, because for many it led to promotion, as discussed in the next chapter. In all the countries in which dictators ruled, fear played a critical role; the story about the humiliation of the minister in front of his cabinet colleagues is just one small example of how terrified people at all levels were of Saddam Hussein's reactions and of his ruthless, efficient, and sinister party machine. Even so, not all Iraqis endorsed the cult or participated in spreading it; there was resistance, but it was mostly ineffective. Adulation of the leader was reinforced in every facet of life and was almost impossible to escape. As Wedeen explains, creating a cult was not the only way "to produce power for a regime," but its absence

---

[111] Batatu, *The Old Social Classes*, p. 836. Batatu quotes Jawad Hashim, Iraq's foreign minister between 1958 and 1963.
[112] Overy, *The Dictators*, p. 119.
[113] Wedeen, *Ambiguities of Domination*, p. 145.

"would probably mean that other disciplinary controls would be needed to sustain obedience."[114]

By the early 1970s, Iraq had suffered prolonged periods of political uncertainty, violence, and insufficient economic growth to meet the needs of the people. Saddam Hussein knew how to exploit this insecurity, and how to sustain it through a combination of rewards and punishments and by creating myths of salvation based on cultural and religious symbols. His control of power, total dictatorship, and cultivation of personality were in many ways similar to the practices of other dictators such as Hitler and Stalin. Richard Overy's succinct summary of the path to dictatorship is very applicable to Saddam Hussein:

> Both [Hitler and Stalin] were driven by remarkable determination to fulfil what they saw as a necessary place in history, but that remorseless will was married to an obsession with the tactical details of political struggle, an unnatural resentment towards anyone who compromised or obstructed their political ambitions, and an unprincipled pursuit of public esteem. This was a merciless combination. It is easy to deplore the weakness of the opposition that they confronted, but it is impossible not to recognize how difficult it was to find ways to obstruct or outmanoeuvre [sic] men who felt they carried the weight of history on their backs and were willing to use it, if they could, to crush the men or circumstances in their path.[115]

Indeed, Saddam's Hussein sense of his place in history was very high. He profoundly believed that the Iraqi people had waited for him for hundreds of years to lead them to prosperity; in a speech to the top leadership of the Ba'th Party in 1981, he asserted that

> the powers that imagine they can make the Iraqi people reject the [Ba'th] system that wants them to have a good living and happy life, these powers will fail, because in my opinion, and in my heart, the Iraqi people, [particularly] those who are faithful, have been searching, over eight hundred years,... for something like this. For someone to come from their offspring and from among them to lead them into a good life, into prosperity, to lead them to be empowered... and to lead them into having full sovereignty.[116]

---

[114] *Ibid.*, p. 153.
[115] Overy, *The Dictators*, p. 53.
[116] Audiotape of a meeting with the party's leadership, 1981 (no specific date), *CRRC*, SH-SHTP-A-000-571.

A final issue, indirect and hypothetical, needs to be addressed: who would have risen to power if Saddam Hussein had died naturally or been assassinated while the Ba'th regime still ruled? Most likely it would have been Qusay, but interestingly, Saddam Hussein told his American interrogator that he had never made a final decision and never promised Qusay the leadership. The reason he gave is instrumental for our understanding of his paranoia and controlling behavior. He said he had learned from what happened in Oman in 1970, when Sultan Qaboos assumed power in a coup directed against his father.[117] The lesson was to refuse to yield too much power to Qusay at an early stage and make himself vulnerable. It is very doubtful that Qusay, at least in his initial years in power, could have built a personality cult like his father's (it is noteworthy that in Syria today the cult for Bashar al-Asad is much less overwhelming than the one that existed for his father). Undoubtedly, Saddam Hussein was a unique phenomenon in contemporary Middle Eastern politics in how he skillfully developed, controlled, and maintained extreme power for such a long time.

[117] U.S. Department of Justice, "Saddam Hussein Talks to the FBI."

7

Control and Resistance

Fear played a major role in sustaining the Ba'th regime for more than three decades, but the party's control of the population was not based only on fear. An elaborate system of rewards and punishments provided a robust framework for the Ba'th Party's domination. Nevertheless, although society as a whole accepted the regime and its relentless demands, a significant number of people did not. Examining the different forms of resistance helps us to understand what "made one person a dissident or resistance fighter and another a collaborator."[1]

Fear and Violence

In Chapter 4, we saw that the Ba'th regime created many security agencies and an extensive security network. In so doing, it was strikingly similar to other tyrannies. Like Stalin, Saddam Hussein was always acutely aware that the people closest to him had the greatest ability to inflict harm: "Near the Tsar, near to death."[2] In his semiautobiographical book, *rijal wa madina*, Saddam Hussein wrote that "he who is not alert, even with a long stick, the dogs will covet him and bite him."[3] Both dictators knew that treachery could arise from within their inner circles, and they understood the need for special guards and organizations that they personally controlled, who would be more loyal than their closest associates but

---

[1] Timothy Garton Ash, "The Stasi on Our Minds," *New York Review of Books*, vol. 54, no. 9 (May 31, 2007).
[2] Quoted from Rigby, "Stalinism and the Mono-Organizational Society," p. 64.
[3] Saddam Hussein, *Rijal wa madina*, p. 24.

193

would remain carefully segregated from their inner circles. Both leaders were closely involved with their security organizations, received direct information from them, and intervened in their affairs. Based on remarks from close associates of Saddam Hussein, Aburish quotes him as saying that "when we take over the government I'll turn this country into a Stalinist state."[4] Both leaders kept changing the organizational structure of the security organs to meet their needs and used fear and violence to keep a firm grip on power.[5]

Given the numerous real and imaginary enemies that flourished under systems like the Baʿth, a central task of the leadership was to decide who its enemies were. Stalin's definition was engagingly simple: "The enemy is anyone the dictator declares to be an enemy."[6] Both Saddam Hussein and Stalin believed they had many enemies and maintained lengthy lists of categories of potential enemies, including spies, saboteurs, and traitors. Crimes could be committed in deed, word, or thought. The Baʿth regime believed in using force, whether it dealt with friends or foes inside Iraq or with its neighbors. As Saddam Hussein told one journalist, "No state could reach peace without utilizing force, and it is not important whether it [the state] uses it, but it is important to own it physically and psychologically."[7] Similarly, Stalin stated in 1937, "We will kill every enemy. If he is an Old Bolshevik, we will destroy his relatives, his family. We will destroy anyone without mercy who with his deeds or thoughts strikes a blow against the unity of the socialist state."[8] Elements that challenged or could have challenged the will of the leadership were brutally removed. *The enemy of the people* was a familiar phrase in Baʿthist as in Stalinist terminology.[9] All those systems shared a common characteristic: paranoia that enemies were lurking everywhere.

During the Baʿth regime's thirty-five-year rule, its enemies ranged from communists, Kurds, and Iranians or those of Iranian origin to members of the Daʿwa Party, prominent Shiʿi religious leaders, ex-Baʿthist Party members, and Baʿth members who at some point or another had planned or conspired to overthrow Saddam Hussein. The security organizations

---

[4] Aburish, *Saddam Hussein*, p. 67.
[5] Gregory, *Terror by Quota*, pp. 51–59.
[6] *Ibid.*, p. 138.
[7] *Al-Jumhuriyya*, April 15, 1975, p. 1. The interview of the then vice president was with the Egyptian magazine *Roz al-Yusuf*.
[8] Quoted in Gregory, *Terror by Quota*, p. 137.
[9] Carl J. Friedrich and Zbigniew K. Brzezinski, *Totalitarian Dictatorship and Autocracy*, paperback edn. (New York: Praeger, 1961), p. 140.

also had the responsibility of protecting the regime's buildings and installations, and with the spread of the Internet in the 1990s they needed to make sure that the communications and Internet systems were not being hacked into by foreign enemies of the state.[10]

Enemies could also be the "marginals of society." Saddam Hussein, like Stalin and Hitler before him, hounded beggars, drunkards, vagabonds, and prostitutes. Members of the SSO enforced a presidential order to arrest any beggar found in central Baghdad and in areas surrounding the presidential palace and the National Council. Beggars were thrown into prison for one month and faced more severe sentences if they were caught again. Members of the SSO were informed that they, too, could be liable for punishment if they were slack in executing those orders.[11] Incredulously, even dreaming of "subversive" action was punishable. Iraqis told me the story of a man who mentioned to some friends in a coffee shop that he dreamed of visiting a shrine in Iran and meeting a famous imam. Two days later he was arrested on the grounds that if he dreamed about it, he must have thought that way.

In both Iraq and similar dictatorships, the regimes "sought merely not to restrain or annihilate their actual enemies, but to destroy even the potential for resistance and dissent."[12] Fighting the enemy manifested itself in many ways: surveillance, instilling fear into the population, and using torture and violence to extract information or to destroy the alleged enemies of the people. Violence and surveillance are, of course, common features of authoritarian systems. By such methods, regimes like the Baʿth sent "a clear signal that those who oppose the authoritarian regime or government will be identified and dealt with harshly."[13] As discussed previously, the Baʿth regime gathered information on almost everyone it could and did not hesitate to use force against its real or alleged enemies. In his memoirs, Minister Jawad Hashim lists nineteen RCC decisions authorizing the death penalty for specific crimes. These included inciting

---

[10] Presidential *diwan* to All Government Offices, "Security of Computers," June 26, 2001, *BRCC*, 151-2-4 (143); Presidential *diwan* to All Government Offices, "Security of Documents and Official Letters," December 26, 1995, *BRCC*, 174-3-2 (085). Government and party bureaus began using the Internet on a wide scale by the end of the 1990s, and party members had to undergo Internet training. See Minister of Communications, "Internet Training for Party Branches," December 3, 2001, *BRCC*, 151-2-4 (175).

[11] SSO Directorate, "Commandments for Preventing the Phenomenon of Beggary and Mendacity," December 23, 2001, *BRCC*, B 008-2-5 (004–008).

[12] Paul Hollander (ed.), *From the Gulag to the Killing Fields: Personal Accounts of Political Violence and Repression in Communist States* (Wilmington, DE: ISI, 2006), p. l.

[13] O'Neil, *Essentials of Comparative Politics*, p. 130.

a revolution or military mutiny, spreading Masonic or Zionist ideas, setting up any organization intended to commit anti-regime activities, and so on.[14] In a meeting with high-ranking officials, Saddam Hussein was unambiguous about his willingness to use violence in dealing with his opponents, as expressed in the discussion with his chief of *al-amn al-'am*: "We are here to serve our nation, not to kill them. Yet, whoever needs to be slaughtered will be slaughtered. We will chop heads off to serve fifteen million [Iraqis]."[15]

Instilling fear, however, was the fundamental condition for success. Whether in the context of the Iraqi security services or Romania's Securitate, putting fear into the hearts of the population "was also reflected in the creation of paranoia about its ubiquity."[16] Fear was cultivated through sending a plethora of messages, to the party elite as well as to the population at large, that dissent would not be tolerated. These messages were graphically and powerfully conveyed through televised trials and public confessions, creating an atmosphere of insecurity throughout the country. The Iraqi people were keenly aware of the repercussions of resisting the regime, and countless stories of torture in the prisons controlled by the different security organizations reinforced this cruel and oppressive image. As in Stalinist Russia, Mao's China, or North Korea, family members were considered guilty by association and were used to inculcate fear or to break down the will of opponents or those considering opposing the regime. Families of "traitors" were severely punished either directly or indirectly (rejection from military colleges, universities, jobs, or even denial of requests to travel abroad). Numerous memoirs by Iraqis describe their lives in the hell of prisons and the brutal interrogations and torture.[17] Al-Hadidi, in writing about the struggles of Shi'i activists, recounts a graphic example of the capricious nature of arrests

---

[14] Hashim, *Mudhakkarat wazir 'Iraqi*, pp. 278–82.

[15] Audiotape of a meeting with the top leadership, May 1987, CRRC, SH-SHTP-A-000-958.

[16] Deletant, *Ceauşescu and the Securitate*, p. xiv.

[17] See, for example, Ahmad al-Habbubi, *Laylat al-harir fi qasr al-nihaya* [The Night of Screaming in the Palace of the End] (London: Dar al-Barraq, 1999); the Iraq Memory Foundation, *Shahadat 'Iraqiyya* [Iraqi Testimonies], Oral History Project, 2006 and 2007; Sha'ul Hakham Sasson, *Fi jahim Saddam Hussein: Thalathma'a wa khamsa wa sittun yawman fi qasr al-nihaya* [In the Hell of Saddam Hussein: 365 Days in the Palace of the End] (Jerusalem: Association for Jewish Academics from Iraq, 1999); Kanan Makiya, *Cruelty and Silence: War, Tyranny, Uprising and the Arab World*, paperback edn. (New York: W. W. Norton, 1994) has an illuminating chapter on the prison experiences of a young Iraqi man called Omar, pp. 105–34. For an engaging comparison with life in Iran's prisons, both under the Shah and under Ayatollah Khomeini, see Ervand

and violence by relating the story of a grave digger who was in charge of collecting corpses from *al-amn*: On March 17, 1980, *al-amn* officers brought some thirty-nine corpses to the grave digger – all university students and all with the first name of Sabah. It transpired that a suspect whom the security agents had caught was severely tortured. Just before his death, he mentioned that his senior in a Daʿwa Party cell was called Sabah and was a university student, but he gave no further details.[18] Unfortunately, the documents rarely mention the local police or the Iraqi prisons during the period under study.[19] "By making everyone afraid that they too can be arrested, the public can be controlled... with everyone fearing that they will be denounced by someone else."[20]

For fear to be truly ubiquitous, the Baʿth regime had to use force. Terrorizing the population had a random quality to it. Citizens never knew when they might be arrested, who would inform on them, and worst of all, whom they could trust. Force was a familiar weapon to Saddam Hussein. In *rijal wa madina* he recounted how at a young age he did not hesitate to brandish the gun his uncle had given him at other youngsters to teach them to respect him. Later in the book he describes how he pistol-whipped someone who did not want to move from his seat on a bus to allow Saddam and his friend to sit down.[21] It seems that Saddam Hussein was happy to write about his violent tendencies because he believed that this would command fear and respect. In 1973, the RCC proclaimed that experience had taught the party that "the only language capable of safeguarding our rights, our honor, our welfare, and our interests... is the language of force and of struggle."[22] Throughout the decades of Baʿth rule, elimination of the opposition went on all over the country to compel subservience to the regime. Indeed, the regime encouraged the culture of violence that permeated the society and led to bloody assaults against the Kurds, Shiʿis, communists, and many others.[23]

Abrahamian, *Tortured Confessions: Prisons and Public Recantations in Modern Iran* (Berkeley: University of California Press, 1999).

[18] Al-Hadidi, *Qabdhat al-huda*, p. 143 (footnote).

[19] For an interesting edited volume of the subject of police and prisons, see Laleh Khalili and Jillian Schwedler (eds.), *Policing and Prisons in the Middle East: Formations of Coercion* (London: Hurst, 2010).

[20] O'Neil, *Essentials of Comparative Politics*, p. 131.

[21] Saddam Hussein, *Rijal wa madina*, pp. 136, 163, and 235.

[22] Bengio, *Saddam's Word*, p. 147, quoting *al-Thawra*, April 20, 1973.

[23] There is a huge volume of secondary sources dealing with the implications of the Baʿth regime's brutal policy against its opponents. In addition to the two basic history texts

Opposition to the regime, however, did not have to be active or violent. Swearing at or cursing the regime and its leaders was taken very seriously by the security organizations and was punishable even if the offender was a party member. An RCC decree of 1986, called *qanun al-tahajjum wa-al-ihana* (the Law of Assault and Insult) announced:

> Anyone who insults the President of the Republic, his deputy, the Revolutionary Command Council, the Arab Ba'th Socialist Party, the National Assembly, or the government is subject to life imprisonment and confiscation of property, both transferable and non-transferable. If the insult took place in public with the intention of inciting public opinion against the authority, the punishment is death.[24]

In one case, a man asked to complete his party forms cursed the party in a moment of anger. A committee comprising representatives of *al-amn*, the *istikhbarat*, the SSO, and a party member representing the *tandhim* of Baghdad met to discuss the case and decided to refer it to a special court.[25] Cursing the president and his family was seen as a more serious offense than fulminating against the regime and was always dealt with more severely.[26] Interestingly, some of the offenders claimed in their defense that they were emotionally unstable or suffering from serious mental problems, an argument that was frequently accepted by the investigating committees, probably on the assumption that only unstable people would risk making offensive remarks against the president or the party.[27] It is remarkable how much time and energy was devoted to dealing with even the most casual swearing at the president; investigative committees made up of representatives from the four major security agencies met to discuss any such incident and to decide whether to refer it to a special court, and it was not coincidental that all files pertaining to assaulting the presidency were handled by the SSO.[28]

---

on Iraq – Tripp, *A History of Iraq*, and Marr, *The Modern History of Iraq* – one can find information in Ibrahim al-Marashi, "An Insight into the Mindset of Iraq's Security Apparatus," *Intelligence and National Security*, vol. 18, no. 3 (Autumn 2003), pp. 1–23. This article is based on some documents from *NIDS* and deals with the "enemies of the state" – the Iranians and Kurds.

[24] RCC, Decree no. 840, April 11, 1986, *CRRC*, SH-PDWN-D-000-590.

[25] SSO Directorate, "Offence," October 2, 1997, *BRCC*, B 004-1-5 (005–007).

[26] SSO Directorate, "Offence," March 3, 1999, *BRCC*, B 004-1-5 (159). In all those cases the curse was recorded verbatim to be used by the special courts in the trials of the accused.

[27] *BRCC*, B 004-1-5 contains many examples of this defense.

[28] *BRCC*, B 005-1-1. The file contains many incidents of *tahajjum* (assault) against the president and how they were dealt with by the investigative committees.

Show trials, public confessions, and announcements of death verdicts became a regular part of life in Iraq soon after the Ba'th seized power in July 1968 and were an essential ingredient in spreading fear. Because authoritarian regimes are characterized by mass slogans, the centrality of confessions in public trials and in the thousands of cases in which Iraqis were imprisoned or sent to the gallows helped to "educate" the public about "the enemies of the people."[29] The same pattern was seen in many communist regimes.[30] Show trials and confessions continued throughout the 1970s, culminating in an infamous party meeting in July 1979 just after Saddam Hussein became president. During this meeting, which was videotaped and distributed to all party members, he revealed a plot in which senior members of the party admitted participating, and later they were executed for "treason" against the country. A party member who attended this meeting told me that the experience left a profound and lasting impression on all members and caused a deep fear of challenging Saddam Hussein.[31] Similarly, Jawad Hashim portrays in his memoirs graphic details of this meeting and how Saddam Hussein, after sending his party associates to their death, lit a large Cuban cigar and used his handkerchief to wipe his tears.[32] Over the next twenty years, whenever a plot was uncovered, an announcement about the execution of the "traitors" was broadcast on radio and television.

Long before any modern tyrant came to power, the Chinese philosopher Han Fei Tzu prescribed to rulers such as Hitler, Stalin, and Saddam Hussein how to gain – and keep – absolute power in their countries:

[29] For a general discussion of trials and confessions, see Friedrich and Brzezinski, *Totalitarian Dictatorship and Autocracy*, pp. 150–65; Gregory, *Terror by Quota*, pp. 133–34. The first show trial began in late 1968 and culminated in the public hangings of fourteen Iraqis, including nine Jews, in January 1969. A public holiday was declared and tens of thousands of Iraqis were called on to participate in the public spectacle. See Makiya, *Republic of Fear*, pp. 46–58. Makiya was among the first to write in detail about the show trials and executions in Iraq.

[30] For a comparison with communist states, see Hollander, *From the Gulag*, pp. lxiv–lxix.

[31] Interview with Minister T., June 16, 2010. In summer 1979, the secretary general of the RCC was shown on television confessing that he was part of a conspiracy against Saddam Hussein organized with the support of the Ba'th regime in Syria. A couple of weeks later, on August 8, 1979, twenty-two senior party and army officers were hanged and dozens were sentenced to prison. See Mu'min 'Ali, *Sanawat al-jamr: Masirat al-haraka al-Islamiyya fi al-'Iraq, 1957–1986* [The Slow-Burning Years: The Journey of the Islamic Movement in Iraq, 1957–1986] (London: Dar al-Masirah, 1993), p. 181; Marr, *The Modern History of Iraq*, pp. 178–80; Makiya, *Republic of Fear*, pp. 70–72.

[32] Hashim, *Mudhakkarat wazir 'Iraqi*, pp. 342–46.

Hide your tracks, conceal your sources, so that your subordinates cannot trace the springs of your action.... Stick to your objectives and examine the results to see how they match; take hold of the handles of government carefully and grip them tightly. Destroy all hope, smash all intention of wresting them from you; allow no man to covet them.

If you do not guard the door, if you do not make fast the gate, then tigers will lurk there. If you are not cautious in your undertakings, if you do not hide their true aspect, then traitors will arise.... Smash their cliques, arrest their backers, shut the gate, deprive them of all hope and support, and the nation will be free of tigers.

The ruler of men must prune his trees from time to time and not let them grow too thick for, if they do, they will block his gate.... Dig them up from the roots, and then the trees cannot spread.... Search out the hearts of others, seize their power from them. The ruler himself should possess the power, wielding it like lightning or like thunder.[33]

The price that Saddam Hussein paid for continually pruning his generals and ministers was that they did not tell him the truth either during the Kuwait invasion and the subsequent uprising in 1991 or in the period preceding the 2003 invasion of Iraq. In a fascinating audiotape of a meeting that took place in 1992 to analyze the invasion and uprising, we hear someone by the name Hussein, most likely Hussein Kamil, tell the president:

Hussein: The truth, we have to tell you [talking about the military] they ran away, most of them except two or three.

President: The honorable people really show their true colors in these situations.

Hussein: We did not provide you with the true picture of the situation due to a variety of reasons, such as fear or someone might think we are going to lose. We had many considerations why we did not tell you the truth. Take Kuwait, the morale was at the lowest level, but when [the generals] came to talk to you, we could not reveal it to you or inform you with the truth about our situation.

President: Were they embarrassed or afraid?

Hussein: Both.[34]

---

33 Han Fei Tzu, *Basic Writings*, translated by Burton Watson (New York: Columbia University Press, 1964), pp. 18, 41–42. Han Fei Tzu (280–233 B.C.) was a prince of the ruling house of the state of Hun, and his handbook for the ruler was used by emperors of China.

34 Meeting of Saddam Hussein with Senior Associates, 1992 (n.d.), *CRRC*, SH-SHTP-D-000-614.

Whereas fear was fundamental to maintaining power, social control was both implicit and explicit.

Control

Printed forms were the essential method for documenting, administering, and controlling the Iraqi population during the decades of Baʿth rule, as was the case in other authoritarian regimes. In the Soviet Union, for example, the state used detailed questionnaires to categorize the population and to help identify "who should be stigmatized as a bourgeois class enemy . . . and who should be trusted and rewarded as proletarian ally."[35] Classifying Iraqi society was a building block for controlling it, and printed forms were created for every possible occasion, constructing a streamlined and relatively efficient system of monitoring citizens. Most were designed in the 1970s, and by the early 1980s the system was fully operational and could be adapted to changes and updated according to circumstances. For example, after the 1991 uprising, two questions were added: one about participation in the "period of betrayal" and the second related to connection to religious movements. Similarly, by the early 1990s, a central question for any party affiliate was whether he had participated in the battles of *qadisiyyat Saddam* (Iran–Iraq War) or *umm al-maʿarik* (the Mother of All Battles) in Kuwait, and if so, whether he had received any award or medal.[36]

The forms were onerous and covered almost every facet of life. For the party itself, as we saw in Chapter 2, documenting memberships, evaluations, and transfers from one grade to another in the hierarchy was a key element of the regime's bureaucratic apparatus. The original forms submitted on joining the party were the basis for each affiliate's membership, and subsequent forms either confirmed or updated his or her status, with answers referenced back to the original questionnaire. Members had to answer detailed socioeconomic questions such as identifying their "class origin," giving a short history of their salaries and total income, and explaining whether they had learned any "production method" or were used to manual labor or whether they were better at organizational or

---

[35] Sheila Fitzpatrick, "Ascribing Class: The Construction of Social Identity in Soviet Russia," *Journal of Modern History*, vol. 65, no. 4 (December 1993), p. 749.

[36] Party Secretariat, "Summary of a Party Membership File," October 2001, *BRCC*, 006-4-3 (002–022).

clerical jobs.[37] Remarkably, many of these questions are similar to ones that appeared on the personal forms for those applying to join the Stasi in East Germany.[38]

But the most important aspect of these forms was to gather as much information as possible about the candidate and his or her family, as we saw in Chapter 4, and whenever or wherever the candidate moved – upward or downward – his or her personal files were there as a reference point. Critical questions included whether the candidate had ever stopped working for the party, and if so, why, and whether at any point he or she had been affiliated with a different political organization or movement.[39] The party was also always interested in documenting whether the member had been disciplined at any point in his or her career and the reasons behind that. Similarly, all rewards, medals, and promotions to a new rank within the party were recorded in detail.[40] For those retired from active duty in the party and joining either *munadhammat al-munadhilin* or *al-sabirin*, a special form was created, as it was for those given party duties in the autonomous region in northern Iraq.[41] As members progressed up the ladder, the thickness of their files expanded correspondingly; in one instance, the file of a member who joined the party in 1966 and became a deputy minister in the Ministry of Transportation in the 1990s was more than a thousand pages, documenting every job, salary increase, sick leave, and all private and official trips outside the country.[42]

Non-Iraqi members had to disclose even more information. They were asked for details of any trip taken outside their country apart from visiting Iraq, the names and addresses of their Iraqi friends and of close associates in their own country, and what their contribution to *qadisiyyat Saddam* had been: did they donate blood, money, or jewelry? The form even asked what model of car the non-Iraqi member currently owned and requested

---

[37] See, for example, the form sent by the party's military bureau, the Branch of National Security, to all secretaries of the party, asking them to distribute copies during party meetings and to supervise the filling in of these forms, making sure that the information was correct, July 6, 1983, *NIDS*, KDP 017, Box 2182 (130021).

[38] For a full set of forms of one member applying to the Stasi in August 1985, see Ministerrat Der Deutschen Demokratischen Republik, Ministerium für Staatssicherheit, BSIU 090095–090110.

[39] *BRCC* contains an extensive number of files about forms for party members. See, for example, 002-5-2; 004-4-6; and B 001-4-1.

[40] See, for example, "Form for Basic Information for Active Members," February 23, 2001, *BRCC*, 122-5-6 (033).

[41] *BRCC*, 004-4-6; *BRCC*, 165-5-5 (087).

[42] *BRCC*, 005-1-6 spans the whole history of S., who occupied many important positions.

details about previous cars.[43] For both Iraqi and non-Iraqi members, an important question was whether they had recruited new members, as this was considered a litmus test of genuine commitment to the party.

Of course, if a citizen happened to be a party member, the data gathering was faster and probably more favorable. The forms facilitated decisions about job applicants, or those on the verge of promotion. Assessing the political leanings of the citizen was critical, and simple questions were asked to solicit direct answers. For example, in forms asking for information about average citizens, the questions about "political trends" were divided into four sections: from 1958 to 1963, from 1963 to *riddat tishrin* (the apostasy of November 1963),[44] from the November apostasy to the July 17 revolution of 1968, and from the July revolution to the current time. Answers to almost all questions were limited to one line, to enable the processing of the huge volume of information.[45] If a citizen was arrested or had a file containing evidence against him or her, the format changed radically. The questions were now directed to when these citizens joined the opponent organization or the Kurdish army, what training they received and what arms they carried, how they were arrested, and whether they had or would have the potential to return to *al-saff al-watani* (national alignment) and be a "good citizen."[46]

A special form was developed for criminals, with an emphasis on religion and nationality. Whereas the standard forms had only two such questions – nationality could be either Arab or Kurd and religion either Muslim or Christian – the form for criminals, however, gave nine choices of nationality: Arab, Kurd, Turkoman, Chaldean, Assyrian, Syriac, Armenian, Kurd Faili, and Other. Under religion, the form had five choices: Muslim, Christian, Yazidi, Sabean, and Other.[47] In almost none of the forms or documents did I find a question about being Sunni or Shiʿi.

---

[43] Party Secretariat to Bureau of *tandhim* Syria, "Form for Information," November 18, 1984, *BRCC*, 006-2-5. This file, in addition to 006-2-2, dealt with the activities of Baʿth members in Arab countries.

[44] *Riddat tishrin* relates to the events of November 1963, when the Baʿth Party was ousted from power nine months after its coup d'état against ʿAbdul Karim Qasim (see Chapter 1). The term *ridda* signified treachery and conspiracy against the party and was given this historical name as a reminder of what happened when a number of tribes conspired against Islam after the death of the Prophet and were returned to the fold by a war launched against them.

[45] See, for example, "Request for Information Form," July 27, 1987, *NIDS*, KDP 021, Box 2225 (280024–280025).

[46] *NIDS*, PUK 034, Box 190 (240033–240034), April 10, 1988; PUK 004, Box 15 (540003–540004), December 30, 1990.

[47] Form, "Subject of Crime," *NIDS*, PUK 011, Box 045 (070019).

There was one instance in which the term *ja'fari* was used in a form for an appointment as chief of staff for the cabinet,[48] whereas in other correspondence, the issue of non-Arab origin was emphasized, and the documents (rather than the questionnaires) dealt with *taba'iyya Iraniyya* (Iranian nationality or origin). Deserters, needless to say, had their own forms, focusing on the reasons for desertion, whether the deserter had joined any "terrorist" group, details of surrender if it took place, and information on his family.[49]

As discussed in Chapter 5, application forms for military colleges and police academies made up a major part of the entry process, and hundreds of files dealing with these applications are found in the documents. In fact, they were the second most extensive questionnaires after party membership forms. Whereas applicants to the party needed to list details about relatives up to the sixth level, those applying for military and police academies were required to provide information on only the third level of relatives: their political association, their affiliation and rank within the party or security forces, and the names of any martyred relatives or those who had received medals and awards from the regime. It is evident that applicants who were well connected received a "fit" decision at the bottom of their forms without too much background information.[50] One reason given for rejection was that the candidate was "independent," which led to further background checks about him and his wider family, and by the 1990s, many of the independent applicants who lacked a deep connection to the party or the military/security agencies either personally or through their families were turned down.[51] There was a very high demand to enter not just the military or police academies but also auxiliary colleges such as those for military medicine or military engineering,

---

[48] Presidential Secretary to Head of SSO, "Nomination," July 5, 1992, *BRCC*, B 001-2-2 (331). *Ja'fari* is part of the Shi'i sect named after Imam Ja'far al-Sadiq.

[49] "Form for Deserters from Military Service," 1987, *NIDS*, KDP 027, Box 2291 (150000; 150019).

[50] See, for example, one applicant's form to the Police College in 1992, *BRCC*, 007-1-1 (150).

[51] See, for example, the application to the Police College. Files were usually split between those accepted and those rejected. For accepted candidates, see *BRCC*, 007-2-4, and for rejected ones, see 007-2-5. One candidate had a family member in the navy and had lost two relatives in the war with Iran and during the invasion of Kuwait yet was rejected. The word "independent" was circled and written in red to explain his rejection. Another was rejected because "his aunt is married [and living] in Kuwait," which disqualified him from the college.

and time and again the files reveal extensive correspondence conveying subtle pressure to gain entrance to those institutions.[52]

The party also created forms for civil servants who were on the verge of being promoted, transferred to another government ministry, or sent abroad. Apart from their existing personal files, a special form evaluating employees and civil servants had to be signed by the relevant senior officials in the branch.[53]

The party processed other forms as well: for example, applications to receive a plot of land or forms related to the national campaign to increase fertility. Receiving land was an important incentive that the party wanted to control to reward its members and selected groups such as martyrs' families.[54] By the 1990s, there was such demand for land in Baghdad that those who had not lived in the city for a long period were excluded from entitlement. A campaign for increasing fertility was launched toward the end of the Iran–Iraq War to counter Iran's demographic advantage over Iraq. Each form related to this campaign carried the slogan, "Giving birth to a new child means killing *bu'ra* [a tumor] of the enemy's tumors established in the malicious brains of the Persians."[55] The questionnaire asked for the number of babies born alive between October 1988 and October 1989 and whether the mother suffered any miscarriages during that period.

Another means of control was expressed in the School Register, which was a separate section of the Ba'th documents. This register for high school students aged sixteen to eighteen brought together tables listing details about these teenagers: their background information, whether they had an association with the party, their families' histories in relation to the party (such as participation in the Iran–Iraq War, the invasion of Kuwait, or the uprising of 1991), whether their families had any martyrs, and their "potential" for recruitment.[56] It demonstrated the importance of young people and children in the philosophy of the Ba'th Party and the

---

[52] See applications to the Military Medical School in *BRCC*, 003-1-3; to the Military Engineering College in *BRCC*, 003-1-6 and 003-1-7.

[53] *BRCC*, 091-3-5 (240). See also the form for candidates to be sent abroad: *BRCC*, 021-2-1 (290).

[54] *BRCC*, B 003-1-3 (033).

[55] An example of the form can be found in *BRCC*, 013-1-1 (025) or 018-2-3 (495). *Bu'ra* is the epicenter of disease.

[56] See *BRCC*, School Registers Dataset. The Hoover Institute has roughly 160,000 documents of the School Register.

emphasis on their recruitment (see Chapter 8), as well as the extensive control exercised by the regime throughout all social classes.

Forms had to be filled in before receiving the awards or medals that paved the way to monetary and other rewards. They asked about privileges already received by the applicant, such as a parcel of land as a gift from the leader or a mortgage, or whether the applicant or his or her spouse had already purchased a piece of land through a government body. Two or three questions reiterated whether there had been any offense against the party or the state at any point.[57]

Bureaucratic documentation was only one means of control and co-optation. Co-opting "by title" was another way of drawing large numbers of citizens into the Ba'th sphere; receiving medals and insignia defined these people as Ba'thists, so that the pool of dependent and compliant citizens grew larger as time went by. A more devious form of control was making as many people as possible accomplices in acts of violence. For example, as the number of deserters grew significantly, Saddam Hussein decreed that other members of the Regional Command of the party besides himself could sign the death warrant. He also ordered that members of the investigative committees deciding the deserter's fate should participate in his execution, if this was what they had recommended. Thus, by the end of the 1990s, many party members had become accomplices, willingly or unwillingly, in the innumerable acts of violence committed against citizens. However, this practice was not new; Saddam Hussein first initiated it in the infamous Ba'th Party meeting of July 1979, when, as a test of loyalty for members, he demanded that they take part in executing their "traitor" comembers.

Medals and Rewards

Medals and rewards were the cornerstone of co-optation. Saddam Hussein's regime, like Stalin's, secured the loyalty of its elite "by offering economic rents, where rents are defined as goods, services, and other privileges below their value or even free of charge."[58] Indeed, the Ba'th managed to co-opt a large number of individuals by making it advantageous, both to those who became part of the organization and even to those who were outside it, to continue supporting the regime. This system co-opted a large segment of the population into dependence on rewards.

[57] Form for the Party Insignia dated 1999, *BRCC*, 002-2-3 (257).
[58] Gregory, *Terror by Quota*, p. 72.

Tens of thousands of Iraqis were the recipients of different medals, badges, certificates, and insignias during the Ba'th rule. All signified status and privileges, which in turn corresponded to whatever medals or badges the recipient already had, and the more medals a citizen or a member of the party accumulated, the higher the rewards.

Sharat al-hizb (the Party Insignia), for example, was a service award given to party members, mostly those who had spent many years – usually twenty-five or more – as active members.[59] The first batch of Party Insignia was distributed in 1984 and was strictly allocated to active members. Later, it was given to officers on active duty, to martyrs, to some prisoners of war and officers missing in action, and, from the 1990s, to tribal leaders.[60] Receiving insignia was by no means automatic; a number of subcommittees discussed and reviewed the files of each potential recipient and presented their findings to a committee of senior members and the president's secretary for party affairs for final approval.[61] The original plan was to give *sharat al-hizb* only to those with years of continuous, uninterrupted work for the party, thus excluding members who left the party after November 1963, when the Ba'th lost power. But because this raised many questions and created serious internal divisions, Saddam Hussein decided to extend eligibility to those with interrupted service who had served the country well during its war with Iran.[62]

Numerous badges were distributed, among them the *nawt al-shaja'a* (Badge of Bravery) and *nawt al-istihqaq al-'ali* (Badge of High Esteem). The former was given especially to military officers, prisoners of war, and the families of martyrs, and recipients received one, two, or three stripes. In granting this badge to an officer, a presidential decree declared that he had shown outstanding bravery in "liberating al-Fao region from the claws of racist magi Persians."[63] It was also given to party members with

---

[59] Many files dealt with *sharat al-hizb* (Party Insignia) and their allocations. See, for example, Party Secretariat, "*Sharat al-hizb* for Class of 1978–79," September 22, 2002, *BRCC*, 003-4-6; for the class of 1974–75 see *BRCC*, 006-5-6.

[60] *Tandhim* Baghdad to Party Secretariat, July 8, 2002, *BRCC*, 131-1-7 (001–002).

[61] Party Secretariat to President's Secretary for Party Affairs, "Party Insignia," April 21, 1987, *BRCC* 006-1-4. The file deals with the 1961 class of members, of whom there were 606, including 35 martyrs and 11 prisoners of war missing in action.

[62] Letter from Saddam Hussein to Members of Regional Command, July 28, 1988, *al-Mukhtarat*, vol. 7, pp. 127–31.

[63] Republican Decree no. 521, May 25, 1988. *Nawt al-shaja'a* law was promulgated in 1982. Here the word *magi* related to the low caste of Zoroastrian priests and had a derogatory connotation.

the rank of division member or higher.[64] On receiving three stripes, the individual was eligible for the highest privilege – possessing the card of "Friends of the President" (see the discussion later in this chapter). An equally prestigious badge was *wisam al-rafidain* (Medal of the Land of the Two Rivers), which was first awarded under the monarchy, predating the Ba'th regime.[65]

The Badge of High Esteem was mostly given posthumously to martyrs who lost their lives during the invasion of Kuwait. In 1993, for example, the RCC approved awarding this badge to 13,280 martyrs.[66] Later on, it was also given to hundreds of government employees and teachers.[67] Another insignia related to the First Gulf War, called *sharat umm al-ma'arik* (the Mother of All Battles Insignia), was given not only to selected soldiers who had fought in the war, but also to any *nasir* (supporter) who had been in the party for four consecutive years without interruption.[68] Many were deprived of its privileges because of disciplinary action taken against them for a wide variety of reasons, ranging from stealing military equipment to being absent without leave, as in the case of one *nasir* who left the north without approval from his branch.[69] After the Mother of All Battles, a special medal was conferred on very senior members and generals; 'Izzat Ibrahim, for instance, the deputy secretary of the party, received this medal for his contribution in deploying the civilian population during the war and the subsequent uprising.[70] It is notable that large numbers of these medals and badges were given years after the war, as they became the guaranteed route to receiving rewards and co-opting large numbers of citizens.

Certain certificates were distributed to soldiers, students, and party activists, and although they carried fewer privileges, they were important in demonstrating that the holder was a loyal citizen. One of these

---

[64] RCC, "Law no. 120," July 17, 1998, *BRCC*, 017-3-2 (010).

[65] *Rafidain* is another word for Iraq, the land of the two rivers – Tigris and Euphrates.

[66] Presidential Decree no. 157, August 16, 1993, *BRCC*, 017-3-2 (108). By the mid-1990s, thousands were given this insignia; see Presidential Decree no. 169, September 7, 1994, which awarded it to more than 10,000 individuals, *BRCC*, 168-2-2 (033).

[67] Republican Decree no. 70, n.d., *BRCC*, 018-5-7 (123). Hundreds of employees in the Ministries of Higher Education, Oil, Justice, and Culture and Information received this badge. See also Presidential Decree no. 73, March 30, 2000, *BRCC*, 017-5-6 (064). Another list containing hundreds of other civil servants from almost all ministries can be found in *BRCC*, 017-2-7 (81–85).

[68] RCC, "Law no. 120," *BRCC*, 017-3-2 (010).

[69] See, for example, *BRCC*, 002-2-3 (0187; 0190).

[70] RCC Resolution 339, September 2, 1991, *BRCC*, B 001-1-7 (007).

certificates was for participating in the special day for military training, another for volunteering in the Jerusalem Army, and an additional one for joining special paramilitary courses for students.[71]

The most coveted medal or identity card, however, was called "Identity Card of the Friends of Mr. President Leader Saddam Hussein, May God Protect him." The front of the card displayed the holder's personal details, but intriguingly, the back featured a headline called *imtiyazat* (privileges), followed by seven items (see Figure 9):

1. Five points to be added to the final average for him [the holder], and his wife and children, for applications to schools, academies, and universities during the [Iran–Iraq] war and for five years after its end.

2. Acceptance of [holder's] sons in military colleges and academies during the war and five after its end, without regard to their average [grades] or ages.

3. The honor of meeting his Excellency [the president] at least once a year.

4. Grants and holiday bonuses to be awarded on the same basis as those granted to employees of the presidential *diwan*.

5. Priority over other citizens in meetings [with government officials].

6. Each holder or his family to have a personal contact with the *diwan*'s secretary, the secretary of Q 'A Q M [initials for general headquarters of military forces], the [president's] senior special assistant, and the minister of defense's secretary, in arranging a meeting for any purpose.

7. An annual gift of two summer suits and two winter suits to be made available from the presidency of the republic.[72]

This card was originally launched during the war with Iran, and its holders benefited from these privileges then and for five subsequent years. However, as the country entered another war and had to contend with a popular uprising in 1991, the validity of the card kept being extended and continued to be effective until the regime fell in 2003. Cardholders whom I interviewed told me they carried this card at all times, as it not only opened doors but also in many ways kept them out of harm's way in their daily lives. In 1998, the RCC decided that disabled soldiers who

---

[71] For a collection of those certificates, see *BRCC*, 007-4-5 (191; 215–217).

[72] For a copy of some of those cards, see *BRCC*, 002-3-3 (0176), and another one dated from 1998 in *BRCC*, 005-4-6.

imtiyazat [Privileges]

1. Five points to be added to the final average for him [the holder], and his wife and children, for applications to schools, academies, and universities during the [Iran–Iraq] war and for five years after its end.

2. Acceptance of [holder's] sons in military colleges and academies during the war and five years after its end, without regard to their average [grades] or ages.

3. The honor of meeting his Excellency [the president] at least once a year.

4. Grants and holiday bonuses to be awarded on the same basis as those granted to employees of the presidential *diwan*.

5. Priority over other citizens in meetings [with government officials].

6. Each holder or his family to have a personal contact with the *diwan*'s secretary, the secretary of Q 'A Q M [initials for general headquarters of military forces], the [president's] senior special assistant, and the minister of defense's secretary, in arranging a meeting for any purpose.

7. An annual gift of two summer suits and two winter suits to be made available from the presidency of the republic.

FIGURE 9. a. "Friends of the President" Identity Card. b. Translation. Courtesy of the Iraq Memory Foundation.

had lost a limb or had a limb amputated during either the war against Iran or the invasion of Kuwait would be granted the status of "Friends of the President."[73] As the number of "Friends" expanded significantly in the 1990s, another more exclusive category was created, called *ittihad al-Saddamiyyin* (Union of Saddamists). This card was signed by ʿUday Hussein as the "supervisor" of the union.[74]

Understandably, most citizens sought these privileges to safeguard their families and futures. By the late 1990s, many personal files carried a table listing all the insignias, medals, and identity cards received, and the party compiled statistics comparing different recipients, not dissimilar from sports league tables.[75]

The rewards were not restricted to "Friends of the President" card-holders. They included a multitude of party members, government officials, members of the military forces and security organizations, and even informers. Like other authoritarian regimes, the Baʿth system was paternalistic to its supporters, offering them opportunities and rewards in every sphere. In one document, an incredibly comprehensive table categorized rewards to all officials from deputies of the president to employees in the different government offices. It listed senior officials, their position, and the size and frequency of the rewards. Also included in the table were tribal leaders, officers from all security organizations, command officers in the armed forces, officials in the large unions, professors at the Saddam Institute for the Study of the Qurʾan, and teachers and excelling students at "special schools" such as the high school in ʿOja, the birthplace of Saddam Hussein. The benefits ranged from about ID5 million (roughly $2,000) for the vice president to less than $40 for *mukhtars*. What is remarkable is the fact that all those bonuses were considered as "gifts" from Saddam Hussein and not the state, thus strengthening the notion that Saddam was Iraq.[76]

Important as the monetary rewards were, the most coveted benefit was obtaining a plot of land or an apartment, particularly in Baghdad

---

[73] RCC Resolution no. 28, April 14, 1998, *BRCC*, 018-4-3 (293).

[74] The identity card carried the slogan, "The Day of God is above Their Days," see *BRCC*, 010-1-3 (101–102).

[75] See, for example, tables of awards split between males and females in *BRCC*, 018-2-2 (018–020) and (046–076). In the party archives, tables for members indicated the reason for medals, such as winning in a local election of a branch or being promoted within the party.

[76] Table of Awards, no specific date but probably created in 2001 or 2002, *CRRC*, SH-MISC-143.

FIGURE 10. Saddam Hussein Dispensing Money, Baghdad, 2000. © -/INA/epa/ Corbis.

and other large cities, especially as property prices became prohibitive; eligibility for this benefit was a significant incentive to attain the party insignia. Even party members who were dislodged from Kurdistan after it became an autonomous state did not automatically receive a plot of land unless they had been awarded insignia or were "Friends of the President."[77] Receiving land was always considered a gift from Saddam Hussein; many members of the security forces and *jihaz al-amn al-khass* were entitled to an allocation of land per the president's instructions.[78] In addition, hundreds of employees in the presidential palaces and the

---

[77] Party Secretariat to Secretary of Autonomous Region, "Report," October 16, 2001, *BRCC*, 002-3-3 (001). According to this report, more than 2,300 party members were expatriated from the north and were living in rented homes in different parts of the country. For allocation of land to party members, see *BRCC*, 005-5-7.

[78] Headquarters of the Republican Guard, "Request for Names," July 9, 1993, *BRCC*, B 01-2-7 (022); (028). In 1993, 109 employees of the SSO received a plot of land (029–031).

intelligence agencies lived in subsidized apartments in Baghdad.[79] Non-Iraqi party members who moved to Iraq, especially those from Syria, were also entitled to apartments in Baghdad; many of these Syrians were appointed to government jobs as a reward for their activities outside Iraq.[80]

Jobs, financial bonuses, and pensions were all part of the rewards system, and without one of the medals or badges it was difficult to get into the compensation structure. Even pensions of civil servants of the same rank were not equal for holders and non-holders of party insignia; each year the presidential *diwan* announced "salary adjustments," which were then implemented by the Ministry of Finance.[81] Martyrs were probably the only recipients of remuneration who were not necessarily holders of insignias or medals. Obviously, families of martyrs who already held these badges of honor received higher compensation.[82] Many of the financial bonuses were distributed on special occasions such as the Prophet's birthday, the Greater Bairam (the second annual Muslim festival, seventy days after Ramadan), and, of course, Saddam Hussein's birthday.

Admission to institutions of higher education and military and police colleges was part of the overall reward structure. In many cases, academic appointments were dependent on political affiliation; in one memo the Party Secretariat decided to "appoint" five new professors with "good credentials" to positions in Suleimaniyya University to replace five teachers who were known to be communists.[83] As we have seen, acceptance at military and police colleges was regarded as one of the incentives for being a loyal party member, and those who were politically independent of this system found that their opportunities dwindled sharply as time went on. "Distinguished" employees in the presidential *diwan*, the SSO, the Party Secretariat, and the Republican Guard qualified to enter universities to

---

[79] Maintaining huge apartment blocks for these employees necessitated significant investments and resources. See issues related to the rents of SSO employees in *BRCC*, B 003-2-6; B 003-2-7; B 003-2-8.

[80] Party Secretariat to Syrian *tandhim*, "Owning Residential Apartments," February 11, 1985, *BRCC*, 006-2-2 (284). According to this memo, more than 200 apartments were allocated to Syrians, mostly in Baghdad and Ninewa. See also the appointment of a number of Syrians in the Ministry of Finance and Ministry of Youth in 1985, *BRCC*, 006-2-2 (368).

[81] Presidential *diwan* to Party Secretariat, "Adjustment of Salaries," November 11, 2000, *BRCC*, 005-4-1 (075–077).

[82] A significant number of files deal with compensation and reward issues spanning many years of the regime and different categories of recipients. See, for example, *BRCC*, 018-5-3 (099–100); *BRCC*, 005-4-6 (574); *NIDS*, PUK 064, Box 441.

[83] Party Secretariat, "Decision," August 9, 1976, *BRCC*, 003-1-1 (080).

study for their master's and PhD degrees with all expenses paid.[84] Even non-Iraqis in the party were exempt from meeting the stringent academic criteria for university admission.[85]

Cars were another form of compensation for loyal members. In 1990, Saddam Hussein ordered that the party's senior cadre could receive their first car as a "gift from the Comrade Leader." This included officers serving in the military bureau of the party or military men who had been affiliated with the party for a long time.[86] In many cases, recipients of the Badge of Bravery were also entitled to receive either a grant toward purchasing a car or a lump sum in lieu of a grant.[87]

Collaborators and informers received many rewards for their work, although there were no rules about entitlement for these special bonuses. Many, however, would receive cars or sums of money "for their participation in the war effort," particularly against Kurdish insurgents in the 1980s. Families of collaborators who had been killed in action also received monthly pensions and financial rewards.[88] For prospective businessmen, compensation came in the form of licenses to open new businesses or authorization for imports and exports.[89] Kurds who supported the regime and remained in the autonomous region of Kurdistan after 1991 received financial support and housing in compensation for the destruction of their properties.[90]

There is no doubt that that the Ba'th regime under Saddam Hussein was generous to its supporters. The carrot-and-stick system was clearly defined, and it was very obvious that those who sided with the regime would be looked after. In the 1990s, the impact of sanctions and the

---

[84] Presidential *diwan*, "Nomination of Those Distinguished for Higher Studies," January 21, 2003, *BRCC*, B 001-2-5 (002). For areas of specialization in graduate studies, see the same file (011).

[85] Party Secretariat, "Acceptances of Syrians," February 11, 1985, *BRCC*, 006-2-2 (466).

[86] Party Secretariat to Regional Command, "Rules of Allocation of Cars," January 21, 1990, *BRCC*, 003-3-7 (155). A memo in the same file, dated March 14, 1990, from the presidential *diwan* indicated that 1,762 individuals received a Toyota Corolla as a gift.

[87] Those who opted for a lump sum rather than a car had to get approval from the presidential *diwan*. Headquarters of National Defense, "Cars for the Badge of Bravery," July 28, 1989, *NIDS*, PUK 004, Box 251 (230003–230033).

[88] Suleimanniyya *amn*, December 19, 1980, *NIDS*, PUK 012, Box 50 (010010). For regulations about compensating collaborators who were injured or killed during their service to the regime, see *NIDS*, PUK 075, Box 563 (030002–030009).

[89] Suleimaniyya Province, "Request for Opening a Restaurant," October 30, 1989, *NIDS*, PUK 012, Box 50 (010093). See also other requests (010031; 010040).

[90] Party Secretariat to Presidential *diwan*, "Situation of Kurdish Comrades," April 28, 1994, *BRCC*, 100-3-5 (060–075).

economic deterioration played into the hands of Saddam Hussein, as the population became more dependent on the regime's carrots. The files contain hundreds of requests for land, financial compensation, and pension adjustments. Petitioners described their contribution to the regime and their personal involvement in "defending the ideals of the Ba'th." It seems that a sense of entitlement developed, such that even when people received their gifts, they felt that they deserved more, and many wrote complaining that others received larger gifts.[91] Numerous appeals were sent to the party and presidential *diwan* asking for coveted places in universities and military colleges.[92] In addition, many privileges extended beyond the lives of beneficiaries. For example, after the death of insignia holders and "Friends of the President," their spouses and children continued to receive financial allowances for a further five years.[93] Saddam Hussein complained to the RCC that he blamed himself for the fact that people had become so accustomed to receiving awards that these gifts had become truly corrupting, and he told his RCC that it made him nervous that every time he stopped by his guards (the Special Republican Guard) to enquire about their well-being, they would badger him with requests for rewards.[94]

As demand increased substantially for all privileges, setting priorities among those entitled became more and more complicated, because the number of university places, for instance, was not unlimited. When the deputy secretary general of the party in charge of military courses responded to a memo about the difficulties of prioritization, he recommended the following: "Elect the best; prefer the members over the

[91] See, for example, a letter from an officer of the Republican Guard asking for a piece of land like his other colleagues, August 7, 1993, *BRCC*, B 001-2-7 (009); a letter from a member in a branch in Baghdad saying that although he had received *ikramiyya* (a bonus) in the past on religious holidays, it had stopped, and he believed that he was qualified to continue getting it, June 7, 2001, *BRCC*, 017-1-7 (094). See also *BRCC*, 021-1-2 (001–010).

[92] For example, see the letter of a father whose son was rejected from the police academy appealing against this decision, November 15, 1994, *BRCC*, 021-1-4 (080). Another case of entitlement can be found in a letter from pensioners and members of an *al-munadhilin* organization who wanted to be considered equal in terms of privileges to those still serving in the military, October 30, 1999, *BRCC*, 017-2-7 (221).

[93] Presidential *diwan*, "Allowances for Religious and National Occasions after Death," August 3, 1999, *BRCC*, 020-1-3 (042). Already in 1986, an amendment to the law dictated that the wives and children of holders of medals and insignias would continue to benefit from the rewards of those medals. See *al-waqa'i' al-'Iraqiyya*, no. 3128, December 15, 1986.

[94] Audiotape of a meeting of the RCC, no specific date but most likely late 1990s, *CRRC*, SH-SHTP-A-000-874.

supporters [of the party]; [give priority to] sons of martyrs and sons of friends of Mr. President Leader; [give preference to] the son of the village over the son of a district over the son of a province, and so on."[95] One of the solutions to prioritization, debated as early as 1980, advocated compensating employees directly without promoting them within the party's ranks, as this triggered further demands for privileges.[96] By the late 1990s the system of allocating rewards had become more sophisticated; forms detailing different categories of activities and social status were created, as well as a table for recording the points accumulated by a potential recipient. The system took into account marital and family status, education, service to the party and the army, medals and badges acquired, gifts already obtained, continuing contribution to the regime, participation in the Popular Army and *yawm al-nakhwa*, and so on.[97]

Whereas the rewards were enticing and led to thousands of citizens becoming deeply vested in the system and compliant with its rules, for anyone who opposed the regime the punishments were equally extensive.

Punishments

To retain power, the Ba'th leadership, like its counterparts elsewhere, needed to drive home the message that its power was irreversible and any kind of opposition would not be tolerated.[98] Punishment was inflicted on all citizens, whether or not they were party members, for a variety of reasons and was ruthlessly applied across all regions of Iraq and all classes of society. In northern Iraq, harsh measures were taken before and after the Kurds gained autonomous status in 1991. Many Kurdish fighters arrested in the 1970s were sentenced to death[99] or "liquidated" at the

---

[95] These comments were handwritten on the margins of a memo from the head of military courses to the deputy secretary general, December 2, 1992, *BRCC*, 017-4-2 (004). The memo detailed the number of applicants, those immediately accepted, and those who were rejected because of "discouraging" information about their backgrounds, leaving a large number of applications undecided, in view of the demand (002).

[96] See Party Secretariat to secretary general regarding the decision of the Regional Command taken on March 25, 1979, to promote party members by one notch, given their contributions, *BRCC*, n.d., 003-1-1.

[97] The form had points and subpoints in nine different categories, *BRCC*, 019-1-3 (275–278).

[98] For rewards and punishments in the Soviet Union under Stalin, see Rigby, "Stalinism and the Mono-Organizational Society," pp. 70–73.

[99] See approval for hanging convicts, June 17, 1979, *NIDS*, UPK 001, Box 3002 (040008).

hands of *al-mafariz al-khassa* (special squads) – groups of Kurdish collaborators operating under the aegis of the Iraqi intelligence services.[100] These squads were themselves heavily disciplined if they did not carry out orders or proved to be "not beneficial" to the Iraqi officers.[101]

One of the extreme punishments meted out to people in the north was destruction of their homes, eviction of their families, and sometimes banishment from the region. In 1988, 'Ali Hasan al-Majid, known as "Chemical 'Ali" for his role in the *anfal* campaign against the Halabja Kurds, ordered that houses of the Shabak minority, who had changed their nationality from Arab to Kurdish, should be destroyed and the residents evicted to special residential locations in Arbil without any compensation.[102] Eviction became a weapon that the regime used forcefully against all supporters of the Kurdish resistance, and many families' pleas to the authorities to spare their homes went unanswered.[103] Arabization of the north was another punitive measure taken against the population and the Kurdish movement, leading to the deportation of many Kurdish families from the north to Baghdad or to other provinces in central and southern Iraq. Many Kurds were also prevented from leaving the country to study or receive medical treatment on the grounds that they constituted a security risk.[104] It seems that no day passed without massive arrests; in the relatively small town of Dokan in northern Iraq, arrest warrants were issued for more than a hundred people in the space of one week in December 1980.[105] Evictions (*tarhil*) were not only used against the Kurds; after the 1991 uprising, the authorities began to deport many families from the south who had supported the uprising to certain areas around Baghdad and its suburbs. By 1994, it was decided to expel all of them from the Baghdad region and force them to return to their provinces without any compensation.[106]

[100] Memo from *al-amn* in Shaqlawa about liquidating an opponent, October 23, 1987, *NIDS*, PUK 005, Box 17 (1930010).

[101] Directorate of *al-amn*, "Administrative Decree," March 23, 1989, *NIDS*, PUK 031, Box 152 (100004).

[102] Head of *amn* Arbil to All Headquarters of *al-amn*, August 31, 1988, *NIDS*, PUK 011, Box 045 (050019).

[103] See examples of orders for eviction and correspondence described in *NIDS*, PUK 008, Box 032 (190085).

[104] Director of *al-amn*, Suleimaniyya to General Headquarters of *al-amn*, January 16, 1979, *NIDS*, PUK 007, Box 024.

[105] Officer of Dokan *amn* to All Security Centers, "Arrests," December 9, 10, and 11, 1980, *NIDS*, PUK 005, Box 016 (120069–120071).

[106] Special committees comprising representatives of the party, the intelligence services, and the local police were given the task of uprooting those families for the second time

In the Soviet Union of Lenin and Stalin, punishing family members
was routine, as it was feared "that class enemies could infect others."[107]
In Iraq, the Ba'th, unlike previous regimes, regarded the families of opponents as legitimate targets for punishment. In 1979, less than a month
after Saddam Hussein became president, a party document detailed measures to be taken against different members of families, corresponding
to the seriousness of the "crime" of resisting the regime. The memo
outlined the different penalties to be applied to the opponents' wives
and children (male and female), to siblings of those punished (both
male and female), and to their nephews. These penalties included barring family members from joining the party and expelling those already
in it; rejecting their applications to any military or police college; preventing them from receiving scholarships to study abroad; limiting their
choice of universities; and finally, barring them from employment in Iraqi
embassies abroad and in many government offices.[108] In addition, families were used to exert influence over suspects and "saboteurs" during and after their interrogations, and many were displaced from their
homes as a punishment for joining one of the antigovernment Kurdish
Parties.[109] Whereas in the Soviet Union, "traitors of the motherland"
were imprisoned and their properties confiscated, in Iraq, and based
on Saddam Hussein's orders, it was decided that "terrorists" had to
divorce their spouses, and the parents of anyone found participating in
an assassination attempt against a member of the party or of a security
organization had their assets sequestered and were evicted from their
homes.[110]

From its earliest days, the regime did not hesitate to use these methods to eradicate resistance. In northern Iraq, when a "terrorist" was
arrested or killed, a diagram of his family members was put together,

and returning them to their region, irrespective of the fact that many of their homes
were destroyed during the events of 1991. See *BRCC*, 003-3-4 (027–033). See also
Presidential *diwan* to Ministry of Interior, "Expatriated Kurds," September 5, 1994,
BRCC, 003-3-4 (013–014). For the party's committees of *tarhil* (eviction), see Memo
to Party Secretariat, August 3, 1994, *BRCC*, 003-3-4 (007–008), and Special Form for
Evicted Families (017).

[107] Gregory, *Terror by Quota*, p. 124.
[108] Party Secretariat to All Headquarters, "Decision," August 13, 1979, *BRCC*, 003-1-1
(290–292).
[109] See, for example, *NIDS*, PUK 013, Box 55; PUK 002, Box 005; PUK 001, Box 001;
and PUK 030, Box 147.
[110] Party Secretariat to Headquarters of Suleimaniyya Branch, "Meeting," *NIDS*, PUK
035, Box 200 (370006).

and evicting them was one of many disciplinary measures.[111] Arresting family members or dismissing them from their jobs was an effective way of putting pressure on the regime's enemies, whether or not they were already arrested.[112] Following a discussion in the RCC in 1983, it was decided to expel from all government ministries the relatives of those convicted and sentenced to death, whereas the relatives of those convicted but not sentenced to death were to be moved from sensitive departments in the public sector to other jobs, or forced to retire altogether. All school teachers were considered part of the civil service.[113]

The party leadership drew up a comprehensive list of punishments for activities concerning the party or the country, although it became increasingly difficult to differentiate between the two. For instance, influencing the population against the reputation of the party, creating "hurdles in the face of the revolutionary programs," or maliciously failing to fulfill the party's commands and ideology all met with severe punishment.[114] What is notable is the lack of detail in these memos, thus opening up broader interpretations of what constituted a "hurdle" or a slackening in fulfilling one's duties to the party, and permitting wider and perhaps harsher penalties. As we saw in Chapter 2, disciplining party members was an important Ba'th priority irrespective of the member's status. The files include hundreds of cases of administrative punishments against party members and various government officials for actions such as not checking the accuracy of forms submitted to the branches, not participating in party meetings or campaigns, and a multitude of other activities deemed unacceptable.[115] However, some of those within the party who were

---

[111] Shaqlawa *amn*, "Report," October 22, 1986, *NIDS*, PUK 041, Box 258; PUK 005, Box 017 (1930059; 1930061).

[112] Suleimaniyya *amn*, July 30, 1985, *NIDS*, PUK 009, Box 039 (190015–190017). A list of forty-one spouses of deserters and opponents of the regime who worked as teachers was collated in order to begin dismissing them from their jobs.

[113] Head of Administration to Party Secretariat, September 12, 1983, *BRCC*, 021-1-5 (684–685).

[114] Party Secretariat to All Party Headquarters, "Decision," March 23, 1978, *BRCC*, 003-1-1 (420–428). The memo contains a table of different levels of punishment for party members for any transgression. The harshest administrative proceeding was expulsion from the party, which obviously had severe ramifications for the individual and his family.

[115] Among those files, see the memo relating to changing *mukhtars*, December 13, 1994, *BRCC*, 005-4-2 (011); administrative procedures in *NIDS*, KDP 020, Box 2215; *BRCC*, B 001-3-6 (006). For an interesting account of the punishment of a military man and a medical doctor, both Ba'thists, see Steavenson, *The Weight of a Mustard Seed*, pp. 47–57.

punished managed later on to redeem themselves and achieve higher and more important jobs; for example, in 1978 Muhammad Sa'id al-Sahhaf was disciplined by having his membership frozen for one year, due to his failure to strengthen the reception of Voice of Iraq Radio so that it could be heard in the Arab world.[116] Later on, however, he rose to become the minister of culture and was the voice of the regime before and during the invasion of Iraq in 2003. In fact, Saddam Hussein used this strategy of banishing party members and generals and stripping them of their bene-fits, only to readmit them after their punishment, reemploy them, or even appoint them to higher positions, as a means of control.

The regime's carrot-and-stick policy was best exemplified in accep-tances to military and police academies; on one hand, offering a place in these institutions was an important reward for the regime's friends, whereas on the other, rejection was a stinging punishment for its foes. This method of rod and reward remained a core policy of the regime to the very end. Allowing or disallowing students and individuals to travel abroad was a further example of the dual policy practiced toward the regime's loyalists and opponents.[117] Another area of punishment and reward was jobs: friends of the regime were rewarded with the best available, whereas its enemies were expelled, demoted, or blocked from progressing to higher and better jobs or locations.[118]

Other severe punishments were imposed on deserters from military service, particularly from the 1980s onward (see Chapter 5). The stick was not only applied to deserters or those actively hostile to the regime; senior officials who did not cooperate had great difficulty getting promoted or transferred to better locations. A memo from the Directorate of *al-amn* about heads of departments in government ministries and large utilities in northern Iraq contained recommendations to block the promotions of, demote, or even fire a number of senior officials for refusing to cooperate with the security agencies; for having a relative who was associated with the two main Kurdish parties or who had fled the country; or for showing sympathy with the Kurdish movement.[119]

---

[116] Party Secretariat to Regional Command, "Party Punishment," February 15, 1979, *BRCC*, 003-1-1 (273).

[117] For a list of senior government officials who were banned from traveling for a period of two years, see RCC to Ministry of Interior, "Banning Travel," January 12, 1982, *BRCC*, 003-3-2 (175).

[118] See, for example, appointing teachers, demoting them, and offering replacements for expelled teachers, in *BRCC*, 001-5-1.

[119] *Al-amn* Directorate, "List of Heads of Departments and Security Information," 1990 (no specific date), *NIDS*, PUK 030, Box 149 (750008–750011).

The regime moved swiftly to withdraw all medals and rewards from individuals whom they felt were no longer sufficiently loyal or compliant. For instance, a law promulgated by the RCC in the mid-1990s stated that that the presidential *diwan* had the right to withdraw all medals for any "honor crimes" committed, such as rape, without providing further details.[120] Similarly, the president had the authority to remove anyone from party membership, including the recipients of rewards and benefits. Perhaps not surprisingly, many of these punishments seem to have been arbitrary or to have emanated simply from irritating a senior official. For instance, one man was arrested and had his car confiscated for a month while he was driving in Tikrit on the president's orders, but no details of his offense were given.[121] Once again, this lack of clarity and ambivalence created fear and wariness of resisting the regime.

Resistance

Resisting tyranny under any regime is inevitably fraught with danger. Opposition manifests itself in many ways; as Václav Havel put it, everything the system "feels threatened by . . . in fact means everything it is threatened by."[122] Many Iraqis did not accept the Ba'th regime; for some, "resistance is made up primarily of mundane transgressions that do not aim to overthrow the existing order."[123] For others, resistance was more active, whether by deserting from the army, failing to comply with party orders, refusing to denounce colleagues or family members, and for some officials, rejecting memos from *al-amn* demanding information about employees – all actions that carried severe retribution ranging from imprisonment to amputation and culminating in death. A minority engaged in a more organized resistance, through political parties such as the Da'wa Party or the Communist Party, participating in the 1991 uprising, or joining the Kurdish political parties.[124] If these individuals were caught, there was no mercy for either them or their extended families; they suffered for a long time afterward.

Even if we assume that the authorities arrested many innocents and a large number of people were falsely accused of subversive activities,

---

[120] RCC, "Decision," February 28, 1996, *BRCC*, 004-5-4 (020–021).
[121] Driver A. to Head of SSO, "Request," March 29, 1994, *BRCC*, B 001-3-1 (051).
[122] Havel, *The Power of the Powerless*, p. 54.
[123] Wedeen, *Ambiguities of Domination*, p. 87.
[124] For a general and theoretical discussion of the different forms of defiance, see James C. Scott, *Domination and the Arts of Resistance: Hidden Transcripts* (New Haven, CT: Yale University Press, 1990).

the fact remains that the number of those who were involved in combating the regime, in one way or another, was still very considerable. However, one should not confuse the resistance in Iraq with many of the civil resistance movements that took place worldwide after the end of the Second World War. Circumstances in Iraq were very different from those in Eastern Europe before the fall of communism, or in other comparable authoritarian states. Although many of these governments were equally ruthless, like Chile's under Pinochet, the consequences in Iraq for participants in a civil resistance would have been far reaching, as witnessed in the 1991 uprising in southern Iraq, when tanks and helicopters were used to defeat a local, mostly civilian struggle.[125] Nevertheless, it is important to underline that not all Iraqis were compliant or actively participated in the Ba'th system, and many people who obeyed its myriad oppressive rules did not privately endorse them.[126] It is impossible to quantify, for example, how many people joined the Ba'th Party – or indeed the Nazi Party under Hitler or the Communist Party under Stalin – out of fear or ambition rather than a commitment to its ideologies.[127]

In any dictatorship, the most effective opposition is to assassinate the dictator. As we have seen, numerous such attempts were made on Saddam Hussein, some of them documented, others not, and a few were fabricated to get rid of opponents. Al-Tikriti details in his book seven specific assassination attempts by the end of the 1970s,[128] and there were at least half a dozen more in the 1980s and 1990s by army officers, members of the Da'wa Party, and others.[129]

Apart from the Kurdish insurgency that absorbed the regime's attention for many years, the two other political groups that the Ba'th was determined to uproot were the Communist and Da'wa Parties. The Communist Party was seen as a major threat, particularly during the 1970s and early 1980s, because Saddam Hussein was worried that the Ba'th Party lacked its intellectual depth. For most of the period discussed in

---

[125] For a general overview of civil resistance, see Adam Roberts and Timothy Garton Ash (eds.), *Civil Resistance and Power Politics: The Experience of Non-Violent Action from Gandhi to the Present* (Oxford University Press, 2009).

[126] Wedeen rightly differentiates between compliance and obedience, *ibid.*, p. 174 (footnote 17).

[127] Overy quotes one teacher who joined the Nazi Party saying that not taking membership would be "a false show of heroism, which would be only a form of suicide." See Overy, *The Dictators*, p. 304.

[128] Al-Tikriti, *Muhawalat ightiyal al-Ra'is*.

[129] For a comparison of assassination attempts against Hitler and Stalin, see Overy, *The Dictators*, pp. 326–30.

this book, the regime hounded Communist Party members and their families and worried about communist infiltration of the military.[130] A more serious challenge, beginning in the 1980s and continuing until the fall of the regime, came from the Da'wa Party and other religious groups. Both should be seen in the context of the rise of the Ayatollah Khomeini and the eight-year war against Iran.

Although Saddam Hussein countered the religious parties' influence with his faith campaign, the regime still saw these groups as a real danger to its power base and popularity. The documents give a remarkable insight into this obsession with the activities of religious groups, in spite of the faith campaign, and into the suspicion with which the regime regarded any person with religious beliefs. Security agencies were instructed to prevent "the spread of pictures of prophets and imams," and to inform printing houses that they were forbidden to produce such pictures.[131] The political departments of *al-amn* monitored mosques and Friday sermons and periodically wrote reports on both large and small religious movements in Iraq, and on others abroad that might influence Iraqis.[132] Already in the late 1970s, the Ba'th regime began arresting Shi'i clerics, and many prominent leaders were put to death, culminating in the execution of Ayatollah Muhammad Baqir al-Sadr and his sister, Bint al-Huda, in April 1980.[133]

Religious ceremonies and special religious processions during Muharram, the first month of the Islamic calendar, particularly in southern Iraq, were mostly prohibited by the security organizations because they attracted large gatherings that could not be easily controlled or infiltrated.[134] On occasion, when the trials of Shi'i activists were known about, small crowds would gather outside to lend support, and the burial of these activists, once their bodies were delivered to their families, was the most serious source of disorder. Except in extraordinary circumstances, the authorities did not prevent activists' families from burying their loved ones, but they were concerned about funerals, realizing that

---

[130] *Al-amn*, "Study: The Iraqi Communist Party and the Military Forces," November 11, 1987, *NIDS*, PUK 017, Box 071 (310013–310021). For the alliance of the Communist Party with the Ba'th, which was followed by an onslaught on the communists by the regime, see Ismael, *The Rise and the Fall*, pp. 166–203.

[131] Presidential *diwan* to *al-amn* Headquarters, November 26, 1988. The memo was distributed to all local *amn* directorates. *NIDS*, PUK 011, Box 045 (050027).

[132] *Ibid.*, (050030; 050054–050056; 050088).

[133] For more details, see Davis, *Memories of State*, pp. 190–91.

[134] Party Secretariat to Party Secretaries, "Religious Practices," March 29, 1997, *BRCC*, 003-2-6 (350–351). See more details in the next chapter.

large processions could develop, especially if the coffin was being taken to Karbala. Time and again the authorities forbade these processions, resulting in many clashes. Similarly, the period of grief that followed the burial was seen as a significant threat, as many would come to console the bereaved families.[135] But it would be wrong to assume that the regime felt threatened only by Shi'ism; in reality, it was worried about any religious activity. A case in point was Wahhabism, which was seen as potentially dangerous, and the party and security organizations were constantly on the lookout for the movement's supporters.[136]

Opponents of the regime faced constant harassment, and the Ba'th leadership repeatedly demanded "increasing the pressure to augment their discomfort wherever they were to be found," which included arrests, ambushes, and assassinations.[137] Violence by the regime's apparatus and the fear that it generated throughout society did not make it easy for any opposition group to develop. Furthermore, any "clandestine organization in a country under the heel of dictatorship is continually engaged in blind and desperate struggle against police infiltration."[138] Political resistance is not necessarily active; in Iraq, thousands were arrested and tortured for sheltering activists and insurgents, in both the south and the north. The security organizations made an example of anyone caught giving help to or sheltering a political opponent or a deserter, and the files provide multiple examples of this.[139]

---

[135] Al-Hadidi, *Qabdhat al-huda*, pp. 134–35. The book contains many details about the arrests, interrogations, and executions of well-known Shi'i activists. In al-Hadidi's opinion there were four milestones in the Shi'i struggle against the Ba'th regime: the execution of five prominent activists, including Hussein Jalukhan, who is the subject of al-Hadidi's book; Shi'i riots in Karbala and Najaf in 1977; the large demonstrations and riots in 1979; and finally the uprising of 1991. See p. 41. For a general overview, see 'Ali, *Sanawat al-jamr*, which deals with the history of the Islamic movement in Iraq.

[136] Party Secretariat to All Headquarters, "Surveillance of Wahhabists and a Study of Wahhabism," February 28, 2002, BRCC, 003-2-6 (357; 616–618). A party memo compared the danger of Wahhabism to that of the Zionist and Masonic movements, concluding that it should be fought as fiercely. See Party Secretariat to *tandhimat* Secretaries, September 5, 2001, BRCC, 003-2-6 (528).

[137] Party Secretariat to Under-Secretary of the Party, "Security Operations," August 5, 1995, BRCC, 008-4-6 (113–119). See also an interesting list of security activities for just one month (September 1997) in one area (provinces of Misan and Wasit), BRCC, 008-4-6 (284).

[138] Silone, *Bread and Wine*, p. 260.

[139] One example is the minutes of a meeting in Suleimaniyya on January 9, 1986, to discuss the president's orders about combating resistance to the regime, NIDS, PUK 035, Box 200 (370006).

Desertion from military service was undoubtedly an act of resistance, directly or indirectly. All deserters realized the severe repercussions if they were caught, and that their families would also suffer. Yet, hundreds of young men absconded before or during their military service, and although it is almost impossible to know their motives, the fact remains that they refused to obey orders and risked their lives and those of their families.[140]

Similarly, those who refrained from participating in the party's activities, or members of the security organizations who just stopped showing up to work, knew the ramifications of their actions but still chose to do it.[141] Fleeing the country rather than submitting to the regime's iron grip was not only done by soldiers; many Iraqi intellectuals and artists fled to avoid being forced to engage in the Ba'th-dominated culture. Once in exile, these intellectuals produced important works about their homeland. Among those who stayed in Iraq, a few chose to express their resistance in very subtle ways without invoking the wrath of the regime.[142]

Other forms of resistance were shown by the families of those arrested or convicted who persevered in writing letters pleading the cause of their relatives, and by those individuals who took risks in protesting about the abuses of the system or the behavior of senior officials.[143] Another subversive activity was spreading rumors and jokes about the regime, both of which were dealt with severely.[144]

---

[140] The deserters came from all socioeconomic groups: one list indicates that a cleaner, a teacher, and a mid-ranking government official all fled the military service in 1988, *NIDS*, PUK 091, Box 710 (070044; 070054).

[141] The files contain numerous examples of party members who were expelled for refusing to fulfill their duties or for "not being loyal to the party and the Revolution." See, for example, Party Secretariat to Baghdad *tandhim*, September 23, 1984, *BRCC*, 006-2-2 (321). Other cases are discussed in Chapter 2. For SSO officials not showing up to work or resigning, see Administrative and Financial Section to Head of Security Section, SSO, November 18, 2001, *BRCC*, B 001-5-6 (018–019). Other examples within the SSO are discussed in Chapter 4.

[142] For a comprehensive discussion of how Iraqi intellectuals responded to the Ba'th regime, see Davis, *Memories of State*, pp. 200–26. See also Fatima Mohsen, "Culture Totalitarianism," in Fran Hazelton (ed.), *Iraq since the Gulf War: Prospects for Democracy* (London: Zed, 1994), pp. 13–19.

[143] The files again provide ample examples of those letters and protests. See one example of letters written by a wife about her arrested husband to the Ministry of Interior, *al-amn*, and the SSO. After five months, on July 11, 1995, she was told that "there is no information about the subject," *BRCC*, B 002-4-3 (231–233).

[144] Although the files have hundreds of cases detailing rumors, jokes were not documented. Once the Law of Assault against the presidency had been issued in mid-1980s, certain files indicated that some people were arrested because of their lack of respect in telling a

Yet the resistance to Saddam Hussein's regime, in all its manifestations, did not manage to unseat him or his party from power. His modes of control were more intrusive, sophisticated, and extensive than the resistance, including those who participated in the popular uprising in 1991, could overcome. In reality, as with similar regimes elsewhere, the vast majority of the population accepted the overwhelming domination of the system to which they were subjected. Most Iraqis, like Russians and Romanians, "surrender[ed] their human identity in favour [*sic*] of the identity of the system."[145] The Ba'th regime succeeded to a large extent in forcing the majority of individuals to adjust their values in order to survive. This was aptly summed up by one Iraqi psychiatrist: "You had to lie against your principles. You had to say things that you did not believe. It was mental conflict. This kind of tension and suppression destroys the superego – I mean that you cannot decide anything; you are directed by the regime, your education, your military service, your job."[146] On a more practical level, the majority just wanted to get on with their lives. As a Romanian artist said about his own oppressive regime, "What most people want to do under a dictatorship is to forget about it, get on with their lives and enjoy themselves."[147]

    joke, but little detail is given. For a comparison with Syria, see Wedeen, *Ambiguities of Domination*, pp. 120–29. For an example of rumors, see Party Secretariat to Presidential *diwan*, October 18, 1997, BRCC, 162-2-2 (019; 104; 270; 488). See also BRCC, 148-4-5 (198–199).

[145] Havel, *The Power of the Powerless*, p. 36.
[146] Steavenson, *The Weight of a Mustard Seed*, p. 8. The author quotes Dr. Hasan al-Qadhani, who worked as a psychiatrist under the regime.
[147] Quoted in Deletant, *Ceauşescu and the Securitate*, p. 167.

8

Bureaucracy and Civil Life under the Ba'th

To understand the complex relationship between the Ba'th Party and the population, one needs to examine the economic management of the country; the activities of the unions; the policy toward women; the focus on youth, students, and children; and finally, the politically motivated transformation from a secular state to a regime emphasizing religion. But first, it is important to analyze how the party interacted with the state bureaucracy and the regime's decision-making process.

Bureaucracy and Decision Making

The Ba'th regime in Iraq was determined from the outset to create "a powerful centralized national authority," unlike many Third World countries in which a weak authority "is devoured by divisions" that render it shaky and ineffective.[1] The party leadership, and in particular Saddam Hussein, succeeded in creating a large, centralized bureaucracy with the president at its apex. Besides his presidential role, Saddam Hussein was simultaneously the chairman of the RCC, secretary general of the Ba'th Party, prime minister, and commander in chief of the armed forces. Like his elaborate security apparatus, which had a systematic overlap in responsibilities in order to diffuse power, Iraq's bureaucracy had multiple organizational layers: the presidential *diwan*, the RCC, the party, and the cabinet, with its numerous ministries and quasi-governmental organizations. Fundamental to this structure was the idea that in the administration of the country no individual was able to know more than the president – or

---

[1] Hizb al-Ba'th, *Thawrat 17 Tammuz*, p. 49.

even as much as him – so that no one else could concentrate power in his hands.

As vice president, Saddam Hussein began establishing *makatib isti-shariyya* (consultancy bureaus) as early as 1969. Although these were under the aegis of the RCC, they reported directly to him. Throughout the 1970s, it became apparent to all concerned that these bureaus, which were supposed to be consulting, began to make decisions pertaining to civilian management in areas such as agriculture, the economy, law, Arab issues, and northern affairs. Jawad Hashim was involved on both sides, first as a minister and then in the economic consultancy bureau, and describes the process: "The bureaus of the Revolutionary Command Council became instruments in covert methods in lieu of scientific management, and in the end led to swallowing the state and dislocating the official protocol, and the fundamental destruction of the bureaucratic hierarchy."[2]

After becoming president, Saddam Hussein began creating a shadow state within the state in the form of the presidential *diwan*, and by the 1990s it had become the nexus of power.[3] Experts and directors in many fields – health, economics, agriculture, culture, education, and so on – were based in the *diwan* with large staffs compiling reports that in many cases conflicted with what the particular ministry was recommending.[4] The numerous *diwan* departments supplied the president with information about different ministries, and its experts competed with the official ministers, thus diluting their powers.[5] The documents indicate the extent of the *diwan*'s vast and intricate network in plotting the path for every decision, from security matters to improving the Arabic language.[6]

By the end of the 1990s, every bureaucratic measure flowed upward to the *diwan*. Saddam Hussein's secretary, 'Abd Hamid Mahmud al-Khattab al-Nasri (known as 'Abd Hammud), became in effect the second most

[2] Hashim, *Mudhakkarat wazir 'Iraqi*, p. 255. See also comments by Qadduri, who presided over the economic bureau from 1972 to 1979, in *Hakadha 'araftu al-Bakr wa Saddam*, pp. 107–09.
[3] In Germany, the shadow state was in the form of the Chancellery. See Overy, *The Dictators*, pp. 164–65.
[4] See in Chapter 6 the account of the minister's dismissal due to clashes with his counterpart in the *diwan*.
[5] For an organization chart of the presidential *diwan*, as of March 1991, see Iraq Survey Group, *Regime Strategic Intent*, vol. I, Regime Finance and Procurement, figure 1, p. 13.
[6] See, for example, a list of some of the bureaus affiliated with the *diwan* in BRCC, B 004-4-6 (022). The RCC proposed the setting up of a new department in the presidential *diwan* called the Department for Care of the Arabic Language, October 25, 2000, BRCC, B 001-1-7 (101).

powerful man in the country. All intelligence reports and ministry updates were sent to him, and he decided what Saddam Hussein would read, whom he would meet, and his daily agenda. People I interviewed told me that ʿAbd Hammud could make or destroy anyone and any plan if he so wished. In the famous deck of cards distributed by the Americans after the invasion, ʿAbd Hammud was number four among the most wanted (after Saddam Hussein, Qusay, and ʿUday). Charles Duelfer, when he was searching for weapons of mass destruction, realized that the best source of information in Iraq was ʿAbd Hammud and devoted considerable time to interrogating him.[7]

In the system that developed, many orders emanated from verbal instructions given by Saddam Hussein to his subordinates, a method that the president preferred mostly for security reasons, which further strengthened ʿAbd Hammud's position, as most subordinates would turn to him for more clarification. As we have seen, many rules and regulations were based simply on presidential orders with scant discussion or consultation. From the audiotapes we can garner how the system of orders worked; Tariq Aziz described it in the meeting following the escape of Hussein Kamil:

> For twenty years, you made it clear to us that if we receive any order from you and we find it objectionable, we can question it and present you with our opinion and facts. If you were convinced, then that would be fine, but if you were not convinced, then the order would remain in effect.... We are all here to assist you... when you give them [your subordinates] the order, they need to execute it.... Yes, it is hard to get in touch with the President, especially in the last few years for security reasons, but you can write a note to ʿAbd [Hammud] to give it to the President.[8]

Saddam Hussein explained that the system was not functioning properly, as the ministers were confused regarding the execution of orders. After Kamil's episode, he promised that he would clearly distinguish between discussions whose purpose were "to educate the ministers and members of

---

[7] Duelfer, *Hide and Seek*, pp. 363–84. In the deck of cards, ʿAbd Hammud was the fourth ace, the Ace of Diamonds.

[8] A fascinating audiotape of a meeting between Saddam Hussein and senior leaders of the party and ministers after Hussein Kamil defected to Jordan sheds light on how the system operated with few written orders. At one point, Tariq ʿAziz claimed that he was the only one who did not wholly trust Kamil, and that he would always revert to ʿAbd Hammud for clarification of orders; August 1995, *CRRC*, SH-SHTP-A-000-762.

the RCC" versus orders "that must be executed."[9] Interestingly, Hussein Kamil took advantage of this system by continually ordering high officials to undertake assignments that benefited him personally, on the basis that the president had given those orders. There was no doubt whatsoever that Saddam Hussein's orders would be executed; in one meeting of the leadership after the cease-fire with Iran (which was considered a victory), Saddam Hussein, in a jubilant mood, announced that it was great "that we [I] ordered the Iraqi people to celebrate. The Iraqi people need to be told."[10]

The RCC was the body that gave orders to the cabinet and its bureaucracy. After becoming president, Saddam Hussein made it clear that a minister's responsibility was "to receive a directive from the RCC and to follow up in its execution with the lower echelons [of his ministry] until it is accomplished in a timely manner."[11] He told ministers that writing the phrase *to be executed* in the margins of RCC orders was not acceptable and that he would hold each minster personally responsible for all activities within his ministry.[12] This mirrored the structure in Syria, where the ministerial bureaucracy was a "junior power institution."[13] In another guideline, all ministers were told that they must accomplish their tasks not only on time but in a cost-effective manner, a tactic that increased competitiveness among the different departments.[14] The RCC was in essence the executive arm of government and not only directed the bureaucracy but promulgated laws. In early 2001, the RCC comprised ten members,[15] and Saddam Hussein had the authority to change them by fiat. For most of the period under study the Quartet (comprised of 'Izzat Ibrahim al-Duri, Taha Yasin Ramadan, Tariq 'Aziz, and 'Ali Hasan al-Majid) was part of the RCC. All four men had been with Saddam Hussein from the beginning of his political life and stayed until the bitter end. None represented a threat: al-Majid was a relative, 'Aziz was Christian, Ramadan was half Kurdish, al-Duri had no real power base, and in reality all four owed their positions to the leader's continuing reign. By integrating the senior

[9] Education as opposed to implementation of orders was discussed more than once in the RCC's meetings. See, for example, *CRRC*, SH-SHTP-A-000-714 and SH-SHTP-A-000-837.
[10] Audiotape of meeting in August 1988, *CRRC*, SH-SHTP-A-000-816.
[11] Saddam Hussein in a discussion with the cabinet, July 31, 1979, in *al-Mukhtarat*, vol. 7, p. 54.
[12] *Ibid.*, pp. 55–57.
[13] Hinnebusch, *Authoritarian Power and State Formation*, p. 190.
[14] Presidential *diwan* to All Ministers, "Guidance," May 3, 1989, *NIDS*, PUK 013, Box 052 (020026).
[15] For the full list of members in January 2001, see Baran, *Vivre la tyrannie*, p. 154.

leadership of the party's Regional Command into the RCC, it became the most powerful executive body in the country.

After the invasion of 2003, captured members of the RCC claimed that Saddam Hussein made all the decisions in the RCC's name after the council had granted him those powers sometime in the 1980s, and that only he could convene an RCC meeting. Furthermore, after 1995 Saddam Hussein would make a decision and have the legal office in the presidential *diwan* draft the details without reference to the RCC or the cabinet. One RCC member emphasized that, even when there was a discussion, it was rare that anyone would object to Saddam Hussein's views.[16] Of course, the president was not making all the decisions related to internal affairs in a vacuum; the *diwan*, the party, and the state bureaucracy were all part of the machinery. However, he treated the country as a personal fiefdom and wanted to make sure that no appointment was ever made without his full blessing. When talking about ministerial appointments, he told his colleagues:

> The framework we follow in the Revolutionary Council is that we say: we need a specific minster, and then [I ask] my brothers: any suggestions? ... and we discuss. But the person I do not know I will not appoint a minister, except on a rare occasion. Even if the whole command and the whole Revolutionary Council will ask for it. ... I told my comrades, it is my literal responsibility. I have a minister, I should know him. ... Also as a President, I have to know my ministers. And the minister who is neglectful, I should know that he is negligent.[17]

Audiotapes of the senior leadership meetings give a revealing insight into how the country was run. It is obvious that during the meetings in the 1990s the president rambled on at length, and many discussions were full of his anecdotes, storytelling, and pontifications about a host of subjects. Saddam Hussein's mood always colored those meetings; for instance, he was somber when discussing his son-in-law's betrayal but jovial when declaring "victory" against the Iranians in 1988. In a somber mood he was more prepared to listen, waiting for others to express their opinions, but when cheerful he would joke and banter with the assembled group.[18] In the middle of the sessions, Saddam Hussein frequently would order cigars and tea to be served to everyone.

---

[16] Iraq Survey Group, *Regime Strategic Intent*, vol. I, pp. 13–14.
[17] Audiotape of the top leadership, no specific date, but dated after the defection of Hussein Kamil in summer 1995, *CRRC*, SH-SHTP-A-000-837.
[18] For the audiotape of the meeting following Kamil's fleeing, see *CRRC*, SH-SHTP-A-000-762; for the meeting in August 1988, see *CRRC*, SH-SHTP-A-000-816.

Iraq followed the pattern of many countries in the Arab world and beyond, with a bloated civil service that provided the regime with a way to "dispense patronage and pretend-jobs to mop up new graduates."[19] The state bureaucracy continued to expand for most of this period, apart from a short time after the Iran–Iraq War, when the regime embarked on privatization (see the discussion later in this chapter), which led to an effort to neutralize the bureaucracy by trimming it.[20] However, the state bureaucracy was dominated by the party apparatus and vulnerable to constant intervention.[21]

Following the First Gulf War, Saddam Hussein created party committees to engage in *raqaba sha'biyya* (popular surveillance) over the activities of ministries. He explained to party cadres that he did not want to "burden the party with the state's detailed duties and affairs," but that these committees were assigned to "conduct monitoring duties." He added that "ever since the party committees assumed their duties, it helped us a lot. Although it is not considered a police surveillance tool, a person who does wrong will recognize the consequences of his mistake, which is a healthy sign."[22] Party committees consisted mostly of members of *munadhammat al-munadhilin* – retired Ba'thists with experience in state bureaucracy – whose role was to oversee the party's activities in each ministry and make sure that all senior officials were following the party line. These committees were the eyes and ears of the party inside the state bureaucracy, not only with regard to political and security issues. For instance, the party committee in the Ministry of Trade informed the Party Secretariat that the construction budget for a new General Company for Trading Seeds building was different from what had been publicly announced, and that an internal committee of the ministry was selecting contractors without open tender.[23] The committees functioned also as a quasi-union for ministry employees, who would file complaints to them about unfair treatment or being blocked from promotion. The committees would look into the matter and make a recommendation to

---

[19] *The Economist*, "Waking from Its Sleep," A Special Report on the Arab World, July 25, 2009, p. 9.

[20] Kiren Aziz Chaudhry, "On the Way to Market: Economic Liberalization and Iraq's Invasion of Kuwait," *Middle East Report (MERIP)*, no. 170 (May–June 1991), p. 17.

[21] This was much like the situation in Ba'thist Syria; see Raymond Hinnebusch, *Syria: Revolution from Above*, paperback edn. (London: Routledge, 2002), pp. 84–85.

[22] Speech by Saddam Hussein to the party cadre during a swearing of allegiance, June 28, 1999, *CRRC*, SH-BATH-D-000-297.

[23] Secretary of Party Committee to Party Secretariat, "New Building," July 5, 2001, *BRCC*, 042-4-6 (073).

the Party Secretariat, which in turn would address the problem directly with the minister or his deputies.[24]

On average, there were between twenty and twenty-four ministries in each Iraqi government, but the total number of party committees was far higher given that the ministries had offices in most of the provinces. For instance, within the Ministry of Education, which had offices in all provinces, there were seventeen committees in addition to the central committee in Baghdad. Furthermore, party committees were established in all utility companies and quasi-government agencies, such as the Youth and Sports Organization and the Central Bank, as well as in all municipalities.[25] A review of these committees in 2000 raised the concern of potential conflicts of interest when committee members, who were sometimes ex-employees of the same ministry, had to investigate other employees and senior officials, which led to an unfortunate "inability to reach the truth."[26]

There is no doubt that these committees created another layer in the labyrinth of bureaucracy and added to the inertia, lack of initiative, and resistance to change that often permeates large bureaucracies in authoritarian regimes. Interestingly, the president was aware of this prevailing atmosphere in government offices and issued a directive stating that it had been noticed that "some officials in the bureaucracy do not express their opinions or make a suggestion but simply raise the matter to higher authorities."[27] The directive attributed this either to lack of knowledge and an unwillingness to study the issues raised or to lack of confidence in their abilities. A case illustrating the party's control over government offices occurred when the party's onslaught on the Ministry of Agriculture ensured Ba'th control by hiving off its most important functions to a parallel body called the State Organization for Soil and Land Reclamation.[28]

An examination of documents indicates that memos sent by the state bureaucracy or the presidential *diwan* sometimes were copied to multiple agencies and organizations with numerous cross-referencing and that the

---

[24] Dozens of files in the *BRCC* deal with these committees, their formation, and the personal files of members. See, for example, *BRCC*, 042-4-6; 039-5-3; 064-5-7.

[25] *BRCC*, 053-3-5 (025; 032–052).

[26] Party Secretariat to Presidential *diwan*, August 13, 2000, *BRCC*, 053-3-5 (195).

[27] Presidential *diwan* to All Ministries and Government Agencies, "Guidance," March 11, 1987, *BRCC*, 003-3-7 (042–043).

[28] Robert Springborg, "Baathism in Practice: Agriculture, Politics, and Political Culture in Syria and Iraq," *Middle Eastern Studies*, vol. 17, no. 2 (April 1981), p. 203.

names of the addressees covered two full pages, reflecting the multilayered Iraqi bureaucratic maze. For example, a directive about setting up a commercial agency was sent not only to all ministries but also to nine addressees, including the presidential palace, all security agencies, the Party Secretariat, and half a dozen quasi-government agencies.[29] Almost every decision or proposal necessitated forming a committee with a large number of participants to make sure that all aspects were covered, but this of course led to inefficiencies and delays in making and executing decisions.[30]

In essence, all major – and sometimes minor – issues percolated upward to the presidential *diwan* and the president himself for a final decision. For example, travel permits of party members outside Iraq could only be approved by the president.[31] By 1990, Saddam Hussein decided that he could not examine every case of punishment of party affiliates and that only the cases of full party members would be brought to his attention.[32] In turn, each minister or organization head wanted to make sure that all correspondence emanating from his office would be controlled by him and no one else.[33] Similar to Ba'thist Syria, heads of ministerial departments were often "stripped of virtually all competence, and some ministers do not allow even their deputies to take routine decisions."[34]

Nevertheless, Saddam Hussein believed in competent management and reiterated that "lack of organization is behind every failure."[35] He paid attention to the many complaints sent by average citizens to the palace about state and bureaucracy officials who refused to deal with them or who were not willing to devote time and effort to solve their problems. He admonished these officials and preached modesty and humbleness

[29] Presidential *diwan*, "Directive for Setting Up the Commercial Agency," November 12, 1994, BRCC, B 003-3-5 (013–014).
[30] In one instance in which posters were to be published to explain national defense topics, representatives of all unions, the Ministry of Higher Education, the party, and other government agencies participated. BRCC, 014-3-3 (005).
[31] In 1991, given the circumstances of the country following the invasion of Kuwait and the uprising, it was decided that one of Saddam Hussein's deputies could grant the approval for travel. See Party Secretariat to Party Secretaries, "Rules of Travel," July 27, 1991, BRCC, 091-3-5 (014).
[32] Party Secretariat to All, "Order," January 7, 1990, BRCC, 021-1-4 (001).
[33] See, for example, a memo written by the SSO director advising the heads of his departments that all correspondence sent to the president or the presidential *diwan* had to be signed by him personally, June 27, 2000, BRCC, B 001-3-3 (008).
[34] Volker Perthes, *The Political Economy of Syria under Asad*, paperback edn. (London: I.B. Tauris, 1997), p. 143.
[35] Saddam Hussein, *Rijal wa madina*, p. 253.

as the appropriate attitudes toward citizens.[36] As mentioned previously, citizen complaints were an important source of information and provided additional supervision of the bureaucracy. In communist regimes, these complaints were also a means of winning the loyalty of the masses and of assessing public opinion.[37]

Because of their constant fear of subversion, both Saddam Hussein and the party leadership were obsessed with centralizing power. In reality, control was more important to them than efficient management, and a state of affairs was created whereby senior officials did not trust their own employees to carry out the leadership's policies. The result was a blurred and overlapping division of labor between the party and government hierarchies. Although the party was supposed to merely guide and oversee the work of government employees, its members ended up being involved in routine administrative work. It is astonishing how many party members were preoccupied with minutiae at all levels; one file shows correspondence about archeology, schools, urban planning, Arabization of words, property transactions, and school fees. In each case, memos were sent for approval to more than a dozen officials, who in turn would send them higher up the pyramid for further authorization.[38] Obviously, policing this bureaucratic army and the party members themselves created another supervisory layer that further impeded decision making.

In describing life in Czechoslovakia, Havel could have easily depicted Iraq during the Ba'th regime:

> life in such a state is thoroughly permeated by a dense network of regulations, proclamations, directives, norms, orders and rules. (It is not called a bureaucratic system without good reason.) A large proportion of those norms functions as direct instruments of the complex manipulation of life that is intrinsic to the post-totalitarian regime. Individuals are reduced to little more than tiny cogs in an enormous mechanism and their significance is limited to their function in this mechanism.[39]

There are a few points to underscore. First, there was no intention throughout the era under study that the Ba'th would replace the state bureaucracy, given the extent and depth of the government machinery. In

---

[36] Party Secretariat to All Headquarters, "Guidance," May 11, 2000, *BRCC*, 004-4-3 (114).

[37] For a fascinating account of creating mass loyalty through accountability in the communist world, see Martin K. Dimitrov, "Building Loyalty: Autocratic Resilience in Communist Europe and China" (manuscript in progress).

[38] *BRCC*, B 001-1-7.

[39] Havel, *The Power of the Powerless*, pp. 72–73.

fact, the bureaucracy, with its talented and experienced cadre, allowed the country to function throughout the upheavals it experienced. "Bureaucratic authority made possible people's continued participation in government, whether working in it as a civil servant or approaching it as a private citizen."[40] The party was always seen as the source of political leadership, and the state bureaucracy as the arm executing orders and directives. Second, the party's involvement in the day-to-day management of the country changed with time, because its own bureaucracy expanded rapidly during the 1980s and 1990s. As the number of party members – who were also employees holding midlevel positions – grew significantly, the lines became increasingly blurred. Third, by the mid-1980s the real decision making was concentrated in the presidential *diwan*, and all other state organs were reduced to conduits of information and resources.

Managing the Economy

The economy was important for Saddam Hussein, because he believed that although the regime could be *damawi* (bloody) in dealing with its enemies, the people would accept the Ba'th rule and "feel happy due to economic growth."[41] Based on interviews with senior Iraqis captured after the fall of Baghdad, the Iraqi Survey Group concluded that financial matters were Saddam Hussein's third priority after security and political management. In his financial discussions he was believed to be "preoccupied with disbursals and cash flow, not fiscal policy or macroeconomic management."[42]

The Ba'th Party realized that economic independence should be a central goal of the revolution and was as important as political independence.[43] In the regime's early years, the Ba'th, following its motto of unity, freedom, and socialism, wanted to build "a united Arab, socialist, democratic society."[44] It saw itself as a "socialist revolutionary party which considers socialism as a decisive necessity for liberating the Arab nation," and it sought to introduce as many steps as possible that would lead to socialism.[45] Nevertheless, it is important to underline the

---

[40] Feldman, *Governing Gaza*, p. 17.
[41] Saddam Hussein, *al-Mukhtarat*, vol. 3, p. 86. This was part of an interview with the journalist Nasir al-Din al-Nashashibi on January 19, 1981.
[42] Iraq Survey Group, *Regime Strategic Intent*, vol. I, p. 18.
[43] Hizb al-Ba'th, *Thawrat 17 Tammuz*, p. 51.
[44] Hizb al-Ba'th, *al-Taqrir al-siyasi lil mu'tamar al-qawmi al-'ashir*, p. 3.
[45] *The Iraqi Gazette*, Law no. 35 of 1977, vol. 20, no. 37, September 14, 1977. The *Gazette* is the English translation of *al-waqa'i' al-'Iraqiyya*.

differences between Iraq and other totalitarian regimes such as communist Russia. In Iraq, there was no centralized economy, no forced industrialization, and no massive, state-run attempt to mold peasants into industrial workers. As Owen explains, authoritarian systems are different from totalitarian ones in that they "lack the powerful institutions that would be needed to control or to transform society by means of bureaucratic methods alone."[46]

Even at the beginning, the Baʿth's socialism was half-hearted and not strictly imposed. Before becoming president, Saddam Hussein talked about his vision, which was neither socialist as in communist states nor a free economy as in the West.[47] He believed that this time – unlike 1963, when the Baʿth lost power before it could make any radical economic changes – the regime would do everything to benefit the people. On another occasion he asked, "What is the point of talking about socialism while people stay hungry?" and, "What is the value of socialism that cannot give security to the people?"[48] Describing his vision of how the Iraqi economy would function, he told his biographer, Fuad Matar, that "we believe the private sector and the socialist sector will go hand in hand forever. They are partners in the service of society."[49] However, in the 1970s more socialist measures, in particular nationalization and land reform, were enacted than in the 1980s. But, similar to Egyptian socialism, Iraqi socialism was "unwilling to sacrifice the needs of the present generation in order to raise money for future development."[50] Modernization and populism in authoritarian states such as Iraq or Syria were "crucial to its consolidation of power," but like Syria and Egypt, the Iraqi regime wanted to achieve rapid growth because it felt the pressure to show fast results.[51]

Iraq's economy can be viewed as divided into three different periods: the 1970s were characterized by higher oil prices and an economic boom; the 1980s were dominated by the eight-year war against Iran, falling oil prices, and huge accumulation of debt; and finally, in the early 1990s

---

[46] Roger Owen, *State, Power and Politics in the Making of the Modern Middle East*, 3rd edn. (London: Routledge, 2008), p. 27.

[47] Speech of Saddam Hussein at al-Bakr University, March 6, 1978, CRRC, SH-PDWN-D-000-341.

[48] Speech of Saddam Hussein at the party preparatory school, May 26, 1976, *al-Mukhtarat*, vol. 7, p. 18.

[49] Matar, *Saddam Hussein*, p. 254.

[50] Roger Owen and Şevket Pamuk, *A History of Middle East Economies in the Twentieth Century* (Cambridge, MA: Harvard University Press, 1999), p. 132.

[51] Hinnebusch, *Authoritarian Power and State Formation*, p. 15. See also Springborg, "Baathism in Practice," p. 195.

until the fall of the regime, the First Gulf War and international sanctions had a devastating impact on the economy and the Iraqi people. We will discuss each period to understand how the regime managed the economy during those phases.

1970s

In the 1970s, Saddam Hussein, true to his word about the importance of the economy for the regime, took a close interest in economic matters, and through the consultancy bureaus that reported to him within the RCC, he was able to take the helm of economic management. Fakhri Qadduri, the minister of economics who ran the economic bureau at the RCC for six years, describes in his memoirs how Saddam Hussein was very involved in all discussions and made sure to be well prepared before the meetings of the Planning Council. He also led all the studies and negotiations that resulted in the nationalization of oil companies, which began in January 1972 and continued until all foreign-owned shares were nationalized in late 1975.[52] With oil prices almost quadrupling after the 1973 October War, oil revenues became significant. This allowed the regime to cement its economic control through a system of patronage and by "creating networks of complicity and dependence."[53] Using oil revenues, the government ploughed large amounts of money into providing free health care and education, expanding the country's infrastructure, organizing large construction projects, and investing in industry and the military.

There is no doubt that by the end of the 1970s Iraq was climbing the modernization ladder and achieving high scores among developing countries in terms of education and health care. Its per capita income rose from ID97 in 1968 to about ID825 by the end of the 1970s, and its gross domestic product (GDP) more than quadrupled during the same period.[54] Raising the standard of living was seen by the party as paving the way for further Ba'thification of the country by proving that the regime would deliver prosperity.[55] Although the ideology was socialist in theory and

---

[52] Qadduri, *Hakadha 'araftu al-Bakr wa Saddam*, pp. 113–19. Qadduri, like many of the Iraqi Ba'th technocrats, lost favor with the regime and, by 1983, found himself in exile in Germany.

[53] Tripp, *A History of Iraq*, p. 207.

[54] Farouk-Sluglett and Sluglett, *Iraq Since 1958*, p. 232. See also Zubaida, "Une société traumatisée," p. 606.

[55] See, for example, a brochure by Wazarat al-Takhtit (Ministry of Planning), *al-Taqaddum fi dhil al-takhtit* [Advancement through Planning] (Baghdad: Central Organization for Statistics, 1975), pp. 49–50.

the country was going through a decade of intense statism, in the 1970s the private sector grew with the expansion of the economy thanks to the huge public expenditure, which stimulated private investment.[56] Even in 1980, the government discouraged state employees from joining the private sector unless they had obtained prior permission, and graduates who were allocated jobs in the state bureaucracy had to honor their placement rather than work in the private sector.[57]

1980s

The 1980s were dominated by the eight-year war against Iran, and the sharp drop in oil prices caused a significant slowdown in all the rentier economies in the region. Many countries launched new liberalization policies intended to stimulate their economies, and Iraq was no exception, introducing liberalization and privatization policies. The agricultural sector was an interesting example of the dramatic shift of policy, in which the regime sold agricultural land to the private sector after years of socialist-style land reform and sequestration that had begun in 1959.[58] This was attributed in part to the labor shortage during the Iran–Iraq War.[59] In fact, the country faced more serious economic issues than just labor shortage, which was partially resolved by importing more than a million workers from Egypt and other countries. Iraq's reserves, accumulated during the boom years of the 1970s, had dwindled by 1983, and as the war continued the country began borrowing heavily, mostly from the Gulf states.

The documents illustrate how the regime was desperately trying to cope during this period, and "mobilization of human resources" became the catchall phrase in correspondence between the party and the state bureaucracy. Austerity measures were imposed, and the party mechanism was given the task of overseeing them. The presidential *diwan* ordered a review of all imports, no new projects were approved, and any proposal had to be forwarded to the *diwan* for authorization. Employment of Arabs and

---

[56] Kamil A. Mahdi, "Iraq's Economic Reforms in Perspective: Public Sector, Private Sector and the Sanctions," *International Journal of Contemporary Iraqi Studies*, vol. 1, no. 2 (2007), p. 220.

[57] RCC Decision no. 700, May 13, 1980, *BRCC*, 003-1-1 (109).

[58] For an interesting comparison with Saudi Arabia and more details about the agricultural sector reforms, see Kiren Aziz Chaudhry, "Economic Liberalization and the Lineages of the Rentier State," *Comparative Politics*, vol. 27, no. 1 (October 1994), pp. 1–25.

[59] Kamil A. Mahdi, "Iraq's Agrarian System: Issues of Policy and Performance," in Kamil A. Mahdi (ed.), *Iraq's Economic Predicament* (Reading: Ithaca Press, 2002), p. 336.

foreigners in all ministries was reduced, and ministries were told to hire pensioners, women, and the disabled. All educational scholarships were halted unless fully paid for by a foreign government, and no payment in cash for any project was permitted unless it was related to the war effort.[60] Another party priority during this decade was the distribution of food and essential supplies, while simultaneously strengthening the blockade against northern villages allied with the Kurdish insurgency.[61] Efforts were made to balance the budget by increasing production and savings while cutting private consumption and employment in government offices.[62]

Throughout the 1980s, whether in agriculture or industry, the regime was engaged in intensive privatization of the socialist state and launched what was considered by Chaudhry as "the most wide-ranging privatization program in the developing world."[63] Its main features were selling state-owned farms and factories to private owners; deregulating labor laws, thus weakening labor unions; promulgating laws to encourage industrialists and entrepreneurs to expand their businesses; and encouraging private investment and exports in the hope that the economy would recover.[64]

Desperate for cash, the government decided to invite foreign companies to invest in oilfields. From the mid-1980s it became clear that Iraq was not going to be either socialist or a free market economy in the true sense. As Saddam Hussein told a meeting in June 1987, the "state should not embark any more on uneconomic activity, and any such activity has to have a return." In the same speech, he said that emphasis would be put on quality of output, and that as part of the liberalization he had ordered the security organizations not to ask people about the source of money for imports, as this led many people to stop importing for fear of the security organizations.[65] In fact, Saddam Hussein's reprimand to the

---

[60] Presidential *diwan* to All Ministries, Unions, and Government Agencies, "Economic Situation," March 20, 1986, *BRCC*, 092-4-4 (298).

[61] See reports of Sarjuk Area Security Committee, March 31, 1987, *NIDS*, PUK 041, Box 251 (250008).

[62] Legal Department, Republic of Iraq, "Proposal for Balancing the State's Budget for 1990," December 23, 1989, *NIDS*, PUK 047, Box 302 (050002).

[63] Chaudhry, "On the Way to Market," p. 14.

[64] See, for example, the RCC's Decision no. 483 to encourage industrialists, *al-waqa'i' al-'Iraqiyya*, no. 3159, July 20, 1987.

[65] Speech of the president during the ceremonies for swearing in the mayors of Najaf, Misan, and Karbala, June 7, 1987, *al-Mukhtarat*, vol. 1, pp. 125–57. The speech was devoted to economic affairs and ended with the prediction that Gorbachev and other

head of *al-amn* during an RCC meeting about this approach illustrates his pragmatism: he argued that it would be better to allow merchants to utilize the money that they had smuggled abroad to import goods to Iraq rather than to persecute them, because these imports benefited everyone.[66] Hence, authoritarianism in Iraq was more comfortable with a mixed economy, because "such an economy blunts class distinctions, thereby inhibiting the formation of firmly based political movements and thus perpetuating the very authoritarian rule."[67]

The cost of the eight-year war against Iran was immense in terms of human and economic losses; its length and severity probably cost the two countries more than one million lives and consumed almost 112 percent of Iraq's gross national product (GNP) annually between 1980 and 1988.[68] The reforms of the 1980s failed to achieve their objectives. They were short lived and indicated "a perennial problem in the economic history of modern Iraq: the inability of the state to regulate a private economy."[69] Part of the failure was due to the opposition of the bureaucracy, but in reality the regime adopted these reforms simply because it was desperately attempting to find a solution to the economic crisis in which it found itself embroiled. One immediate reason for the crisis was the shortage of foreign currency, which was exacerbated by the state's continued policy of allocating a high percentage of the budget to militarization and military industries.[70]

By 1989, Iraq's economy was significantly different from that of 1979: massive destruction of infrastructure (particularly in the south), heavy indebtedness of about $42 billion to Arab and foreign countries, a weak currency, and, worst of all, deteriorating oil prices (crude oil fell from

---

leaders of socialist countries would encounter serious hurdles, because their socialism was a "rigid and hungry socialism."

[66] Audiotape of Saddam Hussein with the country's leadership, May 1987, *CRRC*, SH-SHTP-A-000-958.

[67] Robert Springborg, "Infitah, Agrarian Transformation, and Elite Consolidation in Contemporary Iraq," *Middle East Journal*, vol. 40, no. 1 (Winter 1986), p. 52.

[68] Kamran Mofid, *The Economic Consequences of the Gulf War* (London: Routledge, 1990), p. 135. Mofid estimated the cost at $452 billion (p. 132), whereas Alnasrawi estimated that Iraq spent about $16 billion a year during the war, but that this did not include the value of destroyed assets or allow for lost oil revenues. See Abbas Alnasrawi, "Economic Consequences of the Iraq–Iran War," *Third World Quarterly*, vol. 8, no. 3 (July 1986), pp. 882–83.

[69] Kiren Aziz Chaudhry, "Consuming Interests: Market Failure and the Social Foundations of Iraqi Etatisme," in Mahdi (ed.), *Iraq's Economic Predicament*, p. 261.

[70] For a discussion of costs of militarism and war, see Rohde, *State–Society Relations*, pp. 41–47.

an average high of about $32 per barrel during 1981 to an average low of $12–$14 in late 1988). At the same time, the regime had to continue its militarization and rebuild the infrastructure.[71] Once again, the looming crisis forced the government to change its economic policy, and it increased civil service salaries and offered subsidies on certain products.[72]

Early 1990s to 2003

Given the continuing slump in oil prices, the refusal of some Arab countries to abide by OPEC quotas, and the suffocating burden of the country's debt, Saddam Hussein believed that a quick solution to this enveloping crisis was to invade Kuwait, which he did on August 2, 1990.[73] The consequences of this were dire for the country and its people. Soon after the invasion, Iraq's foreign-held assets were frozen, and an embargo was imposed by the UN on its oil exports, which caused oil output to grind to a halt, resulting in severe loss of revenues. From the time of the allied attack in early 1991 until a ceasefire was signed on February 28, 1991, following the liberation of Kuwait, the country suffered heavy infrastructural damage, to the extent that almost 90 percent of Iraq's electricity grid was destroyed.[74] The popular uprising that erupted in the north and south of the country in March 1991 had many ramifications for the regime, but from an economic standpoint it led to further deterioration, particularly as more resources were allocated to the military to deal with any future upheavals. The strict international sanctions imposed on Iraq after the war profoundly affected the lives of Iraqi citizens and forced policy changes to adapt to their consequences. The regime felt threatened not only by the uprising and the continuing tension with the international community, but also by the ongoing economic deterioration. "Because personalist regimes sustain the loyalty of their supporters by providing access to material rewards, they are vulnerable to economic

---

[71] For a general review of this period, see Muhammad 'Ali Zaini, *al-Iqtisad al-'Iraqi fi dhil nidham Saddam Hussein: Tatawwar am taqhqur* [The Iraqi Economy during Saddam Hussein's Regime: Development or Retraction] (London: al-Rafid, 1995), pp. 251–331. See also *The Economist Intelligence Unit (EIU)*, no. 3, July 6, 1987.

[72] Abbas Alnasrawi, "Iraq: Economic Consequences of the 1991 Gulf War and Future Outlook," *Third World Quarterly*, vol. 13, no. 2 (June 1992), pp. 339–40.

[73] *Ibid.*, pp. 340–44.

[74] *Ibid.*, p. 347. For details of the invasion and the war, see Tripp, *A History of Iraq*, pp. 253–59.

catastrophe."[75] The sanctions, which lasted until the regime's overthrow in 2003, affected the country in many fundamental ways.[76] This echoed the Stalinist experience, in which shortages of consumer goods, long lines to purchase food, and black market speculation were "the most public, the most ubiquitous, and the most challenging" problems that the Soviet regime had to face.[77] The Iraqi regime focused on "how to find an opening in the wall of sanctions,"[78] and hundreds of documents deal with the burning issues of the 1990s: food rationing, smuggling, collapse of the currency in international markets, corruption, and finally the brain drain. We will discuss each of those issues here.

Scarcity of food was an enormous issue facing the population. *The Economist* reported in 1995 that the society was reduced to "penury and semi-starvation" and quoted UN reports that nearly 30 percent of children under five were severely malnourished and that the "social fabric is collapsing."[79] The regime invested considerable financial, administrative, and political resources into administering and maintaining food rationing. Ration cards became extremely valuable, and although each citizen was supposed to receive the same amount of food, party members, senior army officers, and civil servants were entitled to a higher allocation.[80] Party members working in food warehouses and mills were armed to protect these installations from hungry mobs bent on theft.[81] Overall, the food rationing system worked because the regime understood the implications of a hungry population, and hence by "responding in an effective manner to a threat of food insecurity instituted by 'outsiders' (that is,

[75] Barbara Geddes, "What Do We Know About Democratization After Twenty Years?" *Annual Review of Political Science*, vol. 2 (1999), p. 134.
[76] For a very detailed report on the implications of the sanctions, prepared by a special committee of the party in the late 1990s, see CRRC, SH-BATH-D-000-492. The study explained the effects of the economic blockade on the social, economic, nutritional, and psychological health of Iraqi society, and the president's role "in containing this blockade."
[77] Paul Hagenloh, *Stalin's Police: Public Order and Mass Repression in the USSR, 1926–1941* (Washington, DC: Woodrow Wilson Center Press, 2009), p. 305.
[78] From mid-1991 until 2003, many of the meetings of the RCC and the party leadership chaired by Saddam Hussein were devoted to sanctions and to negotiations with the UN-led teams searching for weapons of mass destruction. One audiotape of a meeting of the RCC, November 26, 1994, is a good source for those topics, CRRC, SH-SHTP-A-000-734.
[79] *The Economist*, "King of a Sad Castle," October 21, 1995, p. 45.
[80] Party Secretariat to Ministry of Trade, "Information," November 28, 1992, BRCC, 005-3-5 (001; 007; 086–087; 103).
[81] Party Secretariat, "Ensuring Protection," March 21, 1995, BRCC, 100-3-5 (001; 005; 009–010).

economic sanctions imposed by the UN Security Council), the leadership
would have sought to enhance its claim to political legitimacy within
Iraq."[82] Indeed, as explained in the previous chapter, Saddam Hussein
capitalized on the sanctions to increase support for his regime and to
ensure that his loyal followers were generously rewarded.

A dearth of products such as paper prompted a discussion in the cabinet
that led to an order to all government offices to economize on paper and
use both sides of every page.[83] As shortages of food, cigarettes, and
other essential products intensified, so did smuggling, which yielded wide
profit margins. Because of the "high anxiety of the population," the party
leadership had to take action.[84] Special committees were set up to deal
with smuggling, which was spreading throughout the country, and to
arrest the culprits. Convicted smugglers faced life imprisonment or the
death penalty if their activities were connected to groups or countries
that were considered anti-regime. Interestingly, most of the value of the
smuggled items (80 percent) was distributed in the form of rewards to the
informers and groups that made the arrest.[85] The definition of smuggling
was widened to include those suspected of intending to smuggle, if there
was circumstantial evidence.[86]

The collapse of the Iraqi dinar in the currency markets coupled with
hyperinflation added to Iraq's economic woes. In 1990, on average, $1
was equal to roughly ID4; by 1994, $1 was equivalent to about ID457;
and by 1999 the currency was so devalued that $1 was roughly ID1,200.[87]
The consumer price index rocketed from a base of 100 in 1993 to 3,593
in 1999, depleting savings and causing serious hardship for the large
number of salaried employees such as civil servants and teachers.[88] Commenting on the value of the dinar, Saddam Hussein told the cabinet that
the devaluation reflected the sentiments of the street, given the increase in

---

[82] Haris Gazdar and Athar Hussain, "Crisis and Response: A Study of the Impact of
   Economic Sanctions in Iraq," in Mahdi (ed.), *Iraq's Economic Predicament*, p. 63.
[83] Party Secretariat to All *tandhimat*, "Utilizing Paper," September 10, 1990, BRCC, 003-
   3-7 (072).
[84] See, for example, correspondence of the presidential *diwan* that had begun to deal with
   these shortages during the war with Iran, CRRC, SH-PDWN-D-000-420; SH-PDWN-
   D-000-469.
[85] RCC Decision no. 80, August 30, 1995, BRCC, 020-1-5 (079–080).
[86] Al-Ta'mim Branch to Party Secretariat, "Proposal," April 15, 1997, BRCC, 008-4-6
   (388–394).
[87] Ali Merza, "Iraq: Reconstruction under Uncertainty," *International Journal of Contemporary Iraqi Studies*, vol. 1, no. 2 (2007), table 3, p. 197.
[88] *Ibid.*

expenditure and fall in revenues. He informed his ministers that "discussion of financial matters is sensitive and should be as sensitive as talking about security matters."[89] The lethal combination of hyperinflation and currency devaluation obviously encouraged smuggling and black market dealings. A study prepared by the party underlined that about 43 percent of the population at some point used the black market, whereas 18 percent consistently traded in it. The report identified the scarcity of goods as a major reason for involvement in the black market, but for some citizens it was the long lines to purchase products that prompted them to turn to the black market.[90]

No wonder, in these dire circumstances, that corruption spread into every facet of life, particularly after 1996, when Iraq began selling oil under the UN's Oil-for-Food Programme. Estimates of illicit income from surcharges on oil sales and bribery ranged from $270 million to more than $7 billion.[91] An independent inquiry into the Oil-for-Food Programme estimated that Iraqi surcharges were about $229 million, and that in allocating its crude oil, Iraq had instituted a preference policy in favor of companies and individuals from countries perceived as "friendly," such as Russia and France.[92] The Iraq Survey Report details how the Iraqi government illegally generated billions of dollars in revenue through these unlawful surcharges, using its embassies as a conduit for the transfers, and it describes the contracts awarded to Russian and French politicians and businessmen, who benefited significantly from them.[93] Given the importance of these relationships and their financial weight, Saddam Hussein ordered that no contract with regard to oil or trade could be signed with any friendly entity by any minister unless personally approved by him

---

[89] Cabinet Secretary to Minister of Economic Affairs, "Value of the Dinar versus the Dollar," May 8, 1999, BRCC, 021-2-7 (027).

[90] Al-Fawz al-'Adhim (The Great Victory) Branch, "A Study," May 23, 1998, BRCC, 003-4-4 (270).

[91] Philippe Le Billon, "Corruption, Reconstruction and Oil Governance in Iraq," in Sultan Barakat (ed.), *Reconstructing Post-Saddam Iraq* (London: Routledge, 2008), p. 129. Between 1996 and 2003, the Oil-for-Food Programme allowed Iraq to sell $69 billion worth of oil, of which $38 billion was allocated to humanitarian purchases for Iraq.

[92] Independent Inquiry Committee into the United Nations Oil-for-Food Programme, *Manipulation of the Oil-For-Food Programme by the Iraqi Regime*, October 27, 2005, www.iic-offp.org, p. 9 (accessed October 28, 2010). The committee was headed by Paul Volker, the ex-chairman of the U.S. Federal Reserve. See also Faleh A. Jabbar, Ahmad Shikara, and Keiko Sakai, *From Storm to Thunder: Unfinished Showdown Between Iraq and U.S.* (Tokyo: Institute of Developing Economies, March 1998).

[93] Iraq Survey Group, *Regime Strategic Intent*, vol. I, Regime Finance and Procurement, pp. 39–40. See also Figure 7: Summary of Illicit Iraqi Revenue, 1991–2003.

beforehand.[94] But corruption existed not only at the high international level: the SSO was kept busy tracking government employees and family members of senior officials who were also guilty of corruption.[95]

As the economic situation deteriorated throughout the 1990s, the middle and professional classes suffered debilitating setbacks not only from scarcity of food but even more from the staggering inflation and currency devaluation that depleted their savings. They adopted survival strategies "to maintain consumption level in the face of dramatic declines in their purchasing power," such as working several jobs, having their children operate as petty vendors, bartering for goods, and selling assets and household items.[96] As begging increased on the streets of Iraqi cities, Saddam Hussein believed that only "weak personalities" were pushing their children into this and ordered the police to arrest the parents of begging children and get local councils to name and shame them.[97]

One major consequence of this crisis was the brain drain of Iraq's professionals and educated middle class. During the 1970s and 1980s waves of educated Iraqis had fled the country in search of a better life, among them many of the teaching faculty of Baghdad Medical School and specialist physicians. However, after the events of 1990–91, significant numbers of Iraqis began to leave when they realized that after two wars, the opportunities for professional careers would dwindle dramatically. As the fabric of Iraqi society began to unravel, the demise of the middle class was exacerbated, and some estimates put the number of Iraqis in exile by the time of the 2003 invasion at 4 million.[98]

The government attempted to attract people back to Iraq in the 1970s and 1980s by introducing many incentives, and it intensified its efforts in the 1990s.[99] The party prepared a detailed study recommending steps to

[94] Cabinet Secretary to Security Services, "Information," May 9, 1999, *BRCC*, 021-2-7 (032). Prior to that, Tariq 'Aziz admitted that he himself gave several French individuals substantial oil allotments; Iraq Survey Group, *Regime Strategic Intent*, vol. I, p. 40.

[95] See, for example, SSO documents about Ministry of Agriculture officials who were using their personal positions to accumulate wealth, November 12, 2001, *BRCC*, B 024-4-9 (018). See also information about one minister's son signing a deal with a foreign company, June 11, 1995, *BRCC*, B 002-4-5 (079–080).

[96] Gazdar and Hussain, "Crisis and Response," p. 50.

[97] Cabinet Secretary to Ministry of Labor and Social Affairs, March 24, 1999, *BRCC*, 021-2-7 (233–234).

[98] For more details about the pre- and post-Saddam Hussein brain drain, see Joseph Sassoon, *The Iraqi Refugees: The New Crisis in the Middle East* (London: I.B. Tauris, 2009), pp. 140–51. Even before the Gulf War, Iraqi exiles were estimated at 1.5 million.

[99] For details of the efforts in 1970 and 1972, see Hashim, *Mudhakkarat wazir 'Iraqi*, pp. 327–28.

stem the emigration of academics and created new incentives for those returning. The study emphasized the importance of Iraqi scientists:

> Capabilities such as [the] chemical weapons and long-distance rockets which raised Iraq's profile among the peoples of the world and were the pride of all Arabs and Muslims, determined the battle with the Persian enemy, and shook Israel's structure for the first time, were not the product of illiterate labor but were manufactured by engineers, chemists, physicists and biologists who were graduates of the Iraqi universities.[100]

The party kept an eye on real estate transactions, convinced that many landlords were attempting to liquefy their assets before transferring them abroad, and reported that Swiss banks were coordinating transfers through Iraqis living in Amman.[101] By 1994, the regime had initiated a series of measures to impede sales of assets and to prevent Iraqis who had been out of the country for more than two years from transferring their properties to another person, whether by sale or direct transfer.[102] A study by the Central Bureau of Students in 1995 investigated the departure of educated Iraqis, and although it blamed anti-regime groups outside the country for having "an organized plan to encourage the brain drain," it did propose a long list of measures to encourage citizens to stay. Among these were increasing the salaries of professors to be more competitive with neighboring countries, particularly Jordan; expanding laboratories and science departments; and creating special department stores for academics to provide them with food and products at competitive prices.[103] The presidential *diwan* also ordered a committee to be set up with four delegates from the Party Secretariat, the Ministry of Higher Education and Scientific Research, the Ministry of Foreign Affairs, and the intelligence services to attempt to encourage Iraqis residing abroad, particularly students, to return home.[104] Few of these efforts were crowned with success; one estimate put the number of teachers who left their jobs during

---

[100] Al-Rashid Branch to Party Secretariat, "A Study: The Situation of the Iraqi Academic and Brain Drain," October 27, 1991, *BRCC*, 005-1-2 (646–652).

[101] Party Secretariat, "Economic Phenomenon," December 12, 1991, *BRCC*, 005-1-2 (545).

[102] RCC Decision no. 100, July 31, 1994, *BRCC*, 104-3-3 (672–688).

[103] Central Bureau of Students and Youth to Party Secretariat, March 22, 1995, *BRCC*, 104-3-3 (171–178). According to this study, in Iraq at that time there were 11,658 faculty members across all universities, of whom 8,366 had doctorates.

[104] Ministry of Foreign Affairs, "Presidential Order," April 20, 1995, *BRCC*, 104-3-3 (163).

the 1990s at 40,000, and Iraq's hospitals lost something in the range of 75 percent of their staff.[105]

Although the Iraqi population at large suffered from the sanctions, the regime was not seriously affected. In essence, the sanctions probably "expanded the role of the Iraqi state and increased regime stability."[106] As a result of the success of the rationing system, the Ba'th Party managed to increase its support and empathy among the civilian population during the thirteen years of harsh sanctions. In fact, not only did the authorities manage to reconstruct most of the destroyed infrastructure, but the economy began improving by the late 1990s. Between 1996 and 2000 Iraq's GDP was estimated to have increased from $10.6 billion to $33 billion;[107] the currency stabilized, albeit at a much devalued rate versus the dollar, and inflation was the only continuing problem. The regime itself amassed a vast fortune during the period 1990–2003. According to the Iraq Survey Group and the UN Commission, the regime earned about $10.9 billion from illicit barrel surcharges; received kickbacks amounting to 10 percent from imports authorized under the UN; and benefited from exports, primarily petroleum to buyers outside the UN mandate. The Iraq Survey Group concluded that the regime "filtered the majority of the illicitly earned monies through foreign bank accounts in the name of Iraqi banks, ministries, or agencies in violation of UN sanctions."[108]

The recovery in Iraq's economy in the regime's remaining years should be seen against the impoverishment and destitution since the late 1980s. Still, the regime felt comfortable enough by the end of 2002 to launch a ten-year plan "to bring economic prosperity to the Iraqi citizen,"[109] and in the two years prior to 2003, Iraqi newspapers were full of editorials exalting the regime's economic accomplishments.[110] Although from an economic perspective the regime had survived two wars and many years of sanctions, by 2003 Iraq had an anemic economy, was heavily indebted

[105] Joy Gordon, *Invisible War: The United States and the Iraq Sanctions* (Cambridge, MA: Harvard University Press, 2010), pp. 138–39. The book details the magnitude of the sanctions, the role of the Iraqi government, and U.S. policy.
[106] Nimah Mazaheri, "Iraq and the Domestic Political Effects of Economic Sanctions," *Middle East Journal*, vol. 64, no. 2 (Spring 2010), p. 254.
[107] Iraq Survey Group, *Regime Strategic Intent*, vol. I, Regime Finance and Procurement, p. 23.
[108] *Ibid.*, p. 24.
[109] *Al-Qadisiyya*, no. 7640, January 23, 2003.
[110] *Al-Thawra*, no. 10714, November 4, 2002. The newspaper covered the opening of the Thirty-Fifth International Baghdad Exhibition and pointed out that, in spite of the sanctions, 49 Arab and foreign counties and 1,200 firms participated.

with high inflation and a weak currency, and had lost a significant portion of its educated middle class.

Unions and Professional Organizations

Professional organizations in Iraq had a rich history dating back to 1924, and the first labor law recognizing the power of unions was enacted in 1936. It was amended in 1954 following numerous strikes, particularly in the oil industry, with a violent strike taking place in Kirkuk in 1946.[111] The unions continued to be an important factor after the toppling of the monarchy and were heavily under the influence of the Communist Party. The laws of 1958 and 1964 offered a degree of protection to employees, most of whom were in the government-controlled public sector. All industries had workers' committees, although these were essentially bureaucratic in nature rather than truly representing workers.

After 1968, when Iraq became a Ba'thist state, the unions – as in Syria – were dominated by the party, and popular and professional organizations were created as part of its "populist corporatism" to control different sectors of society.[112] The documents clearly indicate the co-optation of the unions, which were turned into professional associations under the control of the party apparatus to serve its needs. Purging disloyal union members was no different from the same task in any other government ministry. A case in point occurred in 1980, when a new secretary general was appointed to the labor union. On taking up the job, he wrote to the Party Secretariat suggesting that because of the "control of traitors over the secretariat general of the labor union and the general union for Iraqi workers for many years which had affected the workers from educational, disciplinary and moral points of view," the leadership should be purged and replaced by new members. The memo does not explain or indicate why the previous leadership was a group of traitors, but it could be assumed that some of them were connected to the "conspirators" against Saddam Hussein who were exposed in the infamous party meeting of summer 1979.[113]

Before a new labor law was enacted in mid-1987, Saddam Hussein wrote a long article about the decision to promote all workers to the level

---

[111] Davis, *Memories of State*, pp. 106 and 310 (footnote 66).
[112] Hinnebusch, *Syria*, pp. 83–84.
[113] Secretary General of the Labor Union to Party Secretariat, "Proposal," March 29, 1980, *BRCC*, 003-1-1 (183–184).

of white-collar employees. He indicated that previous laws had retained a class distinction that had gravely damaged productivity. He emphasized that the "party has neither promoted class struggle nor made it an ideological platform," and that trade unions in Iraq emerged as a reflection of their counterparts in other countries, but that these unions "have fulfilled their task... thanks to the awareness of the Ba'th Party."[114] In other words, the unions carried out their work due to the support of the party, and now it was up to the party to represent everyone. Labor Law no. 71 of 1987 dissolved the labor unions and confirmed that workers in the public sector would become members of the civil service. It guaranteed every worker the right to earn a wage that was adequate to meet his or her essential needs and those of his or her family and confirmed the rights of working hours and retirement.[115]

In Chaudhry's view, the law was part of a move to undercut opposition to the privatization discussed previously, by banning unions in public sector enterprises and confirming the regime's ownership of strategic and heavy industries.[116] Given the party's control of economic management and production, Iraq was no different from East Germany, where the regime considered that "there were officially no legitimate grounds for worker protest against 'their own' party representatives in 'the people's own enterprises.'"[117] When a real decline in public sector wages and salaries took place in the first half of the 1990s, which Mahdi shows was "more drastic than [in] the private sector," there were no genuine unions to raise the workers' issues, and it was left to party branches to report workers' grievances to the higher authorities.[118]

Even before the 1987 law was enacted, it was hard to find fundamental differences between the unions and professional organizations on the one hand and party branches on the other. For example, it was the party and not the unions that organized visits by labor union members to families of martyrs and advocated strengthening relationships between

---

[114] The full text of President Saddam Hussein's article "Why We Turned Workers into Civil Servants," March 31, 1987, appears in Saddam Hussein, *Economy and Management in Socialist Society*, translated by Naji al-Hadithi (Baghdad: Dar al-Ma'mun, 1988), pp. 197–219.

[115] Labor Law no. 71 for 1987, *al-waqa'i' al-'Iraqiyya*, no. 3163, July 18, 1987.

[116] Chaudhry, "On the Way to Market," p. 17.

[117] Mary Fulbrook, *The People's State: East German Society from Hitler to Honecker*, paperback edn. (New Haven, CT: Yale University Press, 2008), p. 224.

[118] Mahdi, "Iraq's Economic Reforms in Perspective," pp. 215–16.

unions and the families of prisoners of war.[119] Each union had to report on its activities in the different spheres of recruitment, culture, visiting martyrs' families, and so on, in exactly the same manner as any party branch.[120] The presidential *diwan* instructed the central bureau of the Farmers Union to initiate cooperation between the agricultural sector and the commercial sector so as to organize exhibitions with the hope of attracting international companies.[121] In fact, the president's secretary for party affairs received reports from all unions and official organizations, and whenever there was a need to "elect" a candidate for the central bureaus; all names were submitted for approval.[122]

As the lines between membership in the party and in professional associations became confused, many party members refrained from joining these associations, to the party's chagrin. The Secretariat sent a memo to all branches commenting that, based on statistics and surveys it had conducted, a significant number of Baʿthists, such as engineers, doctors, and pharmacists, had not joined the associations that represented their professions, and it warned that the independents were outnumbering the Baʿthists, a phenomenon "which could have ramifications for the workings of those associations."[123] The party wanted to ensure that its control of every facet of professional life was total, and it mobilized its members for every internal association election in case some "independent" members might gain office.[124] Interestingly, in Syria, leadership contests in professional associations were similarly heated, despite the dominance of the Baʿth Party, and party members were a minority in large, professional syndicates such as groups of pharmacists or doctors.[125] Even before

[119] Secretary General of Labor Union to Party Secretariat, December 2, 1986, *BRCC*, 079-4-1 (002–009).

[120] See, for example, a table on recruitment of new members by the Women's Association and Youth Association in a report by the Great Victory Branch, March 1, 1998, *BRCC*, 003-4-4 (463).

[121] Minutes of Meeting between Representatives of the Central Farmers Bureau and the Presidential *diwan*, October 27 and October 30, 1985, *BRCC*, 075-5-3 (003).

[122] Secretary General of the Farmers Union to President's Secretary for Party Affairs, April 24, 1985. See also the memo titled "Candidacy in the Farmers Union," December 10, 1984, *BRCC*, 075-5-3 (077).

[123] Party Secretariat to All Branches' Headquarters, "Joining Professional Associations," November 7, 2002, *BRCC*, 004-5-6 (233).

[124] See, for example, a note from the Party Secretariat calling on all members to participate in the elections of the Lawyers Association in March 2000 to prevent independent candidates from winning those elections, February 28, 2000, *BRCC*, 004-4-3 (311).

[125] Pete W. Moore and Bassel F. Salloukh, "Struggles Under Authoritarianism: Regimes, States, and Professional Associations in the Arab World," *International Journal of Middle East Studies*, vol. 39, no. 1 (February 2007), p. 66.

the labor unions were dissolved, active party members were ordered to move from their branches and become fully active in different unions, to ensure the control of these associations.[126] In certain cases, when members wanted to return to their original jobs, they encountered difficulties, and the Party Secretariat had to intervene on their behalf.[127]

All unions were fully engaged by the regime in its battle to break the sanctions during the 1990s. Professional and populist organizations addressed their counterparts around the world, seeking support for limiting the sanctions.[128] All professional associations were informed of their duty to capitalize on their contacts in the Arab world and elsewhere to encourage them to take an active role in this endeavor. Each of the twelve unions and professional associations that operated in Iraq at the time had to report on their efforts, their contact lists worldwide, and their follow-up measures after initial contact. Saddam Hussein's speeches and reports of the hardship suffered by the Iraqi people were distributed to dozens of organizations worldwide.[129]

Along the same lines, as the drums of war began sounding in 2002, the unions were called on to send a message to the United States about the resoluteness of the Iraqi and Arab people. An urgent memo from the presidential *diwan* to the Party Secretariat cited an order from the president to send a message "from the workers of Iraq to the Arab workers asking them not to unload or load American cargo ships or offer them any help. This should also include all American airplanes at airports of Arab countries."[130] Iraqi unions were told to assess whether it would be easier to call for this boycott if it were based on American support for the "Zionist criminal activities" in the occupied Arab land.[131]

In conclusion, the Ba'th Party in Iraq managed to control economic policy in the public and private sectors, and to neutralize unions and

[126] See, for example, the transfer of a member from the Ministry of Foreign Affairs to the Labor Union, April 5, 1980, *BRCC*, 003-1-1 (124).
[127] Secretary General of the Party to Party Secretariat, "Employing Union's Labor," August 3, 1980, *BRCC*, 003-1-1 (244). The memo interestingly indicated that members were transferred prior to elections in the Labor Union, and once elections were over, the secretary general felt it was only right that they should be allowed to return to their previous jobs, having secured the necessary results in the union. See the list of transferees (246).
[128] Party Secretariat to Presidential *diwan*, "Mobilization," May 2, 1994, *BRCC*, 100-3-5 (488).
[129] *Ibid.*, (500–508). The file contains reports of the Teachers Union and the Youth Association.
[130] Presidential *diwan* to Party Secretariat, April 4, 2002, *CRRC*, SH-PDWN-D-000-473.
[131] *Ibid.*

professional associations and force them to function as state-run organizations in which workers and party members shared the same representatives and aspirations. The changes in the economy from the late 1970s to the fall of the regime did not significantly change these fundamentals.

The Baʿth Party and Women

The Baʿth Party, secular and socialist, saw itself as a movement seeking the resurrection of the Arab nation and was hence bound to encourage Iraqi women to improve their status in society in the conviction that liberating them from economic, social, and legal shackles was necessary for growth and prosperity in Arab society.[132] In 1971, Vice President Saddam Hussein told the General Federation of Iraqi Women (GFIW):

> We are all – in the Party and the Government, and in the social organisations [*sic*] – expected to encourage the recruitment of more women to the schools, government departments, the organisations of production, industry, agriculture, arts, culture, information and all other kinds of institutions and services.
>
> We are called upon to struggle tirelessly against all the material and psychological obstacles which stand in our way along this path.[133]

In analyzing this speech, Marion Farouk-Sluglett observed that it was a good illustration of the party's "basically paternalistic tone" toward women's liberation, with the aim of increasing its popularity among the population.[134] Still, significant achievements were recorded for women, particularly in education and health care. The number of girls attending primary and secondary schools increased sharply throughout the 1970s, and the number of women attending university grew from about 9,000 in 1970 to more than 28,000 by 1979.[135] The party also focused on illiteracy, which was far more widespread among women (70 percent), and as one analysis pointed out, the campaign was unique in the way it struck

---

[132] Hizb al-Baʿth, *Thawrat 17 Tammuz*, p. 153.

[133] Saddam Hussein, *Social and Foreign Affairs in Iraq*, p. 15. The speech titled "Women – One Half of Our Society" was delivered on April 17, 1971, at the Third Conference of the General Federation of Iraqi Women.

[134] Marion Farouk-Sluglett, "Liberation or Repression? Pan-Arab Nationalism and the Women's Movement in Iraq," in Derek Hopwood, Habib Ishow, and Thomas Koszinowski (eds.), *Iraq: Power and Society*, St Antony's Middle East Monographs (Reading: Ithaca Press, 1993), pp. 68–69.

[135] Amal al-Sharqi, "The Emancipation of Iraqi Women," in Tim Niblock (ed.), *Iraq: The Contemporary State* (New York: St. Martin's Press, 1982), pp. 80–81.

a balance "between coercion and voluntarism" and in its "ideological underpinnings."[136]

Whatever the motivation behind these policies, the fact remained that there was considerable progress in the position of women in Iraq. Throughout the 1970s Saddam Hussein continued to advocate women's rights: "We have to focus on equal rights, concentrate on balance in rights, and focus on rejecting the views that put women in a secondary position . . . we reject the feudal and tribalism views and mentality."[137]

Renowned for his ability to adapt his supposedly fundamental views to suit his political ambitions, Saddam Hussein changed his mind on the subject as the war with Iran progressed, in conjunction with his other radical transformations regarding tribalism and religiosity. In an effort to appease religious groups in Iraq, and to counter the appeal of the Ayatollah Khomeini and the looming shadow of Iran's larger population, the regime launched a series of measures that were to have a deep impact on the status of women. One year into the war, the RCC decided to encourage early marriage; interest-free loans were provided to any man under the age of twenty-two who would marry. If the prospective groom was a student, he and his future wife would be entitled to free accommodation in the university dormitories.[138] Encouraging early marriage remained a core policy until the collapse of the regime in 2003; many government offices took part in arranging marriage ceremonies (and circumcision of children) on their premises, together with special bonuses for these families.[139] The second major law, in 1987, encouraged increased fertility. Financial rewards were given to families who gave birth to a fourth child after this law came into effect, and for those who already had four children, bonuses would be paid for future births.[140] The party was enlisted to promote this decision by

---

[136] Christopher J. Lucas, "Arab Illiteracy and the Mass Literacy Campaign in Iraq," *Comparative and International Education Society*, vol. 25, no. 1 (February 1981), pp. 83–84.

[137] Saddam Hussein, in a seminar to discuss the increase in productivity of the working woman, January 27, 1977, *al-Mukhtarat*, vol. 10, p. 190.

[138] RCC Decision no. 632, May 13, 1981, *BRCC*, 021-5-6 (347–348).

[139] See the list of party affiliates approved for early marriage, among them a woman barely eighteen years old in *tandhim* Baghdad, "Early Marriage," June 13, 2002, *BRCC*, 003-5-3 (066); and Presidential *diwan*, "Order," November 10, 2000, *BRCC*, B 001-1-7 (057–058).

[140] RCC Decision no. 881, *al-waqa'i' al-'Iraqiyya*, no. 3179, December 7, 1987.

distributing gifts and rewards to women who responded to the regime's call.[141]

Needless to say, these measures forced many women to stay at home to take care of their children, and once the war had ended, women's employment was further affected by the lack of job opportunities for returning soldiers in a contracting economy, and many women lost their jobs. This, coupled with the growing conservatism, led to a significant loss of women's rights achieved in the 1970s. The regime legitimized the tribal practice of honor killing in 1990, and wives of men arrested and convicted for anti-regime activities were encouraged to divorce their husbands.[142] A law combating prostitution was promulgated in 1988, and divorce laws were amended as part of this wave of conservatism.[143] Interestingly, although not directly criticizing the regime, the GFIW acknowledged the "lacking of commitment of state institutions to gender equality."[144]

The First Gulf War and the ensuing sanctions led to a further erosion of women's achievements. As we have seen, the economic burden on all households was quite heavy, and women suffered even more. Another effect was "the loss of public identity and the domestication of professional women."[145] Employment of women continued to fall, and their wages in real terms, given the hyperinflation, fell precipitously. But as Nadje al-Ali indicated, although women's formal employment decreased, they continued to be "active economically and played a very important role in the increasingly significant informal sector."[146] Recognizing this, Saddam Hussein discussed "women[s'] employment in their houses" in a way that could enhance productivity by establishing commercial relations with both the public and private sectors. Promoting this idea, he argued that "the Iraqi family has a high willingness to work from home; after all not all women work outside their homes, and in fact it is not appropriate

---

[141] Duhok Branch, "Guidance," May 26, 1988, *NIDS*, KDP 029, Box 2305 (080076).

[142] See Suha Omar, "Women: Honour, Shame and Dictatorship," in Hazelton (ed.), *Iraq since the Gulf War*, pp. 63–64.

[143] Law no. 8 for Combating Prostitution, *al-waqa'i' al-'Iraqiyya*, no. 3186, January 25, 1988; for divorce laws, see *al-waqa'i' al-'Iraqiyya*, no. 3190, February 22, 1988.

[144] Rohde, *State–Society Relations*, p. 85. Rohde has an extensive chapter on gender policies in Ba'thist Iraq, mostly based on Iraqi newspapers and journals.

[145] Jacqueline S. Ismael and Shereen T. Ismael, "Living through War, Sanctions and Occupation: The Voices of Iraqi Women," *International Journal of Contemporary Iraqi Studies*, vol. 2, no. 3 (2008), p. 416.

[146] Nadje Sadig al-Ali, *Iraqi Women: Untold Stories from 1948 to the Present* (London: Zed, 2007), p. 187.

that all women work outside their homes, thus we have to think about deploying this potential."[147]

Although the country was in dire economic straits from the end of the 1980s, women's share in the economically active population in the formal economy did not show a significant statistical decline, staying at roughly 11 percent between 1987 and 1997, and women continued to constitute roughly one third of university students between 1989 and 2000.[148] Although their participation in the political domain remained relatively limited during this period, they remained very involved in the field of education and to a lesser extent in business and commerce. Recruitment of women to the Ba'th Party was a second priority after recruiting young men. However, only one woman reached the pinnacle of the Regional Command of the party: Dr. Huda Salih Mahdi 'Ammash, whose father had been active in the Ba'th regime in 1963 and returned to power after July 1968. In September 1971, like many of the old Ba'thists, he was pushed out of his ministerial job and offered the post of ambassador to Finland. Huda 'Ammash obtained her PhD in microbiology at the University of Missouri and became a member of the Regional Command in 2001. Saddam Hussein obviously admired this talented scientist.

The rise of conservatism found its way into the organizational structure of the secular party. Women began to form their own *shu'ab*, which were segregated from male sections and cells. By mid-2002, there were sixty-nine branches across the country, and under their roof there were eighty-seven sections for women. As Table 6 indicates, the total number of women affiliated with the party was slightly less than one million, representing roughly 25 percent of the entire number of party affiliates. Whereas the party elite constituted about 14.5 percent of the total party, the top tier of women members represented only 2 percent of the total female members.

In 2002, when guns were distributed to all those affiliated with the party, one table indicated that Sa'ad branch in Baghdad had 1,019 female affiliates (1 branch member, 11 section members, 126 division members, and 881 cell members), and that only 6 percent of them carried guns. The report warned that this shortage of guns was impacting the missions of many women members even at the cell level.[149] A memo issued by the

---

[147] Speech by the president to the cabinet on June 7, 2000, quoted in a memo from the presidential *diwan* to the Party Secretariat, BRCC, 009-2-4 (037–048).

[148] Rohde, *State–Society Relations*, pp. 101–02.

[149] Sa'ad bin Abi Waqqas Branch (part of al-Rusafa Baghdad *tandhim*) to Party Secretariat, "Shortages of Guns," July 16, 2002, BRCC, 006-2-3 (035–039).

TABLE 6. *Membership Statistics for Women in the Ba'th Party, 2002*

Sections	Cells	Total*	Branch Members	Section Members	Division Members	Active Members	Apprenticed Members	Supporters	Sympathizers	Total**
87	3,430	3,517	83	853	5,128	14,877	35,261	252,263	657,031	965,496

* This total excludes the number of women's divisions that were not reported in the statistics.

** The statistics do not include some categories included in Appendix II, such as candidates and advanced supporters.

Source: "Statistics for Women within the Party Structure for the Country, June 25, 2002," *BRRC*, 108-4-6 (041–043).

Party Secretariat in 1985 detailed the allocation of functions to female comrades; most jobs involved volunteering in education (literacy campaigns); working in the health sector (popular clinics); visiting families of martyrs; and for the younger women, joining either the Popular Army or the civil defense.[150] But their opportunities undoubtedly diminished as branches began to be split into male and female organizations.

Women were enrolled, albeit on a limited scale, as volunteers in *al-jaysh al-sha'bi* (the Popular Army) beginning in 1977 and later in *jaysh al-quds* (the Jerusalem Army) until the 2003 invasion. Some women were allowed to enroll in the army and air force, although Saddam Hussein expressed reservations about this and believed that many countries allowed women to enlist in the armed forces as a masquerade that would not necessarily lead to equality.[151] Women applied regularly for scholarships from the Ministry of Defense, either in civilian colleges (mostly medicine and engineering) or in certain military and police academies. In 1993, for instance, eighty-six female students applied, and their files reveal an interesting depiction of them. First, without exception, all of these candidates had higher grades than the male applicants; second, some were politically independent, but their fathers were "Friends of the President" – one student even attached a personal letter of recommendation from the chief of staff. What is noteworthy is that the minister of defense had decided to allocate only 5 percent of scholarships to women (that is, only fifteen out of eighty-six), which led the head of military courses to write to the under secretary general of the party seeking advice about rejecting such well-qualified students.[152]

On anecdotal evidence it seems that that the leader of the party, Saddam Hussein, had many relationships with single and married women

---

[150] Party Secretariat to All *tandhimat*, October 6, 1985, BRCC, 003-3-2 (108–110).

[151] Saddam Hussein, *al-Mukhtarat*, vol. 10, p. 191. This was part of his speech in 1977, in which he told his audience that the participation of "Zionist women" in the 1967 war had no real impact and was more of a show. For more details about participation in the army, see Rohde, *State–Society Relations*, pp. 86–88.

[152] Head of Military Courses to Under Secretary General (in charge of all military courses), September 28, 1993, *BRCC*, 013-1-6 (019). For some of the women candidates' applications, see (021–068). They had to fill in the same questionnaires as their male colleagues. All the candidates had to sign an agreement stipulating that concealing information on three specific questions carried the death penalty: whether the candidate was affiliated to a political movement other than the Ba'th Party; whether he or she had any connection with conspirators who had opposed the party's July 17–30, 1968, revolution; and whether they had any relatives who were members of non-Ba'th political movements.

during his reign, and numerous stories indicate how he exploited his position to engage in illicit relationships with women.[153]

The Ba'th Party and Religion

Although the regime was secular in nature, at least throughout the 1970s, it was not publicly anti-religious: "Our party does not have a neutral position towards apostasy and faith. It stands with faith, always, but our party is not and should never be a religious party."[154] Saddam Hussein's position on religion and mosque attendance was very clear to his comrades, as he did not mince his words. In one internal party meeting in the early 1980s in which religion was discussed, one member said that "religiosity increases immunity," to which Saddam Hussein immediately replied, "A Ba'thist does not need religiosity for immunity as he has the immunity of Omar [the Caliph]."[155] Similarly, when it was reported to him that some senior officials were attending mosques or praying during working hours, thus forcing subordinates to imitate them, he declared at an internal gathering that members "are not allowed to pray or attend a mosque as a group," as it would create undue pressure on their colleagues (including the non-Muslim ones).[156]

Before he changed his public policy in the 1980s, Saddam Hussein emphasized that the Ba'th should "oppose the politicization of religion by the state and within society."[157] When the issue of sectarianism came to the fore after the 1991 uprising, he told his inner cabinet, which included members of the RCC and the party's Regional Command, that he was completely oblivious to the differences between Sunnis and Shi'is, and the first time that he encountered this issue was when he was living in exile in Cairo and someone asked him whether he was a Sunni or a Shi'i. He mused on the fact that no one from Tikrit would know the difference.[158] It is impossible to tell whether or not this is true, but it is plausible that even in the early 1960s many Iraqis were unaware of the difference. The

---

[153] See, for example, the story about a Foreign Ministry employee who was appointed abroad so that Saddam Hussein could have a relationship with his wife, in Duelfer, *Hide and Seek*, pp. 386–87.

[154] Saddam Hussein, *Nadhra fi al-din wa al-turath* [A Glimpse into Religion and Tradition] (Baghdad: al-Huriyya Publishing House, 1980), p. 7.

[155] Interview with an ex-senior Foreign Ministry official, June 15, 2010.

[156] Interview with an ex-minister and a senior party member, October 17, 2010.

[157] Hussein, *Nadhra fi al-din wa al-turath*, pp. 14–15.

[158] Audiotape of a meeting of Saddam Hussein and the leadership, mid-1990s (exact date unknown), CRRC, SH-SHTP-A-000-714.

exclusion of many Shi'is from senior jobs in government and the military was not "the creation of the Takriti [*sic*] Ba'th Party but rather a policy with a long historical tradition."[159] However, there is no doubt that after the 1991 uprising, repression of the Shi'is increased significantly.

Much has been written about Saddam Hussein's radical policy shifts from anti-tribalism to pro-tribalism and from secularism to religiosity,[160] but the files clearly indicate that the regime remained to the end suspicious of all religions and all religious activities. There was thus a dual policy of public religiosity, on one hand, and monitoring and suppression of all religious activities, on the other hand. Saddam Hussein's attitude to Islam was that superstition had taken over the religion and had "[become] the way to reach religion." He told his top aides in 1980 that "Allah is neither Sunni nor Shi'i. He is neither Catholic nor Protestant," and that most people had moved away from real religion to pursue other philosophies that had no connection to religion.[161]

Saddam Hussein was always wary of any religious movement. In one cabinet meeting in the mid-1980s in which the topic of the Muslim Brothers was mooted, he made his views very clear: "They [the Muslim Brothers] rely on the phase prior to the collapse [of regimes]. . . . So we have to snatch it from them. . . . They do not consider any state, even our country, as Islamic."[162] He warned his colleagues that the Brothers would never accept showing a dancer on television or approve of the bars and restaurants that lined the Abu Nuas Street in Baghdad. In an archetype policy, Saddam Hussein proceeded to tell the cabinet that the regime should not clash with the Brothers or declare that it opposed them. "We should initiate a dialogue with them stating that we will not attack them. We can also tell them that they are our brothers but their talk about the religious state is an attack against us."[163] Discussing the situation in Sudan and the role of the Muslim Brothers, he confused Numeiri (Ja'far al-Numeiri,

---

[159] Davis, *Memories of State*, p. 58.

[160] On tribalism policy, see Baram, "Neo-Tribalism in Iraq," and Bengio, *Saddam's Word*, Chapter 13, "Manipulation of Islam," pp. 176–91.

[161] Audiotape of a meeting held by Saddam Hussein in 1980, CRRC, SH-SHTP-A-000-751. As in many of those high-level meetings, a number of subjects were discussed that were not on the agenda. The agenda for that day listed acquiring weapons, the Soviet Union, Israel, etc., but the conversations invariably drifted onto topics that were on the president's mind.

[162] Audiotape of a meeting of Saddam Hussein with members of the Ba'th Party in the Arab countries. The general secretary of the Sudanese branch of the Ba'th, Badr al-Din Muddathir, was among the attendees, CRRC, SH-SHTP-A-001-167.

[163] *Ibid.*

president of Sudan) with Khomeini, but he immediately laughed and said that these days "everything sounds like Khomeini."[164]

As shown in the previous chapter, the regime was obsessed with all religious movements, be they Wahhabism or Shi'ism, and wanted to infiltrate them to ensure its control. Wahhabism was outlawed because it represented "a deviation from the real Islam." A memo warned that the rapprochement in 2000 between Iran and Saudi Arabia might presage the beginning of conspiracies between the Da'wa Party and Wahhabists.[165] The authorities were convinced that Saudi Arabia was supplying cash to groups acting against the regime. Even throughout the 1990s, anyone showing an inclination toward Wahhabism was considered an enemy of the state.[166] When reports reached the party that an attendant appointed in a mosque in Mosul was suspected to be a Wahhabi, the authorities were alarmed and took steps to replace him.[167] The documents clearly illustrate their concerns about fanatical Islam emanating from Saudi Arabia; two months before the 9/11 terror attacks in the United States, a secret and urgent order from Saddam Hussein was sent to heads of branches ordering that all imams in every mosque must announce that Wahhabism was an infidel movement, and any imam who refused would be punished and dismissed from his job.[168] In early September 2001, the minister of *awqaf* and religious affairs held a meeting attended by academics, religious leaders, and representatives from the different security organizations to discuss Wahhabism – how to fight it and how to show that its teachings had nothing to do with real Islam.[169]

The regime not only monitored Friday sermons and those who attended mosques, but also was involved in every appointment by the Ministry of Awqaf and Religious Affairs in any religious institution, and it tried to impose party loyalists in every position.[170] All imams and

---

[164] *Ibid.*

[165] Al-Karkh *tandhim* to All Heads of Branches in al-Karkh, "Activities of Wahhabists," June 18, 2001, BRCC, 004-3-1 (388).

[166] See, for example, a report by *al-amn* on activities in a district of Baghdad (al-Mashtal), and how owners of stores who were suspected of being sympathizers with Wahhabism were monitored, November 30, 1995, BRCC, 005-1-2 (097–098).

[167] Party Secretariat to Ministry of Awqaf, "Information," November 1, 1997, BRCC, 103-1-5 (041).

[168] Party Secretariat to All Branches, "Guidance," July 23, 2001, BRCC, 004-4-6 (231–235).

[169] Party Secretariat to Heads of *tandhimat*, September 8, 2001, BRCC, 004-4-4 (070). The minister's meeting took place on September 2, 2001.

[170] Party Secretariat to Deputy Secretary of the Party, April 10, 1996, BRCC, 119-4-8 (254).

mosques were under scrutiny. In one case an imam in Arbil was replaced by a more "reliable element"; in another, the SSO arrested an imam and referred him to a psychiatric hospital, and a telephone tap was installed in the house of an imam suspected of anti-regime sentiments.[171] Friday sermons of the imam in al-Hasan Mosque in Saddam City in Baghdad were regularly reported and analyzed, because the party was worried about his views on women. During one sermon the imam spoke out against women working in shops, as this gave them an opportunity to be alone with men. In another sermon he congratulated schools and neighborhoods in his area, claiming that 99 percent of women were wearing the hijab. This was underlined in the report as something to watch out for, as was the imam's criticism of tribal leaders, whom he accused of making decisions based on tradition rather than on Islamic law.[172]

The authorities had a two-pronged approach in dealing with committed religious people. The party called on comrades "to develop relations with religious leaders in mosques in order to influence their positions and attitudes both positive and negative and to induce them to coordinate with the general directorate of *al-amn*."[173] Concurrently, every party branch and section was asked to undertake a survey of all mosques and *husseiniyyat* (Shi'i religious centers) in their areas, and to evaluate all the employees from a security point of view. Each branch reported on its findings. In Salah al-Din province, for example, it was reported that there were 76 mosques, and that 24 out of the 41 imams working in them were associated with the party hierarchy, 4 as full members. The 17 who were independent were given a positive evaluation overall, and the report even recommended nominating a handful of them to be affiliated with the party; only two were put on a watch list, because of rumors that they mixed with "suspicious and Wahhabist elements."[174] At the end of 1998, according to one survey, there were 372 mosques, and Friday sermons took place in 320 of them; 687 people were working in these religious establishments as speakers, attendants, and imams.[175]

[171] Arbil *amn*, December 2, 1982, *NIDS*, PUK 046, Box 046 (550037); SSO to Presidential *diwan*, April 2, 1996, *BRCC*, B 001-2-1 (180–181).
[172] Saddam Branch to Party Secretariat, November 6 and November 13, 1998, *BRCC*, 093-4-4 (077–079).
[173] Party Secretariat to All Branch Secretaries, October 8, 1998, *BRCC*, 093-4-4 (001).
[174] Salah al-Din Branch to Party Secretariat, November 18, 1998, *BRCC*, 093-4-4 (024–026).
[175] Party Secretariat, "A Study," 1998, *BRCC*, 093-4-4 (093–097). It is doubtful that this was a countrywide survey, as the number looks relatively low, and the study does not indicate whether it actually included all provinces.

As early as 1995 the party organized a committee in every province made up of the secretary of the branch, the head of *al-amn* in the province, and the director of the Awqaf Department in the region to evaluate all religious leaders to present everyone involved "the opportunity to continue in the path of the victorious march." A special form was developed, which all employees in religious establishments were asked to complete. Among the questions were the following: What are the worker's political leanings? Does he have any fanatical religious inclinations? Does he have any relationship with an opposition movement? Does he have a relative who has escaped from Iraq? And last but not least, "does he pray for Mr. President May God Protect him in his sermons?" After this form was handed in, each branch had to evaluate the worker and add all other available information on him.[176]

The party was also interested in the attitudes and views of Christian clergy, and a memo commented that although most of the men were independent, they were "good elements" who showed support for the party. Some of the senior clergy were described as "sympathetic to the ideology of the party."[177] The party also regularly reviewed its support among groups of Sufis and *al-takya*.[178]

In addition to monitoring those individuals affiliated with religious institutions, the authorities were wary of religious ceremonies and gatherings of a religious nature (see Chapter 7). A memo sent to all branches asked that a visitors' book be provided at religious ceremonies, so that all information could be checked later. This would enable *al-amn* to monitor those attending and to collect data such as their numbers, ages, and frequency of attendance. Overall, the memo called for discouraging ceremonies in the provinces of Karbala and Najaf, but if these did occur, everyone attending should be thoroughly searched and those found in possession of recording devices should be arrested for at least two weeks for investigation.[179] Another memo warned of certain phenomena that should be watched, or ideally stopped: weddings in which some families

[176] Party Secretariat to All Secretaries of Branches, "Evaluation," December 28, 1995, *BRCC*, 103-1-5 (154; 189).

[177] Party Secretariat to Deputy Secretary General, August 23, 1992, *BRCC*, 141-5-6 (131–138).

[178] *Al-takya* was a house for the needy that had religious support. For the memo, see *BRCC*, 141-5-6 (008).

[179] Party Secretariat to Comrades in Charge of *tandhimat*, "Religious Occasions," March 12, 2000, *BRCC*, 004-4-3 (032–033). The authorities were wary of audiotapes of sermons being distributed outside mosques.

organized readings of poems by people connected with al-Sadr, which
could easily turn into incitement against the regime; funerals that became
processions, with the recitation of religious books while women cried and
ululated; and the worrying occurrence of people visiting the holy sites in
Karbala most Thursday nights for prayers and gatherings. The memo
called on the party apparatus to involve religious leaders in fighting these
"deviants of Islam."[180] One branch reported that it seemed there were
too many "organized religious trips" to holy and tourist sites, and these
needed to be investigated to find out the real reason behind them.[181]

The Party Secretariat sent a detailed document to all branches about
controlling religious occasions and preventing "negative practices."
Among measures taken to counter those practices were directives that
no post-funeral ceremonies should take place without official permission; that food should not be distributed in religious ceremonies, because
it encouraged greater participation; and that information about people attending these functions and staying in hotels should be gathered
immediately.[182] As part of the cultural activities both within and outside
the party, ways of opposing these "negative practices" were emphasized,
and all unions and professional organizations were called on to counter
religious practices with Ba'th ideology and to elevate the motto, "The
Ba'thist and his family are the ideal in behavior and discipline."[183] The
regime was sensitive to its position with regard to religious groups. By
1991, Saddam Hussein was claiming to be a descendant of the Prophet
Muhammad and his cousin Imam 'Ali as part of strengthening his own
personality cult.[184] Because of anxieties about the power of the Shi'i religious establishment in Najaf and Karbala, the RCC decided that anyone,
apart from Saddam Hussein, who claimed that his roots were from the
family of Imam 'Ali would receive a seven-year term of imprisonment.[185]

[180] Party Secretariat to Comrade 'Ali Hasan al-Majid, "Negative Phenomena," February
22, 2000, *BRCC*, 004-4-3 (209–212). A year earlier, in 1999, the Grand Ayatollah
Muhammad al-Sadr was assassinated in what was considered an organized attack by
the Ba'th regime against the independent leadership of the Shi'is.
[181] Al-Ma'mun Branch to Party Headquarters, "Religious Trips," June 6, 1998, *BRCC*,
003-4-4 (260).
[182] Party Secretariat to All Comrades in Charge of *tandhimat*, March 29, 1997, *BRCC*,
003-4-4 (470–472). A copy of this memorandum was sent to all unions and to the
deputy secretary general of the military bureau.
[183] *Ibid.* See also a report on cultural activities and religious practices in *BRCC*, 003-4-1
(177–182). It called for more seminars and distribution of speeches and booklets of the
party dealing with religion and faith.
[184] Ken Ringle, "Iraq, Mother of Metaphor; Flamboyant Imagery Is Carefully Calculated,"
Washington Post, February 13, 1991.
[185] RCC Decision 206, November 27, 2000, *BRCC*, B 001-1-7 (015).

While engaging in all those anti-religious activities the regime continued its faith campaign, publicly supported all religious activities, and called for more conservatism and religiosity within society. The Ba'th party had a complex relationship with Islam: on one hand, it was a secular party whose founder was a Christian, but on the other hand, the party grew in an Islamic environment and was fully aware of the importance religion has in the Arab world. Hence Saddam Hussein found it easy to adopt Islam as part of his political oratory, and used it to great effect. New mosques were built, and Saddam Hussein issued public orders to repair and improve existing mosques in the different provinces.[186] He initiated the construction of the Mother of All Battles Mosque in Baghdad, intended to be the largest mosque in the world, and the Iraqi flag was redesigned to include the inscription "Allahu Akbar" (God Is Great). The authorities also tightened the rules about opening coffee shops and food stores, as well as night clubs and bars, during Ramadan and ordered the closure of all restaurants and even cafeterias in government offices to comply with Ramadan fasting rules. Radio and television were instructed to allot an hour a day to religious programs, particularly before breaking the fast and immediately afterward.[187] The regime devoted a lot of attention to the religious calendar; important dates such as the Prophet's birthday were celebrated under the auspices of the president, and all branches had to organize festivities in their region.[188]

Time and again Saddam Hussein, in speeches and directives, urged Iraqis to observe the Qur'an and underlined the importance of building a generation that would derive its ethics from the Qur'an and whose lifestyle would be based on the rules and customs of the Prophet.[189] Later in the 1990s, over a period of three years, a 605-page Qur'an was written using Saddam Hussein's blood.[190]

[186] See, for example, the order to repair the spiral mosque in Samarra, April 19, 1999, *BRCC*, 021-2-7 (078).

[187] Presidential *diwan* to All Ministries and Municipalities, "Instructions," March 15, 1990, *BRCC*, B 003-4-7 (324–325). For more details about the faith campaign and the trend toward conservatism, see Rohde, *State–Society Relations*, pp. 109–12.

[188] Presidential *diwan* to All Government Offices, April 28, 2002, *BRCC*, 009-2-2 (120–122).

[189] Ministry of Awqaf and Religious Affairs, "Ministerial Order," August 18, 2001, *BRCC*, 004-3-1 (143–145).

[190] *BBC News*, September 25, 2000. After the 2003 invasion, this Qur'an was kept in a vault in a mosque, see Martin Chulov, "Qur'an Etched in Saddam Hussein's Blood Poses Dilemma for Iraq Leaders," *Guardian*, December 19, 2010.

In an intriguing move to ingratiate himself with religious groups, Saddam Hussein set up in 1994 the Saddam Institute for the Study of the Holy Qur'an, ensuring that faculty members were preapproved and that many students were Ba'th Party members. Indeed, the institute functioned as a party directorate and was part of the hierarchy of the Party Secretariat (see Appendix I). Among the institute's most important objectives was interpretation of the Qur'an. Needless to say, these interpretations were highly influenced by the regime.

By early 2000, the institute included three centers – Baghdad, Basra, and Ninewa – with about 1,000 graduates.[191] At least 20 percent of the graduates were active members of the party, and in 2002 the institute began selecting some of its faculty and students to attend the pilgrimage in Mecca, given the importance of knowing "what the pilgrims are thinking and the need to deal with issues raised [during the pilgrimage]."[192] Addressing the seventh class of the institute, the deputy secretary general of the party, 'Izzat Ibrahim, talked about the faith campaign and its importance: "Look at Iraq today ... how the great people under the leadership of this great party, is similar to the manner the Prophet and his associates behaved [and ruled]. We are not a religious party, or a traditional revolutionary party ... we are the party of the Islamic *risala* [message], of the Arab message."[193] Ibrahim informed the new students that the president, following in the steps of the Caliph Omar, would continue to expand Qur'anic studies and that more centers of the institute would be opened soon. He also compared the battles against the Persians during the Caliphates with Iraq's war against Iran under Saddam Hussein.[194]

The institute curriculum, although containing topics such as the biography and history of the Prophet Muhammad, included other elements that were wholly political. Among dissertations graded "excellent" were, "Dimensions of the Ideas of the Comrade Leader" and "Sources in the

---

[191] In Ninewa, 186 participated in the 2000–01 academic year. For the names of students, courses, and grades, see *BRCC*, 004-2-3 (392–396). Among the courses were the Science of Qur'an, the Prophet's Tradition, Poetry and Literature, and *tarhib wa targhib* (Punishment and Rewards) in Islam, which later on was utilized by many observers to describe the system of the Ba'th regime.

[192] Party Secretariat to Deputy Secretary General, "Update," April 2, 2002, *BRCC*, 004-2-3 (085).

[193] Speech by Comrade 'Izzat Ibrahim, October 16, 2001, *BRCC*, 004-2-3 (244–256). The ceremony was attended by members of the Regional Command, among them Huda Salih Mahdi 'Ammash.

[194] *Ibid.*

Faith Speeches of the Leader."[195] During the academic year 2001–02, 241 affiliates of the party, all of them branch and section members (that is, none from the lower echelons), graduated from the institute. They came from a wide range of jobs and backgrounds, were aged mostly between fifty-five and sixty, and were given a year or two of leave to devote to studying at the institute.[196]

In addition to studying in this institute, party members had to participate in the special courses prepared as part of the faith campaign. Each branch and section had to nominate some of its affiliates to enroll in these courses, which lasted up to six months, and graduates received a diploma from the institute.[197] While studying, some students continued with their day jobs. One memo from the party indicated that a member was injured when arresting smugglers and would need a month to recover and would miss his studies.[198]

These public displays of faith and religiosity were part of the effort to enlist support for the regime both in Iraq and in the Muslim world. After the Gulf War of 1991, the party proposed organizing television programs involving religious leaders, particularly those from the south, to explain "the intentions of the imperialist powers against Iraq" and the role that Islam should play in fighting foreign elements.[199] In late 2002, the religious leadership of Najaf issued fatwas emphasizing "the duty of Muslims towards American threats," and "the verdict regarding anyone helping America in its plans to attack Iraq."[200] Another important objective of the faith campaign was to address Saddam Hussein's focus on youth and his belief, even before the Iran–Iraq War, that the Ba'th Party was losing young people to religion and that this constituted a serious

---

[195] For the curriculum of 1998, see *BRCC*, 012-3-4 (074); for a list of dissertations that won accolades at the end of the academic year 2002, see *BRCC*, 004-2-3 (056).

[196] Dean of the Saddam Institute to Presidential *diwan*, July 10, 2002, *BRCC*, 004-4-6 (123).

[197] See the letter from the institute and grades of one of the student graduates, August 21, 2001, *BRCC*, 012-3-4 (073–074). For granting leave to 139 party members for the academic year 2001–02, see Presidential *diwan*, December 30, 2001, *BRCC*, 004-2-3 (195).

[198] Dean of the Saddam Institute for Studying the Holy Qur'an to Party Secretariat, April 25, 2002, *BRCC*, 004-2-3 (155).

[199] Party Secretariat, "Proposal," August 26, 1992, *BRCC*, 005-1-2 (342).

[200] The fatwas were issued by Imam 'Ali Hussein al-Sistani from Najaf and came in response to the two questions put to him by the party. For the fatwas and accompanying letter, see Party Secretariat to Deputy Secretary General of the Party, September 30, 2002, *BRCC*, 009-2-5 (002–003).

threat to its future. Many documents indicate the seriousness of this issue and the resources allocated to countering it.[201]

Children, Youth, and Students under the Baʿth Party

As discussed in Chapter 2, the regime devoted special attention to recruiting youth and students, convinced of their importance for the regime's sustainability and that they were "the most valuable asset we own." In one speech, Saddam Hussein stated that "some fathers slipped away from us for many reasons and factors, but the small boy is still in our hands" and called for transforming those children. He proposed "surrounding" the adults by using their children and insisted that children should learn three important things: to object, but with respect, when their parents discussed party's secrets; to object if their parents were wasting the state's wealth; and finally to be on guard against foreigners. He therefore argued that the role of the primary school teacher was more important than that of the secondary school teacher, which in turn was more important than the mission of the university teacher, because the latter would receive students who were already mature and could not be easily molded.[202] This followed the pattern of many regimes similar to the Baʿth, which made serious and prolonged efforts to "control and direct the energies of young people."[203] Saddam Hussein wanted to assign senior people to guide the youth, given the latter's vulnerability and tendency to imitate others, and he felt that these leaders should be experienced party members.[204] In a discussion about changing the national curricula, he advocated teaching children that the Baʿth Party was an irrefutable fact, and educating them about the party's leadership and achievements.[205] Even the curriculum for kindergartens underwent changes to strengthen "national education" by recruiting more Baʿthist teachers.[206]

---

[201] See, for example, a special meeting at the RCC by the National Security Council to discuss religion and youth, December 31, 1979, *BRCC*, 003-1-1 (411–412).

[202] Speech by President Saddam Hussein in the Ministry of Planning, July 10, 1977. *al-Mukhtarat*, vol. 2, pp. 25–37. See more details on the speech in Makiya, *Republic of Fear*, pp. 77–78.

[203] For East Germany under communism, see Fulbrook, *The People's State*, p. 13.

[204] Speech by Saddam Hussein to the Youth Association, February 11, 1976, *al-Mukhtarat*, vol. 10, pp. 25–29.

[205] Saddam Hussein discussing the report of the educational committee to reform the national curricula, June 3, 1975, *al-Mukhtarat*, vol. 4, p. 88.

[206] Great Victory Branch to Party Secretariat, June 5, 1999, *BRCC*, 003-4-1 (271).

FIGURE 11. Picture of Saddam Hussein Adorning One of His Philosophical Pronouncements. The text reads: "We have to sponsor those who are geniuses, the most intelligent people, and the best educators / We want a perfect person, physically, scientifically, and educationally / (Saddam Hussein's message when schools for the gifted were set up by the Ministry of Education)." Courtesy of the Iraq Memory Foundation.

A number of organizations were established to train children and the youth both physically and politically. *Al-tali'a* (the Vanguards) catered to children aged ten to fifteen; this was later replaced with *ashbal Saddam* (Saddam's Cubs). For those aged fifteen to twenty, there was the *futuwwa* (Youth Organization).[207] In a detailed appraisal of youth training based on data from five camps attended by 1,221 students, it was concluded that although the military training was good, the physical training was less successful, and the weakest link was cultural activities. Ten percent of the students interviewed said that relations with their officers were mediocre, but the majority described their relationship with other students as good.[208] Others in the party complained about the lack of discipline in these camps and the high absenteeism; one table indicated that during a week in August 1986, an average 10 to 30 percent of students did not show up for training. Saddam Hussein concluded that insufficient resources were devoted to educating the students politically and demanded an enhancement of cultural programs.[209] As a result of these reports, the RCC decided that any students who were absent for more than seven days would fail their academic year even if they were to pass their exams. In addition, students who had committed serious breaches would be expelled from their schools, banned from party activities, and drafted into the army.[210]

Political education of the youth had a dual target: it was intended, on one hand, to expand recruitment to the party and, on the other hand, to guard against the "vulnerability" of the youth to other political ideas and in particular to religion, a tendency that the regime constantly feared, even before the war with Iran.[211] Although anxious about religious ideas, the

---

[207] Davis, *Memories of State*, pp. 232–33; Makiya, *Republic of Fear*, pp. 76–77.

[208] Dr. M. (full name is withheld), Center for Educational and Scientific Research and Studies, National Union for Students and Youth, n.d. (probably 1986), *BRCC*, 003-2-7 (257–307).

[209] Party Secretariat to *tandhimat* Bureaus, September 25, 1986, *BRCC*, 003-2-7 (113–120). This followed a report of a special committee ordered by Saddam Hussein, composed of the Party Secretariat, security organizations' representatives, and the presidential *diwan*, to study the shortcomings in the training camps.

[210] RCC Decision no. 720, September 8, 1986. The list contained the names and educational affiliations of 668 students who were absent from training for more than seven days. Another list shows 28 students who had committed gross negligence. Among serious breaches were beating an officer, fighting with other students, and absconding at night from the camp, *BRCC*, 003-2-7 (428–430). For the two lists, see (432–479) and (480–482).

[211] See a memo dated December 29, 1979, warning of the youth being attracted to "reactionary religious movements," and another dated July 7, 2001, to launch a campaign to

party was also concerned about Islamic and traditional values not being followed. For instance, a note circulated to the presidential *diwan* warned about the spread of pornographic videos being shown in some hotels and bars, which attracted a large number of young people.[212]

The party played a pivotal role among youth associations and in higher education institutions, similar to its activities in other spheres of Iraqi society. A special bureau to deal with secondary school students was set up to cater to the many activities organized by the party in the areas of culture, sport, art, and politics, and to be responsible for expanding the party network among fifteen to eighteen year olds.[213] There were many in this age group to keep an eye on; during the academic year 1985–86, the total number of students across all secondary education categories was more than 4 million, a 12 percent increase in comparison to 1979–80.[214] The party was vigilant about teachers who resisted becoming part of the Ba'th system, and it monitored students before their graduation to influence their entrance to universities, using the School Register (see Chapter 7) and the numerous reports it collected from schools and youth organizations.[215] The presidential secretary for party affairs, together with the Party Secretariat, devised plans for activities during the universities' summer holidays to engage students in political education and attract them to the party. In the course of the academic year, party meetings were held immediately after classes, so that students had no excuse to avoid them. The planners grappled with the problem of science students, who needed to work in laboratories after their classes and who genuinely had little time until the evening to be present at such meetings. Female students living in dormitories had to hold their party activities in the dorms to facilitate the students' attendance. Finally, the plan proposed that no party meeting should be longer than one hour, so as not to lose the attention of young people.[216]

---

counter "poisonous religious ideas among the youth." *BRCC*, 003-14 (411); 003-2-6 (637).

[212] Party Secretariat to Presidential *diwan*, February 19, 1997, *BRCC*, 104-3-3 (302–303).

[213] See, for example, a detailed plan of work by the Bureau for Secondary School Students in Suleimaniyya, which was part of the National Union of Students and Youth in Iraq, July 3, 1984, *NIDS*, PUK 047, Box 302 (050084–050090).

[214] Head of National Union of Iraqi Students to the Central Bureau of Students, "Activities of the Union," April 26, 1987, *BRCC*, 161-3-3 (185).

[215] *Dhaw'*, television program based on historical documents. The program quoted documents from northern Iraq dated March 13, 1986, and March 4, 1989.

[216] Presidential Secretary for Party Affairs to Presidential *diwan*, November 29, 1984, *BRCC*, 119-5-6 (425–427).

There is little doubt that the line between academic responsibilities and party tasks became blurred for many academics. For instance, when the dean of the science college at Mustansiriyya University completed his term, he asked that all his benefits and bonuses be paid via his branch, as it used to be before he became dean. In other cases there was friction among academic and party goals; for example, the president of al-Anbar University, himself a party member, wrote a letter complaining bitterly about the intervention of a branch member whose job was to oversee activities in the university. He criticized this comrade because, although he lacked any experience in academic work, he was making academic decisions about student examinations, assigning new teachers, and demoting others in breach of all rules. Furthermore, he accused another comrade of creating a commotion when refused entry to a meeting of the University Council because he was carrying his personal weapon, in spite of the obvious fact that "all members of the council are Ba'thists." The university president ended his letter by reminding the Party Secretariat that "I am a Ba'thist carrying the party insignia, and belong to a Ba'thist family, and without the party I would not have been able to reach my current position."[217]

The activities of the Student Union, another organ dominated by the party, illustrate how the Ba'th attempted to control students' activities not only in Iraq but also when they were studying abroad. The union had branches in all universities, and its representatives sat on councils of universities throughout the country. It also had branches abroad, with its own journals and infrastructure supported by both the Ministry of Higher Education and the party. In 1991 the Student Union was amalgamated with the Youth Association, thus increasing its power and range of influence. Interestingly, a report by the Party Secretariat indicated that the union was adding members by quantity and not quality, and that many of the recruits were not sufficiently steeped in party ideology.[218] A document by *al-amn* about the party structure in the institutions of higher education echoed this criticism of the union and the party, describing its obvious weakness in attracting independent students, and the

---

[217] For the full letter, dated September 25, 2000, and the notes by the *tandhim* of al-Anbar and Diyala provinces, which was responsible for the university, dated September 27, 2000, see *BRCC*, 183-4-1 (081–085).

[218] Baghdad *tandhim* to Party Secretariat, "A Study of Students and Youth," October 28, 1991. The study includes a diagram of the union's structure, *BRCC*, 005-1-2 (662–692).

increasing number of students who avoided attending party activities with the excuses of lack of time or the economic situation.[219]

Abroad, one of the basic tasks of the union was to watch over other Iraqi students. A report by the Scottish Union of Students from the University of Strathclyde accused the Iraqi Student Union of harassing Iraqi students who opposed the regime and even of using physical violence to intimidate them.[220] Another report, written in London and included in the documents, detailed the role of the Iraqi Embassy in London; every new student had to fill in numerous forms, and all information was passed on to the Iraqi Student Union. Each student was marked as either supportive of or against the regime.[221] Unions abroad organized celebrations for Saddam Hussein's birthday and distributed material about the party and its achievements. They also took on the responsibility of supporting Iraqi students; for instance, when stipends were reduced in 1987 as a result of the worsening economic situation, the union in Belgium lobbied hard with the party that the reduction was causing a lot of hardship to students and their families.[222]

As the preceding discussion clearly illustrates, the Ba'th Party's overwhelming dominance in the various areas of civil life in Iraq – the economy, unions, gender, religion, and education – and its influence on all civil activities were quite remarkable. In its consolidation of power, the party managed to weave a network of control across the whole spectrum of Iraqi life.

[219] Headquarters of *al-amn* to Presidential *diwan*, "Party Structure in Universities and Academies," June 9, 1994, BRCC, 100-3-5 (421–422).

[220] Secretary General of Students Bureau to Party Secretariat, June 14, 1987, BRCC, 161-3-3 (003–044).

[221] *Ibid*. See also a report from the union in Madrid about Iraqi students suspected of opposing the regime (319).

[222] National Union of Iraqi Students and Youth to Central Bureau, May 9, 1987, BRCC, 161-3-3 (120).

Conclusion

Saddam Hussein's Ba'thist regime survived the vicissitudes of thirty-five years marked by two major wars, recurrent military conflicts with the Kurds, a major uprising in 1991 after the end of the First Gulf War, and thirteen years of harsh sanctions. By examining the inner workings of the Ba'th Party, the questions that this book has sought to address are as follows: What were the characteristics of this regime? How did it manage to last such a long time? And, finally would it have endured had the U.S.-led invasion of 2003 not taken place?

There are many ways to interpret the regime's durability. Some argue that a dictatorship cannot be run by one man alone, however unrestricted his power. "The recognition that dictatorship flourished on wide complicity fuelled by a variety of motives from idealism to fear, makes great sense of their durability."[1] Whether in Iraq or elsewhere, control by "authoritarian and patrimonial means" paved the way for relative stability and longevity.[2] Václav Havel explains complicity by pointing to the context created by thousands of party slogans, a daily barrage that provides meaning to the lives of ordinary citizens; he points out that

> it reminds people where they are living and what is expected of them. It tells them what everyone else is doing, and indicates to them what they must do as well, if they don't want to be excluded, to fall into isolation, alienate themselves from society, break the rules of the game, and risk the loss of their peace and tranquility and security.[3]

---

[1] Overy, *The Dictators*, p. xxxiv.
[2] Perthes, *The Political Economy of Syria*, p. 133.
[3] Havel, *The Power of the Powerless*, p. 36.

Max Weber asserted that "if the state is to exist, the dominated must obey the authority claimed by the powers that be." He asked the critical question, "When and why do men obey? Upon what inner justification and upon what external means does this domination rest?" In countries that have suffered dictatorship and political personality cults, he says, the answer depends on circumstances and history:

> There is the authority of the extraordinary and personal *gift of grace* (charisma), the absolutely personal devotion and personal confidence in revelation, heroism, or other qualities of individual leadership. This is "charismatic" domination, as exercised by the prophet or – in the field of politics – by the elected war lord, the plebiscitarian ruler, the great demagogue, or the political party leader.[4]

Although the Ba'th Party was a single-party regime, the period under study could also fit the model of "personalist regimes" in which neither the military nor the party is sufficiently strong enough "to prevent the leader from taking personal control of decisions and the selection of regime personnel."[5] However, Iraq's Ba'thist regime combined the characteristics of both single-party and personalist regimes. Benefits were distributed to a larger proportion of citizens than is usual in personalist regimes, but, unlike a one-party system, the regime was dominated largely "by a single familial, clan, ethnic, or regional group."[6]

Authoritarianism in Iraq was somewhat unique, because of the country's history. The seeds of tyranny were planted long before Saddam Hussein and the Ba'th leadership came to power. Instability, numerous power vacuums, and a need to find a new direction all contributed to the rise of the Ba'th Party. Once it had gained control of the levers of power, it managed to subjugate its opponents and eliminate opposition. Unquestionably, the regime was tyrannical, dictatorial, and repressive almost from its first day until its dramatic collapse in 2003. Like Stalinist Russia, the Iraqi regime had no tolerance for any form of dissent, real or imagined, subversive or peaceful. Its security organizations operated systematically to repress the population and conducted massive surveillance both inside and outside the party. Here, there is a need to remind

---

[4] Max Weber, "Politics as a Vocation," in *From Max Weber: Essays in Sociology*, translated, edited, and with an introduction by H. H. Gerth and C. Wright Mills, paperback edn. (Oxford: Routledge, 2007), p. 79.

[5] Geddes, "What Do We Know about Democratization," p. 132.

[6] *Ibid.*, p. 133.

ourselves that not only non-Baʿthists suffered at the hands of the regime; party members and thousands of officers and soldiers endured hardships ranging from banishment to death for what the authorities interpreted as acts against the regime, although sometimes these punishments were motivated by jealousy and rivalry. Akin to Stalin, Saddam Hussein did not want anyone, even those who were with him from the beginning, to feel too comfortable or to be able to acquire enough power to constitute a personal threat.

Economically, the country was blessed with a huge increase in oil revenues in the 1970s, leading to a prosperity that strengthened the Baʿth's support base. Furthermore, the regime's longevity and its centralization of decision making provided reasonable coordination at the macro level. As shown in this book, there was no consistent economic policy; the regime allocated resources and catered to certain interest groups, and laws were passed to accommodate vested interests, such as the labor law of 1987 that curtailed labor rights.

There is also no doubt that a large number of talented and educated Iraqis played a major part in maintaining the country and the system in spite of the widespread destruction of the First Gulf War. To take one example, by the end of the 1991 war, almost 90 percent of the electricity grid was destroyed, yet by the end of the 1990s, and in spite of strict sanctions, Iraq had managed to repair the grid and reconstruct the economy. Ministries such as oil or military industrialization were able to draw on a large pool of talented engineers and technicians, who rebuilt their country with ingenuity and skill.

In reality, the Baʿth's ideology was not as dominant as communist ideology, and none of its three slogans of unity, freedom, and socialism was ever enacted. This ideology was also malleable according to circumstances, and by the 1990s it had transmuted into a personality cult around Saddam Hussein with little resistance from the party's ideologues. In fact, ideological issues were rarely the basis for internal conflicts; rather, conflicts centered around clashes of personalities or ambitions for jobs and promotion. Scouring the party's archival material, one would be hard pressed to articulate its ideology and substance. An important point to underline is that Saddam Hussein was not keen on political theories and general discussions, and he continuously called on the party to deal with practical issues of governance. Given its weak intellectual and theoretical base, the Baʿth ideology lent itself to authoritarian rule. In fact, there was no support within the party (both its Syrian and Iraqi branches) for "the concept of responsible parliamentary government."[7] The regime did have priorities and policies, but most, even foreign policy, changed with time. Arab countries that were seen as friends of Iraq during the war with Iran in the 1980s became foes in the 1990s, and similar changes took place in relations with non-Arab countries. The one constant was probably the animosity toward the other Ba'th regime in the area – Syria. This lack of ideology distinguished Iraq from most totalitarian regimes but did not affect the Ba'th's durability. Its directives were focused on coup-proofing, ensuring control by instilling fear, and creating a system of rewards that co-opted large numbers of citizens. In a way, the ideology – or realpolitik – concentrated on staying in power, and policies were adapted accordingly. After every crisis the Ba'th Party managed to rejuvenate itself, even after the 1991 uprising, which it did not expect and was ill prepared to deal with.

The party's membership recruitment was relatively successful, adding uncritical supporters of the system even though some recruits did not agree with every aspect of official policy. The pyramid of power, which was developed on a relatively large support base, led to difficulties in communications between the leadership and the grass roots; many orders were imprecise, given orally and without much forethought. Often they were put into effect in a convoluted and bureaucratic way, whereas some orders were rarely followed at all. Interestingly, many supporters accepted the emphasis on discipline, although the lower levels of the cadres were not informed of disciplinary action taken against senior party officials.[8] "Society was kept down by millions of tiny Lilliputian threads of everyday mendacity, conformity and compromise."[9] At the top of the pyramid sat Saddam Hussein, assisted by what constituted the leadership: a quartet of comrades who were with him most of his political life and who posed no threat. To this quartet one could add his younger son, Qusay, who in the 1990s was put in charge of the powerful Republican Guard and the SSO.

Thus, the durability of the regime can be explained by the determination of the leadership to eradicate all opposition, whether military or civilian; its willingness to use violence and fear to control the population; its comprehensive system of rewards; its success in recruiting large

---

[7] Devlin, *The Ba'th Party*, p. 214.
[8] A similar situation existed in the Soviet Union; see Merridale, *Moscow Politics and the Rise of Stalin*, pp. 224–25.
[9] Timothy Garton Ash, "The Truth About Dictatorship," *New York Review of Books*, vol. 45, no. 3, February 19, 1998.

numbers of supporters even though many were not fully active; its ability to exploit the talent and ingenuity of educated Iraqis in rebuilding the country and maintaining its systems; and finally, Saddam Hussein's own shrewdness and ability to outmaneuver his opponents and competitors and keep them in a state of flux until the end. He never allowed even his two sons, 'Uday and Qusay, to become powerful enough to challenge his position. In fact, during his interrogation after being captured, Saddam Hussein made it very clear that he did not give much thought to this issue, given his relatively young age and good health. In the mid-1990s, after the defection to Amman of his son-in-law Hussein Kamil, he told the RCC that the problem with Kamil was that he was too ambitious, wanting to be his deputy and then his successor. He emphasized, however, that Iraq was not a monarchy but a republic, and just because Kamil became a family member, this did not entitle him to any high position.[10]

Saddam Hussein's role in shaping the history of Iraq over those three-and-a-half decades was paramount. Chapter 6 discusses his personality cult and modus operandi, but it is worth reiterating here. He was a very complex man, and any attempt to depict him in one sentence is bound to fail. Although he was ruthless and determined to uproot any opposition, many of those who worked with him said he was also caring and attentive. The audiotapes of the RCC meetings and those of the army and party leadership are uniquely insightful; he was in complete control of all meetings without exception, and all attendees respected and feared him, yet he was polite and rarely interrupted anyone, and if he did, he would immediately apologize. At the beginning of each meeting his mood could immediately be sensed, and no one dared to contradict him or to say anything that might infuriate him if he was in a gloomy mood. On the other hand, he often sounded jovial, ordering cigars for all participants, and loved to tell stories and anecdotes, prompting the others to join in. Sometimes he would dwell on an issue in detail and then suddenly become bored, and the subject was immediately changed or dropped.

Saddam Hussein unquestionably viewed himself not only as the leader but also as the father of the nation and of the Ba'th family. He was convinced that no one understood the Iraqi people or knew their deep aspirations as he did. Although this was true to a certain extent, given his mastery of the art of manipulating different groups and that he ran the

---

[10] Audiotape of the top leadership, no specific date, but dated after the defection of Hussein Kamil in summer 1995, *CRRC*, SH-SHTP-A-000-837.

country as a personal fiefdom, his instinct sometimes betrayed him, as witnessed by the unexpected uprising after the end of the First Gulf War.

Saddam Hussein confronted struggles and defeats with full composure and control, due partly to his strong personality and partly to his delusional state of mind. He convinced himself (and his people) that he had won the war against Iran in spite of the enormous human and material losses. At the end of the First Gulf War he faced what appeared to be the end of his regime, but luck was on his side, and the Americans let him remain. He immediately turned the situation to his advantage and would tell his comrades that no country except Iraq could face thirty-three other countries and emerge without being completely destroyed. He boasted, in one meeting of the RCC, that Egypt, the largest Arab country, would not have endured such an onslaught more than a couple of weeks, whereas Iraq not only survived but also managed to "cut off the heads of the traitors" after the end of the war.[11]

Saddam Hussein was deeply hurt when Hussein Kamil defected to Jordan in 1995, and many who knew him or worked with him detected changes in his personality: he became more paranoid and less trusting, more inclined to solitude and less interested in detail. Following the defection, he went around apologizing for Kamil's behavior as a minister in his government and a family member. Yet again he exploited the new situation, telling his audience that he knew they had accorded Kamil respect because "you have a lot of love and respect for me [Saddam Hussein] and you thought you were doing the proper thing."[12] His relationship with the Ba'th Party was multidimensional; he saw himself – as he often repeated – as "the son of the party" and claimed that he never stopped believing in Ba'thism. On the other hand, he was the leader of the party from 1979 and needed it to bolster his own position and as a springboard for his personality cult. In reality, there was never any competition between the party and Saddam Hussein, and the symbiosis worked to their mutual benefit.

The question of whether his regime would have collapsed without the invasion of 2003 is obviously hypothetical but is important to our understanding of its structure and duration. Although it is impossible to know

[11] [...] nking officials talking to Saddam Hussein, date unspecified, but probably [...] C, SH-SHTP-A-000-834.
[12] Audiotape of a meeting between Saddam Hussein and senior employees of the Ministry of Military Industrialization, which was headed by Hussein Kamil before his defection, date unspecified, but probably late summer 1995, *CRRC*, SH-SHTP-A-000-834.

for sure, it is doubtful that the regime would have disintegrated. Domestically, Saddam Hussein was in effective control of the major enclaves of power. Within the party and the inner circle there was no serious competitor, and no one seems to have amassed enough influence to challenge him. Finally, it is important to remember that, by late 2000, Iraq's economy was improving and its infrastructure was more or less back to its pre-First Gulf War strength.

A critical aspect in Iraq, as in other authoritarian regimes, was that for the vast majority of Iraqis who were not direct victims of repression, daily life was generally more normal than the image we have of such systems.[13] Unlike the communist systems of Eastern Europe, repression in Iraq did not decline with the regime's maturity, and violence characterized it to the end. This may be partly due to the turbulent events in Iraq, particularly in the 1980s and 1990s, which differed greatly from the relative stability of Eastern Europe in the 1970s and 1980s. Hence, there was no compelling reason for the inner circle to overthrow the regime. At the same time, all outside opposition groups were weakened or infiltrated, thus reducing the possibility of toppling the regime. If Saddam Hussein were to be assassinated, it would have to have been someone very close to him, which was virtually precluded by his tight security. Nor was Saddam Hussein's powerful aura ever dented, and listening to the many audiotapes of the RCC meetings, the overwhelming impression is that he was in total control of the decision-making process for the country and its people.

As for the swift collapse of the regime, it should be remembered that authoritarian systems like the Iraqi Ba'th emanate masterfulness and strength, and their underlying weakness does not become apparent until after their downfall. The lack of cohesiveness of the Soviet and Eastern European communist systems became exposed only after the fall of the Berlin Wall in 1989, and few anticipated that they would collapse so soon. The realization that Iraq's industry was badly damaged and that its military forces and popular militias were not as threatening as they seemed before the 2003 war came too late to save the country from the ravages of invasion and its aftermath.

During the years of Ba'thist rule, Iraq wasted a historical opportunity to become a developed country whose citizens reaped the rewards of its natural wealth. Instead, under Saddam Hussein's leadership, the country experienced extreme violence, its infrastructure wrecked by his wars

---

[13] See a similar conclusion reached by Overy about people's lives under Hitler's and Stalin's dictatorships. Overy, *The Dictators*, p. 209.

and conflicts. I could not find any statistics for the total number of people killed or injured in the service of their country, or a tally of those killed by the regime's cohorts during those thirty-five years. However, it would not be unrealistic to assume that both categories are in the hundreds of thousands, in a population that averaged about 15 million during this period.[14] Economically, the country slipped backward, and apart from the 1970s, the plight of the people was more miserable than before the Ba'th came to power. Under the baleful influence of oil wealth, the regime expanded its militarization and squandered these riches and the talents of its people in two major wars. The illusion of economic growth was perpetuated by continually tapping oil resources, in a manner not dissimilar from many other oil-rich states. By 2003 Iraq was greatly weakened, and when the Americans imposed regime change, the institutional disintegration was aided by mass de-Ba'thification and the ill-judged disbanding of the army.[15]

The relationship between Saddam Hussein's Iraq and the United States changed fundamentally over time. As explained in the Introduction, Saddam Hussein did not always see the United States as an adversary. In fact, the two countries enjoyed relatively strong cooperation in the 1980s, when Saddam Hussein distanced himself from the Soviet Union and countries such as East Germany. Some even argued that he managed to escape from Iraq after the assassination attempt on Qasim in 1959 "with the help of the CIA and Egyptian intelligence."[16] There has not, so far, been any confirmation of this from Iraqi or American sources. The relationship became, of course, extremely hostile after Iraq's defeat in the Gulf War of 1991 and the recurrent bombing of Iraqi installations in the 1990s by U.S. and British forces.

The regime reacted to the terror attacks of 9/11 in two ways: first, an immediate joy and feeling of schadenfreude that America had got what it deserved and, second, a more rational response expecting that Washington would change its policy toward Baghdad and realize that Iraq, a secular state that had banned Wahhabism, could be a trusted ally in fighting Islamic extremism. This was a classic example of Saddam Hussein misreading the signs; he underestimated the psychological

[14] Iraq's population was about 10 million in 1970 and roughly 25 million in 2000, see the World Bank, *Economic Data Indicators*, http://data.worldbank.org/country/iraq (accessed November 15, 2010).

[15] For a discussion of the institutional disintegration from a sociological point of view, see Marc Garcelon, "Trajectories of Institutional Disintegration in Late-Soviet Russia and Contemporary Iraq," *Sociological Theory*, vol. 24, no. 3 (September 2006), pp. 255–83.

[16] Yevgeny Primakov, *Russia and the Arabs: Behind the Scenes in the Middle East from the Cold War to the Present* (New York: Basic, 2009), p. 69.

repercussions of 9/11 on Americans, and instead of sending cordial signals and expressing a willingness to cooperate, he continued with his grandiose anti-American rhetoric.

On the issue of sectarianism and religion, the multiple official forms in the archives do not reveal questions referring to applicants or suspects being Sunni or Shiʿi, even after 1991. My first reaction was that a high official had ordered these words to be excluded, and that in most cases a person's full name, place of birth, and residency would indicate their sect. Although this may be correct, many names were neutral, and mixed names and families were common particularly in large cities like Baghdad. Even so, I could not understand why sectarian identification was not referred to in the audiotapes of the leadership's private meetings when the Shiʿi intifada – or, as they called it, "the period of betrayal" – was discussed. One explanation might be that among the higher echelons of the party, army, and security organizations, there were some Shiʿis serving the regime until 2003, and as we have seen, Saddam Hussein placed emphasis on loyalty rather than religious affiliation. However, there were documents discussed in Chapter 2 that described the origins of members, applicants, or suspects by indicating that the individual in question belonged to *tabaʿiyya Iraniyya* (Iranian nationality). Indeed, Saddam Hussein's persecution and repression of the Shiʿis stemmed from his incorrect belief that many would be influenced by the ideology of his real bête noire, Ayatollah Khomeini, and hence they were a potential threat to his regime. Saddam Hussein's obsession with Iran and Khomeinism went far deeper than his animosity to the United States or even to Israel and stayed with him until his demise. Many insiders and analysts believe that one of the reasons for the lack of serious opposition to the invasion was that Saddam Hussein was far more worried about another uprising in the south supported by Iran, or even a general insurgency, than about invading forces and thus did not concentrate on defending Iraq's strategic outposts. This grew out of the Baʿth's paranoia about being removed from power again, and contingency plans were made as early as the 1970s for a return to power if this happened.

One of the most divisive issues in post-Baʿthist Iraq has been how to deal with former members of the Baʿth Party and known informers. The term *Baʿthist* is as "malleable as it is incendiary, and the quandary it represents has underlined the growing dispute over the credibility of Iraq's parliamentary elections in March [2010]."[17] Baʿth Party membership has

[17] Anthony Shadid, "How an Inflammatory Term, Baathist, Bars Candidates in Iraq," *New York Times*, January 20, 2010.

divided the country since 2003, because it has been assumed that everyone who was a member of the party participated in the regime's atrocities during its long rule. As my research has shown, by the end of 2002 the party had approximately 4 million affiliates, but the vast majority was inactive and did not possess a party card, and probably no more than 3 to 4 percent were involved in carrying out the regime's policies. In addition, even among this low percentage there is no evidence whatsoever that all of them, or even the majority of them, were involved in violence against the population. The history of post-communist regimes has proved that a blanket punishment of all party members is unjustified.

This book has shown that the majority of citizens were intent on getting on with their lives, and that out of necessity they had to adapt to the structures of reward and punishment imposed on them irrespective of age or socioeconomic status. It is unreasonable to judge the Iraqi people harshly, because of the near impossibility of understanding the constraints under which they lived, or the impact of the three turbulent decades they endured. Based on the regime's own archives, we now know that a comprehensive system of repression and surveillance existed, and that many thousands paid a heavy price for refusing to bend to the will of the Ba'th Party. The Iraqi people suffered tremendously during Saddam Hussein's rule, and because violence unfortunately begets violence, injustice and suffering have continued unabated since 2003.

My hope is that the historical perspective offered by this remarkable trove of documents will be utilized by many to learn valuable lessons about authoritarianism and the need to avoid further vengeance. It is vitally important to look to the future when dealing with Saddam Hussein's legacy, as one senior Iraqi official appointed after the invasion eloquently expressed:

> He [Saddam Hussein] was there and he ruled and he impacted on [*sic*] the world. But he was a part of our history. He was a bad part of our history, but he made a huge difference, whether we like it or not. We need not bury the legacy of that period. We need to remember it, all what is bad and what is good and learn lessons. And the most important lesson is that dictatorship should not return to Iraq.[18]

---

[18] Muwaffiq al-Rubay'i, a national security advisor from 2004 to 2009, quoted in Chulov, "Qur'an Etched in Saddam Hussein's Blood."

Appendix I

Chart of the Structure of the Baʿth Party Secretariat
(*maktab amanat sir al-qutr*)

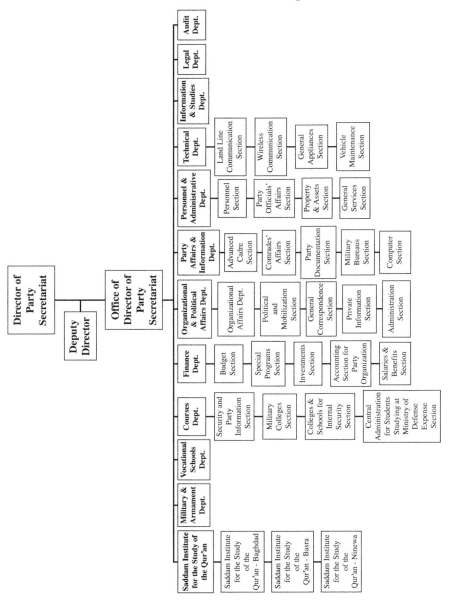

Appendix II

Ba'th Party Statistics as of September 2002

Name of tandhim (Structure)	Branches	Sections	Divisions	Cells	Secretary Generals	Branch Members	Section Members	Division Members	Active Members	Apprenticed Members	Candidates	Supporters	Sympathizers	Grand Total
Baghdad (al-Karkh)	9	57	331	2,760	8	101	564	4,198	23,517	18,363	3,074	73,139	208,547	331,511
Baghdad (al-Rusafa)	7	57	386	3,187	6	84	600	4,606	19,686	17,733	2,760	119,365	332,414	497,254
Ninewa	5	50	290	2,539	4	71	501	3,813	17,798	16,690	1,051	71,014	125,113	236,055
Salah al-Din	6	57	391	3,188	6	82	626	4,516	19,090	23,383	3,534	50,436	73,617	175,290
Al-Ta'mim*	5	31	196	1,568	5	52	315	2,244	9,581	9,068	799	44,667	126,356	193,087
Diyala	6	34	200	1,453	5	55	340	2,302	8,721	17,600	866	57,352	144,035	231,276
Al-Anbar	2	28	184	1,502	2	40	294	2,330	14,474	8,315	1,235	45,872	80,096	152,658
Wasit	4	31	165	1,326	4	47	282	1,943	9,957	6,462	1,351	48,895	113,624	182,565
Misan	3	20	93	470	3	33	175	821	3,781	3,630	0	23,067	64,809	96,319
Dhi-Qar	4	35	203	1,417	4	53	349	2,162	14,098	11,072	1,620	136,077	166,258	331,693
Al-Muthanna	2	13	87	468	2	22	139	737	3,351	4,370	1,797	30,964	117,258	158,640
Basra	5	44	237	1,799	5	66	414	2,743	12,016	12,463	1,161	196,117	290,409	515,394
Najaf and al-Qadisiyya	4	27	170	1,141	4	45	280	1,739	7,073	12,543	264	56,723	116,938	195,609
Karbala	2	17	92	658	2	26	159	1,054	3,238	4,806	336	22,915	60,392	92,928
Babil	4	26	170	1,388	4	45	274	1,920	6,498	16,163	1,328	36,578	111,993	174,803
Professional Unions and Others	1	3	18	115	1	113	34	194	1,022	78	20	479	238	2,179
Military Bureaus	n/a	82	574	7,873	11	92	782	8,215	49,761	71,342	6,046	99,551	195,983	431,783
GRAND TOTAL	69	612	3,787	32,852	76	1,027	6,128	45,537	223,662	254,081	27,242	1,113,211	2,328,080	3,999,044

* al-Ta'mim statistics were inclusive of the autonomous region in the north.

Source: "Statistics for Party Organization for the Country," September 29, 2002, BRCC, 108-4-6 (004-025).

Notes on Sources

The main sources of this book are the Iraqi archives, which consist of the following:

- *Ba'th Regional Command Collection (BRCC)*
- *North Iraq Dataset (NIDS)*: There are two subsets – PUK and KDP – which represent material originally taken by or related to the two Kurdish parties
- Special Security Organization (SSO)
- Ministry of Information Dataset

The first three sets of documents were mostly used when they were at the Iraq Memory Foundation, Washington, DC, before being moved to the Hoover Institute, Stanford University, California. As a result, my citations may differ from the current Hoover system of citation. However, it is easy to convert them utilizing a guide prepared by the Iraq Memory Foundation/Hoover Institute.

The book also draws on the *Conflict Records Research Center (CRRC)* Collection, National Defense University (NDU), Washington, DC. The following categories of the collection were used in this book:

SH-BATH: Ba'th Party Correspondence
SH-FSDM: Fedayeen Saddam
SH-MISC: Saddam Regime Miscellaneous
SH-PDWN: Saddam Hussein's Presidential *diwan*
SH-RVCC: Iraqi Revolutionary Command Council
SH-SHTP: Saddam's Tapes (Audio)
SH-SPPC: Saddam's Personal and Political Correspondence
SH-SSOX: Iraqi Special Security Organization

The research is also supported by interviews with senior Iraqi officials and generals of the period under study. Some interviewees agreed to having their names published, others did not, and I respected their wishes. The first set of interviews took place in Amman, followed by numerous telephone conversations with interviewees residing in Jordan and Egypt. All interviews are on file.

Saddam Hussein published his books under the subtitle "a novel by its author." For simplicity reasons, I put those novels under his own name in the footnotes and the Bibliography.

Al-Mukhtarat contains Saddam Hussein's speeches, letters, and interviews up to 1987 in ten volumes and is a helpful collection that was used extensively.

British Foreign Office documents were accessed via Cengage Learning EMEA, Middle East Online Series 2: Iraq 1914–1974.

For comparison between Stasi forms and Iraqi forms, the archives of the Federal Commission for the Records of the State Security Service of the Former German Democratic Republic were used: Ministerrat Der Deutschen Demokratischen Republik, Ministerium für Staatssicherheit.

The Iraqi currency, Iraqi dinar (ID), underwent significant devaluation from the late 1980s until the 2003 invasion. For conversion to the U.S. dollar, I used The Economist Full Converter, which can be found at www.economist.com/markets/currency.

For many issues of *al-Waqa'i' al-'Iraqiyya* and the English *Iraqi Gazette*, I found the following website of al-Kufa University very useful: www.kuiraq.com/waqqae.

Bibliography

ʿAbboud, Salam, *Thaqafat al-ʿunf fi al-ʿIraq* [The Culture of Violence in Iraq], Köln: Al-Kamel Verlag, 2002.

Abdul Majid, Saman, *Les années Saddam: Révélations exclusives* [Saddam's Years: Exclusive Revelations], Paris: Fayard, 2003.

Abrahamian, Ervand, *Tortured Confessions: Prisons and Public Recantations in Modern Iran*, Berkeley: University of California Press, 1999.

Abu Jaber, Kamel S., *The Arab Baʿth Socialist Party: History, Ideology and Organization*, Syracuse, NY: Syracuse University Press, 1966.

Aburish, Saïd K., *Saddam Hussein: The Politics of Revenge*, New York: Bloomsbury, 2000.

Al-Ali, Nadje Sadig, *Iraqi Women: Untold Stories from 1948 to the Present*, London: Zed, 2007.

ʿAli, Muʾmin, *Sanawat al-jamr: masirat al-haraka al-Islamiyya fi al-ʿIraq, 1957–1986* [The Slow-Burning Years: The Journey of the Islamic Movement in Iraq, 1957–1986], London: Dar al-Masirah, 1993.

Alnasrawi, Abbas, *Financing Economic Development in Iraq: The Role of Oil in a Middle Eastern Economy*, New York: Praeger, 1967.

———, "Economic Consequences of the Iraq–Iran War," *Third World Quarterly*, vol. 8, no. 3 (July 1986), pp. 869–95.

———, "Iraq: Economic Consequences of the 1991 Gulf War and Future Outlook," *Third World Quarterly*, vol. 13, no. 2 (June 1992), pp. 335–52.

Arab Baʿth Socialist Party, *Revolutionary Iraq 1968–1973: The Political Report Adopted by the Eighth Regional Congress of the Arab Baʿth Socialist Party–Iraq*, Baghdad: The Party, 1974.

———, *Some Theoretical Principles: Approved by the Six National Congress October 1963*, Beirut: Dar al-Taliʿa, 1974.

Askari, Hossein, and John Thomas Cummings, *Middle East Economies in the 1970s: A Comparative Approach*, New York: Praeger, 1976.

Balaghi, Shiva, *Saddam Hussein: A Biography*, Westport, CT: Greenwood Press, 2006.

Baram, Amatzia, "Qawmiyya and Wataniyya in Baʿthi Iraq: The Search for a New Balance," *Middle Eastern Studies*, vol. 19, no. 2 (April 1983), pp. 188–200.

_____, *Culture, History and Ideology in the Formation of Baʿthist Iraq, 1968–89*, New York: St. Martin's Press, 1991.

_____, "Neo-Tribalism in Iraq: Saddam Hussein's Tribal Policies 1991–96," *International Journal of Middle East Studies*, vol. 29, no. 1 (February 1997), pp. 1–31.

_____, *Building Toward Crisis: Saddam Husayn's Strategy for Survival*, Washington, DC: Washington Institute for Near East Policy, Policy Paper No. 47, 1998.

_____, "Saddam Husayn, the Baʿth Regime and the Iraqi Officer Corps," in Barry Rubin and Thomas A. Keaney (eds.), *Armed Forces in the Middle East: Politics and Strategy*, London: Frank Cass, 2002, pp. 206–30.

Baran, David, "Iraq: The Party in Power," *Le Monde Diplomatique*, December 2002.

_____, *Vivre la tyrannie et lui survivre: L'Irak en transition* [Life and Survival under Tyranny: Iraq in Transition], Paris: Mille et une nuits, 2004.

Bashkin, Orit, *The Other Iraq: Pluralism and Culture in Hashemite Iraq*, Stanford, CA: Stanford University Press, 2009.

Batatu, Hanna, *The Old Social Classes and the Revolutionary Movements of Iraq: A Study of Iraq's Old Landed and Commercial Classes and of Its Communists, Baʿthists, and Free Officers*, Princeton, NJ: Princeton University Press, 1978.

Bengio, Ofra, *Saddam's Word: Political Discourse in Iraq*, Oxford University Press, 1998.

_____, "Saddam Husayn's Novel of Fear," *Middle East Quarterly*, vol. 9, no. 1 (Winter 2002), pp. 9–18.

Bruce, Gary, "The Prelude to Nationwide Surveillance in East Germany: Stasi Operations and Threat Perceptions, 1945–1953," *Journal of Cold War Studies*, vol. 5, no. 2 (Spring 2003), pp. 3–31.

Central Intelligence Agency, *Iraq: Foreign Intelligence and Security Services*, Report No. 276, August 1985, MORI DocID: 1127938, pp. 12–19.

Chaudhry, Kiren Aziz, "On the Way to Market: Economic Liberalization and Iraq's Invasion of Kuwait," *Middle East Report (MERIP)*, no. 170 (May–June 1991), pp. 14–23.

_____, "Economic Liberalization and the Lineages of the Rentier State," *Comparative Politics*, vol. 27, no. 1 (October 1994), pp. 1–25.

_____, "Consuming Interests: Market Failure and the Social Foundations of Iraqi Etatisme," in Kamil A. Mahdi (ed.), *Iraq's Economic Predicament*, Reading: Ithaca Press, 2002, pp. 233–65.

Chubin, Shahram, and Charles Tripp, *Iran and Iraq at War*, Boulder, CO: Westview, 1988.

Chulov, Martin, "Qur'an Etched in Saddam Hussein's Blood Poses Dilemma for Iraq Leaders," *Guardian*, December 19, 2010.

Darle, Pierre, *Saddam Hussein maître des mots: Du langage de la tyrannie à la tyrannie du langage* [Saddam Hussein the Master of Words: From the Language of Tyranny to the Tyranny of Language], Paris: L'Harmattan, 2003.

Davis, Eric, *Memories of State: Politics, History, and Collective Identity in Modern Iraq*, Berkeley: University of California Press, 2005.

Deletant, Dennis, *Ceauşescu and the Securitate: Coercion and Dissent in Romania, 1965–1989*, 2nd impression, London: Hurst, 2006.

Devlin, John F., *The Ba'th Party: A History from Its Origins to 1966*, Stanford, CA: Hoover Institution, 1976.

———, "The Baath Party: Rise and Metamorphosis," *American Historical Review*, vol. 96, no. 5 (December 1991), pp. 1396–1407.

Dimitrov, Martin K., "Building Loyalty: Autocratic Resilience in Communist Europe and China" (manuscript in progress).

Duelfer, Charles, *Hide and Seek: The Search for Truth in Iraq*, New York: Public Affairs, 2009.

Al-Dulaimi, Khalil, *Saddam Hussein min al-zanzana al-Amrikiyya: Hadha ma hadath!* [Saddam Hussein from the American Cell: This Is What Happened!], Khartoum: al-Manbar, 2009.

Eppel, Michael, *Iraq from Monarchy to Tyranny: From the Hashemites to the Rise of Saddam*, Gainesville, FL: University Press of Florida, 2004.

Fainsod, Merle, *Smolensk under Soviet Rule*, Cambridge, MA: Harvard University Press, 1958.

———, *How Russia Is Ruled*, revised edn., Cambridge, MA: Harvard University Press, 1963.

Farouk-Sluglett, Marion, "Liberation or Repression? Pan-Arab Nationalism and the Women's Movement in Iraq," in Derek Hopwood, Habib Ishow, and Thomas Koszinowski (eds.), *Iraq: Power and Society*, St Antony's Middle East Monographs, Reading: Ithaca Press, 1993, pp. 51–73.

Farouk-Sluglett, Marion, and Peter Sluglett, "From Gang to Elite: The Iraqi Ba'th Party's Consolidation of Power 1968–1975," *Peuples Mediterranéens*, no. 40 (July–September 1987), pp. 89–114.

———, *Iraq Since 1958: From Revolution to Dictatorship*, London: KPI, 1987.

Feldman, Ilana, *Governing Gaza: Bureaucracy, Authority, and the Work of Rule, 1917–1967*, Durham, NC: Duke University Press, 2008.

Fisk, Robert, "Saddam Hussein: The Last Great Tyrant," *The Independent*, December 30, 2000.

Fitzpatrick, Sheila, "Ascribing Class: The Construction of Social Identity in Soviet Russia," *Journal of Modern History*, vol. 65, no. 4 (December 1993), p. 745–70.

———, *Everyday Stalinism: Ordinary Life in Extraordinary Times: Soviet Russia in the 1930s*, paperback edn., Oxford University Press, 2000.

Friedrich, Carl J., and Zbigniew K. Brzezinski, *Totalitarian Dictatorship and Autocracy*, paperback edn., New York: Praeger, 1961.

Al-Fukayki, Hani, *Awkar al-hazima: Tajribati fi Hizb al-Ba'th al-'Iraqi* [The Dens of Defeat: My Experience in the Iraqi Ba'th Party], London: Riyadh al-Rayyis Publishing House, 1993.

Fulbrook, Mary, *The People's State: East German Society from Hitler to Honecker*, paperback edn., New Haven, CT: Yale University Press, 2008.

Garcelon, Marc, "Trajectories of Institutional Disintegration in Late-Soviet Russia and Contemporary Iraq," *Sociological Theory*, vol. 24, no. 3 (September 2006), pp. 255–83.

Garton Ash, Timothy, "The Truth About Dictatorship," *New York Review of Books*, vol. 45, no. 3, February 19, 1998.

_____, "The Stasi on Our Minds," *New York Review of Books*, vol. 54, no. 9, May 31, 2007.

Gazdar, Haris, and Athar Hussain, "Crisis and Response: A Study of the Impact of Economic Sanctions in Iraq," in Kamil A. Mahdi (ed.), *Iraq's Economic Predicament*, Reading: Ithaca Press, 2002, pp. 31–83.

Geddes, Barbara, "What Do We Know About Democratization After Twenty Years?" *Annual Review of Political Science*, vol. 2 (1999), pp. 115–44.

Getty, J. Arch, and Oleg V. Naumov, *The Road to Terror: Stalin and the Self-Destruction of the Bolsheviks, 1932–1939*, New Haven, CT: Yale University Press, 1999.

Gordon, Joy, *Invisible War: The United States and the Iraq Sanctions*, Cambridge, MA: Harvard University Press, 2010.

Gregory, Paul R., *Terror by Quota: State Security from Lenin to Stalin (An Archival Study)*, New Haven, CT: Yale University Press, 2009.

Al-Habbubi, Ahmad, *Laylat al-harir fi qasr al-nihaya* [The Night of Screaming in the Palace of the End], London: Dar al-Barraq, 1999.

Al-Hadidi, Salah, *Qabdhat al-huda: Hussein Jalukhan tarikh wa rihla* [The Guiding Hand: Hussein Jalukhan's History and Journey], 2nd edn., Karbala: al-Hadidi Center for Studies and Research, 2009.

Hagenloh, Paul, *Stalin's Police: Public Order and Mass Repression in the USSR, 1926–1941*, Washington, DC: Woodrow Wilson Center Press, 2009.

Al-Hamdani, Ra'ad Majid, *Qabla an yughadirana al-tarikh* [Before History Leaves Us], Beirut: Arab Scientific, 2007.

Han Fei Tzu, *Basic Writings*, translated by Burton Watson, New York: Columbia University Press, 1964.

Hashim, Ahmed, "Saddam Husayn and Civil–Military Relations in Iraq: The Quest for Legitimacy and Power," *Middle East Journal*, vol. 57, no. 1 (Winter 2003), pp. 9–41.

Hashim, Jawad, *Mudhakkarat wazir 'Iraqi ma'a al-Bakr wa Saddam: Dhikrayat fi al-siyasa al-'Iraqiyya 1967–2000* [Memoirs of an Iraqi Minister with al-Bakr and Saddam: Reflections on Iraqi Politics, 1967–2000], Beirut: al-Saqi Publishing House, 2003.

Havel, Václav et al., *The Power of the Powerless: Citizens against the State in Central-Eastern Europe*, 2nd printing, New York: M.E. Sharpe, 1990.

Helms, Christine Moss, *Iraq: Eastern Flank of the Arab World*, Washington, DC: Brookings Institution, 1984.

Hemingway, Ernest, *The Old Man and the Sea*, paperback edn., London: Triad Grafton, 1988.

Hinnebusch, Raymond A., *Authoritarian Power and State Formation in Ba'thist Syria: Army, Party, and Peasant*, Boulder, CO: Westview Press, 1990.

_____, *Syria: Revolution from Above*, paperback edn., London: Routledge, 2002.

Hiro, Dilip, *The Longest War: The Iran-Iraq Military Conflict*, New York: Routledge, 1991.

Hirst, David, "The Terror from Tikrit," *Guardian*, November 26, 1971.

Hizb al-Ba'th al-'Arabi al-Ishtiraki, *al-Taqrir al-siyasi lil mu'tamar al-qawmi al-'ashir* [The Political Report of the Tenth National Conference], Baghdad: The Party, 1970.

_____, *Thawrat 17 Tammuz: Al-tajriba wa al-afaq* [The 17 July Revolution: The Experience and the Horizons], (Political Report of the Eighth Regional Conference of the Arab Ba'th Socialist Party–Iraq Region), Baghdad: The Party, 1974.

_____, *al-Taqrir al-markazi lil-mu'tamar al-qutri al-tasi'*, *Huzairan 1982* [Central Report of the Ninth Regional Congress, June 1982], Baghdad: The Party, 1983.

_____, *Lamahat min nidhal al-Ba'th 1947–1977* [Glimpses from the Ba'th's Struggle 1947–1977], 4th edn., Baghdad: Ministry of Information and Culture, 1986.

Hollander, Paul (ed.), *From the Gulag to the Killing Fields: Personal Accounts of Political Violence and Repression in Communist States*, Wilmington, DE: ISI, 2006.

Holquist, Peter, "State Violence as Technique: The Logic of Violence in Soviet Totalitarianism," in David L. Hoffmann (ed.), *Stalinism: The Essential Readings*, Malden, MA: Blackwell, 2003, pp. 129–56.

Hottinger, Arnold, "Personality Cult and Party in Iraq," *Swiss Review of World Affairs* (June 1984), pp. 12–16.

Human Rights Watch, *Bureaucracy of Repression: The Iraqi Government in Its Own Words*, February 1, 1994, www.hrw.org/en/reports/1994/02/01/bureaucracy-repression (accessed November 10, 2010).

Hussein, Saddam, *Rijal wa madina* [Men and a City], *riwaya li-katibiha* [a Novel by Its Author], Baghdad: Ministry of Culture, n.d.

_____, *Zabiba wa al-Malik* [Zabiba and the King], *riwaya li-katibiha* [a Novel by Its Author], Baghdad: al-Bilad Publishing House, n.d.

_____, *al-Thawra wa al-tarbiya al-wataniyya* [The Revolution and the National Education], Baghdad: al-Maktaba al-Wataniyya, 1977.

_____, *Hawla kitabat al-tarikh* [About Writing History], Baghdad: Dar al-Huriyya, 1979.

_____, *Social and Foreign Affairs in Iraq*, translated by Khalid Kishtainy, London: Croom Helm, 1979.

_____, *Nadhra fi al-din wa al-turath* [A Glimpse into Religion and Tradition], Baghdad: al-Huriyya Publishing House, 1980.

_____, *Economy and Management in Socialist Society*, translated by Naji al-Hadithi, Baghdad: Dar al-Ma'mun, 1988.

_____, *al-Mukhtarat*, 10 volumes, Baghdad: Dar al-Shu'un al-Thaqafiyya al-'Ammah, 1988.

_____, *al-Qal'a al-hasina* [The Immune Castle], *riwaya li-katibiha*, [a Novel by Its Author], Baghdad: al-Huriyya Publishing House, 2001.

Independent Inquiry Committee into the United Nations Oil-for-Food Programme, *Manipulation of the Oil-For-Food Programme by the Iraqi Regime*, October 27, 2005, www.iic-offp.org (accessed December 6, 2010).

Iraq Memory Foundation, *Shahadat 'Iraqiyya* [Iraqi Testimonies], Oral History Project, 2006 and 2007.

———, *Prospectus 2008*, Washington, DC: 2008.

Iraq Survey Group, *Regime Strategic Intent*, Comprehensive Report of the Special Advisor to the Director of Central Intelligence, 3 volumes, September 30, 2004.

Iskander, Amir, *Saddam Hussein: The Fighter, the Thinker and the Man*, translated by Hassan Selim, Paris: Hachette Réalités, 1980.

Ismael, Jacqueline S., and Shereen T. Ismael, "Living through War, Sanctions and Occupation: The Voices of Iraqi Women," *International Journal of Contemporary Iraqi Studies*, vol. 2, no. 3 (2008), pp. 409–24.

Ismael, Tareq Y., *The Rise and Fall of the Communist Party of Iraq*, Cambridge University Press, 2008.

Jabbar, Faleh A., Ahmad Shikara, and Keiko Sakai, *From Storm to Thunder: Unfinished Showdown Between Iraq and U.S.*, Tokyo: Institute of Developing Economies, March 1998.

Karsh, Efraim, and Inari Rautsi, *Saddam Hussein: A Political Biography*, New York: The Free Press, 1991.

Al-Khafaji, Isam, "State Terror and the Degradation of Politics in Iraq," *Middle East Report (MERIP)*, no. 176 (May–June 1992), pp. 15–21.

———, "War as a Vehicle for the Rise and Demise of a State-Controlled Society: The Case of Ba'thist Iraq," in Steven Heydemann (ed.), *War, Institutions, and Social Change in the Middle East*, Berkeley: University of California Press, 2000, pp. 258–91.

Khalili, Laleh, and Jillian Schwedler (eds.), *Policing and Prisons in the Middle East: Formations of Coercion*, London: Hurst, 2010.

Kienle, Eberhard, *Ba'th v Ba'th: The Conflict between Syria and Iraq 1968–1989*, London: I. B. Tauris, 1991.

Kotkin, Stephen, *Magnetic Mountain: Stalinism as a Civilization*, paperback edn., Berkeley: University of California Press, 1997.

Le Billon, Philippe, "Corruption, Reconstruction and Oil Governance in Iraq," in Sultan Barakat (ed.), *Reconstructing Post-Saddam Iraq*, London: Routledge, 2008, pp. 121–39.

Leland, John, "Iraq Mends a System to Treat Trauma," *New York Times*, January 30, 2010.

Lewis, David, *The Temptations of Tyranny in Central Asia*, New York: Columbia University Press, 2008.

Lucas, Christopher J., "Arab Illiteracy and the Mass Literacy Campaign in Iraq," *Comparative and International Education Society*, vol. 25, no. 1 (February 1981), pp. 74–84.

Mahdi, Kamil A., "Iraq's Agrarian System: Issues of Policy and Performance," in Kamil A. Mahdi (ed.), *Iraq's Economic Predicament*, Reading: Ithaca Press, 2002, pp. 321–39.

———, "Iraq's Economic Reforms in Perspective: Public Sector, Private Sector and the Sanctions," *International Journal of Contemporary Iraqi Studies*, vol. 1, no. 2 (2007), pp. 213–31.

Makiya, Kanan, *Cruelty and Silence: War, Tyranny, Uprising and the Arab World*, paperback edn., New York: W.W. Norton, 1994.

———, *Republic of Fear: The Politics of Modern Iraq*, paperback edn., Berkeley: University of California Press, 1998.

———, *The Monument: Art and Vulgarity in Saddam Hussein's Iraq*, London: I. B. Tauris, 2004.

Malovany, Pesach, *Milhamot Bavel ha-Hadashah* [The Wars of Modern Babylon], Tel Aviv: Ma'rakhot, 2009.

Al-Marashi, Ibrahim, "Iraq's Security and Intelligence Network: A Guide and Analysis," *Middle East Review of International Affairs (MERIA)*, vol. 6, no. 3 (September 2002), pp. 1–13.

———, "The Struggle for Iraq: Understanding the Defense Strategy of Saddam Hussein," *Middle East Review of International Affairs (MERIA)*, vol. 7, no. 2 (June 2003), pp. 1–10.

———, "An Insight into the Mindset of Iraq's Security Apparatus," *Intelligence and National Security*, vol. 18, no. 3 (Autumn 2003), pp. 1–23.

Al-Marashi, Ibrahim, and Sammy Salama, *Iraq's Armed Forces: An Analytical History*, London: Routledge, 2008.

Marr, Phebe, *The Modern History of Iraq*, 2nd edn., Boulder, CO: Westview Press, 2004.

Martin, Bradley K., *Under the Loving Care of the Fatherly Leader: North Korea and the Kim Dynasty*, paperback edn., New York: Thomas Dunne, 2006.

Matar, Fuad, *Saddam Hussein: The Man, the Cause, and the Future*, London: Third World Centre, 1981.

Mazaheri, Nimah, "Iraq and the Domestic Political Effects of Economic Sanctions," *Middle East Journal*, vol. 64, no. 2 (Spring 2010), pp. 253–68.

Merridale, Catherine, *Moscow Politics and the Rise of Stalin: The Communist Party in the Capital, 1925–32*, New York: St. Martin's Press, 1990.

Merza, Ali, "Iraq: Reconstruction under Uncertainty," *International Journal of Contemporary Iraqi Studies*, vol. 1, no. 2 (2007), pp. 173–212.

Meyer, Alfred G., "USSR, Incorporated," *Slavic Review*, vol. 20, no. 3 (October 1961), pp. 369–76.

Ministry of Defense, the Political Guidance Bureau, *The Iraqi Army Sixtieth Anniversary 6th January 1921–1981*, Baghdad: Al-Adeeb Press, 1981.

Mofid, Kamram, *The Economic Consequences of the Gulf War*, London: Routledge, 1990.

Mohsen, Fatima, "Culture Totalitarianism," in Fran Hazelton (ed.), *Iraq since the Gulf War: Prospects for Democracy*, London: Zed, 1994, pp. 7–19.

Moore, Pete W., and Bassel F. Salloukh, "Struggles Under Authoritarianism: Regimes, States, and Professional Associations in the Arab World," *International Journal of Middle East Studies*, vol. 39, no. 1 (February 2007), pp. 53–76.

Mu'alla, 'Abd al-Amir, *al-Ayyam al-tawila* [The Long Days], Baghdad: Wizarat al-I'lam, 1978.

Mufti, Malik, *Sovereign Creations: Pan-Arabism and Political Order in Syria and Iraq*, Ithaca, NY: Cornell University Press, 1996.

Nakash, Yitzhak, *The Shi'is of Iraq*, Princeton, NJ: Princeton University Press, 1994.

Nicolae Ceauşescu: The Genius of the Carpathians, Milton Keynes, UK: Filiquarian, 2008.

Nordlinger, Eric A., *Soldiers in Politics: Military Coups and Governments*, Englewoods Cliffs, NJ: Prentice-Hall, 1977.

Omar, Suha, "Women: Honour, Shame and Dictatorship," in Fran Hazelton (ed.), *Iraq since the Gulf War: Prospects for Democracy*, London: Zed, 1994, pp. 60–71.

O'Neil, Patrick, *Essentials of Comparative Politics*, New York: W.W. Norton, 2004.

Overy, Richard, *The Dictators: Hitler's Germany and Stalin's Russia*, paperback edn., London: Penguin, 2005.

Owen, Roger, *State, Power and Politics in the Making of the Modern Middle East*, 3rd edn., London: Routledge, 2008.

Owen, Roger, and Şevket Pamuk, *A History of Middle East Economies in the Twentieth Century*, Cambridge, MA: Harvard University Press, 1999.

Pedersen, Susan, "Getting Out of Iraq – in 1932: The League of Nations and the Road to Normative Statehood," *American Historical Review*, vol. 115, no. 4 (October 2010), pp. 975–1000.

Perthes, Volker, *The Political Economy of Syria under Asad*, paperback edn., London: I.B. Tauris, 1997.

Post, Jerrold M., "Saddam Hussein of Iraq: A Political Psychology Profile," in Jerrold M. Post (ed.), *The Psychological Assessment of Political Leaders: With Profiles of Saddam Hussein and Bill Clinton*, paperback edn., Ann Arbor: University of Michigan Press, 2005.

Post, Jerrold M., and Amatzia Baram, "Saddam Is Iraq: Iraq Is Saddam," Maxwell Air Force Base, AL: USAF Counterproliferation Center, Paper No. 17, 2002.

Primakov, Yevgeny, *Russia and the Arabs: Behind the Scenes in the Middle East from the Cold War to the Present*, New York: Basic, 2009.

Qadduri, Fakhri, *Hakadha 'araftu al-Bakr wa Saddam: Rihlat 35 'aman fi Hizb al-Ba'th* [This Is the Way I Knew al-Bakr and Saddam: A Journey of 35 Years in the Ba'th Party], London: Dar al-Hikma, 2006.

Quinlivan, James T., "Coup-proofing: Its Practice and Consequences in the Middle East," *International Security*, vol. 24, no. 2 (Fall 1999), pp. 131–65.

Rakowitz, Michael, "Strike the Empire Back," an exhibition at Tate Modern, London, 2010.

Reid, Donald Malcolm, "The Postage Stamp: A Window on Saddam Hussein's Iraq," *Middle East Journal*, vol. 47, no. 1 (Winter 1993), pp. 77–89.

Rigby, T. H., "Stalinism and the Mono-Organizational Society," in Robert C. Tucker (ed.), *Stalinism: Essays in Historical Interpretation*, New Brunswick, NJ: Transaction, 1999, pp. 53–76.

Ringle, Ken, "Iraq, Mother of Metaphor; Flamboyant Imagery Is Carefully Calculated," *Washington Post*, February 13, 1991.

Roberts, Adam, and Timothy Garton Ash (eds.), *Civil Resistance and Power Politics: The Experience of Non-Violent Action from Gandhi to the Present*, Oxford University Press, 2009.

Rohde, Achim, *State–Society Relations in Ba'thist Iraq: Facing Dictatorship*, London: Routledge, 2010.

Ronson, Jon, *The Men Who Stare at Goats*, New York: Simon & Schuster, 2009.

Rubin, Barry, "The Military in Contemporary Middle East Politics," in Barry Rubin and Thomas A. Keaney (eds.), *Armed Forces in the Middle East: Politics and Strategy*, London: Frank Cass, 2002, pp. 1–22.

Saghieh, Hazem, "Saddam Hussein, quel totalitarisme?" [Saddam Hussein: What Totalitarianism?] in Chris Kutschera (ed.), *Le Livre Noir de Saddam Hussein* [The Black Book of Saddam Hussein], Paris: Oh! Editions, 2005, pp. 119–38.

Al-Samarra'i, Wafiq, *Hutam al-bawwaba al-sharqiyya* [Ruins of the Eastern Gate], Kuwait: al-Qabas Publishing House, 1997.

Sasson, Sha'ul Hakham, *Fi jahim Saddam Hussein: Thalathma'a wa khamsa wa sittun yawman fi qasr al-nihaya* [In the Hell of Saddam Hussein: 365 Days in the Palace of the End], Jerusalem: Association for Jewish Academics from Iraq, 1999.

Sassoon, Joseph, "Industrialization in Iraq 1958–1968," *Ha-Mizrah he-Hadash*, vol. 30 (1981), pp. 21–49.

_____, *The Iraqi Refugees: The New Crisis in the Middle East*, London: I.B. Tauris, 2009.

Scott, James C., *Domination and the Arts of Resistance: Hidden Transcripts*, New Haven, CT: Yale University Press, 1990.

Sha'ban, 'Abd al-Hussein, *Man huwa al-'Iraqi? Ishkaliyat al-jinsiyya wa alla-jinsiyya fi al-qanunayn al-'Iraqi wa al-duwali* [Who Is Iraqi? Complexities of Nationality and Lack of Nationality in Iraqi and International Laws], Beirut: Al-Kanuz Publishing House, 2002.

Shadid, Anthony, "How an Inflammatory Term, Baathist, Bars Candidates in Iraq," *New York Times*, January 20, 2010.

Al-Sharqi, Amal, "The Emancipation of Iraqi Women," in Tim Niblock (ed.), *Iraq: The Contemporary State*, New York: St. Martin's Press, 1982, pp. 74–87.

Silone, Ignazio, *Bread and Wine*, translated by Gwenda David and Eric Mosbacher, New York: Harper & Brothers, 1937.

Simon, Reeva S., *Iraq Between the Two World Wars: The Creation and Implementation of a Nationalist Ideology*, New York: Columbia University Press, 1986.

Slackman, Michael, "Baath Party Is Bedrock of Hussein's Power Base," *Los Angeles Times*, April 5, 2003.

Sluglett, Peter "Le parti Baas: panarabisme, national-socialisme et dictature" [The Ba'th Party: Pan-Arabism, National-Socialism and Dictatorship], in Chris Kutschera (ed.), *Le Livre Noir de Saddam Hussein*, Paris: Oh! Editions, 2005, pp. 75–104.

_____, *Britain in Iraq: Contriving King and Country 1914–1932*, paperback edn., New York: Columbia University Press, 2007.

Springborg, Robert, "Baathism in Practice: Agriculture, Politics, and Political Culture in Syria and Iraq," *Middle Eastern Studies*, vol. 17, no. 2 (April 1981), pp. 191–209.

_____, "Infitah, Agrarian Transformation, and Elite Consolidation in Contemporary Iraq," *Middle East Journal*, vol. 40, no. 1 (Winter 1986), pp. 33–52.

Stansfield, Gareth R. V., "The Kurdish Dilemma: The Golden Era Threatened," in Toby Dodge and Steven Simon (eds.), *Iraq at the Crossroads: State and Society in the Shadow of Regime Change*, Adelphi Papers 354, Oxford University Press, 2003.

Steavenson, Wendell, *The Weight of a Mustard Seed: The Intimate Story of an Iraqi General and His Family During Thirty Years of Tyranny*, paperback edn., New York: Harper, 2010.

Stewart, Rory, *Occupational Hazards: My Time Governing in Iraq*, London: Picador, 2006.

Al-Ta'i, Ghazy Dir', *al-Bahr al-akhdhar* [The Green Sea], Baghdad: Cultural Affairs Department, 1988.

Tarbush, Mohammad, *The Role of the Military in Politics: A Case Study of Iraq to 1941*, London: Routledge and Kegan Paul, 1982.

Al-Tikriti, Barazan, *Muhawalat ightiyal al-Ra'is Saddam Hussein* [Attempts to Assassinate the President Saddam Hussein], Baghdad: Arab Publishing House, 1982.

Tripp, Charles, *A History of Iraq*, paperback edn., Cambridge University Press, 2000.

Tucker, Robert C., "The Rise of Stalin's Personality Cult," *American History Review*, vol. 84, no. 2 (April 1979), pp. 347–66.

U.S. Department of Justice, Federal Bureau of Investigation, "Saddam Hussein Talks to the FBI," National Security Archive Electronic Briefing Book No. 279, www.gwu.edu/~nsarchiv/NSAEBB/NSAEBB279/index.htm (accessed February 25, 2010).

Wazarat al-Takhtit [Ministry of Planning], *al-Taqaddum fi dhil al-takhtit* [Advancement through Planning], Baghdad: Central Organization for Statistics, 1975.

Weber, Max, "Politics as a Vocation," in *From Max Weber: Essays in Sociology*, translated, edited, and with an introduction by H. H. Gerth and C. Wright Mills, paperback edn., Oxford: Routledge, 2007, pp. 77–128.

Wedeen, Lisa, *Ambiguities of Domination: Politics, Rhetoric and Symbols in Contemporary Syria*, Chicago: University of Chicago Press, 1999.

Wien, Peter, *Iraqi Arab Nationalism: Authoritarian, Totalitarian, and Pro-Fascist Inclinations, 1932–1941*, London and New York: Routledge, 2006.

Woods, Kevin M., *The Mother of All Battles: Saddam Hussein's Strategic Plan for the Persian Gulf War*, Annapolis, MD: Naval Institute Press, 2008.

Woods, Kevin M., with James Lacey, *Iraqi Perspectives Project: Saddam and Terrorism: Emerging Insights from Captured Iraqi Documents*, 5 volumes, Alexandria, VA: Institute for Defense Analysis (IDA), 2007.

Woods, Kevin M., James Lacey, and Williamson Murray, "Saddam's Delusions: The View from the Inside," *Foreign Affairs*, vol. 85, no. 3 (May/June 2006), pp. 2–26.

Woods, Kevin M., Williamson Murray, and Thomas Holaday, with Mounir Elkhamri, *Saddam's War: An Iraqi Military Perspective of the Iran–Iraq War*, McNair Paper 70, Washington, DC: National Defense University, 2009.

Woods, Kevin M., with Michael R. Pease, Mark E. Stout, Williamson Murray, and James G. Lacey, *The Iraqi Perspectives Report: Saddam's Senior Leadership* on *Operation Iraqi Freedom from the Official U.S. Joint Forces Command Report*, Annapolis, MD: Naval Institute Press, 2006.

World Bank, *Economic Data Indicators*, http://data.worldbank.org/country/iraq (accessed November 15, 2010).

Zaini, Muhammad ʿAli, *al-Iqtisad al-ʿIraqi fi dhil nidham Saddam Hussein: Tatawwar am taqhqur* [The Iraqi Economy during Saddam Hussein's Regime: Development or Retraction], London: al-Rafid, 1995.

Zubaida, Sami, "Une société traumatisée, une société civile anéantie, une économie en ruine" [A Society Traumatized, a Population Crushed, an Economy in Ruins], in Chris Kutschera (ed.), *Le Livre Noir de Saddam Hussein*, Paris: Oh! Editions, 2005, pp. 601–27.

Newspapers and Journals

Alif Ba
The Economist
The Economist Intelligence Unit (EIU)
Al-Jumhuriyya
Al-Qadisiyya
The Telegraph
Al-Thawra
Al-Waqaʾiʿ al-ʿIraqiyya [Iraqi Official Gazette]

Summary of Broadcasts and Newspapers

Foreign Broadcast Information Service (FBIS), Washington, DC

Film

Joel Soler Film, *Uncle Saddam*, Xenon Pictures and Frog Entertainment, 2003

Television and Radio

BBC News
Dhawʾ

Index

'Abd Hammud, 228–9, 229n8, 230
abuses of power
  in armed forces, 142–3
  by *fida'iyyu Saddam*, 150
  by SSO, 110–11, 111nn69–70
active member (*'udhu 'amil*), 46
affiliation (*intisab*), 45–6
'Aflaq, Michel, 19–20, 26, 30–1
age policies, 53–4, 54t, 56
al-Ali, Nadje, 255
American invasion 2003, 40, 85, 159–61, 187n100
'Ammash, Huda Salih Mahdi, 36n11, 256, 266n193
al-amn al-'am (General Security)
  intelligence gathering by, 115
  monitoring of religious institutions by, 261n166, 262–4
  overview, 95–6
  on recruitment, 72
al-amn al-'askari (Military Security), 97
Anglo–Iraqi Treaty of 1930, 18
Anglo–Iraqi War, 18
Arab Ba'th Socialist Party. *See* Ba'th Party
Arab Glory, 80n46, 85–6, 86n72
Arabization of Kurdistan, 39–40, 83, 83n61, 84, 84n64

Arab student recruitment, 119–20, 120nn112–14, 121
Arab unity, 9–10, 22–3, 66–7
'Arif, 'Abd al-Rahman
  exile of, 31–2
  Nasserite coup, 28
  policies generally, 30
  rise to power, 28
'Arif, 'Abd al-Salam
  arrest, sentencing of, 20
  consolidation of power by, 27–8
  death of, 28
  economic policies, 27
  Egypt, relations with, 27
  ousting of Ba'th Party by, 26
  policies toward military, 26–7
  political violence as policy, 32, 32n55
armed forces
  abuses of power in, 142–3
  Ba'th domination of, 7, 13
  deserters in (*See* deserters)
  education (Ba'thification) of, 133–5, 134n20, 135nn21–22, 136n24, 137
  historical role of, 23, 129–30
  Iran–Iraq War, hanging of senior officers during, 141–2
  marriage approvals in, 144–5
  martyrdom (*See* martyrdom)

elections, 73–4, 80–1, 187–8,
251n124, 252n127
finances, 85–7, 119–20
al-hamla al-ʾimaniyya (the faith
campaign), 80, 80n46, 177–8,
265–6, 266n191, 268
initiatives, 90
Kurdistan, Arabization of, 39–40,
83, 83n61, 84, 84n64
leaders, daily activities by, 89
membership, recruitment (*See*
membership, recruitment)
militia enlistment, 81
al-muʿaisha (cohabitation), 121
organizational activities, 72–5
overview, 13, 71, 71n1, 72, 94
party unit daily life, 90–3, 93n102,
94
political, security activities, 81–5
(*See also* intelligence gathering)
public relations duties, 78–81
referendums, national censuses,
80–1
rumors, counter-rumors, 84, 225
tribal policies, 78
university student recruitment,
78–9, 268–73
weapons training, 84–5, 256–8
Baʿth Regional Command, 4, 30, 32,
98, 99
Baʿth Regional Command Collection
(BRCC), 2, 71–2, 98
bayʿa (pledge of allegiance), 175,
175n41
al-Bazzaz, ʿAbd al-Rahman, 28
beggars, 194–5, 246
birthday celebrations (Saddam
Hussein's), 184–5, 187–9
al-Bitar, Salah al-Din, 19–20
Boutros Ghali, Boutros, 117
bureaucracy, decision making
citizen complaints, 234–5
final decision making in, 234,
234n31, 281
makatib istishariyya (consultancy
bureaus), 228
memos, 233–4, 234n30
ministerial appointments in, 231

overview, 227–8, 235–6
party committees, 232–3
party control of, 233, 235
presidential *diwan* (*See* presidential
diwan)
raqaba shaʿbiyya (popular
surveillance), 232
Saddam Hussein's moods in, 231,
259–60n158
system of orders, 229, 229n8, 230
travel visas, 234, 234n31

Caliph al-Mansur, 177n56
cars, 214, 214nn86–7
Ceauşescu, Nicolae, 179–80
censorship, 69
Chaldeans, 102, 102n25, 103, 203–4
children, youth
Arab student recruitment, 119–20,
120nn112–14, 121
focus of Saddam Hussein's
personality cult, 181, 181n73,
268–73
university student recruitment,
78–9, 268–73
Christians
form entry for, 203–4
as part of system, 11
requirements of, 73
in Saddam Hussein's inner circle,
230–1
surveillance of, 102–3, 203–4, 263
Clemenceau, Georges, 7, 7n11
cohabitation (*al-muʿaisha*), 121
collaborators, 214. *See also* informers
commands of the president (*wasaya
al-raʾis*), 179
Communist Party, 21, 23n23, 222–3
confessions, 199, 199nn29–31
Conflict Records Research Center
(CRRC), 1, 287
consultancy bureaus (*makatib
istishariyya*), 228
co-optation
executions, public participation in,
206
medals, rewards in, 206–16
of unions, 249–53

Made in the USA
Middletown, DE
09 November 2020